POLITICS IN NEWFOUNDLAND

Politics in Newfoundland

S. J. R. NOEL

University of Toronto Press

© University of Toronto Press 1971
Toronto and Buffalo

Printed in Canada
ISBN 0-8020-5246-0
Microfiche ISBN 0-8020-0036-3
LC 73-151382

To my parents

CANADIAN GOVERNMENT SERIES

General Editors

R. MACG. DAWSON, 1946–58/J. A. CORRY, 1958–61
C. B. MACPHERSON, 1961–

Preface

THIS BOOK is a study of the political life of Newfoundland in the twentieth century. In it I have sought to analyse the forces shaping the politics of the island during its decline from independent dominion status to bureaucratic dictatorship and its subsequent conversion into a province of Canada. It will be obvious to the reader that my approach to the study of politics permits no sharp distinction between the political and the economic and social. What I have attempted to do, therefore, is to relate the operation of governmental institutions and processes to a wider historical context. The issues and personalities of contemporary provincial politics are dealt with only in so far as they reflect certain themes of continuity and change in Newfoundland society which to me seem particularly significant.

The most serious deficiency in the material upon which this book is based, and the greatest handicap in its writing, was the paucity of economic studies. Before confederation the Newfoundland government employed neither economists nor statisticians, and not since the death of H. A. Innis has there been an ingenious economic historian to piece together the economic picture from the many uncorrelated sources which exist. Innis was mainly concerned with an earlier period, but I have no doubt that Newfoundland's economic history since 1900 would prove an equally rewarding subject.

In the preparation of this study I have received much help which it is now my pleasure to acknowledge. The staffs of the Public Record Office, British Museum, Newfoundland Archives, Bodleian Library, Rhodes House Library, Bonar Law–Bennett Library of the University of New Brunswick, and the libraries of the Royal Military College of Canada and the Memorial University of Newfoundland have all at various times rendered valuable assistance. I am grateful to Professor Frederic F. Thompson of the Royal Military College for giving me access to the papers of Sir Robert Bond and for his many personal kindnesses during my visit to Kingston. I owe a special debt to Dr A. F. Madden of Nuffield College, Oxford, for his thoughtful criticism and encouragement. It was under his supervision that a major part of the manuscript was originally written as a doctoral thesis.

There is no part of my work which has not benefited immensely from the knowledge and insight of Peter Neary. Were it not for our discussion of innumerable points over many years I do not think this book would ever have been written. My gratitude to him goes beyond conventional acknowledgement. I would be remiss if I did not thank Jim Devereux for his eccentric contribution: in the midst of his own research on English translations of Erasmus he characteristically took enough interest in mine to drag me to the UNB library and insist that I examine the R. B. Bennett papers, which turned out to contain much important material. At the University of Toronto Press Rik Davidson and Gerry Hallowell have given me the benefit of their advice and skilful editorial assistance. And last, though not least, I am grateful to Elizabeth, who typed the manuscript and created an environment in which I was able to write. All of the above have helped me to avoid errors I would otherwise have committed; for those that remain I alone am responsible.

Research for this study was financially assisted by the Rothermere Fellowships Trust, the Canada Council, the Institute of Social and Economic Research of Memorial University, and the University of Western Ontario. This book has been published with the help of a grant from the Social Science Research Council of Canada, using funds provided by the Canada Council, and with the assistance of the Publications Fund of the University of Toronto Press.

S.N.

Contents

APPENDICES

POLITICS IN NEWFOUNDLAND

1 The land, the people, and the constitution

THE ISLAND OF Newfoundland is a far more 'northern' place than its location on the globe would seem to suggest. It lies between the same lines of geographical latitude as southern England and northern France and nowhere is its elevation very high; yet in almost all its observable features it more closely resembles the sub-arctic regions of North America. The land is heavily, and in places spectacularly, glaciated. The great Pleistocene ice-cap covered it completely and in retreating, some ten thousand years ago, carried out to sea so much of its soil that today over vast areas only the bare windswept rocks remain. Departing glaciers filled its valleys with debris, dammed back its rivers, and left behind a landscape thickly strewn with lakes and marshes; while the deep bays and rounded headlands so characteristic of its coastline were likewise sculptured by irresistible movements of ice.

In contrast to western Europe, which is warmed by the Gulf Stream, the shores of Newfoundland are chilled by the Labrador Current which comes sweeping down from the Arctic and blockades a large part of the coast with drift ice for several months of the year. Hence the climate is cooler at all seasons than that of other lands of comparable latitude, and the winters longer. Over much of the interior the only vegetation is the sparse and stunted growth associated with tundra, though in the lower-lying areas, where adequate drainage exists, the land typically sustains a growth of boreal forest consisting mainly of small spruce and fir.

The island covers an area of approximately 43,000 square miles (about twice the size of Nova Scotia) and protrudes into the Atlantic some 350 miles beyond the easternmost tip of Cape Breton Island. It also lies on the edge of a large undersea plateau, the southern part of which is known as the Grand Banks, which means that its coastal waters abound in the cold-water species of fish for which the banks are famous, particularly the ubiquitous cod. And though it was among the first parts of North America to be frequented by Europeans – from at least the sixteenth century, English, French, Spanish, and Portuguese ships made annual voyages to its shores – for centuries they came to fish rather than to settle.

In the entire history of Newfoundland there has been but one brief period of substantial European colonization and that occurred in the early nineteenth century. In other times, both before and after, the great waves of immigrants that flooded across the Atlantic to America passed the island by in favour of other more richly endowed lands further south. But during and immediately after the Napoleonic Wars economic conditions in Europe were such that the Newfoundland fishery became sufficiently attractive to induce permanent settlement. The wars disrupted the transatlantic ship fishery, raised the price of fish to unprecedented heights, and so brought to Newfoundland an influx of settlers who hoped to earn a prosperous livelihood, in spite of the rigours of climate and soil, by basing their fishery on the land nearest the fishing grounds. They came predominantly, and in about equal number, from Ireland and the west of England, and it is from them that the present population of the island is largely descended.

In the eighteenth century Newfoundland had existed as a curious hybrid of the British Empire, being something more than a fishing station, something less than a colony. The total year-round population was small, probably less than ten thousand in all, and even these few had no right of habitation, for it was the policy of the imperial government to discourage colonization in order to preserve the English ship fishery as a 'nursery for seamen' for the Royal Navy. By 1830, however, the status of the island was no longer in doubt. Regardless of imperial policy, the population had increased to around fifty thousand, and in the process a new and unique colonial society had haphazardly taken root.

Inevitably, the nature of that society was largely determined by the cultural norms and patterns of social organization and behaviour of the two founding groups, the Irish and the English. Their cultural backgrounds in large measure shaped their responses to their new environment – and to each other. The latter is particularly significant. For the Irish brought with them a national heritage of poverty, Roman Catholicism, and hatred of their English oppressors; while the English brought with them from the west country a heritage of puritanical Protestantism, social deference, and semi-feudal economic relationships. Thus the constituent elements of the new community from the very beginning contained in their respective traditions and memories from the old world the seeds of social conflict in the new.

Yet although their traditions were divisive, it was also the case that the harsh physical and economic environment against which the vast majority of English and Irish alike had to struggle provided at least the minimum conditions for the growth of the forces of social and political integration. Indeed, the observable differences between them were far less striking than their similarities. Both groups were predominantly composed of shore fishermen who, with their families, were the basic units of production in the cod fishery; as fishermen they necessarily led similar lives in small, though for the most part separate, settlements; they experienced the same hardships and deprivations which the vagaries of nature undiscriminatingly imposed upon them; as producers they were part of the same economic class, sharing a common position at the base of the island's trading and financial structure; and both suffered grievously from the unsatisfactory state of the island's government.

It is not surprising, therefore, that the politics which developed in this nascent colony reflected not only the traditional cleavages of ethnicity and religion but also the underlying potential of the people to realign their loyalties on the basis of economic class. Indeed, the subsequent history of Newfoundland may be viewed as a struggle between those who sought to preserve the existing economic system by maintaining and exploiting existing social cleavages and those who sought to bring about social and economic changes by persuading the majority of the people of the paramountcy of their common class interests. But for this to be properly understood it is necessary to view the rise of politics in a social and economic context.

Politically, the most significant change that took place in Newfoundland during the Napoleonic Wars was not the increase in population as such but its concentration in St John's, which emerged as the island's first town. This was no small achievement, for the growth of urban communities in fishing areas is made a slow and difficult process by the availability of cheap water transport from other centres, which tends to obviate their commercial necessity.[1] This tendency, however, was largely inoperative during the long years of war, much to the advantage of St John's. By 1815 it was a town of more than ten thousand inhabitants, a ramshackle frontier port, crowded with newly arrived settlers and transients, and already enjoying some of the amenities of civilization that lack of population had previously made unobtainable. A post office had been in operation since

1/H. A. Innis, *Essays in Canadian Economic History* (Toronto, 1962), p. 38.

1805; a newspaper, established by John Ryan, a United Empire Loyalist, since 1806;[2] a grammar school and two charity schools provided education;[3] and dozens of taverns and coffee houses provided convivial meeting places for gossip, business, and – inevitably – politics.

For if the rise of St John's made political life possible, the despotic naval régime under which its inhabitants were forced to live made it necessary. In Newfoundland, in contrast to the other settled parts of British North America, population expansion and economic growth had not been accompanied by significant constitutional advancement. Though British sovereignty in the island had been acknowledged by France ever since the Treaty of Utrecht in 1713, the British government, under pressure from the west country merchants who dominated the English fishery in Newfoundland and who were strongly supported by the Royal Navy, continued to regard colonization in the island as contrary to the imperial interest. Newfoundland's rôle was to serve the Empire as 'a great ship moored near the Banks for the convenience of English fishermen.' Consequently, those who had defied the imperial authorities and settled there were allowed none of the usual rights of British colonists. Even in 1815 they had no legal status, no title to the lands they occupied, and no civil government. The governor was still a naval officer who lived in the island only during the summer,[4] and even while there was bound to carry out his government's policy of discouraging settlement; and the administration of justice, in spite of the existence of a Supreme Court at St John's, was hopelessly corrupt and chaotic.[5] Under a bizarre system of 'surrogate courts' naval officers of even the most junior rank had the authority to act as judges, with the rights of hearing and determining all cases of civil jurisdiction. No set rules of law were observed, the decisions of the Supreme Court were commonly ignored, and decisions in even minor civil cases were not infrequently enforced by the brutal punishments of the quarterdeck.[6]

2/E. J. Devereux, 'Early Printing in Newfoundland,' *Dalhousie Review*, vol. 43, no. 1 (Sept. 1963), pp. 57–66.

3/F. W. Rowe, *The History of Education in Newfoundland* (Toronto, 1952), pp. 31–2, 55–6.

4/The first governor to winter in the colony was Admiral Pickmore, who died in the attempt in 1817.

5/See A. H. McLintock, *The Establishment of Constitutional Government in Newfoundland, 1783–1832* (London, 1941), pp. 130–2; for the development of the judiciary in the eighteenth century, see J. Reeves, *History of the Government of the Island of Newfoundland* (London, 1793).

6/In 1820 a particularly horrific case of flogging for a trivial offence brought reform agitation to the boil. The 'Landergan Case' became the 'Peterloo' of Newfoundland's history. See C. R. Fay, *Life and Labour in Newfoundland* (Cambridge, 1956), pp. 113–15.

It was widespread revulsion against these conditions – which in many respects were worse even than those the Irish immigrants had left behind in their native land – that turned St John's into a centre of political agitation. By the 1820s a substantial reform movement had grown up under the leadership of two exceptionally gifted men: William Carson, a Scottish surgeon, and Patrick Morris, a young Irish merchant.[7]

The reformers put to good use all the contemporary tactics of British radicalism: pamphlets, political committees, petitions, and test cases before the courts.[8] And if, on the whole, their efforts form one of the more edifying chapters in Newfoundland's history it is because they never allowed their struggle to degenerate into the mean politics of a rude colonial backwater. By constantly bringing the debate back to the level of human rights and high constitutional principle they were able to win the advocacy of Joseph Hume and other humanitarian radicals in the British House of Commons, and thus were able ultimately to take advantage of the changing political climate within Britain. 'Three hundred years is in all conscience a sufficient minority,' wrote Patrick Morris in 1827; 'we are now of sufficient age to take care of our private affairs.'[9] He had not long to wait. In England the struggle for the great Reform Bill was nearing its climax and affairs in Newfoundland were carried in its wake. 'Surely,' declared Joseph Hume, 'the British House of Commons which is about to give representation to the people and property of this country will not refuse it to the inhabitants of Newfoundland.'[10] Nor did it. On 7 June 1832 – the very day the Reform Bill received the royal assent – a bill was introduced to confer upon Newfoundland the benefits of representative government.

The constitution of 1832 gave Newfoundland no more than the traditional system of colonial government which neighbouring Nova Scotia, by contrast, had enjoyed since 1758. The governor and the Legislative Council were to be appointed by the Crown; the Assembly, comprising fifteen representatives of nine electoral districts, was to be chosen by the people on a household franchise. That this arrangement had not proved an unqualified success in other parts of the Empire did not make it any less attractive to the Newfoundland reformers. On the contrary, the more

7/For biographical sketches of Carson and Morris see McLintock, *The Establishment of Constitutional Government*, pp. 145–9, and Fay, *Life and Labour*, pp.116–27.

8/In one such case, *Rex* v *Keough*, 1819, it was ruled that occupancy of land for purposes other than the fishery was legal on grounds of undisturbed possession – an important victory for the colonists.

9/Quoted in McLintock, *The Establishment of Constitutional Government*, p. 175.

10/*Ibid.*, p. 183.

radical of them appear to have regarded it from the beginning as doomed to failure, but none the less welcome as a useful stepping stone to further constitutional advance. In his address to the electors of St John's the young radical candidate, John Kent, put these aims explicitly:

Our Constitution has as yet only half developed itself ... In a Council nominated by the Governor, composed of those holding offices under Government, or expectants for place ... oligarchical principles must prevail. The task of prostrating those principles ... now devolves upon the People ... Your extensive franchise, amounting almost to universal suffrage, will enable you to do this.[11]

In the event, the new legislature had no sooner assembled than the unsuitability of the new constitution became manifest. An acrimonious quarrel immediately arose between the Council and the Assembly over the Assembly's right to pass revenue bills, and in the total absence of any spirit of compromise a deadlock ensued which brought the normal business of government to a premature end.[12] (*Punch* satirized the legislature as the 'Bow Wow Parliament' in a cartoon depicting a chamber full of howling Newfoundland dogs.) The harshness of the conflict was due in part to the nature of the constitution, but even more to the deep social and religious antagonisms which existed in the colony and which in the new legislature came bubbling to the surface.

Nowhere else in North America had colonial society evolved in quite the same way as in Newfoundland, and nowhere were social classes more sharply polarized. With the decline of the English west country influence virtually the entire export and import trade of the country had fallen into the hands of a small group of St John's merchants,[13] who, with the government officials, churchmen, and others they supported, formed the dominant social class. They were invariably English and Protestant. And not only were they wealthy, they were also immensely powerful, for the financial structure of the fishery had become totally dependent upon their capital. As J. D. Rogers has observed: the merchant 'acted as bank, mint, and clearing-house, besides acting as money-lender, export-agent, and import-agent. He combined six or more functions of capital, and represented the integration of capital.'[14] A middle class of small traders and

11/*Public Ledger*, St John's, 11 Sept. 1832.
12/Various experiments were tried in an effort to break the deadlock, including (1842–8) an 'amalgamated' legislature consisting of both houses sitting in one chamber thereby placing the radicals in a minority, but without notable success. See Gertrude E. Gunn, *The Political History of Newfoundland, 1832–1864* (Toronto, 1966), pp. 89–109.
13/McLintock, *The Establishment of Constitutional Government*, p. 100.
14/*Newfoundland: Historical and Geographical* (Oxford, 1911), p. 206.

artisans was numerically insignificant; and the lower class, which included the vast majority of the population, consisted almost entirely of fishermen, roughly half of whom were Irish Roman Catholics. Over this class the merchants held practically unlimited power, based upon the operation of a truck system of credit trading. Under it the merchant set both the price of the goods he supplied to the fishermen on credit and the price of the fish he accepted in payment of their debts. In consequence, the use of cash was practically eliminated from the transaction; one bad season could place a fisherman hopelessly in debt, and by refusing him further credit the merchant had it in his power to destroy a fisherman's livelihood.[15]

During this unhappy era of representative government political parties emerged that had their basis in the economic and class divisions of society and stood for essentially different forms of government. Those who opposed any further change in the constitution, a group dominated by the St John's merchants, became the 'Conservative' party; the original reform movement of Carson and Morris, dedicated to securing responsible government, became the 'Liberal' party.[16] The former was a party of patronage and influence, the latter a channel of popular agitation. Its popular base, however, was both its strength and its weakness, for only in St John's and the Avalon Peninsula was there a sufficient density of population to make popular agitation effective. As a result Liberal support was heavily concentrated in those areas.[17] The rest of the population was for the most part scattered in tiny villages along a thousand miles of coast, far removed from the influence of radical orators, newspapers, and the general turmoil of the capital. Consequently, Liberal support diminished in roughly inverse proportion to the distance from St John's.

This pattern, however, also coincided with the ethnic and religious distribution of the population; for although the country was about equally divided between Irish Roman Catholics and English Protestants, the former greatly predominated in St John's and the east, and the latter elsewhere.[18] Not a single constituency outside the Avalon Peninsula had a Catholic majority. As a result, the Liberal party, while not a 'Catholic' party in either policy or leadership (Carson was a Protestant), nevertheless received the bulk of its support from Catholic voters. The Conservative party, on the other hand, as representative of the merchant class, was

15/There are numerous descriptions of this system and the social evils it produced. See, e.g., McLintock, *The Establishment of Constitutional Government*, pp. 121–4; H. A. Innis, *The Cod Fisheries: The History of an International Economy* (rev. ed., Toronto, 1954), pp. 152–5; and for its continuation into more modern times, see W. T. Grenfell, *A Labrador Doctor* (London, 1919), pp. 150–7.

16/Both names were commonly in use by 1836.

17/See, e.g., the 1848 election results in Gunn, *The Political History of Newfoundland*, Appendix B, Table v.

18/*Ibid.*, Appendix E, Table III.

numerically small but exclusively Protestant. In these circumstances it is little wonder that 'Protestant Unity' became the Conservative rallying-cry.[19]

In 1854 the Assembly, which contained a Liberal majority, demanded legislation to guarantee fishermen the payment of their wages from the proceeds of the voyage – a direct attack on the merchants' system of credit. The Council refused, and the Assembly retaliated by withholding supply. The imperial government was thus faced once again with the problem of adjudicating the affairs of the troublesome colony, and this time rather ungraciously conceded the Liberal demands for self-rule:

Her Majesty's Government had come to the conclusion that they ought not to withhold from Newfoundland those institutions and that civil administration which under the popular name of responsible government had been adopted in all Her Majesty's neighboring possessions in North America; and that they were prepared to concede the immediate application of the system as soon as certain necessary preliminary conditions had been acceded to on the part of the legislature.[20]

These conditions, which involved the payment of pensions to ousted officials and the enlargement of the Assembly from fifteen members to thirty, were acceded to, and in 1855 Newfoundland became internally self-governing.

Under the new constitution, as under the old, the governor was to be appointed by the Crown, and the legislature was to consist of a Legislative Council and an Assembly. But henceforth executive power was to reside in an Executive Council (that is, a Cabinet) whose members were to be responsible to the Assembly, to hold office only so long as they retained the support of a majority in the Assembly. Members of the Legislative Council were to be appointed for life on the nomination of the Executive Council. The Assembly was to be elected as before, upon a household franchise.[21] In the legislature was vested the power of making

19/Unfortunately for the Liberals, other events also tended to favour the growth of sectarianism. The death of William Carson in 1843 and of Patrick Morris in 1849 deprived the party of their experienced leadership just as the struggle for responsible government was entering its final phase. Moreover, the Roman Catholic bishop of St John's developed an unfortunate taste for active Liberal politics, and the new leaders of the party, John Kent and P. F. Little, were both Catholics. See *ibid.*, pp. 120–7.

20/Quoted in Innis, *The Cod Fisheries*, p. 391.

21/J. Little, *The Constitution of the Government of Newfoundland in its Legislative and Executive Departments* (London, 1855). New Letters Patent and Royal Instructions were issued in 1876. These are conveniently reproduced in *Constitutions of All Countries* (London, 1938), I, 222–42.

laws, jurisdiction over the public debt and property, the power of taxation and of raising loans upon the colony's credit, and the conduct of all
public services. The legislature could not, however, enact any law repugnant to the law of England or inconsistent with any obligations imposed
upon the Crown by treaty.[22] It was this latter provision that was to be the
source of much subsequent discord between the colony and the mother
country.

For the constitution of 1855, while it placed Newfoundland legally on
an equal footing with the other colonies of British North America, did
nothing to relieve the island of its greatest burden – the 'French Shore,' a
damnosa hereditas of eighteenth century diplomacy. Under article 13 of
the Treaty of Utrecht, 1713, the subjects of France, while not permitted to
settle, had been allowed the right

to catch fish, and to dry them on land, in that part only, and in no other besides that, of the said island of Newfoundland, which stretches from the place
called Cape Bonavista, to the northern point of the said island, and from thence
running down by the western side, reaches as far as the place called Point
Riche.[23]

In other words, although the treaty ceded the island to Britain, France had
nevertheless retained for her subjects important rights of easement upon
nearly a thousand miles, or roughly one-third, of its coast.

There were, however, a number of serious ambiguities in this provision.
Were the French rights exclusive or were they concurrent with the rights
of British fishermen on the same coast? Did the word 'fish' as used in
article 13 mean 'codfish,' as the phrase 'to catch fish, and to dry them'
seemed to indicate, or was it used in a general sense to include other species such as salmon and lobster? How far inland did the rights extend?
And where exactly was Point Riche? These and other equally vexing questions ensured from the beginning that the rights of France in Newfoundland would be a source of dissonance and potentially of war so long as they
remained in existence.

In 1783, under article 5 of the Treaty of Versailles, it was agreed that
'in order to prevent the quarrels which have hitherto arisen between the
two nations of England and France' the rights of France should cease on
the Newfoundland coast between Cape St John, where the French had
increasingly come into conflict with English fishing ships and illegal set-

22/See R. A. Parsons, 'Our Former Constitution,' in J. R. Smallwood, ed.,
The Book of Newfoundland (St John's, 1937), I, 32–42.
23/As quoted in F. F. Thompson, *The French Shore Problem in Newfoundland:
An Imperial Study* (Toronto, 1961), Appendix 1 A.

tlers, and be replaced by an extension of identical rights on the west coast as far south as Cape Ray.[24] Although this arrangement excluded French fishermen from two large and valuable eastern bays it also meant that the total extent of the French Shore was considerably enlarged. Moreover, the west coast of Newfoundland, though practically unknown in the eighteenth century, was by no means uninhabitable. Indeed, in some ways it was the richest part of the whole island; it included the estuary of the island's second largest river, while its hinterland contained considerable areas of forest and some well-drained valleys that were capable of sustaining certain types of agriculture.[25]

Responsible government in Newfoundland was therefore severely handicapped from birth. In 1855 the ambiguous treaty rights of France were still in existence between Cape St John and Cape Ray, a constant source of friction and an affront to the principle of internal self-rule. Because of these rights a large part of the colony's territory and more than three thousand of its inhabitants (out of a total population of approximately 130,000) were placed effectively beyond the jurisdiction of the colonial government, for English settlement on the French Shore had not been completely prevented by the virtual state of anarchy that reigned there.[26] Moreover, since the economy of Newfoundland was entirely dependent upon the fishery, responsible government was inevitably weakened if the colony could not regulate its most vital natural resource. In such important matters as fisheries conservation the French could ignore colonial legislation with impunity. Also, Newfoundlanders bitterly resented the fact that the government-subsidized French fishery, by selling its produce at an artificially low price in southern Europe, tended to depress the value of Newfoundland's stable export in its largest market.[27]

In these circumstances it is little wonder that the French Shore was perpetually an area of conflict. To preserve the peace, both France and Britain were compelled to employ warships on the coast during the fishing season – the former to defend French lives and property, the latter to restrain the colonists from provoking an international incident. In an effort to reduce this tension, the two great powers agreed in 1857 to separate the combatants by partitioning the shore into two equal spheres, and a convention

24/*Ibid.*, p. 15.
25/The west coast is also the part of the island nearest the mainland of North America. The extension of the French Shore to this area naturally strengthened the tendency of the colony in the nineteenth century to orient itself towards the Atlantic and Britain rather than towards the St Lawrence and the other British North American colonies. This was undoubtedly one of the underlying reasons why it remained outside the Canadian federation.
26/See Rogers, *Newfoundland*, p. 217 ff.
27/See Innis, *The Cod Fisheries*, pp. 414–16.

was signed to that effect.[28] Its advantages were obvious: France would gain a secure and clearly defined foothold in Newfoundland, which was more than the ambiguous treaties of the eighteenth century had ever offered, and Britain would at least be absolved of the responsibility for maintaining order in a concurrent fishery.

In fact, the only party that stood to loose from the convention was the colony of Newfoundland. For as long as the fishery on the French Shore remained concurrent, and the rights of France obscure and disputable, the colony, with its rising population, could look forward to ousting the French in due course, just as earlier it had ousted the English ship fishery. Also, as F. F. Thompson points out, 'the presence of good land, rumours of mineral deposits, the hope for west coast trade, and colonial pride were against any concessions on the treaty coast.'[29] The convention was therefore regarded in Newfoundland as a perfidious betrayal of colonial interests, and the publication of its terms caused a furore. Citizens flew the British flag at half-mast; others hoisted the 'Stars and Stripes' in protest. There were 'indignation meetings,' reports Prowse, 'as hot and fiery as the Tea riots of Boston.' More to the point, the legislature passed a resolution condemning

any attempt to alienate any portion of our fisheries or our soil to any foreign power, without the consent of the local legislature. As our fishery and territorial rights constitute the basis of our commerce and of our social and political existence, as they are our birthright and the legal inheritance of our children, we cannot under any circumstances assent to the terms of the convention ...[30]

The prime minister, Philip Little, and the leader of the opposition, H. W. Hoyles, together led a delegation to London to try to persuade the British government to abandon the convention, while John Kent, a Liberal minister, and F. B. T. Carter, a Conservative, were despatched to arouse support for Newfoundland's case in the other North American colonies.[31]

Faced with this determined and unanimous opposition, the British colonial secretary, Henry Labouchere, agreed to withdraw the convention, and further, in a despatch to the governor of Newfoundland, conceded the principle that

28/Rogers, Newfoundland, pp. 220–1.
29/The French Shore Problem, p. 34.
30/D. W. Prowse, A History of Newfoundland (London, 1895), p. 474.
31/A. M. Fraser, 'The French Shore,' in R. A. MacKay, ed., Newfoundland: Economic, Diplomatic, and Strategic Studies (Toronto, 1946), p. 284.

the rights enjoyed by the community in Newfoundland are not to be ceded or exchanged without their consent, and that the constitutional mode of submitting matters for that consent is by laying them before the colonial legislature; and that the consent of the community of Newfoundland is regarded by Her Majesty's government as the essential preliminary to any modification of their territorial and maritime rights.[32]

This was an important constitutional victory for Newfoundland as well as for every other colony, although in Newfoundland's case at least the British government later had frequent cause to regret the wording of Mr Labouchere's letter. No colonial secretary thereafter was ever allowed to forget that a settlement of the French Shore problem was impossible without the consent of Newfoundland; and time after time, at every suspected encroachment of the imperial government, Newfoundland politicians appealed to it as to a Magna Carta.

In the decades following the Labouchere despatch the issue of French rights on the treaty coast hung like a cloud over the turbulent domestic politics of Newfoundland, overshadowing all other issues, for it alone called into question the very basis of the colony's existence – control over its fisheries. As long as this was denied the colonial government found itself in the intolerable position of having assumed responsibility for the welfare and good government of its citizens without power commensurate with that responsibility. Therefore, in a way that Downing Street was never able to appreciate, the sanctity of imperial treaties inspired no feeling of awe in the aggrieved colony. Newfoundlanders lost no opportunity to harrass the French at every turn, and their government in St John's, regardless of which party was in power, never relented in their determination to see those treaties abrogated.

In pursuing this policy, by means that were sometimes direct, sometimes devious, the representatives of Newfoundland earned for themselves an unsavoury reputation with the Colonial Office for their lack of regard for the 'obligations of the Empire.'[33] But Newfoundland could not afford to wait for a diplomatic rapprochement that might never come. Its population was growing, and the French Shore, besides handicapping the fishery, was also holding up the development of agriculture, mining,[34] and

32/Labouchere to Governor Darling, 26 March 1857, as quoted in Innis, *The Cod Fisheries*, p. 396.

33/See Thompson, *The French Shore Problem*, p. 112.

34/When molybdenum deposits were discovered on the west coast in 1881 the American State Department issued a warning to investors not to risk their capital in a disputed territory, thus providing the colony with yet another illustration of the ruinous influence of the French treaty rights. See Fraser, 'The French Shore,' p. 293; also J. S. Winter *et al.*, *The Case for the Colony Stated by the People's Delegates* (London, 1890).

even the building of a transinsular railway by denying it a western terminus. As a matter of urgency, therefore, the colony was obliged to use whatever leverage it possessed in attempting to prize the French off its territory.

Yet in any serious test of strength Newfoundland's position was inevitably weak. Alone of the parties involved in the dispute, she could neither afford to make concessions nor had the strength to impose her own solution. It was therefore not until 1904, when conditions in Europe made an Anglo-French entente mutually desirable, that the rights of France in Newfoundland were finally abrogated as the colony had long maintained they should be: at the expense of the Empire in whose interest they were first created. The Anglo-French convention of that year,[35] although it dealt entirely with colonial and other overseas issues, owed its genesis not so much to colonial or overseas pressures as to an altered balance of power in European politics. In Britain there was a growing awareness of the dangers of diplomatic isolation, first aroused by the hostility of European opinion to the South African War, and given immediate relevance by the growing naval power of Germany. A similar anxiety was aroused in France by the preoccupation of Russia, her principal ally, with a war against Japan. The concomitance of these circumstances tended to produce on both sides of the Channel a climate favourable to an entente cordiale.[36]

The terms of the 1904 convention were designed to effect a worldwide balancing of accounts by the two signatories, thereby eliminating with a single stroke a tangle of unrelated disputes which intermittently over two hundred years had caused friction between them. Thus, the recognition of British hegemony in Egypt was exchanged for the recognition of French hegemony in Morocco, and French fishing rights in Newfoundland under the Treaty of Utrecht and succeeding treaties were exchanged for territorial concessions in West Africa (comprising part of the present-day Republic of Chad) and a monetary compensation to displaced French interests.[37] It was an imaginative solution, readily agreed to when the immediate self-interest of the two powers happened to coincide, to problems each of which taken individually had proven intractable, and which, in the case of Newfoundland, generations of agitating colonists and half a century of diplomatic wrangling had failed to resolve.

With the signing of the convention the prolonged struggle of the New-

35/Cd 2383, *Convention between the United Kingdom and France Respecting Newfoundland and West and Central Africa*, signed at London, 8 April 1904, ratifications exchanged 8 Dec. 1904.

36/See S. B. Fay, *The Origins of the World War* (New York, 1930), pp. 152–68.

37/Cd 2737, *Agreement between His Majesty's Government and the French Government for the Constitution of an Arbitral Tribunal and Statement of Sums Allotted by the Arbitrators* (London, 1905).

foundland colonists to control the island's territory and resources came to
an end. Newfoundland was at last master in its own house, politically as
well as constitutionally the equal of the other self-governing dominions of
Canada, Australia, and New Zealand. St John's was *en fête* for several
days and Newfoundlanders everywhere looked forward with Prime Minister Sir Robert Bond 'to the time when even the memory of the French
presence will fade like a fevered dream before the brightness of a new
day.'[38]

Yet if, in the nineteenth century, Newfoundland was burdened by the
problem of the French Shore, and if years of frustration led its government to adopt desperate measures which sometimes rebounded to the
colony's disadvantage, it must also be said that the struggle against France
– and occasionally against Britain as well – had a generally maturing and
beneficial effect upon the island's public life. For as long as the French
Shore remained a burning issue colonial politics could never be completely
confined to the level of the parish pump, no matter how strong the forces
tugging in that direction. Also, by emphasizing the uniqueness of Newfoundland's interests, the dispute with France helped to forge among the
people of the colony a keen awareness of their own separate identity. This
was encouraged in any case by natural insularity, the absence of substantial or varied immigration, and especially by the singular character of the
island's economic life. On the other hand, Newfoundland society also contained deep-seated sources of social conflict, and in such circumstances
the existence of a single great issue on which merchant and fisherman,
Protestant and Catholic, could at least suspend their differences was of
inestimable value in helping to create a distinct political entity.

38/Quoted in Fraser, 'The French Shore,' p. 332.

2 The political system

BY THE BEGINNING of the twentieth century there had evolved in Newfoundland, after forty-five years of responsible government, a political system that was unique in North America. Though archetypally 'British' in its formal institutions and outward trappings, in practice it also clearly reflected the island's history, distinctive geography, and socio-economic structure. In the first place, although the construction of a transinsular railway had furnished the island with an 'iron backbone' it was still, in J. D. Rogers' picturesque metaphor, primarily an 'exoskelton.'[1] Scarcely a Newfoundlander lived out of sight and sound of the sea.

The basic problem of government, therefore, was not how best to administer a compact though thinly populated land no larger than England, but rather how to provide even the most essential services of the state to a population scattered in tiny communities around roughly six thousand miles of coast, often linked to one another only by the sea – resembling, in fact, some vast triangular archipelago.

This peculiar distribution of population was responsible in no small measure for the emergence during the course of the nineteenth century of a highly centralized system of administration, and not, as might *prima facie* be supposed, a decentralized one. For instead of encouraging the growth of local government, the inescapable isolation of the great majority of 'outports'[2] militated strongly against it. The country did not divide

1/'Its heart,' wrote Rogers in characteristic style, 'is on the outside; there its pulse beats, and whatever is alive inside its exoskelton is alive by accident. The sea clothes the island as with a garment, and that garment contains the vital principle and soul of the national life of Newfoundland.' *Newfoundland: Historical and Geographical* (Oxford, 1911), p. 190.

2/'Outport' is a convenient word used in Newfoundland to denote any small coastal community.

easily into natural regions, and outside St John's there were few communities of sufficient size to support any form of local government.[3] Those that were large enough were faced with other formidable handicaps, not least of which was a scarcity of hard currency caused by the ubiquity of the truck system of credit trading. Direct taxation as a means of financing local government was therefore out of the question.[4] Nor was there any deeply rooted tradition of locally managed institutions which might have helped to overcome these handicaps, for the early settlers were for the most part Irish peasants or English west countrymen who had emigrated to Newfoundland before the movement in Britain towards modern municipal organization had made much progress. Consequently, with the single exception of St John's, which because of its size must be regarded as a case apart,[5] local government existed, if at all, only in embryo.

Under a Local Affairs Act passed in 1890 it was made possible for outport districts to elect 'district boards,'[6] responsible for such matters as roads, bridges, lighting, and sanitation. But the money so spent had to be provided entirely by the central government, by means of direct grants assigned for specific purposes in the annual Public Service Act. Control over the 'pork-barrel,' in other words, remained with the politicians in St John's. District boards themselves had no power to impose taxation of any sort, nor could they spend money or incur debts without authorization. Within these extremely narrow limits, elective boards were functioning in several areas by the turn of the century, though in the great majority of outports it was still true that local government did not exist in any shape or form.

This weakness at the bottom of the governmental structure had as its (perhaps inevitable) counterpart an extraordinary concentration of power at the top, in the cabinet and the House of Assembly. For besides the inchoate nature of municipal organization there were also historical factors which encouraged the growth of a strong centrally directed administration. First, the colony had inherited from the pre-1832 naval régime the habit of looking to St John's as the sole fount of political and legal

3/In 1901, of a total of more than 1,300 communities only 18 had a population of 1,000 or over. *Census of Newfoundland and Labrador, 1901.*

4/Public opinion was always violently hostile to the idea of direct taxation on property. One of the arguments used in 1869 by those opposed to confederation with Canada was that union would mean the levying of local rates. J. C. Crosbie, 'Local Government in Newfoundland,' *Canadian Journal of Economics and Political Science*, vol. 22, no. 3 (Aug. 1956), pp. 332–46.

5/The municipal institutions of St John's date from 1837 and it was incorporated as a city in 1888.

6/These districts normally coincided with electoral districts, which themselves had a distinctly nautical flavour: the District of Bonavista, for example, was defined as the area lying between Cape Freels and Cape Bonavista. There was no third dimension. It was taken for granted that no one would live away from the coast.

authority, and a habit so deeply ingrained was slow to fade. Secondly, each of the great struggles of the nineteenth century – for recognition as a colony, for responsible government, and for control of the French Shore – had tended, for various reasons, to accentuate the importance and enhance the prestige of the central government. Thus, the democratic parliament so long desired by the colony's politically conscious element, when finally attained, became the natural focus of every political ambition, the one instrument of government worth fighting to control, whose powers were jealously guarded and not easily circumscribed or even delegated. Although the constitution of 1855 had established a bicameral parliament with an appointed seventeen-member Legislative Council with wide formal powers,[7] it was always the elected House of Assembly that was the dominant chamber.

Moreover, the entire machinery of the state, from the highest official in St John's to the postmaster in the most distant outport, came under the direct command of a single executive – in theory the Governor-in-Council, in practice the cabinet. This was the focus of power in the system and at its centre stood the prime minister, always much more than *primus inter pares*. It was he who commanded the largest following in the House of Assembly, which enabled him, at the governor's invitation, to choose the other ministers. They therefore owed their positions to him; if he resigned, their resignations were automatic. The security of the government rested upon his ability to maintain the support of his party followers in the Assembly, which was never an easy task in the intimate and fractious world of St John's politics, where political fortunes rose and fell with bewildering suddenness. Party loyalties were as uncertain as they were fierce, and support was generally something a prime minister had to purchase, or reinforce, by the judicious use of patronage, whether political, personal, or purely commercial.

As in Britain, not all ministers were entitled to cabinet seats. Typically, the cabinet would consist of nine members, four of whom would be ministers without portfolio with two of these being the government leader in the Legislative Council and one other senior party supporter in that chamber. The colonial secretary (whose responsibilities were roughly those of the home secretary in Britain), minister of justice and attorney general,

7/Until the passage of the Legislature Act of 1917 the Legislative Council had the formal power to amend or reject any bill, but thereafter it was empowered only to delay a money bill for one month or any other bill for three consecutive sessions of the legislature. Legislative councillors were nominally appointed for life by the Crown, which meant in reality that all appointments were patronage appointments under the control of the prime minister and like all such patronage were distributed in accordance with the denominational principle (see p. 24). Though there were some exceptions, councillors were typically elderly St John's merchants or lawyers.

and minister of finance and customs, were invariably included; the holders
of one or two departmental posts of less prestige, such as the minister of
public works and the minister of marine and fisheries, usually were not.

Since the only effective unit of administration was the electoral district,
the individual district member in the House of Assembly had acquired the
crucial function of intermediary between the government at St John's and
the people of his district.[8] In the legislature he was the guardian and
spokesman of local interests, the sole liaison between the governors and
the governed. In addition, he was customarily expected to perform a mul-
titude of local duties that made him, for practical purposes, an unofficial
mayor and councillors rolled into one; and at the same time he was looked
upon by his constituents as the provider of free legal advice and other welfare services of every kind. As a former governor disapprovingly observed:

They regard their member as one who has to look after their personal interests
in every detail. He must be ready to watch over them when they are ill and get
them free medical treatment; he must get them free tickets for the seal fishery
[that is, a berth on a sealing ship], employment on the railways, free passes
from place to place, billets for their sons and daughters, and must even strive to
sell their fish above market price at the bidding of any ignorant or mischievous
agitator. In fine, there is nothing too ridiculous for electors to expect of their
member, and failure in any single case may send back a constituent to the outport to which he belongs, to become the centre of a clique resolved to displace
the member from his seat in Parliament.[9]

From the affluence and security of Government House these practices no
doubt appeared to be shocking deviations from the Westminster ideal:
from Bonavista or Fortune Bay they could be viewed in a different light.
For the really significant fact about Newfoundland society was not that
the member performed these functions but that if he did *not* perform them
there were no other channels through which they could be performed at all.

Yet if the member's responsibilities were great, so also were his powers.
Above all, he was the main channel through which public money flowed
to his district. The central government's revenue, for all purposes, was
raised almost entirely by indirect taxation (more than 80 per cent normally
being derived from customs duties alone), and in its annual distribution he
was instrumental in determining the allocation of funds within the area he
represented. It was an established convention that in each district locally

8/See H. B. Mayo, 'Municipal Government in Newfoundland,' *Public Affairs*,
March 1941, pp. 136–9; also Cmd 4480, *Newfoundland Royal Commission 1933
Report* (London, 1933), pp. 82–3.
9/Sir Ralph Williams, *How I Became a Governor* (London, 1913), pp. 412–13.

applicable grants, subsidies, contracts, concessions, and appointments were all made upon the recommendation of the district member. If the member happened to belong to the party in opposition, however, matters were more involved, not only because his district as a whole was unlikely to be favoured with more than a bare minimum of government patronage, but also because the defeated candidate of the governing party, or a government member in an adjoining district, often played a dominant part in its distribution. As can easily be imagined, this was a perennial cause of party strife.[10] But whatever the party situation, at the local level 'politics' and 'patronage' were virtually synonymous.

Moreover, this relatively simple, personal, and highly centralized system functioned within a society that to a remarkable degree had retained its original social and economic structure from the early nineteenth century, including its sharp cleavages of class and religion. There was still no substantial middle class: a gross inequality of wealth continued to separate the upper class of merchants, the 'fishocracy,'[11] from the lower class of fishermen. The credit structure of the fishery was unchanged: the city of St John's was still the financial as well as the political capital, its relationship to the outports being that of creditor to debtor. Water Street, the sea-front thoroughfare along which the leading merchant houses had their premises, was an object of hatred and fear in the outports, its name a synonym for exploitation.

Nor had the gulf separating Irish Catholics from English Protestants lessened with the passage of time. Instead it had become institutionalized. There was now scarcely an area of social life into which organized religious sectarianism did not in some way intrude, sustained and reinforced by a system of education that was totally church-controlled. There were no state schools: only Roman Catholic, Church of England, Methodist, Presbyterian, Congregational, and Salvation Army schools – all maintained with the aid of per capita government grants.[12]

Thus, although the members of the governing élite were recruited from a narrow stratum of society composed almost entirely of merchants and those members of a small professional class, particularly lawyers, who depended for their livelihood upon merchant patronage, their positions of

10/See, e.g., *Proceedings of the House of Assembly, Newfoundland, 1914*, p. 239 ff.

11/A word used (if not coined) by P. Tocque, *Newfoundland: As it was and as it is in 1877* (Toronto, 1878), p. 86. 'There is no colony belonging to the British Empire where influence and name tend so much to form a caste in society, and where it is more regarded than in St. John's.'

12/For an account of the development of this system, see F. W. Rowe, *The History of Education in Newfoundland* (Toronto, 1952); there is also a brief but accurate description of the system by J. D. Rogers in the *Oxford Survey of the British Empire* (Oxford, 1914), IV, chap. 10.

power were relatively secure. For the dominant institutions through which the political attitudes, values, and behavioural expectations of the community were inculcated and transmitted were all of a sort which tended to emphasize religious and ethnic differences rather than economic and social inequalities. That is to say, churches, schools, and organized groups, such as the Orange Lodge and the Benevolent Irish Society, all tended to maintain the sectarian status quo.

The effect of this upon the party system was far-reaching, but for this to be properly understood it is necessary to refer briefly to the development of political parties after the introduction of responsible government in 1855. Up to that time the division between the Liberal and Conservative parties, in terms both of policies and sources of support, was clear and unmistakable: the Liberals were for self-government and were supported mainly by Irish Catholics; the Conservatives were opposed to self-government, which they feared would allow power to fall into the hands of the lower classes, and were supported almost entirely by English Protestants, who feared it would allow power to fall into the hands of the Irish. At the urging of the Colonial Office, various experiments were tried in an effort to construct a viable constitution,[13] but the ineluctable fact remained that in any democratically elected chamber the Liberals could normally control a majority of seats by virtue of their appeal to a radical minority of Protestants. The merchant Conservatives had therefore to rely upon Crown appointees to safeguard their economic and class interests, and as long as this was the case any move in the direction of popular government was anathema to them.

There was, however, another variable present in the situation: what the constitution-writers of the Colonial Office could not accomplish the forces of demographic change could, for the Protestant population was growing more rapidly than the Catholic. The explanation of this is probably to be found in the higher rate of Irish Catholic emigration to the United States; but, whatever the reason, by 1855 the balance had tipped decisively in the Protestants' favour. In the census of 1857, the first after the granting of responsible government, it was confirmed that of a total population of 119,304 no less than 54.1 per cent were Protestant.[14] Thus, even though the Liberals were able to win the first two general elections after the introduction of responsible government, by 1860 the prospect of a Conservative government based wholly upon Protestant support had become more than a mere mathematical possibility. The Liberal Protestant minority was small and under extreme pressure from their co-religionists to conform to

13/See Gertrude E. Gunn, *The Political History of Newfoundland, 1832–1864* (Toronto, 1966), pp. 89–109.
14/*Ibid.*, pp. 149–50, and Appendix E, Table IV.

sectarian norms. They were, for example, vilified in the Conservative press as 'nominal Protestants ... poverty-stricken "anythingarians" who would support Atheism as soon as Romanism if thereby their purses felt the heavier.'[15] Their numbers had not grown proportionately with the growth of the Protestant population, and were no longer sufficient to keep their party in power should the rest of the electorate divide along sectarian lines.

Meanwhile, too, the Liberal government, after five years of able, constructive administration, had run into internal dissension over both leadership and policy and had also – most ironically in view of the Conservative charge that they were puppets of the Catholic hierarchy – incurred the wrath of the Roman Catholic Bishop of St John's. The temperamental Dr Mullock took a broad view of his episcopal duties: while on a visit to New York he had engaged, on behalf of the government but without the government's consent, a steamship he had taken a fancy to for service on the Newfoundland coast; when the government refused to honour his personal commitment he launched a scathing public attack upon them![16] Nevertheless, the Liberals might have been able to overcome their difficulties had they been allowed to serve their full term, but in the event, in February 1861, while still commanding a clear majority in the House of Assembly, they were arbitrarily dismissed from office by the governor. The latter was Sir Alexander Bannerman, a grossly prejudiced near-octogenarian who had shown nothing but malice towards his Liberal ministers and who had almost certainly engaged in a conspiracy with the Conservative opposition to remove them. The only justification an alarmed Colonial Office could find for his illegal and unconstitutional behaviour was that it had better succeed – meaning that the Conservatives had better secure a majority in the elections that were bound to follow.[17]

The governor had, in effect, delivered a coup de grâce to the idea that the political system could be legitimately operated in the interest of any but the dominant economic class. After a virulently sectarian campaign, and elections marred by violence, intimidation, and irregularities of every sort, the Conservatives emerged with a dubious victory: sectarian lines had sharpened sufficiently to alter the balance in the two constituencies with Protestant majorities which had previously returned Liberals. Burin now returned two Conservatives, while Harbour Grace was disfranchised by the refusal of the local magistrate to open the poll.[18]

To the Liberals this result, not unnaturally, looked fraudulent. And though the governor and his new Conservative ministers were backed by a garrison of British troops, even these could not keep order in predomi-

15/Quoted in *ibid.*, p. 143.   16/See *ibid.*, pp. 154–5.
17/*Ibid.*, pp. 157–61.   18/*Ibid.*, pp. 163–4.

nantly Liberal and Catholic St John's. On the day the legislature opened
a mob formed around the Colonial Building, stoned the governor's carriage, and were finally dispersed only after the troops had opened fire. The
loss of life was not great – three were killed and twenty wounded, one of
the latter being a Catholic priest[19] – but the effect on the community was
profound. Sectarianism had reached its inevitable nadir. Thereafter the
Conservatives could govern alone if they were determined to do so, but
only with military support and at considerable risk to their lives and
property.

Newfoundland, however, was not to become simply a colonial microcosm of Ireland, for, unlike Ireland, political oppression was not in the
economic interest of the Protestant ruling élite. Rather, the events of 1861
taught them that their economic interests could be effectively safeguarded
even under a system of responsible and democratically elected government
if they accepted the system and learned to operate it to their own advantage. In this sense, 1861 converted the Conservatives into liberal demo-
crats. They could accept majority rule once it had been successfully demonstrated that the electorate could be divided along sectarian lines. The
only remaining problem was the danger of open insurrection or terrorism
by the Catholic minority, but in a very short time that problem too was
solved.

The solution was an obvious one: to purchase security for themselves
and undisturbed conditions of trade the merchant Conservatives were prepared to give a generous share of the spoils of office to defeated Catholic
politicians. Since the cost of such a share-out fell upon the general revenue
it cost the merchants nothing directly. Accordingly, after 1865, when two
Catholic Liberals accepted office in the Conservative government of F. B.
T. Carter, positions in the cabinet, the civil service, and all other patronage
posts were awarded on a roughly proportional basis among the adherents
of the various religious faiths. In time this 'denominational principle,' as it
came to be called, acquired the status of a constitutional convention.[20] It
also signalled the breakdown of the old party system and the disappearance of Liberal radicalism, a process soon to be further accelerated by the
movement of events on the North American mainland.

The debate over confederation with Canada shattered old political al-
legiances. The St John's oligarchy naturally feared Canadian commercial
competition and the imposition of a federal authority which would be

19/For vivid contemporary accounts of this incident, see Anon. [H. Winton?],
A Chapter in the History of Newfoundland for the Year 1861 (St John's, 1861); also
R. B. McCrea, *Lost Amid the Fogs* (London, 1869), pp. 127–32.

20/This solution is an interesting early example of what has since come to be
labelled 'consociational democracy.' See Arend Lijphart, 'Typologies of Democratic
Systems,' *Comparative Political Studies*, vol. 1, no. 1 (April 1968), pp. 3–44.

beyond their control. Ironically, however, they found their main support not among the English Protestant community but among the Irish Catholics, whose bitter folk memories were stirred by such effective propaganda as the comparison of confederation to the 1801 Act of Union between Britain and Ireland. Thus in 1869 the anti-confederation party, with the support of every Irish Catholic (and therefore traditionally Liberal) constituency, swept to victory under the leadership of Charles Fox Bennett – an extreme Tory, a Protestant, a wealthy mine-owner, and an absentee landlord![21] For more than thirty years thereafter there was little to distinguish one party from another. Parties, in so far as they may be said to have existed at all, were mere *ad hoc* creations, cabals of politicians whose association with one another signified nothing more than their common desire to capture the government. And each government in turn stood on a quicksand of shifting alliances within the Assembly, where the real struggle for power took place.[22] Sectarianism was by no means dead, but its value was symbolic rather than substantive. There were no major issues of church-state relations, no 'separate schools' question or any other involving religion that could produce clear party differences. Elections were frequently highly competitive, but it was a competition between teams recruited from the same narrow élite. Elections gave the people a choice, went a popular aphorism, 'between merchants and lawyers and lawyers and merchants.'

The basic power structure was therefore relatively simple: a small merchant-dominated oligarchy ruled a community in which the denominational compromise of the 1860s had crystallized into an established principle of government and denominational segregation had become an unwritten law of social organization.

Around the turn of the century, however, important changes were beginning to take place, and new political patterns were beginning to emerge. There were a number of contributory factors involved in this – improved communications within the island and with the outside world, the consequent spread of outside ideas and influences, and the general growth of population – but above all there was the impact of the railway, or more accurately, perhaps, the *financing* of the railway, upon almost every aspect of Newfoundland's political life.

21/G. F. G. Stanley, 'Sir Stephen Hill's Observations on the Election of 1869 in Newfoundland,' *Canadian Historical Review*, vol. 29, no. 3 (Sept. 1948), pp. 278–85; see also H. B. Mayo, 'Newfoundland and Confederation in the Eighteen-Sixties,' *Canadian Historical Review*, vol. 29, no. 2 (June 1948), pp. 125–42.
22/For a valuable account of Newfoundland politics in this period, see H. Mitchell, 'The Constitutional Crisis of 1889 in Newfoundland,' *Canadian Journal of Economics and Political Science*, vol. 24, no. 3 (Aug. 1958), pp. 323–31.

3 The railway and politics

THE 'age of iron and steam' came late to Newfoundland. The island's small population, rugged terrain, and meagre resources made railway construction at best a financially dubious undertaking. Yet, after many vicissitudes, including the British government's veto of any western terminus which infringed upon French treaty rights, and the bankruptcy of the company to whom the original construction and operating contract had been given, a narrow-gauge line was at last completed between St John's and Port-aux-Basques in 1896.

The builder was R. G. Reid,[1] a Canadian engineer and capitalist, who received in part payment from the Newfoundland government substantial concessions of land. His stake in the island thus assured, he soon became a political power to be reckoned with: railway construction pumped millions of dollars in cash into what had previously been an almost exclusively credit economy, all of it emanating from or channelled through Reid, whose personal empire began to rival the government as a source of patronage. For the first time fortunes could be made by supplying goods and services to an enterprise unconnected with the fishery; for the first time lawyers and other functionaries who had previously served the merchant class both professionally and politically were able to earn lucrative fees from another source. And since some of the recipients were cabinet ministers and members of the Assembly it is not surprising that Reid was soon able to obtain uniquely favourable terms in his negotiations with the government. Ultimately, the question of Reid's place in the economy and politics of the island split the traditional governing élite into pro-Reid and anti-Reid factions. On the basis of this split a new party alignment took

1/Mr (later Sir) Robert Gillespie Reid, 1842–1908. *Dictionary of National Biography, 1901–11* (London), pp. 176–8.

shape, and, more importantly, a new form of political party emerged. The flashpoint which set off these reactions was the Railway Contract of 1898.

In that year the Conservative government of Sir James Winter, a lawyer and former judge, negotiated a contract with Reid which gave the government a cash payment of a million dollars, thus enabling it to avoid an imminent financial crisis,[2] but which in return gave Reid concessions of the most sweeping nature. For operating the railway for fifty years he was to receive approximately three million acres of land, bringing his total in the island to more than five million acres; for $1 million, and the eventual reassignment of a portion of his lands to the government, he was to become the owner of the railway at the end of the operating period; he was to purchase the publicly owned St John's dry dock; he was to provide a coastal steamship service, aided by a government subsidy of nearly $100,000 per annum; and he was to purchase and operate the publicly owned telegraph network.[3] In short, the colony's entire communications system was to be handed over to a private individual. 'Although all men agreed,' wrote J. D. Rogers, 'that the essence of the contract was to convert the State into a Man, they differed as to whether the Man should be looked on as an incarnate Atlas or Leviathan.'[4]

When a bill authorizing this astonishing covenant was submitted to the House of Assembly it provoked an unprecedented storm. The governor, Sir Herbert Murray, was so aghast at the implications of the contract that he immediately sought permission from the Colonial Office to refuse the royal assent; but Joseph Chamberlain, secretary of state for the colonies, though equally aghast, deemed that it would be unconstitutional to interfere in a matter of local finance – even though 'such an abdication by a Government of some of its most important functions is without parallel.'

The Colony is divested for ever of any control over or power of influencing its own development, and of any direct interest in or benefit from that development. It will not even have the guarantee for efficiency and improvement

2/According to the minister of finance at the time, 'Debentures of the Colony amounting to $943,000 had been called in for payment, and money was being borrowed temporarily from the banks at 6% to pay such as were presented. The public were alarmed at conditions, and borrowing publicly would have necessitated embarrassing explanations.' A. B. Morine, *The Railway Contract, 1898, and Afterwards* (St John's, n.d. [1933]), p. 9.

3/There were a number of other provisions. The actual contract was an involved document, and certainly no model of good legal draftsmanship: it stipulated payments both by and to the contractor, but failed to make any clear distinction between his rights and obligations. For a useful summary of its terms, see Cmd 4480, *Newfoundland Royal Commission 1933 Report* (London, 1933), pp. 32–3.

4/*Newfoundland: Historical and Geographical* (Oxford, 1911), p. 178.

afforded by competition, which would tend to minimise the danger of leaving such services in the hands of private individuals.[5]

Nevertheless, the 'abdication' duly took place. But in the process the existing loosely knit parliamentary factions were forced to divide on a fundamental question of principle: whether the government or a private industrial empire was to be the greatest power in the land. In effect, the ancient battle over responsible government flared up again in a new and incredible form.

In the Assembly the governing party, which had a clear majority of five, unanimously supported the contract, despite the fact that their leader had been elected in 1897 on a pledge of 'no more concessions to Reid'! The thirteen opposition members were almost evenly divided. A group of six, led by Edward Morris, supported the contract; the remaining seven 'Liberals' under Robert Bond's leadership were implacably hostile towards it. It should not be thought, however, that in the controversy that raged throughout the summer of 1898 the Conservatives were without a case. To Bond's charge that Reid had been made a 'czar' they plausibly replied (*pace* Chamberlain) that Reid's railway, steamship, telegraph, and other holdings could return a profit only if his lands were developed, and by such development the entire country would benefit.[6]

But whatever the strength of the government's case, it was soon obscured by scandal. In November it was revealed that A. B. Morine,[7] the minister of finance – the person most responsible for negotiating the contract and its most forceful advocate in the legislature – had been *at the same time*, and was still, the solicitor of R. G. Reid at a yearly retainer of $5,000.[8] Though Morine was dismissed from office, Sir James Winter would neither resign nor call for a dissolution of Parliament. Instead, he and the remainder of his ministry clung to power throughout the following year until finally, amid a rising crescendo of public protest, their parliamentary support began to disintegrate. In this the faction led by Edward Morris played a crucial rôle. These six members now found themselves in

5/Public Record Office, Colonial Office Papers, series 194, vol. 240, Chamberlain to Governor Murray, 23 March 1898.

6/See A. B. Morine, *The Railway Contract*, pp. 22–4.

7/Mr (later Sir) Alfred Bishop Morine, 1857–1944, a Nova Scotian who became editor of the St John's *Mercury* in 1883, but later read law at Dalhousie University, was called to the bar, and entered the House of Assembly in 1889; minister of finance, 1897–8. His political career, which lasted until 1927, was divided between Newfoundland and Canada and in both was marked throughout by violent controversy. See the speech by the Hon. F. B. Carvell, *Canada, House of Commons Debates*, vol. CVI, cc. 6528–43, 29 March 1912; also *Who's Who in Canada* (Toronto, 1922), p. 966.

8/CO 194/241, A. le C. Berteau to Murray, 31 Oct. 1898.

an invidious position – they had gambled and appeared to have lost. Their leader had not been given office, and worse still, they had become identified with a discredited régime that was almost certainly doomed to annihilation at the polls. Such, however, was not to be the fate of the ambitious Morris. At an opportune moment he and his followers switched sides once again, and carried with them a sufficient number of Winter's own supporters to bring down the government on a vote of confidence.[9]

Thus, when on 7 March 1900 Robert Bond was called upon to form a government he was immediately faced with the problem of how best to deal with Morris who, besides controlling the balance of power in the Assembly, was also the leading Catholic member with a large personal following in St John's and among Irish Catholics generally. But if Bond needed the support of Morris to avoid a denominational split, Morris needed the endorsement of Bond to avoid being returned to opposition in the next election as the head of a minority Catholic party. For, given the state of public opinion, he could not reasonably have hoped for a better result. A coalition was therefore possible and even necessary. Morris was included in Bond's ministry as minister without portfolio and a general election was set for 8 November.

Meanwhile, in the country at large the furore over the 'Reid Deal' had scarcely abated since 1898. The people of Newfoundland were overwhelmingly hostile, and the man who more than any other shaped and directed their hostility was Robert Bond, an aristocratic young politician who combined intellect with moral passion in a brilliant 'Gladstonian' campaign. Ultimately, however, the most significant development in this period was not Bond's leadership but the sharp impetus that agitation over the Reid contract gave to the development of a Liberal party organization. Lord Birkenhead's remark that 'the islanders stopped fishing and took to petitions'[10] is not complete: they also formed or reactivated constituency Liberal associations whose functions were to assist in the drafting and circulation of petitions and to organize public meetings and other forms of protest.[11] By such means the Liberal party became the first to acquire an effective reality which extended beyond the traditional limits of the

9/Morine claims in his apologia that he and Sir James Winter had an 'understanding' that upon the close of the legislature in 1898 Sir James was to be appointed chief justice of the Supreme Court and he (Morine) was to succeed him as prime minister. Had this arrangement been followed, he claims, he would have invited Morris to join the cabinet, 'but coalition was never discussed between us, as leadership never came to me.' *The Railway Contract*, p. 32.

10/*The Story of Newfoundland* (London, 1920), p. 148.

11/Associations were organized in practically every constituency. For accounts of their meetings, activities, names of officers, and other information, the local press of the period is an invaluable source, particularly the *Twillingate Sun, Harbour Grace Standard*, and the St John's *Evening Telegram*.

House of Assembly. It became, in fact, the island's first 'modern' political party in the sense that its structure came to resemble (with due allowance for the more primitive and rural nature of Newfoundland society) the structure of parties then existing in England.[12] It was, of course, in an incipient state of development, and in any case the combination of a spoils system with a democratic franchise might have produced similar results in the long run, just as it had elsewhere in North America. Nevertheless, the immediate stimulus was provided by local agitation against the Reid contract, which Bond and his party astutely turned to their advantage. Hence the Liberal party that entered the 1900 general election not only had an able leader with a strong moral case to present: it was also the best organized party that Newfoundland had ever seen.

The opposition Conservative party, on the other hand, had no organization whatever. It was not even the traditional 'Tory' party of Water Street merchants, many of whom supported Bond. Instead it was the party of R. G. Reid, the railway contractor, who owned it body and soul. *The Times'* correspondent reported:

One of Mr. Reid's sons has been accompanying him [A. B. Morine] through his constituency, and is mooted as a candidate. Two captains of Reid's bay steamers are running for other seats. The clothier who supplies the uniforms for Reid's officials is another, and a shipmaster, who until recently was ship's husband for the Reid steamers is another. His successor, who is a member of the Upper House, has issued a letter warmly endorsing Mr. Morine's policy, and it is now said that one of Reid's surveying staff will be nominated for another constituency.[13]

For Reid, politics had naturally become a means of protecting his vast holdings, and in 1900 these were clearly in danger. He had therefore installed the irrepressible Morine as his party leader and lavishly financed a campaign to persuade the electorate of the public benefits of the 1898 contract.[14] But even had the Liberal party been less well organized and less ably led, the result would probably have been much the same. In the event, it was almost a clean sweep. Bond's government was returned with thirty-two of the thirty-six seats, giving it the largest majority ever held in

12/Cf. M. Ostrogorski, *Democracy and the Organization of Political Parties* (New York, 1922), I, 161–82.

13/Quoted in Birkenhead, *The Story of Newfoundland*, p. 158.

14/A fascinating glimpse into the financing of the Reid campaign is to be found in the report of the case of *Reid* v *Morine*, 1906. In 1899 Reid purchased the St John's *Daily News* anonymously through Morine, who later refused to transfer the ownership to him. Reid sued and won. *Evening Telegram*, 1–16 March 1906.

the House of Assembly. For Reid and Morine the result was an over-whelming expression of popular condemnation.

It was thus from a position of great strength that Robert Bond set about the task of forming a new government. The election, however, had failed to settle the question of his relations with Edward Morris, who had prudently played down the issue of the Reid contract in his own election campaign and had been returned at the head of the poll in the important three-member district of St John's West.

As Bond well knew, Morris was a political renegade who owed allegiance to no one and no party. Yet in forming his first ministry Bond had had no choice but to include him since the government was dependent for its majority upon the votes of Morris' personal followers in the Assembly. But in the new House, with a majority of twenty-eight seats, he was under no such compulsion. Even if Morris crossed the floor once again he could not have carried with him, this time into the certain wilderness, more than four or five members. Still, he remained a formidable political force. With his unconcealed ambition for the highest office, his platform eloquence, and his proven hold on the Irish-Catholic vote, Morris was a danger to any ministry. What Bond had to decide was whether he would be more dangerous inside the cabinet or outside. On the one hand, his exclusion would have created no immediate problem. The majority of Catholic members were loyal to Bond and would not have bolted the party with Morris. Moreover, Bond, a Methodist, was a personal friend and confidant of Dr Michael Howley, the Roman Catholic archbishop of St John's, whose main concern in the matter was to *prevent* the appointment of his co-religionist Morris, whom he heartily disliked and distrusted.[15] On the other hand, Bond undeniably owed Morris a political debt, not only for his aid in toppling the régime of Sir James Winter, but also for his contribution to the party's electoral victory, especially in the predominantly Catholic constituencies. And there was also the additional consideration that if he included Morris his government would be the strongest, most broadly based aggregation the country had ever seen, able to govern practically without opposition.

After some hesitation, Bond finally made up his mind. When the new Executive Council was sworn in on 30 November 1900, Edward Morris took office as minister without portfolio.

So far little mention has been made of Bond or Morris apart from a consideration of their political rôles. Yet in describing the political life of a community as small as Newfoundland it can be seriously misleading to allow its politicians to appear only as impersonal instruments of policy

15/Bond Papers, Archbishop Howley to Bond, 29 Nov. 1900.

or as 'rôle-occupants.' To do so is to run the risk of distorting or even missing altogether those quintessential elements of character and personal background without an understanding of which the nuances and subtleties of political life so often become unintelligible. To understand, for example, the nature of the gulf which separated Robert Bond from Edward Morris is to understand a great deal of the social background to Newfoundland politics in the early twentieth century.

Robert Bond was born in St John's in 1857,[16] the second son of a wealthy merchant, one of the traditional island élite. He was sent for his early education to a west country public school (Queen's College, Taunton), and later studied law. But independent wealth made practice at the bar unnecessary; instead he became the protégé of William Whiteway, the dominant political figure of the time (prime minister, 1878–85, 1889–94, 1895–7), and in 1882, at the age of twenty-five, took his seat in the House of Assembly as member for Trinity.

In 1859, two years after Bond, Edward Patrick Morris[17] was born on Lime Street, in a working-class area of St John's, where his father, an Irish immigrant, was a cooper and later keeper of the poorhouse. From there, by some combination of wits and ambition and good fortune, he rose through a school of the Irish Christian Brothers to a degree in law at the University of Ottawa. He was called to the Newfoundland bar and in 1885, at the age of twenty-six, entered the House of Assembly as member for St John's West.

Both obtained their first office under Whiteway in 1889, Bond as colonial secretary, Morris as minister without portfolio. But thereafter Bond's rise had been rapid and spectacular, Morris' much less so. In 1890 Bond had been responsible for negotiating a reciprocity treaty with the United States,[18] and in 1894 he had become a national hero by his success in ne-gotiating an emergency loan in London which saved the colony from in-solvency after a catastrophic bank crash.[19] By 1900 he had reached the very pinnacle of success: at the age of forty-three he was prime minister, with the greatest majority ever seen in the House of Assembly. Morris, meanwhile, held the same office he had held eleven years before.

16/For brief but useful biographies, see the *Dictionary of National Biography, 1922–30*, pp. 87–9; and J. R. Smallwood, ed., *The Book of Newfoundland* (St John's, 1937), I, 263–5. Also of interest is an article in the *Review of Reviews* (London), vol. 26, no. 152 (Aug. 1902), pp. 138–9, and the impressions of Sir Ralph Williams, *How I Became a Governor* (London, 1913), p. 410 ff.

17/See the *Dictionary of National Biography, 1931–40*, pp. 631–2; and Smallwood, *The Book of Newfoundland*, I, 265–7.

18/See below, pp. 36–7.

19/D. W. Prowse, *A History of Newfoundland* (rev. ed., London, 1896), pp. 544–6.

In other respects, too, their careers and lives presented a sharp contrast. Morris, through forensic astuteness (and the Newfoundlander's love of litigation) had built up a large practice at the St John's bar, which mixed well with his political activities. For in St John's, as elsewhere in North America, the law and politics were natural avenues to advancement for an ambitious and talented Irishman. He was a voluble and out-going man, deeply involved in the life of the city, and possessed an instinctive understanding of its inhabitants. He was at his best in the rough-and-tumble of an election campaign, but his political strength was also well rooted in a host of remembered names, personal kindnesses, cases taken without hope of fees, attendance at wakes and baptisms, and other assiduously cultivated contacts. He was, in fact, the darling of the St John's Irish, one of their own who had risen high, and throughout his career their loyalty to him never wavered.

Bond could not have been more different. Though a brilliant speaker and debater, and relentless in his pursuit of a political career, he was personally a quiet and reserved man. And though he was *from* the St John's merchant class, he was not *of* it. His home was a scenic country estate at Whitbourne, some sixty miles from the city, where, as a bachelor, he lived the life of an intellectual country squire, devoted to his library, progressive agriculture, and a small circle of close friends. Yet if his private life was serene, his public life was characterized by immense vigour. For him the reality of politics was found not, as it was for Morris, in the mundane business of dealing with local people and their local or private problems. It was found in a different sphere: in the relations between sovereign governments, and in those issues which affected the country as a whole. If Morris resembled a New York congressman, Bond was more like a British cabinet minister.

Given these various factors, it is easy to understand why Bond occupied an ideal vantage point from which to lead the Liberal party, and why, at the beginning of the century, the Liberal party was able to reconcile the diverse elements within Newfoundland society. For Bond was a Methodist, yet had the rare asset of possessing the full confidence and support of the Catholic hierarchy; he was the wealthy scion of a merchant family, yet a Liberal; he was an urbane and educated man, yet his deepest personal interests lay outside the St John's milieu. Finally, his alliance with Edward Morris brought to the Liberal party the undivided loyalty of the Newfoundland Irish.

This unique combination of forces in a single party did not fail to live up to its early promise. The first years of the new administration were distinguished by political stability, prosperity, and orderly progress. Bond's reputation grew both at home and abroad, while Morris was apparently content to serve in the cabinet, of which he was the acknowledged deputy leader.[20]

In 1901 the Liberal pledge to modify the Reid contract was fulfilled. Reid was compelled to surrender absolutely his claim to ownership of the railway; the telegraph system was immediately returned to public owner-ship and operation; and title to all those lands he had been granted in 1898 reverted to the Crown.[21] As A. B. Morine himself sadly observed, this amounted to 'a virtual repeal of the 1898 Contract.'[22] Under a new agree-ment, however, the newly incorporated Reid Newfoundland Company was given a concession to operate the railway and steamship services for fifty years, and provide electric street lighting and tramway services for St John's. Reid's million dollar payment to the Winter government was re-turned to him with 6 per cent interest, and his claims respecting rolling stock and the telegraph system were settled by arbitration. Despite Reid's open political hostility, the Liberal government's treatment of him was scrupulously fair and even generous. In all, it cost the colony some $2.5 million to repurchase assets which, in the opinion of the vast majority of its citizens, should never have been surrendered in the first place.

For Bond, success followed upon success. After 1900 the island's eco-nomy began to enjoy a modest boom with the rapid expansion of new timber and mining industries, while a combination of large catches and high prices in foreign markets produced a series of prosperous fisheries. With revenue swelled to unprecedented heights, the government was able to operate from year to year with a budget surplus.[23] Finally, in 1904, with a general election approaching, the signing of the Anglo-French conven-tion bestowed upon the colony the greatest boon of all – undisputed pos-session of the French Shore. Naturally, as the party in power, the Liberals were able to claim credit for the settlement, and the election which fol-lowed was remarkable only for the ineffectiveness of the opposition.

In 1902 the government had surprisingly lost two seats in by-elections and this was hopefully interpreted in some quarters as a sign of widespread dissatisfaction.[24] There was consequently a small stampede among the

20/Other than Bond, Morris was the only member of the cabinet to attend the coronation of Edward VII in 1902. He also took part in discussions with the British government on the French Shore question. In the same year he became attorney general.

21/Cmd 4480, *Report*, p. 36.

22/*The Railway Contract*, p. 34.

23/For an expert contemporary review of the island's economic and financial position, see *The Times*, London, 7 Sept. 1904.

24/It was more likely due to a strong personal vote for the two young opposition candidates, William Warren and Robert Watson, who were standing for the first time and were thus untainted by the scandals of 1898.

ousted politicians of earlier régimes to obtain the leadership of the 'anti-Liberal' forces. Sir James Winter ended his brief retirement in the hope of replacing A. B. Morine, who had led the opposition in the Assembly; and Donald Morison, a leader of the Orange Lodge, resigned a Supreme Court judgeship in the hope of replacing them both. In addition, A. F. Goodridge, an ex-premier who had held office briefly at the time of the 1894 bank crash, also announced his candidacy, as (for unclear reasons) did an aged William Whiteway. Unable to agree upon either a single leader or a common statement of policy, they finally settled upon a name – the 'United Opposition Party.' The outcome was predictable. The Liberals held all thirty of their seats while of the five opposition 'leaders' four were defeated. The exception was the politically durable Morine, who managed to hold his seat in Bonavista.[25]

Robert Bond's first term in the premiership had thus been one of unmitigated triumph. Now, at the age of forty-seven, he stood at the very height of his powers. Under him the Liberal party was strong and united, and demonstrably the only effective political organization in the land. There was every reason to believe that its stay in office would be long and fruitful.

25/Morine attributes the defeat of the opposition party to 'the feeling that it had no definite policy and was led by men whose part in public life had been played.' *The Railway Contract*, p. 33.

4 The Liberal party and relations with the United States and Canada

IN THE euphoric wake of the French Shore settlement, the Liberal government, with its mandate newly endorsed, turned with an air of confidence to the one outstanding problem of external relations still confronting the colony: the repeated thwarting of its desire for commercial reciprocity with the United States. But this was a problem of formidable complexity, demanding caution rather than confidence. For any change in Newfoundland's relations with the United States necessarily involved both Britain and Canada, and affected not only their relations with Newfoundland but with each other and with the United States as well.[1] Nor, in a matter of such far-reaching importance, could the internal politics of Newfoundland remain untouched, as the Liberal party was to learn to its sorrow.

The immediate background to the reciprocity question may be traced back to 1890, when Robert Bond, then colonial secretary in Whiteway's administration, succeeded in negotiating with the American secretary of state, James G. Blaine, a comprehensive agreement covering both reciprocal trade and American fishing rights in Newfoundland waters.[2] For Newfoundland and for Bond personally this was a major diplomatic coup. But to the Canadian government, whose own hope of obtaining reciprocity had collapsed with the Senate's rejection of the Chamberlain-Bayard Treaty in 1888, it was a source of intense chagrin. Newfoundland's suc-

1/For an outstandingly perceptive general study of the interplay between Great Britain and North America, see J. B. Brebner, *North Atlantic Triangle* (Toronto, Carleton Library Edition, 1966). See also Peter F. Neary and Sidney J. R. Noel, 'Newfoundland's Quest for Reciprocity, 1890–1910,' in Mason Wade, ed., *Regionalism in the Canadian Community, 1867–1967* (Toronto, 1969), pp. 210–26.

2/See A. M. Fraser, 'Fisheries Negotiations with the United States, 1783–1910,' in R. A. MacKay, ed., *Newfoundland: Economic, Diplomatic, and Strategic Studies* (Toronto, 1946), pp. 359–72.

cess was an embarrassing contrast to their own failure; but even worse, it was feared that if the reciprocity agreement strengthened Newfoundland's economy it might well end all hope of bringing the island into confederation, or, worse still, might encourage in Newfoundland a movement for annexation to the United States.[3] Consequently, Canadian pressure upon the British government to refuse the necessary imperial ratification of the agreement was persistent and unrestrained, and despite Newfoundland's protests against Canadian interference, the greater influence of Canada prevailed. In January 1891, in accordance with Canada's wishes, the British government informed Newfoundland that the Bond-Blaine convention could not be ratified on the grounds that Newfoundland's negotiations with the United States must proceed *pari passu* with those of Canada.[4]

Outraged at having the plum of reciprocity so rudely snatched from it, Newfoundland retaliated by prohibiting the sale of bait to Canadian fishermen. This in turn provoked a minor but unpleasant tariff war with Canada – Newfoundland imposing a prohibitive duty on Canadian flour, Canada on Newfoundland fish.[5] In an effort to improve relations, a conference was held at Halifax in November 1892, but by ending in failure served only to aggravate matters. Newfoundland-Canadian relations were thus at an extremely low ebb when, in the spring of 1895, the Newfoundland government was forced by the imminence of financial collapse, and the British government's refusal to lend practical aid, into the humiliating position of having to supplicate for entry into confederation. Negotiations opened at Ottawa on 4 April, but quickly broke down when Canada's MacKenzie Bowell administration, with characteristic ineptitude, sought to take advantage of Newfoundland's desperation by driving an excessively hard bargain.[6] Ultimately the colony was saved from collapse only by the timely success of Robert Bond (who had been a delegate at the Ottawa negotiations) in floating a loan in the City of London, but neither he nor his countrymen could easily forget the niggardly attitude shown by Canada at a time of crisis. A lesson had been learned, however, and Newfoundlanders turned more than ever towards the United States, where the

3/There is evidence to suggest that Blaine was well aware of the possibility of annexation, and facilitated an agreement with Bond in order to create tension between Canada and Newfoundland. See T. Dennett, *John Hay: From Poetry to Politics* (New York, 1933), p. 423.

4/Fraser, 'Fisheries Negotiations,' p. 368.

5/H. A. Innis, *The Cod Fisheries: The History of an International Economy* (rev. ed., Toronto, 1954), p. 452.

6/A. M. Fraser, 'Relations with Canada,' in MacKay, *Newfoundland*, pp. 449–59; also H. Mitchell, 'Canada's Negotiations with Newfoundland, 1887–1895,' *Canadian Historical Review*, vol. 40, no. 4 (Dec. 1959), pp. 277–93.

thwarted Bond-Blaine convention had afforded them 'a tantalizing glimpse of riches behind the American tariff wall.'[7]

The chief proponent of reciprocity was naturally Bond himself, and in 1900, as prime minister, he had reopened the question by asking the British government to ratify the 1890 convention or, if Washington considered it defunct, to permit Newfoundland to begin negotiations for a new treaty. His request came at an opportune moment. After a full decade Canada could no longer credibly blame Newfoundland for her own failure to obtain reciprocity, and though Sir Wilfrid Laurier, like his predecessor, feared that a separate agreement between Newfoundland and the United States would further imperil the prospects of bringing the island into confederation, his protests were in vain. With British approval, Bond opened discussions with the State Department in Washington in August 1902.[8]

On 8 November he and the American secretary of state, John Hay, concluded a draft convention similar to the one of 1890. Under it Newfoundland was to obtain free admission to American markets for a wide range of fishery and mineral products, and in return American fishing vessels were to have 'the privilege of purchasing herring, caplin, squid, and all other bait fishes at all times, on the same terms and conditions, and subject to the same penalties as Newfoundland vessels,' and 'the privilege of touching and trading, buying and selling fish and oil, and procuring supplies in Newfoundland, conforming to the Harbour Regulations, but without other charge than the payment of such light, harbour, and custom dues as are, or may be, levied on Newfoundland fishing vessels.'[9] In addition, the treaty listed a number of manufactured goods and foodstuffs that Newfoundland was to admit from the United States duty free. But before the treaty could take effect it required ratification both by the British government and by the president and Senate of the United States. Britain reluctantly gave its consent; the Senate proved more troublesome. A vociferous opposition had been raised by the New England fishing interests, whose chief spokesman in Congress was the influential senator from Massachusetts, Henry Cabot Lodge. Hence, when on 4 December 1902 the Bond-Hay Treaty was referred to the Senate Foreign Relations Committee, Lodge, as chairman of the committee, seized the opportunity to block its further progress, which he succeeded in doing for more than two years. When finally, in January 1905, at the urging of President Roosevelt, he

7/C. S. Campbell, *Anglo-American Understanding, 1898–1903* (Baltimore, 1957), p. 259.
8/*Ibid.*
9/*Proceedings of the North Atlantic Coast Fisheries Arbitration* (Washington, 1912), IV, 79–82.

agreed to report the treaty out of committee, it was in so drastically amended a form as to be totally unacceptable to Newfoundland.[10]

For Bond the loss of the treaty was a bitter disappointment, though hardly a surprise. As early as January 1903 he had anticipated this result and when it became clear that Senator Lodge was completely adamant, he was ready to retaliate. His plan was to employ what had by this time become Newfoundland's standard diplomatic sanction: the withholding of bait supplies to fishermen of the offending country.[11] It had previously been used, with varying degrees of effectiveness, against both France and Canada: Bond now threatened to employ it against the United States. At first sight, he would appear to have been on firm ground, for although the United States possessed certain fishing rights on the south and west coasts of Newfoundland under an Anglo-American treaty of 1818, for economic reasons the American fleet was almost completely dependent upon supplies of bait purchased in Newfoundland, the use of Newfoundland port facilities, and even upon Newfoundland crews.[12]

Thus, when the last hope of ratification faded, the Newfoundland government had its policy ready. In April 1905 it introduced an amendment to the Foreign Fishing Vessels Act of 1893 designed to prohibit American vessels from purchasing bait or supplies, or engaging crews, within Newfoundland's territorial waters. Newfoundland customs officials were empowered to board and inspect all American vessels within the three-mile limit, and the presence on board a vessel of prohibited goods was to be considered *prima facie* evidence of their illegal purchase.[13] In introducing this amendment in the Assembly, Bond strongly emphasized that Newfoundland's quarrel was not with the government of the United States:

They have treated us with the greatest courtesy whenever we have approached them, and have manifested both a friendly and just attitude towards the colony. It was not the fault of the Administration in Washington that we are where we

10/E. E. Morison, *The Letters of Theodore Roosevelt* (Cambridge, Mass., 1951–4), IV, 1031; and *Journal of the Executive Proceedings of the Senate*, XXXV, 495, 499–502.

11/See F. F. Thompson, *The French Shore Problem in Newfoundland: An Imperial Study* (Toronto, 1961), p. 93 ff.

12/An understanding existed, based upon a temporary diplomatic protocol of 1888 which was extended from year to year by mutual consent, that American fishing vessels, upon payment of an annual licence fee of $1.50 per ton, could enter Canadian and Newfoundland ports for the purpose of purchasing bait, ice, and other supplies, and for the shipping of crews. See Innis, *The Cod Fisheries*, pp. 421–2.

13/*Proceedings of the North Atlantic Coast Fisheries Arbitration*, II, 184–5.

are today in the matter; the fault lies solely at the door of those who for petty personal reasons have deceived those who represent them in the senate of their country.[14]

In moving so decisively against the New England fishing interests, Bond probably hoped that a dramatic disruption of their trade would teach them the value of the concessions Newfoundland was prepared to make in order to obtain reciprocity, and thus compel them to reverse their stand on the issue. It was a daring policy, and in the circumstances not an unreasonable one. An influential body of opinion in the United States was likely to sympathize with Newfoundland; the New York *Evening Post*, for example, was vociferously supporting the Newfoundland case for reciprocity; and, in view of the relatively small importance of the Bond-Hay treaty to the United States, opinion in Washington had been sharply divided by its rejection.[15]

Yet events were soon to show that Bond had miscalculated wildly. Far from responding as he had hoped, the Roosevelt administration rallied to the defence of American fishermen, while the imperial government at the time was in no mood to allow a carefully nurtured Anglo-American rapprochement to be suddenly endangered by the belligerent acts of a minor colony.

The ingenuity of the New England fishing captains had prevented a crisis from developing in 1905 – they had evaded the law by hiring New-foundland fishermen *outside* the three-mile limit to fish for bait *inside* the limit. But when the Newfoundland government closed this loophole by a further amendment to the Foreign Fishing Vessels Act passed in May 1906, the American fishing interests were faced with the prospect of a major disruption of their industry. They were at last beginning to feel the pressure of Newfoundland's policy. The effectiveness of that policy, how-ever, was never finally tested. For before it could be properly put into effect it was undermined by the action of the British government, which became thoroughly alarmed by the vehemence of diplomatic protests from the United States, and withheld imperial assent to the new amendment. More severely still, the British colonial secretary, Lord Elgin, informed Newfoundland that in order to avoid 'a highly undesirable and even dangerous situation' it was necessary for Britain to arrange a modus

14/Cd 3262, *Correspondence Respecting the Newfoundland Fisheries* (London, 1906), p. 60.

15/Secretary of State Hay was so incensed by Lodge's obstruction in the Senate that the issue was responsible for the final breach in their personal friendship. See Dennett, *John Hay*, pp. 426–9.

vivendi with the United States for the 1906 winter fishing season.[16] This was duly arranged by an exchange of notes between London and Washington which, in essence, guaranteed that the American fishing fleet would not be denied bait by Newfoundland legislation. The most strenuous protests of the colony were disregarded.

At this point any likelihood there may have been of forcing the New England fishing interests to accept reciprocity vanished. To be effective Newfoundland's action had to be swift and absolute. The modus vivendi ensured that it would be neither. In retrospect it is very easy to see that Newfoundland should therefore have accepted defeat as gracefully as possible, and adopted a policy of conciliation. But by the autumn of 1906 Sir Robert Bond had so deeply committed himself and the Liberal party to a policy of restricting the American fishery that any retreat was bound to be both humiliating and politically damaging. To persist in the face of British hostility, however, was to court disaster. Already the cost of antagonizing the imperial authorities had been higher than Bond realized. Newfoundland's independent attitude in dealing with foreign powers had long been a sore point in London, and it is therefore not surprising that the thought again arose that Newfoundland might be less troublesome if less independent.

As early as 23 May Lord Grey, the governor general of Canada, had written to Lord Elgin on the assumption

that H.M.G. agree with me that it is desirable that Newfoundland should become a province of the Dominion as soon as possible. Sir W. MacGregor [governor of Newfoundland] understands the importance in view of the prospect of cleaning the slate between Canada and the U.S., as well as for general considerations of preventing any action on the part of the government of Newfoundland which may prejudice the friendly treatment by the U.S. of the points at issue between us. He appears to think that a visit from me would assist the party in Newfoundland who favour confederation.[17]

Grey subsequently visited Newfoundland on the pretext of spending a holiday there, and upon his return to Ottawa reported to Elgin on the prospects of union. Among the forces in favour of it, he found, were the governor, the Roman Catholic archbishop, the Bank of Montreal, the Canadian iron ore companies, and the Reid railway monopoly. The opposition, he believed, came from 'the few two penny ha'penny industries at

16/Cd 3262, *Correspondence Respecting the Newfoundland Fisheries*, p. 18.
17/Public Archives of Canada, Grey Papers, Grey to Elgin, 23 May 1906.

St. John's' and from 'Bond himself.' Thus, Grey concluded, confederation could be brought about in one of two ways: either by persuading Bond that it was necessary for his political survival, or, significantly,

> by persuading Sir E. Morris to break with Bond and to place himself at the head of the Confederationists. Morris is R.C., much liked and respected, and I believe at heart a confederationist. Whether he has the little bit of courage required to break with Bond, of whom he, and I believe all his colleagues are to some extent afraid, I know not, but that he has the power of knocking out Bond and winning the Island to confederation if Bond remains obdurate, I feel pretty certain.[18]

Grey had perceptively pointed to the one potential flaw in Bond's ministry: the crucial question was whether the time was now ripe for it to be exploited.

Within Newfoundland the political situation gave Bond's enemies good reason to feel optimistic. Although economically the country was prospering as never before, the Liberal government's fortunes were noticeably in decline. Even the hitherto remarkable cohesion of its supporters in the Assembly had begun to crack when in March 1905 Michael Cashin, the member for Ferryland – and, ominously, a personal supporter of Edward Morris – resigned from the Liberal party in protest against the government's American policy.[19] Among the public generally Bond's attempt to force reciprocity on the United States had caused considerable apprehension, while those most directly affected, the west coast fishermen, were openly hostile. The sale of bait fish, of which they always had a large surplus, was for them a profitable sideline. Moreover, they were on friendly terms with the American fishermen, who always paid well for their purchases and in cash, which provided a welcome measure of relief from the truck system of the local merchants. Again it was the case that a total prohibition against bait sales to American ships, if swiftly applied, might have won support and been successful, whereas a prolonged campaign in the face of an imperial veto was likely to backfire upon its protagonist.

Bond, however, refused to accept the inevitable. His reaction to the imposition of the modus vivendi was to test its validity before the courts. Accordingly, in spite of the grave warnings of Lord Elgin, a case was insti-

18/*Ibid.*, Grey to Elgin, 16 Aug. 1906.

19/Cashin later claimed that the 1905 amendment to the Foreign Fishing Vessels Act had been introduced in the Assembly before the Liberal party caucus had had a chance to discuss the matter, in order to forestall criticism. See *Proceedings of the House of Assembly, Newfoundland, 1911*, p. 164.

tuted against two Newfoundland fishermen who had signed on as 'crew members' aboard an American vessel outside the three-mile limit. Both were convicted and fined, leaving an embarrassed British government to pay their fines in order to forestall an appeal to the Privy Council,[20] whose confirmation of the court's decision would have given the Newfoundland government authority to frustrate the modus vivendi by a policy of whole-sale arrests. Newfoundland thereupon offered to refrain from pursuing the matter if Britain would arrange with the United States to prevent any further attempts to employ Newfoundlanders on American vessels,[21] and it was only by delaying a negative reply until after the end of the fishing season that Britain was able to avoid a serious crisis.

Bond's decision to persist in his retaliatory policy marked a critical turning-point both in the course of the fisheries dispute and in the political fortunes of the Liberal party. There was no longer any hope of forcing the issue of reciprocity: the only vital issue now turned upon the broad legal questions of the extent of American fishing rights in Newfoundland waters under the treaty of 1818, and the liability of American fishermen to colonial law, which the bait controversy had elevated to prominence. By making a solution difficult to achieve, and thereby prolonging an awkward situation between Britain and the United States, Bond was playing straight into the hands of those who wished to destroy him.

These 'anti-Bond' or 'anti-Liberal' forces were essentially those which Lord Grey had identified as confederationists, but with the notable exception of the archbishop of St John's, Dr Michael Howley, whose support for union was subordinate to his high personal regard and political support for Bond.[22] Opposing Bond were, first, the remnants of the old 'Reid' party of 1900, as represented by Reid's newspaper, the St John's *Daily News*, who were doing their utmost to turn public opinion against the government. They had long awaited the first sign of vulnerability in the Liberal party's position, and in the 'American question' they thought they had found it. And to add to the Liberals' misfortune, the Reid family also owned the *Western Star*, the only newspaper published on the west coast. Its thunderings against the government, by virtue of coming from the very

20/Fraser, 'Fisheries Negotiations,' p. 390.
21/Public Record Office, Foreign Office Papers, series 371, vol. 185, MacGregor to Elgin, 23 Nov. 1906.
22/Dr Howley was also a strident defender of the government's policy towards the United States. In his view Newfoundland was 'on the brink of the greatest crisis that has ever occurred in her history; a crisis on the outcome of which depends her future as a country.' He therefore appealed for national unity to meet the threat of 'an insatiable American rapacity on the one hand, and a compromising British diplomacy on the other.' Letter to the *Evening Telegram*, St John's, 14 Jan. 1907.

centre of the American fishery in Newfoundland, carried considerable force both at home and abroad.[23] Secondly, opposing Bond in a different way, were the highly placed advocates of confederation, working quietly and privately towards union, strongly represented in Canada by Lord Grey, in Newfoundland by Governor Sir William MacGregor. In their eyes the anti-confederate Bond was an obstacle that had to be removed, and, if they thought it necessary, neither Grey nor MacGregor was particularly scrupulous about interfering in the domestic politics of the colony.

Already Grey had made a point of discrediting Bond before the imperial government. Writing to Lord Elgin in September 1906 he expressed the view that MacGregor was doing his best to restrain his ministers,

but Bond is a difficulty – there is madness in his family, and madmen are not easy to control. My apprehension that Newfoundland might at any moment, by an unfriendly act against the United States over the fisheries, make the white heart of America black towards Canada, has been confirmed by what I heard of Bond during my visit to Newfoundland. I shall not feel safe until the Newfoundland fisheries are controlled from Ottawa.

Grey concludes this remarkable letter by advancing what amounts to a psychological explanation of Newfoundland's policy:

Bond complains that Laurier in allowing his people to sell bait to American fishermen is nullifying his policy. Laurier complains, with much reason, that Bond in pin-pricking the United States is nullifying his. As Newfoundland's only chance of securing what she wants would appear to be by taking hold of the rope behind Canada, Bond's attitude towards the American fishermen is only to be explained by his madness.[24]

Governor MacGregor, though scarcely more sympathetic towards his Liberal ministry, was somewhat more subtle. He had been highly critical of the bait policy from its inception, and by the spring of 1907 had adopted the tactic of sending to the Colonial Office batches of newspaper articles that were uniformly hostile to the government – without mentioning who owned the newspapers in question, an absolutely vital point where the Newfoundland press was concerned. But for those in London who were unlikely to be aware of this, the impression naturally given was that public opinion in the colony overwhelmingly disapproved of the government's policy, which was far from the actual truth.

Such reports, however, could only have contributed to a general hard-

23/See, e.g., the correspondence in *The Times*, London, 14 Nov. 1906.
24/Grey Papers, Grey to Elgin, 8 Sept. 1906.

ening of the British attitude at a time when Bond was about to encounter his last chance to extricate himself from the quagmire: the 1907 Colonial Conference in London. By making use of this occasion, with its opportunities for personal diplomacy, to come to terms with the British government, Bond might yet have escaped the worst consequences of his policy towards the United States. But, in the event, his reception in Downing Street was not encouraging.

By this time the British government was strongly in favour of submitting the fisheries dispute to international arbitration, a procedure Bond objected to in a speech before the conference on the grounds that the treaty of 1818 was not ambiguous, while to submit Newfoundland's statutes to arbitration 'would be degrading to the Crown, and in contravention of the constitutional right of self-governing Colonies.'[25] Later, however, under pressure from the Foreign Office, and perhaps realizing he was to be given no choice in the matter (for if a modus vivendi could be imposed against his wishes so also could arbitration), he finally agreed.

This was Newfoundland's grudging contribution to a settlement. Yet without the co-operation of Canada it was likely to prove futile, for even though Canada was not directly concerned in Newfoundland's quarrel with the United States, she was necessarily concerned with any question affecting national jurisdiction in the North Atlantic fisheries. Under the treaty of 1818 the United States had been given the same fishing rights in what later became part of Canada's territorial waters as in part of Newfoundland's; therefore Canada also had to be persuaded to accept arbitration. This proved to be no easy task. The Dominion was still smarting from the consequences of the Alaska boundary award of 1903, and inclined to look with suspicion upon any arrangement that could conceivably lead to another American coup. Consequently, when the Colonial Conference ended on 14 May Sir Wilfrid Laurier still had not consented to arbitration, and though both he and Bond remained in London for further consultations, no agreement could be reached. Meanwhile, the possibility of a quick settlement vanished, leaving the British government with no alternative but to negotiate another modus vivendi with the United States for the 1907 winter fishery. To Bond this was anathema. He vehemently protested, maintaining that Britain should either refer the dispute to The Hague tribunal or support the colony in the enforcement of its laws.[26] But Lord Elgin, on 18 June, brusquely set aside his contentions:

25/Cd 3523, *Correspondence Respecting the Newfoundland Fisheries* (London, 1907), p. 600.
26/Cd 3765, *Further Correspondence Relating to the Newfoundland Fishery Question* (London, 1908), pp. 184–8.

It is the duty of His Majesty's Government to deal with international relations, and while we should prefer in a matter of this kind to rely upon Colonial legislation, we shall not hesitate if necessary to use such other means as are open to us to obtain sanction for the arrangements which we consider essential for the preservation of relations of peace and amity with a friendly nation, and for the settlement of disputes in an orderly fashion.[27]

Two days later, with the crisis deepening around him, Bond sailed for St John's.

He was to find that affairs had not stood still in his absence. The colony had followed the progress of his negotiations in London with mounting anxiety, for failure almost certainly meant a revival of the quarrel with the Americans and another humiliating imposition of an Anglo-American modus vivendi. The most severe strain naturally fell upon the Liberal party, and within the party it inevitably focused upon Sir Edward Morris, for he alone had the political strength to force a major split. As Bond's strength declined, his increased proportionately, a change noted with satisfaction by the advocates of confederation, who still hoped to use him as their standard-bearer.

The wish is growing [Lord Grey wrote to James Bryce, the British ambassador in Washington, on 29 June] of Sir E. Morris as Bond's successor. Morris is an R.C. and a keen confederationist, but a cautious mover who dislikes taking any risk. If he decided to break with Bond and fight him at the next General Election which must take place in November, 1908, we may look forward, I hope with some confidence, to a reopening of negotiations for Confederation. ...

I hope to see W. D. Reid this afternoon. He is the Rhodes of Newfoundland and he hates Bond. With the R.C. vote, the Protestant educated and disinterested vote represented by Judge Prowse, Sir W. Whiteway, etc., and the Railway and mining interests all against Bond, it would appear that all that was wanted is a leader to secure a smashing victory. Morris I hope will be that leader.[28]

With Bond's star in decline, and an election year approaching, the time was obviously propitious for a challenger to declare himself. On 20 July Morris took the crucial step.

Revealingly, he chose to resign from the cabinet without committing himself on either the American fisheries question or on confederation. In his letter to Bond he advanced but one purely local reason for his action: a misunderstanding with the minister of public works over who should

27/Ibid., pp. 188–9.
28/Bodleian Library, Oxford, Bryce Papers, Grey to Bryce, 29 June 1907.

take credit for the granting of a pay increase to road labourers.[29] The full impact of his resignation was not immediately obvious, since the House of Assembly was not in session and there could thus be no dramatic confrontation between the rebel and his former colleagues. Yet there could be no doubt that the split in the party was no mere surface crack, but an irremediable fissure that would be found in time to cut deep into the constituencies, to the very grass roots where Morris' appeal had always been most potent.

Nor were Liberal prospects improved by the turn of events in the fisheries dispute. By the time Canada finally agreed to submit to arbitration the opening of the winter fishery was only two months away. Already on 10 August Newfoundland had been informed by the Colonial Office that

the provision necessary to secure a *modus vivendi* during the interval until the decision of the Hague Tribunal is obtained should be the act of the Colonial Government and Legislature, but, in the absence of any assurance to this effect, His Majesty's Government must proceed to take whatever measures are necessary to provide for it, as Imperial interests of great importance are involved.[30]

Though still adamantly opposed to an Anglo-American modus vivendi, Bond, under pressure from a section of the Liberal party, offered to arrange a compromise which would permit American fishermen to purchase bait while maintaining the prohibition against the hiring of Newfoundland crews. But since nothing less than complete acceptance of the modus vivendi could satisfy both Britain and the United States, his offer was rejected. On 6 September the two powers signed an agreement guaranteeing American vessels the right to employ Newfoundlanders, and on 9 September the British government issued an order-in-council (under an act passed in 1819) designed to assist the officers of the Royal Navy in their task of enforcing the modus vivendi by providing that legal process against Newfoundland citizens could not be served on board American ships, and that neither these vessels nor their boats or tackle could be liable to seizure.[31] At the same time, having wielded the stick, Britain dangled the carrot: the order would be revoked, Lord Elgin promised, if Newfoundland

29/E. B. Foran, 'Battle of the Giants: Bond and Morris,' in J. R. Smallwood, ed., *The Book of Newfoundland* (St John's, 1967), III, 160–1.
30/Cd 3765, *Further Correspondence Relating to the Newfoundland Fishery Question*, p. 157. The actual arbitration took place at The Hague during the summer of 1910. On all important points the international court upheld the Newfoundland contentions.
31/*Ibid.*, pp. 168–9.

would unreservingly accept the modus vivendi. Still Bond refused, angrily protesting that the order-in-council was undermining the colony's case before The Hague tribunal by yielding to the Americans in advance the very point that was to be decided. Furthermore, he added, the law officers of the Crown in Newfoundland advised that an order-in-council 'cannot be operated against the Laws of the Colony.'[32]

With Newfoundland apparently as intransigent as ever, and with the New England fishing fleet inexorably on its way, a new crisis seemed imminent. In Washington, the British ambassador was fearful of the consequences: if Newfoundland attempted to prevent her fishermen from shipping on board American vessels, he warned Lord Grey, 'there might be an outburst of popular feeling which would embarrass the U.S. Government, and encourage the Senate, if that body is maliciously disposed, to raise difficulties regarding the terms of the Arbitration.'[33] He therefore urged the governor general to use any means at his command to prevent Bond from disrupting the modus vivendi. Sir Wilfrid Laurier had already declined to intervene: 'I wish I could persuade myself that I could influence Bond,' he wrote, 'but I cannot thus flatter myself.'[34] He did, however, pass on the suggestion of Chief Justice Fitzpatrick that pressure might be put on Bond through the Bank of Montreal, the largest bank in the island and the holder of the government's account. But in his reply to Bryce, Grey expressed the view that the influence of the bank might be more effectively applied in another direction: 'My view,' he wrote on 26 September, 'is that neither Shaughnessy [Sir Thomas Shaughnessy, a director of the Bank of Montreal and of the Reid Newfoundland Company] or Clouston [William Clouston, first vice-president of the bank] will be able to move Bond – Bond is mad and cannot be diverted from his settled purpose. But Shaughnessy and Clouston can be very useful in putting backbone into Morris.'[35]

On 1 October, having been in touch with Clouston, Grey reported to Elgin on the prospects of getting rid of Bond at the next general election: 'The case against Bond that could be made by a clever fighter is one that if properly pressed ought to carry the Island. I wish we had a clever and hard fighter in Sir E. Morris – and Sir Wilfrid wishes he were a Protestant – for he is afraid that the fact of his being an R.C. may enable Bond to rally the Orangemen behind him.' The bankers, however, had evidently been more encouraging. Grey's letter continues: 'The Canadians who have interests in Newfoundland can be relied upon to do whatever is possible to

32/Quoted in Fraser, 'Fisheries Negotiations,' p. 398.
33/Bryce Papers, Bryce to Grey, 21 Sept. 1907.
34/*Ibid.*, Laurier to Grey, 25 Sept. 1907 (copy).
35/*Ibid.*, Grey to Bryce, 26 Sept. 1907.

stiffen Morris and to assist him in the battle against Bond. All the money he wants to enable him to conduct an educational campaign will be forthcoming, so I have been privately informed.'[36] In this context, there can be no doubt that 'educational' was but Grey's transparent synonym for 'political.' Two weeks later he wrote hopefully to Bryce:

Re Newfoundland: All is going well. Bond, I am told, is killed. A newspaper edited by McGrath (the only good journalist on the island) will be shortly started to nail down his coffin ... I hear Morris has a stout Protestant colleague who will join him in the fight against Bond, and this combination with the help of McGrath and the unseen forces of the railway interest and the Bank of Montreal etc. hope in any case to do for Bond whatever he may do.[37]

Thus, although in St John's the political surface remained ostensibly unruffled, with Morris eschewing public controversy, and the legislature not due to reassemble until January, already the Morris bandwagon was quietly beginning to gather steam.

Meanwhile, the harbingers of the New England fleet were beginning to arrive in Newfoundland waters. Fearing a hostile incident, the British government, undergoing a last minute change of heart, hurriedly sought to have Bond's earlier offer to allow the sale of bait substituted for the modus vivendi;[38] but when the State Department objected, there was nothing more that could be done. Since the imperial order-in-council gave Newfoundland fishermen no immunity from prosecution *after* disembarking from American vessels, the colonial government could still have seriously disrupted the American fishery had it wished to do so. In the event, however, British anxiety proved groundless. Rather than provoke a conflict, which would have been to invite the intervention of the Royal Navy, Newfoundland chose instead to permit the sale of bait under licence even though the modus vivendi was not withdrawn. This served the dual purpose of preserving at least the fiction of the colony's right to regulate the fishery (which was regarded as important if the case before The Hague tribunal was not to be prejudiced), and allowing the Americans to obtain bait supplies without having to contravene the Foreign Fishing Vessels Act of 1906 by employing Newfoundlanders.

36/ Grey Papers, Grey to Elgin, 1 Oct. 1907.
37/ Bryce Papers, Grey to Bryce, 14 Oct. 1907. The McGrath referred to was P. T. (later Sir Patrick) McGrath, a party propagandist of considerable talent. He had formerly been editor of the Liberal *Evening Herald* but had bolted the party after Morris' defection. He subsequently emerged as the editor of a new paper, the *Evening Chronicle*, founded to support Morris.
38/ FO 371/390, Sir E. Grey to Bryce, 3 Oct. 1907.

Nevertheless, in spite of the satisfactory working of this arrangement, it was unavoidably damaging to the beleaguered Liberal party. The more extreme advocates of bait restriction were bound to regard it as a capitulation, while the opposition could point with scorn to the futile policy which made it necessary. 'The appeals of the west coast fishermen during the last two years for free fishing have been refused by the Government,' complained the *Daily News*, 'and a concession is only made now because such a step is part of the Government's policy of trickery and deception.'[39] Only if the imperial government rescinded the order-in-council, as Bond requested on 2 November, could the Liberals have hoped to salvage so much as a minor victory; but even that was denied them when on 12 December Bond's petition was turned down.[40]

As the year drew to a close there was thus no glimmer of improvement in the Liberal party's position. Lord Grey, after a meeting in Montreal with Sir Robert Reid, the patriarch of the Reid family, wrote to Bryce on 7 December:

Sir R. Reid is greatly confident that Bond is finished. The forces which will sweep him out of political existence are slowly but surely gathering force ... The head of the Orange Lodge has joined political hands with Morris – and though the idea is still prevalent that Bond has been used harshly by the Home Government ... my impression is after talks with Sir R. Reid and William Clouston, that Bond is politically a very sick man.[41]

A partisan view, no doubt, but not inaccurate. It was abundantly clear that whatever the subsequent course of events, the glowing future that seemed to await Bond and his party in 1904 had been finally and irretrievably lost.

39/St John's, 12 Oct. 1907.
40/FO 371/390, Elgin to MacGregor, 12 Dec. 1907.
41/Bryce Papers, Grey to Bryce, 7 Dec. 1907.

5 The fall of the Liberal party

THE NEW YEAR of 1908 brought no revival in the declining fortunes of Sir Robert Bond's Liberal administration. The imperial order-in-council continued to cast its shadow over all other issues, while Lord Grey's 'unseen forces of Confederation' hovered discreetly in the background. In the constituencies the full extent of the damage done to the Liberal party by Edward Morris' resignation remained uncertain, for he had yet to take a public stand in opposition.

Nevertheless, the Liberals had no reason to believe that events had already overtaken them. The Liberal members in the Assembly, almost without exception, had remained loyal to their leader, and in the final session before the general election he was assured of a continuing majority. For the first time he would have to face an opponent whose political talent rivalled, and in some ways exceeded, his own; but Morris was as yet a man without a party, while Bond had a prime minister's prestige and control of all the patronage that belonged to a government in power. Also, as the general election was not due until November, there was still time for political 'fence-mending.' Therefore, no matter how low the government's popularity may have fallen, it did not appear to be on the brink of losing office, nor did it behave as though it were.

Beyond a pious hope that 'the prosperity that has attended upon a wise administration of our public affairs may long continue,' the speech from the throne contained little to indicate that a dissolution was in sight. The government's programme was a modest one, containing proposals to establish an experimental farm to provide instruction in agriculture, to encourage shipbuilding, and to enact more stringent measures for the protection of workmen against industrial accidents. The two items mentioned in the speech which might have been put to party advantage – free elementary education and old age pensions – were handled so scrupulously as to escape even the faintest suspicion of electioneering. After careful consideration, the idea of free education was rejected on the ground that there was a greater need to use the funds available to provide schools in localities where there were none; while the question of old age pensions was referred for further consideration to a royal commission to be appointed for that purpose.[1] It is safe to say that only a government confident at least of survival would dare to face the legislature in an election year with such an unambitious programme.

Whether such a display of confidence would later appear as wisdom or folly rested very much in the hands of Edward Morris, for whom the final session of Parliament was a crucial test. Having resigned on a transparent pretext after nearly seven years in office, he could hardly condemn the government's past record; nor, for that matter, could he convincingly justify his resignation from it. Yet in an election year he could not dismiss the valuable publicity afforded by the parliamentary spotlight. His answer, with the aid of an enthusiastic daily press,[2] was to make his seat in the Assembly a platform from which to address the country without appearing too prominently in the rôle of an opposition critic. He preferred instead to present himself as a statesman-like alternative to Bond, advocating policies not essentially different from the government's but generally more 'progressive' in outlook or more daring in application,[3] content to leave the task of attacking the government in the hands of Michael Cashin, his aggressive colleague.

Compared with these two, the official Conservative opposition was weak and ineffectual. It had suffered overwhelming defeat in two successive general elections, and now, after eight years without office, most of its former leaders had died or retired from active politics. Even the controversial A. B. Morine, after 1900 the only effective opposition voice, had resigned in 1906 to seek his political fortune in Canada. Of the six Conservative members in the House only Donald Morison was widely known, and then mainly because of his earlier reputation as a sectarian pamphleteer and militant Orangeman.[4] The nominal leader of the opposition was

1/ *Journal of the House of Assembly, Newfoundland, 1908*, p. 5.

2/ In addition to Reid's *Daily News*, a morning paper, which was strongly supporting him, the newly established *Evening Chronicle*, edited by P. T. McGrath, was serving as his personal vehicle of propaganda.

3/ For example, he supported the government's proposal to increase the Poor Districts Education Grant, but commented that he would like to have seen 'a larger measure increasing the grant all round and benefitting teachers'; and while he was in favour of legislation to protect workmen, he 'would like to see fishermen and others covered as well.' *Evening Telegram*, St John's, 15 Jan. 1908.

4/ He was a former grand master (1886, 1888–96) of the Orange Lodge and was

Captain Charles Dawe,[5] a respected mariner, but an ultra-conservative who was totally unsuited to the task of reviving a dormant party. He was, moreover, at this time nearing the end of his life, too ill even to take his place in the legislature. On the opening day he resigned as leader and in an interview with the *Daily News* expressed his desire for a 'united opposition.' He appealed to those opposed to the government to 'forget differences, whether of a personal or a party character, and to fight unitedly for one policy, under one banner, and with one leader.' He did not state explicitly who that leader should be, but there can be little doubt that he had Morris in mind:

Sir Edward Morris and Mr. Cashin represent the best and ablest elements of the Liberal Party. United with the men who have fought so well and ably at my side during the past sessions, and with the Liberals, Conservatives and others outside the House who are desirous of effecting reforms in the administration of affairs, a new party could be formed that should be invincible.[6]

Despite this benediction from the Conservative leader, the formation of a new party did not come about immediately, although what might be considered a 'united opposition' emerged during the course of the session. Morris and Cashin sat apart from the Conservatives as 'Independent Liberals,' but this distinction, it seems, was due largely to their reluctance to lend credence to the charges that they had 'gone over to the Tories.' In fact, there was a close alliance between the two opposition groups, and, in the absence of a Conservative leader, Morris soon came to be regarded, both within the House and outside it, as the *de facto* leader of the opposition.[7] Not until the legislature had closed was it revealed that early in the session he had received a petition signed by every opposition member inviting him 'to assume the leadership in the Assembly and to take immediate steps for the reorganization of the opposition forces throughout the Colony on broad and comprehensive lines.'[8] But by prudently declining to

prominently connected with the *Banner of Progress* and other anti-Catholic pamphleteering activities as late as 1904. In 1906 he was returned to the House of Assembly as Conservative member for Bonavista in a by-election caused by the resignation of A. B. Morine.

5/ A Conservative supporter of the 1898 railway contract, minister of marine and fisheries 1897–1900, who lost his seat in Harbour Grace in the 1900 election, but returned to the House by means of a by-election in Port de Grave in 1906, caused by the death of the sitting Conservative member.

6/ *Daily News*, 9 Jan. 1908.

7/ This was how the governor described his position, adding that it was 'a post he filled with much tact and sagacity under very difficult circumstances.' CO 194/272, MacGregor to Elgin, 13 April 1908.

8/ *Daily News*, 5 March 1908.

accept while the House was still in session, Morris managed to preserve the fiction of his 'independence,' or, what was perhaps more important, managed to avoid the stigma still attached to the 'Conservative' label.

This was particularly wise in view of the anticipated debate on the imperial order-in-council, when the whole question of the government's policy towards the American fisheries was bound to arise – with awkward consequences for the opposition. The Conservatives had consistently opposed the government's policy; Morris, as attorney general, had been actively associated with it. In the event, however, there were undeclared interests on both sides of the House in favour of restricting the debate to the constitutional implications of the order-in-council: the government hoped that a unanimous resolution petitioning for its withdrawal might carry more weight with the imperial government, while Morris was anxious to avoid an open breach with his Conservative allies. To make matters easier, the prime minister himself played a minor part in the debate, entrusting the main government speech to W. F. Lloyd,[9] a capable Liberal backbencher, who chose a direct non-party line of attack. The order-in-council, he said, was 'an outrage on the Constitution of Newfoundland, an insult to the Legislature and an infringement of the Labouchere despatch.' And by being 'in conflict with the contentions concurred in by both the Imperial and the Newfoundland Governments,' it was 'prejudicial to the case to be submitted to the Hague Tribunal on behalf of Newfoundland.' In conclusion, he moved the adoption of a series of resolutions calling upon the imperial government to 'recognize the justice and expediency of cancelling the said Order-in-Council and Modus Vivendi.'[10]

Any hopes, or fears, that the opposition might oppose the resolutions in order to censure the government were quickly extinguished when Morris rose to speak:

No one could possibly take exception to the remarks of the honourable member who had lifted the question out of the sphere of party politics and had made it possible for every member of the Opposition to vote with the Government for the resolutions. This is not a question of party policy nor are these resolutions party resolutions, the question is rather for the Legislature as a whole to stand united in asserting the rights of a Colony and in upholding the laws by which the Colony is governed.[11]

9/ William Frederick Lloyd, 1864–1937; b. Stockport, England; ed. Victoria University, Manchester; editor of the *Evening Telegram*, 1890–1914; MHA for Trinity, 1904–8, 1913–19; prime minister, 1918–19.
10/ *Evening Telegram*, 4 Feb. 1908.
11/ *Ibid.*

There were slight rumblings of discontent from some of the Conservatives, but Lloyd tactfully refused to be drawn, and in the end the resolutions were passed unanimously by both branches of the legislature. Critics of the government were far from satisfied with this unexpected result; but, in view of the stand taken by Morris, they were unable to exploit the situation as fully as they might otherwise have done. The *Evening Chronicle* was non-committal, merely pointing out that:

The speeches of Dr. Lloyd and Sir Edward Morris make it perfectly clear that only the constitutional position was affirmed and that the political side of the problem, the policy of the Government on the subject, and the difficulties and troubles in which the Colony has become involved, did not enter into the debate at all, so that the views of different members as to these matters was not in any way affected by last night's vote.[12]

The other newspapers generally welcomed what they hoped would be the end of a long and tedious dispute. Only the *Daily News* was unable to resist a final gibe: 'By Bond's bungling,' it commented sourly, 'the interpretation of our rights is now handed over to Dutchmen to be arbitrated on.'[13] It was thus apparent that the American fisheries dispute was unlikely to be a major issue in the forthcoming election campaign.

One effect of the government's success in obtaining a unanimous resolution, however, was to overshadow an electorally more significant omen – the sudden defection to the opposition of one J. R. Bennett, a Liberal backbencher. Ostensibly, the cause of his break with the party arose from the unlikely source of an item in the annual supply bill which provided for the payment of relief to stranded ships' crews. At this time, it should be explained, it was the practice of certain sealing ships, if a voyage ended in failure, to discharge their crews, consisting of hundreds of men who worked on a share system, at St John's. These men were often left penniless, and had to be housed, fed, and given transportation to their homes at the public expense. Sir Edward Morris introduced an amendment calling upon the government to negotiate with the shipowners in order to 'render the introduction of legislation dealing with the subject unnecessary.' The prime minister replied that the government could not accept the amendment as legislation was contemplated. But Bennett, the junior member for St John's West, followed with a speech praising Morris' suggestion as 'humane, considerate, and reasonable.' He would not be 'whipped into line,' he announced, and promptly crossed the floor of the chamber to join

12/1 Feb. 1908.
13/3 Feb. 1908.

the Independent Liberals. Bond dismissed his defection as of no importance, revealing that when Morris first left the cabinet every member of the
Liberal party came to him unsolicited and assured him of their loyalty,
except Bennett, so his action was not unanticipated.[14]

Yet it is highly revealing that a young and ambitious politician, who
had begun his career on the St John's municipal council and had strong
roots in his constituency, felt compelled to make such a move. There could
have been no clearer indication of the extent to which the Liberal party's
strength had been undermined, for Bennett could not have failed to see
that the party organization in his constituency was loyal not to him, nor to
Bond, but only to Morris. And therefore without the support of Morris his
political existence was in peril.

The remaining weeks of the parliamentary session were filled with
relatively uncontroversial business. In his eighth budget speech Finance
Minister Jackman revealed a surplus for the past year of more than
$125,000 and cautiously forecast a reduced surplus for the fiscal year
ending in June; the Reserve Fund was gradually rising; the country continued to show a favourable balance of trade; and, beyond a few minor
adjustments in the tariff designed to encourage shipbuilding and agriculture, there were to be no changes in taxation. The drastic tariff cuts frequently associated with a pre-election budget were conspicuously absent.
Even Sir Edward Morris was reduced to observing that 'there was very
little in the speech to comment upon or to criticize as a financial proposi-
tion,' though he did point out that there were hidden increases in the tariff
because the prices of goods taxed *ad valorem* had risen. Furthermore, he
remarked, 'looking at many items on the tariff we find the very poorest
classes have to pay the highest duty.' But his proposed remedy – to add
tea and sugar to the free list – the minister of finance could lightly dismiss
as 'an attempt to make political capital.'[15]

However, when the governor's speech closing the session made no mention of old age pensions, there was no dismissing the fact that a solid plank
was gratuitously given to the opposition platform. 'The policy of Old Age
Pensions,' declared the *Daily News*, 'demands more serious treatment than
a frothy paragraph in the opening speech, contemptuous indifference
during the session, and absolute silence at the close.'[16] The Liberal press
was evidently unperturbed. 'The session might fittingly be termed the
workingman's session,' the *Evening Telegram* commented with satisfaction, 'for his interests have been specially and particularly considered and
looked after. The present Liberal Government has been long recognized

14/*Evening Telegram*, 4 Feb. 1908.   15/*Ibid.*, 5 March 1908.
16/19 Feb. 1908.

as the Workingman's Party.'[17] Thus, for the Liberals the close of the Assembly foreshadowed the course of the election campaign. The government proposed no startling new measures and made no new promises. After eight years in office they were prepared to stand on their record.

Any disability Morris may have suffered when facing his former cabinet colleagues across the floor of the House vanished with the prorogation, and two weeks later, on 5 March, the rationale of his refusal to become the official leader of a predominantly Conservative opposition was made brilliantly clear. With an appropriate fanfare from the press, he issued a manifesto launching a new 'People's Party.'[18]

The timing of this announcement was calculated to coincide with the presence in St John's of several thousand men from the outports who had come to 'sign on' as crews of the sealing ships. By placing his manifesto before them and by addressing them at a huge public meeting Morris ensured that his new party and its platform would immediately and dramatically reach a representative selection of outport voters. Again demonstrating his electioneering virtuosity, he stridently defended his action in breaking with the government in terms familiar to his audience:

What they really have against me is that I committed the unpardonable crime of leaving them. You are hardly the men to go with a skipper who missed the seals every spring. And you can take it from me that when I left the Government, when I gave up the highest office the Government could offer ... I did not give it up without good cause ... It would have been of no value to me to have left the Bond Government if I did not feel that the great army of Liberals who follow me were with me in my act ... I am as much a Liberal today as I ever was ... and in the party we have now formed, the *People's Party*, Liberals and Conservatives alike are united to do good for this country.[19]

This speech, reaffirming his 'liberalism' but also appealing for support from all parties, and the extensive thirty-point programme outlined in his 'preliminary manifesto,'[20] established the character of the new party.

17/21 Feb. 1908.
18/The birth of the new party was not unanticipated. On 22 February the *Daily News* had given considerable prominence to a pseudonymously signed letter which called for the formation of 'a *People's Party*, representative of the true interests of all the people, without distinction of class, creed or position in society. The only man in the community who is able ... to command such a party is Sir Edward Morris.' Sir Robert Bond, the writer claimed, 'has no sympathy with the labouring man. He is a blue-blooded aristocrat from the tops of his curly locks to the soles of his patent leather shoes.'
19/*Daily News*, 7 March 1908.
20/Published in full in the *Daily News*, 5 March 1908.

It was clear from the beginning that it would not be based upon or in-corporate any particular principle. It was, in fact, in the general pattern of North American politics, an organization of the 'outs' to replace the 'ins,' and bore no relation to those groups with the same or similar names that had appeared as symptoms of popular discontent in western Canada and the United States. In no sense could Morris be considered a radical, and above all else it was his leadership that gave the new party its raison d'être. It would be wrong, however, to conclude that the People's party was therefore simply the old 'Tory' or 'Merchant' party disguised under a new name, as the Liberal press was quick to assert. Its avowed aim was to appeal to all classes of the community, and in drafting its programme on the basis of 'something for everyone' it more closely resembled the national parties of the United States and Canada.

Many of the thirty points in its manifesto were carefully directed at specific sections of the electorate: fishermen were promised a daily tele-graphic service supplying weather reports and the latest information on fishing conditions, more cold storage bait depots, and more navigational aids and other marine works; farmers were to receive a bounty for clearing land; 'proper housing' was to be provided for labourers at mines and in-dustrial centres; trade unions were to be given the same legal status as in Great Britain; poor relief was to be paid in cash instead of in purchase orders; and an old age pension scheme was to be introduced. At the other end of the scale, important business interests were also catered for: fish exporters were promised a subsidized steamship service to the West Indies; and a promise to construct more railway branch-lines had an obvious appeal to the railway contractors as well as to all those who stood to profit in various ways from another railway boom. Other promises reflected the wider anxieties of people generally: taxation was to be reduced; educa-tional grants and teachers' salaries raised; school buildings improved; out-port hospitals constructed; and there was even an undefined 'industrial policy' which, it was claimed, would 'keep workers at home.'

External relations were largely excluded from the area of party conflict: in the fisheries dispute with the United States the People's party was un-equivocally committed to 'a strict maintenance of every position taken by this Colony in defence of our constitutional rights under the Treaty of 1818,' and in relations with Canada to 'the maintenance of self-govern-ment and NO CONFEDERATION.'[21]

Although it contained a number of ambiguities, taken as a whole the party's initial statement of policy presented an impressive challenge to the government. It dealt with genuine problems in a confident manner and with a view to the future. This latter characteristic, especially, was placed

21/*Ibid.*

in sharp relief by the tactics of the Liberal press. The *Evening Telegram*, in a series of leading articles entitled 'Deeds not Words,' ineptly countered the People's party manifesto by listing the past achievements of the Bond administration,[22] while the *Evening Herald* tried desperately to identify the new party as the Tories in disguise and supported by Canadian money.[23]

These and similar charges were to be persistently levelled at the People's party throughout the campaign, but in the early stages the issue arousing by far the greatest public excitement was also extremely damaging to the government. It arose from the scandalous disclosures in the report of a grand jury investigation into conditions in public institutions, and coming from this source it was more effective than any opposition attack in discrediting the government. Among the grand jury's findings were that children under sixteen years of age were imprisoned in the same penitentiary, and sometimes in the same cells, with hardened criminals, some of whom were serving sentences for sexual crimes; that the lunatic asylum was dangerously overcrowded; and that the poorhouse was in an even more deplorable condition, crowded with the old and dying, and without isolation of inmates suffering from disease. 'It is the saddest place in Newfoundland,' the report stated, 'and no one can visit it without feeling chastened and distressed.'[24] Hurriedly the government announced that land had been acquired on which to build a new asylum, and when this was completed it was hoped to convert the old asylum into a poorhouse. This announcement, however, merely added fuel to the flames, for the opposition press gleefully seized the occasion to charge that the land in question had been purchased from a prominent supporter of the Liberal party at an exorbitant price.[25] The Liberals emerged badly shaken from this first unexpected skirmish and subsequently never managed to recover the initiative. The central plank in their platform – their record – had been suddenly and shockingly tarnished.

As the campaign gathered momentum it became increasingly dominated by the two most consistently potent factors in Newfoundland politics – sectarianism and confederation – although this time both occurred in strangely convoluted and paradoxical forms.

Predictably, politicians and party workers were most tempted to play

22/6–11 March 1908.
23/14 March 1908.
24/The grand jury report was published in full in the *Daily News*, 14 March 1908. Ironically, only a week earlier the *Evening Herald* had complacently asked: 'What does Sir Edward Morris propose to do for the people which has not already been done, or is in the process of doing [*sic*], or that cannot be done, by the Bond Party?'
25/*Daily News*, 16 March 1908.

upon religious prejudice (or, for that matter, to resort to bribery or other corrupt practices) in marginal constituencies, where a handful of votes, however acquired, could mean the difference between victory and defeat. Almost every constituency of this nature contained a mixed population of Protestants and Catholics, and in four of the most important – the adjoining Conception Bay North constituencies of Bay de Verde, Harbour Grace, Carbonear, and Port de Grave, which between them returned seven members to the Assembly – the tradition of denominational rivalry was especially strong.[26] In the previous general election the Liberals had won five of these seats by majorities of less than one hundred, the Conservatives two, by equally small majorities. Of the total popular vote in the four constituencies the Liberals obtained a mere 51.5 per cent, as compared to more than 60 per cent for the country as a whole.[27] Each constituency contained a majority of Protestants, so if voting took place strictly on denominational lines, the 'Protestant party' would win all seven seats. Yet these were the very seats the People's party, with its Catholic leader, had to win as a matter of necessity if it was to have any hope of forming a government. The conjunction of these circumstances naturally produced a desperate struggle for votes. And since both parties had adopted impeccably Protestant candidates, the main controversy centred inevitably upon the religious affiliations of the party leaders.[28] A graphic illustration of this is provided by the following account of a People's party caucus in Carbonear:

A meeting of the local committee of the People's Party was held in the old Methodist Day School on Saturday night. Over a hundred representatives from all parts of the district were present ...

Mr. John R. Goodison, who was the Conservative candidate at the last General Election, in a few well chosen and complimentary words, moved that the meeting endorse the leadership of Sir Edward Morris, and the policy outlined in the manifesto of the People's Party ...

Mr. Goodison called the attention of the meeting to the strenuous and indecent efforts which the Government Party were employing in Carbonear, and, he feared, in other districts also, to raise the Sectarian issue ...

Referring sarcastically to what he termed the impudent assumption of cer-

26/The area was the scene of sectarian violence as late as 1883. See
D. W. Prowse, *A History of Newfoundland* (London, 1895), pp. 513–14.

27/These statistics are calculated from the total vote cast for the candidates of each party; i.e., in two- and three-member constituencies voters are represented as having two and three votes respectively.

28/There had not been a Catholic premier since John Kent in 1861. His grandson, J. M. Kent, Liberal member for St John's East, became attorney general after the resignation of Morris in 1907.

tain shouting partisans, who apparently imagined that all true Protestantism in the town centered in themselves, and that they were its sole inheritors ('a new role for them', he added) he stated that men had come to him who had been warned by the Liberal heelers (notably by certain road board men ...) that it was their duty to vote against the candidate of the People's Party ... because the Leader, Sir Edward Morris, was a Roman Catholic.[29]

Similarly, 'anti-sectarianism' featured prominently in Morris' personal campaign, which opened in May with a 'whistle-stop' tour of these key Conception Bay constituencies. On every platform he was conspicuously accompanied by Donald Morison, his 'Orange' colleague, who joined him in repeatedly condemning the Liberals as 'fomenters of sectarian strife.'[30] Finally, upon his return to St John's, Morris had this to say in an interview with the *Daily News*:

The question which was usually put to the voters by these emissaries of peace and good will was: 'Surely you are not going to vote for a Catholic Premier?' At each meeting held by me I pointed out the absurdity of this cry ... I showed them that even if I were disposed to act unfairly to my Protestant fellow countrymen ... I could not do so for the reason that if every district in the country elected candidates to support the People's Party it would mean that I would have a following of 23 Protestants and 13 Catholics; and that in any Government which I would form there would have to be six Protestants as against three Catholics. Further, no matter what the result may be, the Legislature must always have on the basis of population 23 Protestants and 13 Catholics.[31]

Such an apparently candid acknowledgment of political reality might *prima facie* be taken as simply an attempt to reassure dubious Protestant voters, which on one level it no doubt was. But on another level it was highly disingenuous. Sectarianism was a knife that cut both ways, and by no means favoured the Liberal party. On the contrary, though Protestant bigots were certainly active, the clamorous publicity given to their (always anonymous) bigotry by the Reid newspapers, by People's party candidates on the hustings, and even (as has been shown) by Morris himself, cannot escape the suspicion that it was calculated primarily to arouse the strongest possible reaction among Catholic voters.[32] For only if these

29/*Daily News*, 5 May 1908.
30/*Ibid.*, e.g. 21–3 May 1908.
31/*Ibid.*, 25 May 1908.
32/It is remarkable that some of the most vocal 'anti-sectarians,' such as Donald Morison, had earlier in their careers been notorious for their anti-Catholic campaigning. This alone would be enough to render their motives highly suspect, as

could be persuaded to desert the Liberal party in predominantly Catholic districts, and to vote en bloc for the People's party in marginal districts where they formed a large minority, could the latter hope to secure enough seats to form a government. It was simply not in the Liberal interest to alienate the Catholic vote, nor is it conceivable that Sir Robert Bond, who valued Archbishop Howley's friendship and support, would have permitted a sectarian campaign by his party. Further, and most significant of all, there is no hint of sectarianism in the Liberal press. Morris was vilified for many things – for being a 'traitor to his party,' an 'agent of the Reids,' a 'secret confederate' – but never was it suggested that voters should spurn him because of his Catholicism. Hence the paradox that the condemnation of sectarianism must in many cases be regarded as indistinguishable from the preaching of it.

The question of confederation with Canada may be considered in a similar light, for it too, though differing from sectarianism in that it was genuinely a political issue, came to be exploited as a political stalking-horse. Originally, as has been seen, Lord Grey and the Canadian banking, railway, and other interests, had favoured Morris as the likely leader of a new confederation party.[33] Yet contrary to their expectations, his manifesto in March had unequivocally pledged his new party to the maintenance of self-government and no confederation.[34] There is nothing to suggest that Morris himself actively encouraged the confederates to think he would do otherwise – he was much too canny a politician to openly declare his intentions – though obviously he could have done nothing to *dis*courage them. In any case, by March he undoubtedly had all the 'educational' funds he required to launch the People's party and sustain it through a long and lavish campaign.[35] Also, by this time the Canadian financial and industrial interests had little choice but to support him whatever his attitude towards union, so anxious were they to be rid of Bond; while the politically most influential of them – the Reids – could be placated in other ways, notably by the promise of new contracts implied in his pledge to expand the railway system.[36] Thus, with consummate skill, Morris made

the Liberal press repeatedly pointed out. See, e.g., the *Evening Telegram*, 10 Sept. 1908.

33/See above, pp. 48–9.

34/*Daily News*, 5 March 1908.

35/Much later, Sir W. D. Reid claimed in a letter to Sir Thomas Shaughnessy that he himself had contributed enough to finance Morris's entire election campaign. See the *Evening Telegram*, 8 Jan. 1918; for a comment, see A. B. Keith, *Responsible Government in the Dominions* (2nd ed., Oxford, 1928), I, 133–4.

36/Such a pledge was included in his manifesto and further expanded in the *Evening Chronicle*, 5 Oct. 1908.

use of the unseen support of the confederates without allowing himself to become their prisoner.

It is only when viewed against this background of pressure, intrigue, and sharp dealing, that confederation becomes understandable as an election issue. The Liberals were naturally suspicious of Morris' anti-confederation pledge when he was known to be favoured by the Reids and other Canadian moneyed interests, and their reaction was to raise loud and persistently the cry of a 'confederation plot.' It would be pointless to go into the many variations of this which may be found scattered through the pages of the Liberal press, or to treat seriously the attempt of the People's party to turn the tables by accusing Bond of being the 'real' confederate and of having a secret agreement with Laurier, for neither side could substantiate its charges. As the St John's correspondent of *The Times* reported:

The very idea [of confederation] is cordially detested, and the political party which can succeed in convincing the electorate that its opponents are confederates plotting union with Canada is certain to secure an enormous majority at the polls. For forty years this question has been doing duty ... and it is being worked as strongly now as ever before.[37]

Hence the seemingly curious spectacle of confederation being an issue not, as might be expected, between a 'pro' and an 'anti' party, but between two 'anti' parties – each insisting upon the other's insincerity.

The publication of Bond's manifesto in September marked the concluding stage of the campaign. It also removed any likelihood there may have been of the Liberals suddenly introducing some enticing new item into their platform in a last-minute attempt to outbid their rivals. Instead, the prime minister produced a proudly defiant statement of his party's record in office – 'a record,' he said, 'that has never been equalled in the whole history of this land.' He reviewed the catastrophes which the last Tory government had visited upon the country and reminded electors that under his administration the railways, telegraphs, and crown lands granted to the Reids in 1898 had been restored to public ownership, taxes had been reduced, expenditure on education increased, the pulp and paper industry induced to begin operations in the interior, and the general earning and purchasing power of the people had risen. In the fisheries dispute with the United States, he said, 'the present government may also justly claim the approval of the electors of this country. They have been waging a battle against American aggression, and the difficulties of the situation have

37/*The Times*, London, 3 Nov. 1908.

been increased by the attitude of His Majesty's Government in relation thereto.' It was only by the Liberal government's 'firm and decided action' that an agreement had been reached to submit the dispute to the arbitration of The Hague tribunal, he continued. Returning to domestic matters, he warned against his opponents' railway policy. 'I believe,' he said, 'that the course of an honest and economic Government should be to go cautiously and enquiringly, and not commit the country to a vast expenditure which neither existing nor prospective conditions warrant.' In other respects their policy 'for the most part ... merely rehearsed the policy that the present Government has been so successful in carrying out during the past eight years.' Sir Edward Morris, he said, 'seems to be labouring under the strange delusion that the Liberal Party's policy can be best carried out under his leadership, with the assistance of those who have ever been most bitterly opposed to it!' He concluded by rebuking his opponents for trying 'to hide from the people the conspiracy ... to bring this country into the Canadian Dominion,' declaring that he himself was 'entirely opposed to Confederation' and pledged 'unreservedly to consider no proposal in that direction unless the people of Newfoundland demand such a consideration at the polls.'[38]

It was a remarkable manifesto, containing but one promise of the usual sort – to reduce the tariff 'until the workingmen of this country are provided with a free breakfast table' – but what made it even more remarkable was that the economic outlook in the autumn of 1908 had suddenly become bleaker than at any time for nearly a decade. This hard fact was bound to blunt the edge of what was essentially a conservative appeal, and by ignoring it to concentrate upon *past* prosperity and *past* achievements Bond gave his otherwise attractive manifesto the appearance of being out of touch with the present reality.

The immediate cause of the economic uncertainty was a familiar one: a sharp decline in the price of fish in European markets. For despite the introduction of new land-based industries after the turn of the century, the island remained overwhelmingly dependent for its livelihood on the fishery, the value of whose produce in 1908 still accounted for more than 70 per cent of total exports.[39] Prices paid to fishermen for the various grades of dried salted cod, still the staple export commodity, after reaching their highest level for almost a century in 1905, fell slightly in 1907, and in the autumn of 1908 collapsed to only half of what they had been a year previously.[40] So sudden and icy an economic blast carried with it

38/*Evening Telegram*, 29 Sept. 1908.
39/*The Times*, 3 Nov. 1908.
40/*Annual Report of the Department of Marine and Fisheries, 1908* (St John's, 1908), p. 24.

an unmistakable scent of depression, which inevitably tended to undermine popular confidence in the government. This was not without a certain ironic justice. The responsibility the Liberals so blithely accepted for the high prices prevailing during the fat years now returned to haunt them in the lean, and Bond's disclaimer that it was a 'silly but malicious falsehood'[41] to charge the government with being responsible for low prices met with a singularly unsympathetic response. He gave potentially sound advice to the fishermen to hold back their supplies because 'demand in foreign markets is growing and prices are fairly remunerative. Merchants [that is, St John's merchants] at present are timid in buying.' But even this proved embarrassing when the opposition press got hold of the story that a Liberal member of the Assembly, a Twillingate merchant, was quietly selling and had not sufficient confidence in the market, or in his leader's assessment of it, to withhold his stocks.[42]

Only one event appeared to favour the Liberals. In his manifesto Bond was able to announce that he had succeeded in persuading the imperial government to rescind the 1907 order-in-council. This was hailed by his supporters as a great victory, even as 'the crowning triumph of Sir Robert's political career,'[43] but by then the issue was politically dead, and despite strenuous efforts, could not be resuscitated before a largely uninterested public. There had been no disagreement between the parties on the decision to submit the dispute with the United States to arbitration, and as the withdrawal of the order-in-council was regarded as following naturally from that earlier settlement, it failed to arouse any great enthusiasm; nor would Morris allow himself to be lured into a personal quarrel over it, despite strong provocation.

Nevertheless, in the absence of any clear principle dividing the parties, personal rather than political factors became increasingly pre-eminent in setting the tone of the electoral struggle. As the *Evening Telegram* observed: 'when no important political question is brought before the electorate, as at the present election, it becomes a question of MEN. And the keynote of the present election is this: DO YOU TRUST MORRIS?'[44] With the essential issue viewed in these terms it is not surprising that, in the course of a long campaign, debate on measures came gradually to be replaced by attacks on men. The unscrupulous and almost absurdly venal press practically ensured that this would be so. At various times Bond was accused, without the slightest evidence being produced, of everything from personally writing vituperative articles for the Liberal newspapers to distributing campaign literature at government expense and even of destroying public records, while his hapless minister of finance was pilloried in

41/*Evening Telegram*, 7 Oct. 1908. 42/*Daily News*, 10 Oct. 1908.
43/*Evening Telegram*, 29 Sept. 1908. 44/7 Oct. 1908.

cartoon and story as 'Reid's Tailor' and as 'Minister of Graft and Corruption' after it was discovered that his private firm had been awarded contracts to supply uniforms for railway employees and public officials.[45] Like any party in office, the Liberals were handicapped in a muck-raking duel by the fact that their opponents could claim to have clean hands – if only by virtue of being without the opportunity. Nor could they accuse Morris of wrongdoing without the charge reflecting to some extent upon themselves. Not even this thought, however, could deter the *Evening Telegram* from publishing a list of fees paid to Morris as minister of justice which totalled over $20,000 in addition to his salary.[46]

It was in this atmosphere of ludicrous scurrility that the long campaign finally exhausted itself. The *Daily News* wound up the debate for the People's party by posing a question to the electors – 'Will you vote to continue in power the band who have been living on you the past eight years, who have looted the public treasury of millions of dollars ...?'[47] While the *Evening Telegram*, not to be outdone, once again admonished voters to 'beware confederation,' and by way of warning left them to ponder the undoubtedly sinister but scarcely relevant question of 'Who Sold Ireland?'[48]

The election results came in slowly and at first seemed to indicate a victory for the People's party, but as the returns from first one and then another of the outlying constituencies reached the capital, amidst growing excitement, the balance swung back in favour of the government. It was not until 11 November, nine days after polling day, that the final result became known – the election had ended in a draw, each side electing eighteen members.[49] In the country as a whole there had been a powerful swing against the Liberals, their share of the popular vote falling from 60.4 per cent in 1904 to 49.8 per cent. They lost twelve seats to the People's party, gained none, and retained fifteen of their eighteen by reduced majorities (only in the three-member district of Twillingate, where Bond himself was a candidate, did the Liberal share of the vote increase). No cabinet ministers were defeated, although the minister of marine and fisheries managed to hold his seat in Harbour Grace by but a single vote. Predictably, the newly elected Assembly mirrored with exactitude the convention that representation in Parliament should be according to reli-

---

45/*Daily News*, 18 April, 20 June, 9 July 1908; *Evening Chronicle*, 11 Feb. 1908.
46/10 Oct. 1908.
47/31 Oct. 1908.
48/31 Oct. 1908. The allusion is to a well-known anti-confederation simile: that the union of Newfoundland and Canada would be as unhappy as the union of Ireland and England.
49/*Ibid.*, 11 Nov. 1908.

gious denomination, by tradition twenty-three Protestants (twelve Church of England and eleven Methodist) and thirteen Catholics. However, of the Catholic seats, every one of which had been Liberal in 1904, six now belonged to the People's party.[50] Also, in the Conception Bay North constituencies, where religion was most openly an issue, of the seven seats, the Liberals were able to win only two (one in Harbour Grace and one in Carbonear, by majorities of one and fourteen respectively) as against five in 1904. The Liberal losses here may be reasonably ascribed to the existence of a Catholic 'block vote' for the People's party. It is remarkable that of the twelve seats lost by the Liberals no less than nine were in predominantly Catholic or 'mixed' constituencies. As these were certainly no more (and in some cases considerably less) affected by the depression in the fishing industry than the northern constituencies, then, assuming that all other factors also were roughly equal, an analysis of the results indicates that religion rather than economic conditions or any other issue was the single most important factor in determining the outcome of the election, although by no means the only one. The fact that the Liberal vote fell by 6.2 per cent in Protestant constituencies compared with 16 per cent in Catholic ones lends further support to this inference.

The greater swing against the Liberals in Catholic districts may be explained by the understandable inclination of Catholic voters to favour the party with a Catholic leader – even though the head of the church in Newfoundland was a known supporter of the other side. Never was there a sharper demolition of the myth that the Catholic hierarchy, rather than local Catholic politicians, could deliver the 'Catholic vote.' Morris, the local politician par excellence, knew the truth and cultivated the latter. This is not, however, to suggest that the priest was without influence; but generally he was obliged to exercise a certain public restraint for fear of antagonizing the Protestant majority, if for no other reason. As the *Daily News* remarked on the result in Ferryland, a predominantly Catholic two-member constituency that returned one candidate of each party: 'the explanation is too self-evident to need comment. Many, acting on the advice of the Rev. Father O'Brien, refrained from voting for Cashin and P. F. Moore [People's party candidates] but refused to vote against them.'[51] Elsewhere, it would appear, clerical support was of even less value to the Liberal party.

50/Ferryland, 1; Harbour Main, 2; St George's, 1; St John's West, 2.
51/7 Dec. 1908.

6 The People's party and the constitutional crisis of 1908-9

THE IMMEDIATE aftermath of the electoral deadlock of November 1908 was a furious constitutional battle which continued for six months and was finally settled only after another general election. At the very centre of this struggle was the representative of the Crown, Governor Sir William Mac-Gregor, for the deadlock made it practically inevitable that he would be called upon to exercise the royal power of dissolution of Parliament in difficult, indeed almost unprecedented, circumstances.[1]

In the colonial context, however, it would be misleading to regard the governor as a strictly impartial representative of the Crown, for in reality his rôle was ambiguous: though *legally* a representative of the Crown, he was at the same time *politically* an agent of the British government, in constant touch with his superiors in the Colonial Office. Consequently, when no established legal precedent for a situation existed, the governor was in a position to exercise the royal prerogative in a politically partisan way if he, or his superiors, wished – and thought they could get away with it. This was exactly the situation following the 1908 tie election.

The constitutional controversy began with a letter from Sir Edward Morris to the governor which claimed that the results of the election were 'decisive against the Government Party,' and that 'from the granting of representative government in this Colony the invariable practice has been for the leader of the Government Party, on his return from the country, having failed to secure a majority, to tender his resignation to the Governor. This, I respectfully submit, the present leader of the Government

1/See Eugene A. Forsey, *The Royal Power of Dissolution of Parliament in the British Commonwealth* (Toronto, 1943), pp. 60–4; S. J. R. Noel, 'Politics and the Crown: The Case of the 1908 Tie Election in Newfoundland,' *Canadian Journal of Economics and Political Science*, vol. 33, no. 2 (May 1967), pp. 285–91.

Party should be called upon to do.' He then proceeded to expound the highly controversial and, in view of the critical importance of patronage in Newfoundland politics, tactically vital theory that

> as the Government has failed to receive the confidence of the electorate at the polls, Your Excellency would not be justified in being a party to the filling of any offices in the civil service now vacant, or the making of any contracts. In other words, the present Administration, pending the assumption of office by their successors, should be limited entirely to the transaction of ordinary routine business ...[2]

Governor MacGregor sent a copy of this letter to the prime minister, who indignantly replied that he regarded it as an 'impertinent intrusion' on the part of Morris. Nevertheless, he took care to deal with the arguments it contained, first drawing attention to the contradiction between what Morris presented as the 'invariable practice' and the course which he advised. He further pointed out that 'a tie can scarcely be regarded as a "decisive result." ' The suggestion that the Crown would not be justified in sanctioning appointments or contracts he dismissed as 'a perfect absurdity, for there can be no limitation of confidence between the Crown and its responsible advisors, and so long as Ministers retain their positions under the Crown, they of right exercise full executive power and authority.'[3] Finally, he produced a telegram from the clerk of the British House of Commons which stated: 'Sir Courtenay Ilbert's clear opinion is that Government retains office and full executive authority until defeated in Legislature, which must meet in regular way. Governor will exercise his discretion as to dissolution if and when circumstances arise necessitating this course.'[4] MacGregor cautiously replied that he did not think he would be justified in allowing himself 'to be guided to a decision on such questions by the opinion of any expert, however experienced,' for 'such an opinion is given on abstract principles ... and without full knowledge of local circumstances, which in this case deserve most careful consideration based on the fullest possible information ...'[5]

2/co 194/273, Morris to MacGregor, 12 Nov. 1908.
3/This was not the view of the colonial secretary, Lord Crewe, who was inclined to agree with Morris on this point: 'under existing circumstances,' he wrote to the governor, 'you must exercise your personal discretion in making appointments or agreeing to contracts because your Ministers cannot claim your full support inasmuch as they have no Parliamentary Majority. Such contracts or appointments should therefore be confined to routine matters ...' *Ibid.*, Crewe to MacGregor, 16 Nov. 1908.
4/*Ibid.*, Sir Robert Bond to MacGregor, 17 Nov. 1908.
5/*Ibid.*, MacGregor to Bond, 24 Nov. 1908.

Meanwhile Morris and his People's party, strong on the scent of office, returned to the attack with a ferocity which made the election campaign seem mild by comparison. The most powerful assault of all came from Morris himself, in a speech at St John's on 26 November. In language which vividly portrays the temper of political life, he told his audience 'the story of a crime.'

Sectarianism, Confederation, the Reid cry, added to the vilest personal slander, were deseminated [sic] in every district. Nothing was too sacred to drag in the mire of party politics ... The Government stood to-night beaten, discredited and humiliated all over the land. The Government had the work and policy of eight years behind them; they had the prestige and influence of a Government; they had the expenditure of $60,000 for the carrying out of the election, the hire of steamers and crafts for the distribution and collection of ballots and ballot boxes, the officers acting as canvassers. From the earliest summer months no one was employed to take the Voters' List unless he was a Government supporter, and in this way patronage was given to thousands of supporters all over the country. Added to this, hundreds of thousands of dollars on roads, bridges, dredges, breakwaters and public wharves were expended in every district. Further, the Government service was demoralized; civil servants were encouraged by promises of an increase in pay and promotion to come out and fight and canvas for the Government candidates. The public offices [that is, the civil service departments] were used to frank party literature to go free through the post office, whilst at the same time the Opposition Party had to pay postage on the same kind of literature. Thousands of dollars were spent in printing of election literature and men paid to address this literature and all out of Government funds at the public expense.

Force, fraud, coercion, threats, intimidation, bribery and corruption had done their work.[6]

The constitutional debate was carried on in a more dignified and erudite manner but with scarcely less intensity. Governor MacGregor could hardly fail to see the dilemma that was taking shape before him.

I am not aware [he wrote to the colonial secretary, Lord Crewe] of any precedent in which the point of dissolving a House before a Speaker has been appointed has ever arisen. If, as at least some members of the Assembly anticipate, no Speaker can be appointed, the question in that case would be: whether and how, I can dissolve or prorogue a House that has no Speaker; a

6/ *Daily News*, St John's, 26 Nov. 1908.

House, moreover, that I have not opened; and to which I have not communicated the purposes for which it was called together.[7]

This, as it happened, was exactly the question which arose. On 18 February Bond advised the governor to dissolve the House on 25 March, the day it was due to be opened, 'so as to afford the constituencies an opportunity to establish the Government of the Colony upon a firm and proper basis.' It was obvious, in his view, that 'a deadlock must ensue on the motion of either party to elect a Speaker, both parties being firm in their allegiance to their respective leaders,' and consequently 'there is no probability of any Ministry that can be formed being able to meet the House and to carry on public business.'[8]

But was a parliamentary deadlock inevitable? This was clearly the crux of the matter. Although a great deal of hard bargaining had taken place among the elected members, it had failed to produce a break in the discipline of either party. As Governor MacGregor noted, 'a change from one side of the House to the other is necessarily attended by great notoriety, which in the present intense state of party feeling could hardly fail to assume such a bitter personal character as would go a long way to act as a deterrent.'[9] The solidarity of the party ranks was further emphasized by the publication of a pledge of loyalty to Sir Robert Bond signed by all the Liberal members of the Assembly.[10] It appeared on the day following Bond's request for a dissolution ('a remarkable coincidence in dates,' the governor drily observed) and on the next day there appeared in the opposition press a similar pledge to Sir Edward Morris signed by all his supporters.[11] In spite of this, the governor refused to accept the inevitability of a deadlock and therefore refused to grant a dissolution. He explained: 'It is not improbable that members of the House may be influenced by the fact that the Speaker presides over the deliberations of the Assembly and represents the House, not a party; and this consideration, coupled with the desire to avoid a dissolution, a General Election in the Spring, and a second session, may make the election of a Speaker possible, and even easy.'[12]

Faced with the rejection of his advice, the prime minister had no option but to tender his resignation. But since it was clearly impossible for a suc-

7/co 194/275, MacGregor to Crewe, 7 Jan. 1909.
8/*Ibid.*, Bond to MacGregor, 18 Feb. 1909.
9/*Ibid.*, MacGregor to Crewe, 7 Jan. 1909.
10/*Evening Telegram*, St John's, 18 Feb. 1909.
11/*Evening Chronicle*, St John's, 19 Feb. 1909.
12/co 194/273, MacGregor to Bond, 20 Feb. 1909.

cessful ministry to be obtained without his co-operation (provided that all his colleagues remained loyal), he not unnaturally sought to elicit from the governor some indication of what he proposed to do in the event of an alternative ministry failing. The question of which party held office at the time of dissolution was of considerable importance, for control of the state machinery with its attendant patronage was no small asset in an election campaign, and Bond was anxious to establish his claim to it. He wrote:

In accordance with constitutional practice, your Ministers may retain office until they are defeated in Parliament or are dismissed by the Representatives of the Crown. They cannot be defeated in Parliament, because the Opposition are not in a majority. Seeing then that they voluntarily relinquish their right under the Constitution may I be permitted to enquire if "when it is made clear that by no other constitutional means can a Ministry be obtained which can induce Parliament to vote Supply and carry on the business of the country," you will grant your present Ministers a dissolution, or if it is your intention under such circumstances to grant a dissolution to their political opponents? I think I am entitled to this information and justified in anticipating the most perfect frankness between the Representative of the Crown and his Ministers.[13]

'I am not sure that I fully understand the question that is thus stated.' replied the governor warily, adding that in his opinion 'the prerogative of dissolution should not be committed to hypothetical cases, but left free to meet events when they actually present themselves.'[14] On the following day he asked Sir Edward Morris if he could 'form a Ministry that would meet the House at an early date, with a reasonable prospect of being able to induce Parliament to pass Supply, and to carry on the business of the country.'[15] Morris immediately gave an assurance that he could, but without offering to explain how, a critical omission in the circumstances and one which for the governor raised an obvious difficulty – a difficulty he chose to ignore. 'I have not deemed it necessary,' he wrote to Lord Crewe, 'to make detailed inquiry as to how Sir Edward Morris expects to be able to induce Parliament to grant Supply, but have thought that I was bound to accept his written assurance that he has a reasonable prospect of being able to do so.'[16] But what was 'a reasonable prospect'? This was not a question of semantics. Either Morris had some plan by which he expected

13/*Ibid.*, Bond to MacGregor, 22 Feb. 1909.
14/*Ibid.*, MacGregor to Bond, 24 Feb. 1909.
15/*Ibid.*, MacGregor to Morris, 25 Feb. 1909.
16/co 194/275, MacGregor to Crewe, 26 Feb. 1909.

to break the deadlock or he did not, in which case he was deliberately misleading the governor in order to gain office. In the absence of further evidence, it can only be said that if he did have a plan he never revealed it, nor is it easy to imagine what it might have been.[17]

Events quickly proved that the new ministry had not the slightest chance of obtaining supply. It met the House on 30 March but in the face of uncompromising obstruction from the Liberals failed even to elect a Speaker. Morris then advised the governor that 'the only solution to the present difficulties is a dissolution of the Legislature and an appeal to the country,'[18] thereby confronting him with an acutely embarrassing choice: could he accept from Morris the very same advice he had refused to accept from Bond? On the one hand, circumstances were different, for Morris had at least tried to obtain supply before advising a dissolution; but on the other hand, he had only been allowed the opportunity to do so because he gave a firm assurance that he had a 'reasonable prospect' of success. His assurance was now shown to have been groundless, and his weak and unhelpful explanation that in accepting a commission to form a ministry he had acted on the belief 'that if the Legislature were asked for Supplies they would be granted'[19] merely confirmed that Bond had been right in the first place. Even had the government succeeded in electing a Speaker they would only have placed themselves in a minority, liable to be defeated on a vote of confidence. Bond later pointed this out in a letter to the governor: 'I chose to hasten the process by defeating them on the motion for a Speaker as the opportunity was afforded me to do so, and as I conceived it to be in the best interest of the public that an appeal should be made to the constituencies without delay.'[20]

Nevertheless, the governor was inclined to grant the dissolution to Morris. He had accepted without question an unsupported assurance from him and therefore could not now, without casting doubt upon his own judgment, dispute its good faith, even had he wished to do so. Morris, moreover, had made another notably awkward omission – nowhere in

17/Shortly thereafter it was reported that 'certain members of the Liberal Party' were offered 'thousands of dollars' to alter their allegiance, and that 'some of these offers have been increased since Sir Edward's advent to power two days ago' (*Evening Telegram*, 5 March 1909). However, in the tense political atmosphere then prevailing it was improbable that any Liberal members could have been thus persuaded even to absent themselves from the Chamber while supply was being passed. Bribery remained a possibility, but without some positive indication that it would succeed it was hardly sufficient ground on which to base a firm assurance to the governor.

18/co 194/273, Morris to MacGregor, 31 March 1909.

19/*Ibid.*

20/*Ibid.*, Bond to MacGregor, 6 April 1909.

his letter did he offer to resign. MacGregor at once sent a telegram to the Colonial Office indicating his intention, the result of which was temporarily to remove the matter from his hands and shift the scene of the debate to Whitehall. There also opinion was sharply divided. In a departmental minute written on 1 April, A. B. Keith[21] forcefully presented the case for granting a dissolution to Bond. He asked: 'How can Sir E. Morris complain if the Governor says to him "I have given you a chance, you have failed and advise a dissolution, but I must give one rather to Sir R. Bond whose advice to dissolve I rejected only because I hoped for a Ministry which could get Supply. I should be acting unfairly to Sir Robert if I gave you a dissolution after refusing him." '[22] His colleague Mr Dale disagreed. While admitting that there was 'considerable force in Mr. Keith's arguments,' he did not believe that it was any part of the governor's duty to take into account the advantage to a party of being in power at the time of a dissolution. 'Questions of fairness or unfairness as between Sir R. Bond and Sir E. Morris do not therefore appear quite relevant,'[23] he wrote. Mr Just took a similar line: 'I do not think we can take cognisance of the advantage (? corruption) given to the Premier in office at dissolution.'[24]

Lord Crewe, however, was not so unmindful of political factors. His primary concern was to ensure that the preparation of Newfoundland's case before The Hague tribunal should not be interrupted by an election, for he instructed Governor MacGregor to press this view upon both party leaders before dissolving Parliament. He did not state in so many words that the dissolution must be given to Morris, merely that he did not dissent from such a course, but before the telegram to MacGregor was sent he added the following enquiry: 'Do you hold that the man to whom the dissolution is granted would have a great advantage in the campaign? On the other hand in the event of Bond's not being recalled for the purposes of giving him a dissolution can he after what has taken place between you and Morris make with any show of reason such a grievance as to considerably enhance his prospects at the polls?'[25] The implication was clear, for there was no doubt as to how the governor would answer these questions. Bond's advocate, Mr Keith, reluctantly acquiesced, summarizing the situation thus:

21/Mr (later Sir) Arthur Berriedale Keith, at this time an official in the Dominions Division of the Colonial Office.
22/co 194/275, minute by A. B. K[eith], 1 April 1909.
23/Ibid., minute by H. E. D[ale], 1 April 1909.
24/Ibid., minute by H. W. J[ust], 1 April 1909.
25/Ibid., Crewe to MacGregor, 3 April 1909.

I understand that a victory for Sir E. Morris is preferable to one for Sir R. Bond, and the victory of the latter is practically certain if he gets a dissolution in office.

I think we can now let Sir W. MacGregor act on his discretion – we know how he will act and – tho' I think Sir R. Bond preferable to Sir E. Morris – there is much to be said for the latter on the score of newness.[26]

The House of Assembly was dissolved on 16 April with a general election set for 8 May. Inevitably, the brief campaign was fought mainly on the issue of the dissolution, other matters receiving but scant and sporadic attention. Bond published his correspondence with the governor, who was then attacked by the Liberal press for his 'partisan' conduct. The *Evening Telegram* angrily declared that 'no unbiased man who has read carefully the correspondence ... can arrive at any other conclusion than that the Governor from the very outset was determined "by hook or by crook" to give the dissolution to the Reid-Morris Combination,'[27] and went on to denounce in the strongest possible terms not only his handling of the constitutional crisis but the whole of his personal conduct as governor.

All such protests had about them an air of apoplectic impotence, for nothing could alter the fact that in an unprecedented situation the Crown had exercised its unhindered discretion. The dissolution could have been given to either Bond or Morris and justified with equal plausibility. By giving it to Morris the governor, and his superiors in the Colonial Office, made a political choice, but one which in the circumstances was legitimately theirs to make.

It remains to be said that Keith's assertion that a victory for Bond was 'practically certain' if he were granted a dissolution in office is of questionable validity, for if the trend towards the People's party so evident in the November election had continued to develop, they might well have overtaken the Liberals by May in any event. Possession of the government at the time of dissolution, however, guaranteed them victory. The bulk of the electorate could not be interested in constitutional niceties; in terms of electoral influence what mattered far more was who had local patronage to dispense, and that was Morris' party not Bond's. In innumerable ways, in every town and hamlet, the shift in the seat of power was made manifest. The Liberal candidates could only promise where once they could perform, and those who hoped for government contracts or civil service appointments, or the more humble who wanted nothing more than

26/*Ibid.*, minute by A. B. K[eith], 5 April 1909.
27/26 April 1909.

seasonal employment on the roads, or even poor relief, had now to seek the favour of the People's party.

If sectarianism and economic depression weighed heavily against the Liberals in November, in May patronage and a widespread feeling of 'give Morris a chance' combined to produce a landslide victory for the People's party. Eight Liberals lost their seats and the government was returned with a majority of sixteen. Four more 'Catholic' seats fell to the People's party, bringing their total to ten (out of thirteen), and the two marginally held Liberal seats in Conception Bay North (Carbonear and Harbour Grace) also changed hands. Liberal representation in the Assembly was reduced to five members from the extreme north, two from Burin, and three from the (Catholic) Liberal stronghold of St John's East.

After more than a year of rancorous political warfare Morris and his party had at last obtained both office and power. For the Liberal party the defeat was even more catastrophic than it might at first have appeared; the electoral tide had swept away its once enormous majority in the Catholic south, and with it the traditional foundations of the party that stretched back to the beginning of representative government and beyond. Only at the zenith of its power, under Bond's leadership, had it managed to capture the north, and even then the important and populous constituency of Bonavista steadfastly returned three Conservatives. Now no less than half the Liberal representatives in the House of Assembly came from north of Cape Freels, from the remote districts of Fogo, Twillingate, and St Barbe – a geographical distribution later to have far-reaching political consequences.

7 The rise of the union movement

BY THE END of the first decade of the twentieth century Great Britain and most of the self-governing British colonies had witnessed, to varying degrees, the rise of mass-organized and politically conscious labour movements. Though sharing certain characteristic attitudes and tendencies, these movements were not otherwise linked to one another. Rather, each was basically indigenous to the society that gave it birth. It was thus in Newfoundland. Nowhere was the rise of a labour movement more sudden or unexpected than it was there, or more suitably adapted to its surroundings. And nowhere, in North America in particular, has there ever been a labour movement that is so little known or so fascinating in its evolution.

At the turn of the century the only trade unions in Newfoundland were the various craft unions in St John's – the coopers, mechanics, railway workers, longshoremen, and a few others of a similar sort – none of which were politicallly active, beyond exercising a limiting influence in municipal affairs. Though progressive in spirit, these tiny unions were essentially marginal to the economic life of a fishing country, and therefore of little general significance. No attempt had ever been made to organize a fishermen's union, for the fishermen of the country were commonly believed to be, and indeed to a certain extent were, almost archetypally individualistic, largely self-employed, in debt to their merchants perhaps, but still supremely self-reliant. They were, in fact, more closely akin to an agrarian peasantry than to an industrial proletariat. Moreover, they were scattered around the coast in hundreds of tiny villages, with apparently little or no contact with one another. And in a country where most men were fishermen, the mere fact of belonging to that category was not *per se* a strong bond of unity. Sectional differences generally managed to obscure the underlying homogeneity of occupation and economic class. In no sense, therefore, could Newfoundland be considered a promising field for union endeavour – at least not on the normal industrial pattern.

Yet if the right seeds were planted the field possessed a latent fertility, as one remarkable man was soon to demonstrate. He was William Coaker, a young farmer, who saw in the principle of unionism an economic panacea, and who, incongruously, in the seclusion of his farm, gradually conceived a plan for a fishermen's union that was at once both original and brilliantly simple. By the autumn of 1908 he was ready to put his plan into action; but before discussing this phase of his career – and the next phase of his country's political development – it is illuminating first of all to look in some detail at the background and personality of the man himself.[1]

Coaker was born in St John's on 19 October 1871 of parents who had recently moved to the city from Twillingate. Little is known of his early life other than that he left school at the age of eleven to work on the St John's waterfront, and five years later moved to an outport near Twillingate where he was employed in the branch store of a firm of St John's merchants. He never again took up residence in his birthplace, and indeed throughout his life evinced nothing but the deepest aversion towards it. It was perhaps to avoid returning to St John's that he became a farmer, for when his employers went out of business, Coaker, lacking the skills of a fisherman, turned to the soil. Or, more accurately, he turned to the forest, for the uninhabited islet on which he chose to locate his farm was densely wooded. Even to think of such a place in terms of agriculture was an act of boldness. But at the time William Coaker was a bold young man of twenty.

For the next decade he was to lead the simple, laborious life of a pioneer homesteader. In the early years, to raise money for equipment and livestock, he sometimes took winter employment elsewhere; but he always returned, and in due course became one of Newfoundland's few full-time farmers. A suitable ending to a pioneering story – had Coaker been an ordinary pioneer.

He was, however, a pioneer with a difference: in him pioneering individualism was paradoxically mixed with a radical turn of mind and a passionate interest in trade unionism. Where these surprising aspects of his character had their origin is obscure, though it is possible to surmise that as a boy on the St John's waterfront he had perhaps seen the work and absorbed the ideals of the early trade unionists. Whatever the source

1/Unfortunately, Coaker's life has not received the attention it deserves. There is but one brief biographical sketch: J. R. Smallwood's *Coaker of Newfoundland* (London, 1927). A more accurate treatment of Coaker's life and career is to be found in J. Feltham, 'The Development of the F.P.U. in Newfoundland (1908–1923),' unpublished MA thesis, Memorial University of Newfoundland, 1959.

of his unionism, it was demonstrably of a practical nature. In 1894–5, during one of his periodic money-earning excursions, he was employed as a telegrapher at Port Blandford, Bonavista Bay, and, noting the absence of a telegraphers' union, promptly set out to remedy the deficiency. His efforts apparently met with success, for he was soon the editor of a new union journal, the *Telegrapher*. But after this promising start, his career as an organizer-editor came to an abrupt end. In St John's the receiver general, the minister responsible for telegraphs, began to suspect with good reason that the new union which was badgering him with its demands had been organized by the surreptitious use of the government telegraph system! With dismissal imminent, Coaker hastily retreated to his farm.

He had soon no need for outside employment, but even as a full-time farmer one problem dominated his thoughts. As he later explained: 'The winter evenings and stormy Sundays gave me the leisure for reading and study, and whatever I worked at I always found myself drifting away to thoughts of the toiler's life and its hardships, while so many lived lives of ease and luxury without toil or producing.'[2] In Coaker's mind the remedy for these ills was equally commonplace: he believed as an article of faith that productive workers could obtain a fair share of the wealth they produced only through collective action. His one problem, the one truly daunting question, was *how*, in a land of fishermen, could this general principle be applied? None of the preconditions normally required for successful industrial organization were present. The fishermen were not wage-earners; they were geographically dispersed; they had no tradition of unity and no élite to whom they could look for leadership.

Coaker was naturally aware of these obstacles, for although his farm was isolated he was by no means a recluse. He was well known to, and knew well, the fishermen of the neighbouring villages in whose community life he played an active part, especially in matters of education. His knowledge of the fishery and of outport society was therefore solidly based upon his own experience of many years. However, the fact that he was not himself an outport fisherman never lost its significance. His untypical upbringing and occupation served to sharpen his awareness of the society in which he lived, while his radical instincts gave him the boldness to question existing social and economic assumptions.

Thus, his plan for a new union, as it gradually emerged, was both finely attuned to the realities of Newfoundland society and conceived on a scale

2/*Evening Advocate*, St John's, 12 Dec. 1917, quoted in Feltham, *ibid.*, p. 22. It would be interesting to know the nature of Coaker's reading, but unfortunately he does not elaborate the point.

so ambitious as to stir the imagination of the outport people as it had never been stirred before.

Like a good doctor, or social reformer, Coaker based his prescriptions upon careful diagnosis: each of his ideas can be seen as an attempt to remedy a particular ailment of outport society. First, it was glaringly obvious that in Newfoundland's credit-based laissez-faire economy the fishermen were as surely at the mercy of the merchant oligarchy as workers in an industrial society would have been at the mercy of their employers if each individual had to negotiate his own separate wage agreement – and purchase all his basic supplies at his employer's store at his employer's prices. The financial structure of the fishery had changed but little since the early nineteenth century, when St John's finally succeeded in replacing the west of England as Newfoundland's financial and political capital. After the 'crash' of the St John's banks in 1894, Canadian banks had moved in to take their place as the chief suppliers of credit to the merchant fish exporters, but this change had not appreciably affected the lower levels of the credit pyramid. Small merchants still depended upon the credit of large merchants, as did outport traders, planters, and schooner captains. And in turn every fisherman depended absolutely upon credit, either directly from a St John's merchant or indirectly through an intermediary, for his season's supplies.[3] Prices were not established at the time the supplies were given, but were 'adjusted' when the fisherman 'sold' his catch to the same merchant in payment of his debts. If the fisherman happened to be illiterate (as many were), he then had no means of checking the annual account rendered to him. A favourable balance could, like a debt, be 'carried forward' on the merchant's books. And always the fisherman lived in dread of being 'cut off,' for his merchant had absolute power to refuse him further credit. This power was invoked for a number of reasons: persistent failure to secure a good catch being the most common, but also for political reasons, or (the most heinous crime of all) selling fish for cash to an independent trader instead of surrendering it to the merchant.[4] Furthermore, in addition to selling supplies and buying fish, and setting the price of both, the merchant also had absolute discretion in the grading or 'culling' of fish. There were basically seven grades, Choice, Merchantable, Madeira, West India, Labrador no. 1, Labrador no. 2, and Cullage, each with a different price. The culler was invariably

3/See above, pp. 8–9.
4/'To prevent such frauds, a kind of espionage had to be exerted, and the catches of a suspected planter were watched as the season progressed. Convicted planters were turned off from their merchants and no one would take them on. Thus resulted in the end the worst cases of poverty, – cases, to my mind, not caused by the bad fishery, but by the bad system.' W. T. Grenfell, *Labrador* (New York, 1922), p. 310.

an employee of the merchant, thus enabling an unscrupulous merchant to 'reward' or 'discipline' a fisherman by manipulating the cull.[5]

Exploitation was inherent in such a system, and the reason the fishermen bore their exploitation with passivity, or else emigrated to escape it, was, in Coaker's view, because they were not conscious of their own economic importance or of the power they could wield if they acted in unison as the country's productive class.[6] The best means of arousing them to effective class-consciousness, he concluded, was through a massive general union, which, though open to all workers, would necessarily in Newfoundland be a union overwhelmingly composed of fishermen. That such a union, in the short run at least, could not hope to effect substantial reforms in the fishery – for a start, even the most normal avenues of trade union endeavour, such as collective bargaining, were closed to it – did not matter. It could perhaps show useful results in other spheres more amenable to industrial organization: the sealing ships were an obvious target, and the expanding paper-making and timber industries, with their growing numbers of loggers, more obvious still.

In any case, the one vital point was that a mass union should be brought into existence, however limited its initial powers. For the union, as Coaker saw it, was not to stand alone, but was to function as the core of an even larger organism. It was, in fact, to be the trunk of a union 'tree,' whose value was to consist less in its activity than in its solid strength, and whose primary duty was to be the maintenance of a number of fruitful branches, the union's active arms. These were to fall into three broad categories: co-operative, educative, and political.[7] And, like the union itself, each branch was to be designed to combat a particular weakness of Newfoundland society. First, the main instrument by which the merchant class dominated

5/ Most of a fisherman's output would fall clearly into one grade or another, but marginal cases could be graded up or down with serious effect upon the fisherman's income. 'The culler was under oath to do justice to his assessment; instead, however, of being an independent man, he was an employee of the merchant buying the fish. Unless, therefore, he gave satisfaction to the merchant, he was in danger of losing his livelihood. It is obvious that in these circumstances the scales were heavily weighted against the fisherman.' Cmd 4480, *Newfoundland Royal Commission 1933 Report* (London, 1933), p. 104.

6/ This theme of the 'community of interest' of all primary producers runs through his speeches. See W. F. Coaker, ed., *The History of the Fishermen's Protective Union of Newfoundland* (St John's, 1920), pp. 1–4 and passim. The title of this book is a misnomer. Its contents consist mainly of the proceedings of the FPU supreme council, 1909–19. These are continued to 1929 in W. F. Coaker, ed., *Twenty Years of the Fishermen's Protective Union of Newfoundland* (St John's, 1930).

7/ Plans for each were introduced by Coaker at the first meeting of the FPU supreme council in 1909. See Coaker, *The History of the Fishermen's Protective Union*, pp. 3–4.

the economic life of the country was the credit system; and the way to attack the very root of the problem, Coaker believed, was through the institution of consumer co-operatives, not struggling in isolation as the few co-operatives then in existence were doing, but linked to one another through the agency of the union. Secondly, in order to counteract the parochialism and apparent lack of solidarity of the fishermen it was imperative that the union should have a branch devoted to education and propaganda, working mainly through a union newspaper. Thirdly, since in Coaker's view many of the problems of the fishery could be solved only by government action, and since the outport constituencies were represented in Parliament for the most part by lawyers and merchants who normally lived in St John's, the only way the fishermen could safeguard their interests was by securing the election of representatives of their own class. Therefore the union would have to sponsor its own political party.

These, briefly, were the component parts of Coaker's scheme. Taken together they constituted nothing less than a blueprint for a labour movement, to be built in a country that so far lacked even the barest foundations. Coaker of course drew upon outside sources for ideas and inspiration, but the plan as a whole bears the plain imprint of his own creative and audacious personality. And though it was conceived slowly, it was released in a torrent, beginning on the evening of 2 November 1908, three hours after the closing of the polls in the general election held that same day.[8]

The occasion could hardly have been less auspicious. In the quaintly named village of Herring Neck, about five miles from Coaker's home, some two hundred fishermen gathered into the Orange Hall to hear the local farmer make his first public speech. The scene is described by J. R. Smallwood:

He spoke for an hour, and stopped then, not because he had said all that he had to say, but because a voice unused to speaking could stand no more strain such as he was putting upon it. He was one of the most forceful speakers they had ever heard. A man in his early thirties [he was in fact thirty-seven], short, very thick-built, strong as an ox, eyes flashing, dressed in the kind of clothes that would be worn by a farmer ... Coaker appeared that night every inch one of the people ... Nor was his speech suave, polished, like that of the professional politician to which they were accustomed to listen each four years. He paid them no oily compliments, which was a novelty to them. Had they not

8/W. F. Coaker, *Past, Present, and Future* (St John's, n.d. [1932]), a reprint of a series of articles contributed to the *Fishermen's Advocate*.

recognized the rugged simplicity and sincerity of every word he uttered they would most surely have resented the taunts and gibes he threw passionately at them for what he termed their slavish acquiescence in the conditions imposed for centuries upon their forefathers and themselves. He pointed out to them their impotence, their weakness, their powerlessness. They were the prey of professional politicians, of profiteering merchants, of shark lawyers, of a whole horde of parasites who were living in St. John's and even in the outports, in their midst, upon the wealth which their hard and dangerous toil created. The country was a fishing country, he told them, 'an Empire built upon fish,' in which the last man who had a chance was a fisherman.[9]

Coaker's remedy was union, and on the following evening the fishermen again assembled to hear the positive side of his programme. This he had prepared to the last detail, even to a written constitution which he put before his audience for their consideration.[10] Its structure was simple and hierarchical, easily within the grasp of even the least educated of its potential members. Each settlement was to have a Local Council, open to all workers, to meet weekly, with democratically elected officers. Each local was to be represented on a District Council (the boundaries of the districts corresponding to the established administrative divisions of the island) by its chairman, deputy chairman, secretary, and treasurer, who were to elect the district officers. At the apex, the district officers plus the chairman of the local councils were to comprise the Supreme Council, with responsibility for electing the president and other officers of the union as a whole. In his peroration Coaker urged the fishermen to embrace the principle of unity and called upon those who shared his faith to remain behind at the close of the meeting. Only nineteen were sufficiently convinced, *and* sufficiently courageous to risk the merchants' wrath, to do so. These nineteen men of Herring Neck proceeded to form the first local council of the Fishermen's Protective Union (FPU), with Coaker as their provisional president.

In the morning Coaker set out for the next village, driven – quixotically – by horse and waggon by one of his converts, where again the story was much the same: a meeting of fishermen, a rousing speech, the birth of a new union branch, and on to the next village, a pattern repeated in dozens of unchronicled meetings from one end of Notre Dame Bay to the other. 'His voice grew stronger, his speeches longer, and his fame spread before him to the fishing settlements,' writes Smallwood.[11] Winter arrived and he took to snow-shoes, travelling alone, through forests and across frozen

9/*Coaker of Newfoundland*, pp. 20–1.   10/*Ibid.*, p. 23.
11/*Ibid.*, p. 24.

bays, working his way with incredible stamina along that wild and stormy northeast coast.

The coming of spring forced him to return to his farm, leaving in his wake a tenuous string of newborn FPU branches containing altogether perhaps a thousand members.[12] But in the autumn, his crops harvested, he was again free to devote his prodigious energy to the task of union organization. This time, however, the task was easier, for during the summer news of the union had spread like an epidemic wherever fishermen gathered. One of the very few natural advantages on the side of the nascent union, it appears, was the tendency of its original members to be activists and proselytizers, encouraged perhaps by the example of Coaker, but also no doubt by the simple urge to self-preservation. For it must be emphasized that a fisherman who cast his lot with the FPU in its early days was taking no small risk: in short, he took the risk of having his credit cut off by the merchant who supplied him, with consequent loss of livelihood. Therefore it was only by making the FPU so large that a merchant could not refuse to supply its members without damaging his business that union fishermen could obtain a measure of security – a thought that must have given the early unionists a grim incentive to missionary endeavour. Thus, by the time Coaker resumed his travels the movement he had set in motion during the previous winter had already acquired something of its own impetus, and his second tour, coinciding with the return of the schooners from the Labrador fishery where union activists had been at work among the crews, gave it more impetus still. By late autumn, all along the northeast coast fishermen were flocking to enroll in the FPU, creating new but welcome problems for its founder.

For a whole year Coaker had kept the infant union alive and active, and the branches in touch with one another, by himself writing a weekly circular letter raising various topics for discussion, spreading information about the activities of local branches, and about the work of organized labour in other parts of the world. Smallwood describes a typical meeting:

This circular would be read aloud by the Chairman of the branch; and then, for the purpose of greater accuracy, would be read a second time. Then it was thrown open for discussion. The members, almost to a man unaccustomed to standing up and speaking, joined in the discussions now with great heartiness, and the branch meetings became something in the nature of night schools ... Coaker, having all his life observed things and thought about them, had much information to impart, and many novel viewpoints to express. For the first time in the history of the country fishermen were getting educated as to the

12/*Ibid.*, p. 25.

inner affairs of their government, the fish industry, and many other matters of
first importance to them.[13]

To maintain the interest and enthusiasm of branch officers he wisely coun-
selled them to take an active interest in local affairs, and to act as spokesmen for their localities by such means as the initiation of petitions to the
House of Assembly on any grievances that arose. A skilfully directed
union branch could thus make itself the focus of public life in an outport
community, a rôle made easier for it in most places by the virtual absence
of local government.[14] But since this was not to be the ultimate function
of the union, towards the end of 1909 Coaker decided that the time was
ripe to convene the first meeting of the supreme council in order to con-
solidate the gains of the first year and to make plans for the union's next
phase of development.

There had not yet been time to establish district councils, although
there were already more than thirty branches spread over three districts
(Twillingate, Fogo, and Bonavista). Consequently, the first supreme
council consisted simply of nine branch chairmen, hastily assembled at
Change Island, Notre Dame Bay, on the first three days of November
1909,[15] the anniversary of the union's founding. Though impeccably democratic in form, the meetings were dominated by Coaker, who tirelessly
led the delegates through one lengthy session after another.

The problems dealt with were vital to the union's future success. First,
there was the question of finance, which was settled by fixing the annual
membership dues at twenty-five cents, fifteen cents to go to the local council and ten cents to the supreme council. Secondly, since the union was
now of sufficient strength, it was decided that two of its projected auxiliary
branches should be started at once. These were a union newspaper and
a co-operative buying system, both of which the president was authorized
to establish. Thirdly, it was decided to have the FPU incorporated as soon
as the new Trade Unions Act then before the legislature passed into law.
Finally, in his closing address, Coaker prophetically advised the delegates
that though the time to act had not yet arrived, 'if we are to have the
wishes of the fishermen of the Country respected, it will be necessary to
elect eight or ten union members for [sic] the House of Assembly.'[16] He
also at this time announced his decision to abandon his farm in order to
devote his full attention to the work of the union.

13/*Ibid.*, p. 28.
14/See above, pp. 17–18.
15/For the proceedings of the council, see Coaker, *The History of the Fishermen's
Protective Union*, chap. 1.
16/*Ibid.*, p. 2.

The convention over, he embarked at once upon another incredibly arduous winter campaign of speaking and organizing, this time working his way southwards through the districts of Bonavista and Trinity, keeping in touch with the older union branches while on the move, and somehow also finding time to establish, edit, and largely write, a two-sheet weekly newspaper – the *Fishermen's Advocate* – the first issue of which appeared on 12 February 1910. It was small and crudely produced, but the fishermen loyally subscribed in thousands, giving the union a powerful new organ of education and propaganda. Moreover, the *Advocate* quickly acquired the invaluable function of a union 'cement,' each week reinforcing the bond that held its widespread members together. They eagerly awaited its arrival and read it, or had it read to them, over and over.

During the summer of 1910, while the outports were, as usual, seasonally preoccupied with the fishery, Coaker took advantage of the lull to establish a rudimentary co-operative buying organization, as the supreme council had authorized.[17] The organization was simple. A union purchasing office was opened in St John's to act as a clearing house. Through it, each local branch that wished to do so could function as a consumer cooperative by placing bulk orders for a narrow range of goods – basic fishing supplies, such as salt and line, and staple foods, such as flour, tea, sugar, barrelled salt beef and pork. By co-ordinating the orders the purchasing office could buy in even greater bulk, and so pass on to the fishermen the benefit of wholesale prices – incidentally eliminating the retail merchants' profit. All transactions were to be in cash, and fishermen were urged to participate in the scheme no matter how small the amount of goods they could afford to purchase, for the effect of co-operative buying was expected to be cumulative, each purchase so made reducing the purchaser's indebtedness to the credit merchant, thus freeing more of his cash in the following year.

By late autumn 1910 the co-operative experiment was a distinct, if qualified, success. The chief difficulties were the limited range of goods that could be supplied and the high cost of small shipments which made it impracticable to despatch orders from St John's to the local branches of any district more often than once or twice a year. Nevertheless, the general response had been encouraging and the question of improving and extending the union's commercial activities was high on the agenda of the second annual convention of the supreme council which met in December at Catalina, Trinity Bay. 'I have had some correspondence with a Fishermen's Association in Scotland,' Coaker remarked in his opening speech,

17/For an account of the union's co-operative and commercial activities, see Feltham, 'The Development of the F.P.U.,' chap. 5.

'which will show us what those fishermen are doing regarding the advancement of their affairs.' One of their ideas he soon adapted to the needs of the Newfoundland outports: 'I strongly recommend,' he said, 'the establishment of cash stores to accommodate the business of members at settlements where branches contain at least two hundred members.'[18] A committee of the supreme council set up to study the matter advised that the first such stores should be opened as soon as possible, under the direction of the president.

Meanwhile, the union had sustained its rapid rate of expansion. There were thirty-eight delegates to the 1910 convention representing sixty-six local and two district councils (Twillingate and Fogo). Its newspaper, the *Advocate*, was such an immediate success that in March its printing had to be transferred to a larger press in St John's. The union was on a rising tide, it seemed, increasingly confident, and ready even for politics. Though the FPU had been tacitly political from the moment of its origin (perhaps inevitably so, given its social context), politics was the one major sphere in which Coaker's ideas had yet to be precisely formulated. However, it is clear from the *Advocate* that political problems were much on his mind during the summer of 1910. The activities of the British Labour party were avidly reported; while most of the front page of one issue was devoted to a lengthy eulogy (obviously written by Coaker himself) on the political success of organized labour in Australia. By July the *Advocate* was thinking in terms of a union party of half a dozen members 'to serve as opposition watchdogs,' but it was not until October that a definitive statement emerged: the duty of union members elected to Parliament, wrote Coaker, would be 'to act exactly as the Labour Party in England – support the Government that will do the most for the masses.'[19] Subsequently, at the Catalina convention of the supreme council in December, he urged the delegates 'to formulate plans for the establishment of a Union Party to take the field in 1913.'[20] His recommendation was enthusiastically adopted, and it was further decided that responsibility for the selection of candidates should rest with the district councils. The matter of party policy was left in abeyance until the next meeting of the supreme council.

It could safely be postponed, for it was unlikely to cause any serious difficulties. The union had already articulated its views on a wide range of topics through its practice of initiating petitions to the government.

18/Coaker, *The History of the Fishermen's Protective Union*, p. 16.
19/*Fishermen's Advocate*, 29 Oct. 1910, quoted in Feltham, 'The Development of the F.P.U.,' p. 42.
20/Coaker, *The History of the Fishermen's Protective Union*, p. 17.

This at first had been little more than a clever, if rather obvious, device for sustaining the militancy of local officers; but such was the enthusiasm shown at branch meetings for the discussion of the problems raised that a broad but distinctive 'union attitude' began to emerge and to find expression in progressive resolutions. These were, on the whole, remarkably well-informed and even sophisticated, especially when it is remembered that the fishermen had not previously been accustomed to having their views heard with respect on such matters as educational policy or foreign trade. As early as March 1909, for example, the union was demanding the appointment of Newfoundland trade agents in Souh America, and thereafter produced a series of carefully considered recommendations on such matters as adult education, pension schemes, and the conservation of natural resources, in addition to a host of recommendations for technical and marketing changes in the fishery.[21] Taken together, these constituted a practical basis for a comprehensive political programme.

With the beginning of co-operative purchasing, the publication of the *Advocate*, and the formal birth of the 'Union Party,' the skeletal structure of the union movement was complete. It had taken a Herculean effort by William Coaker to make it so, and inevitably it bore in each of its aspects the sharp imprint of his overpowering personality. Under him the FPU became more than a union: it became a crusade. He in turn became more than a leader: he became a symbol. 'The Moses of the North' he was derisively dubbed in St John's, but to the northern fishermen such an allusion had no satirical connotation. In the words of one union song:

> We are coming Mr. Coaker, men from Green Bay's rocky shore,
> Men who stand the snow white billows down on stormy Labrador;
> We are ready and a-waiting, strong and solid, firm and bold,
> To be led by you like Moses led the Israelites of old.[22]

Indeed, to a truly remarkable extent Coaker exemplified in his person the qualities of Weber's charismatic leader.[23] J. R. Smallwood has written of one of his speeches: 'It stirred those phlegmatic fishermen as they had never been stirred before, *even at religious revival meetings.*'[24] This choice of words is significant and revealing, for it touches upon a point that is

21/*Ibid.*, pp. 11–13.
22/Quoted in Feltham, 'The Development of the F.P.U.,' p. 170; other doggerel in a similar vein is quoted in Joshua Stansford, *Fifty Years of My Life* (Ilfracombe, Devon, n.d.).
23/M. Weber, *Theory of Social and Economic Organization*, trans. Talcott Parsons (New York, 1947), pp. 147, 300–1.
24/*Coaker of Newfoundland*, p. 30 (italics added).

central to a proper understanding of the union's phenomenal growth: the quasi-religious nature of its appeal. Though the union gospel itself was strictly secular, holding out the promise not of heavenly reward but of earthly social and economic improvements, in the minds of the northern people the leader who made it part of their understanding was nothing less than a messiah on snow-shoes. He spoke to them 'in a way that they understood – a thing which but few have ever known how to do, and none since the country began knew how to do as Coaker did.'[25] They idolized and revered him, and came to trust in him as they trusted in no other man:

> We are with the fight for freedom, and union is our song,
> We are coming Mr. Coaker and we're forty thousand strong.

Their actual number was not nearly so high, but it was steadily rising. By November 1911 there were more than 12,500 dues-paying FPU members, organized into 116 local and four district councils; the *Advocate*, now the product of the Union Publishing Company, had reached a weekly paid circulation of over six thousand; and the co-operative movement, now the Union Trading Company, was firmly established and prospering, with four new outport cash stores already in operation.[26] Apart from these tangible results, however, it is at least as important to convey some idea of the union's emotional and psychological impact. For the first time a substantial body of outport people were awakened to effective class-consciousness, prodded and spurred on by the tireless Coaker, who again and again hammered home a single point: 'You are the producers,' he told them, 'the country collapses without you.'[27] While on the masthead of the *Advocate* appeared an ominous new motto: *suum cuique*, 'to each his own.'

From the beginning it was part of Coaker's aim to encourage fishermen to take pride in their occupation; in effect, to transform their oilskins and guernsey sweaters – for centuries the caste-marks of social inferiority – into emblems of solidarity and fraternity. And in order to inculcate these values the FPU consciously adopted some of the characteristics of a fraternal order, with officers' sashes, flags, emblems, annual parades, and fêtes. The local council of a union village was typically a hub of social activity, often the only institution in the community with the vigour to arouse excitement and controversy. It provided a natural focus for the discussion of local affairs and – most important of all – it supplied the

25/*Ibid.*, p. 20.
26/Coaker, *The History of the Fishermen's Protective Union*, p. 29.
27/Smallwood, *Coaker of Newfoundland*, p. 25.

ladder by which fishermen of intelligence and character could rise to positions of formal and institutional, as distinct from purely personal, influence.

In his study of social movements, Rudolf Heberle has written:

The growth and diffusion of a social movement or of a political party in a given area depends upon the strength, solidarity, and social importance of other social groups: the family and kinship group, the neighbourhood, the village community, the church, vocational or occupational associations, special-purpose organizations as well as clubs, social circles and other informal groups without a special purpose. These groups serve as conductors or channels which facilitate the diffusion of political opinions and attitudes.[28]

This theoretical statement is confirmed by the actual pattern of union development on Newfoundland's northeast coast, for the type of society indigenous to this area contained many of the 'conductors' or 'channels' to which Heberle points. The communities were small and isolated, but many were long-established (dating for the most part from the early nineteenth century, although a few were of eighteenth or even seventeenth century origin), and their residents possessed a strong sense of community identity. By North American standards they were poor, but not generally primitive in the sense that the remote settlements on the coast of Petit Nord (which only a few years previously had been part of the French Shore) were primitive. They had such amenities as churches, schools, and occasionally a meeting hall. Local weekly newspapers were published at Twillingate (the *Sun*)[29] and Trinity (the *Enterprise*),[30] and for nine months of the year the larger settlements were connected to St John's by a regular coastal steamship service. Hence, their isolation was not so great as to impose social stagnation. Within each village and between villages kinship was normally an important social link, but there were also church groups, informal social circles, and such wider institutions as the Orange Lodge, which in the Protestant north was especially strong. Each of these acted as a natural conductor for Coaker's electrically charged union message.

However, by far the most important conductors were occupational. To say this is not merely to state the obvious, for the Newfoundland cod fishery was (and is) an industry carried on in three distinct branches:

28/*Social Movements* (New York, 1951), p. 217.
29/Politically Liberal, owned by G. H. Roberts, Liberal MHA for Twillingate.
30/Politically Conservative, supporter of Sir Edward Morris and the People's party.

inshore, Banks, and Labrador. The first (as its name implies) was carried on from the shore in small boats. It was practised to some extent in every part of the island, though generally with greater success on the south and southwest coasts where the catch also included salmon, lobster, and other species more valuable than cod, or in other areas where fishing could be combined with agriculture. The Banks fishery belonged to an entirely different category. It was practically a year-round fishery, relatively heavily capitalized, and undertaken by large 'bankers' sailing from ports along the southeast coast and the Avalon Peninsula. Finally, the Labrador fishery was a branch of the industry confined entirely to the northeast, to the fishermen of Conception, Trinity, Bonavista, and Notre Dame bays.[31] Though less famous than the Banks, it was the most adventurous fishery of all. Late each spring thousands of fishermen[32] ventured forth from the villages of this region bound for the Labrador coast in two- and three-masted schooners, swift and graceful sailing craft whose unladen weight rarely exceeded a hundred tons.[33] Their course was set straight north for up to a thousand miles, hugging the coast as far as possible, yet facing every conceivable Atlantic peril from drifting ice to uncharted rocks once the tip of Newfoundland was passed. As sailors, in the twentieth century, the crews of these schooners were unmatched. If they had equals they were found in another age, among their ancestors in the west of England who centuries before had annually crossed the Atlantic in similar vessels.

It was thus among a unique breed of fishermen (they were commonly known as 'floaters') that the FPU was born, and the relevance of their occupation to the union's precipitous advance is that they alone of Newfoundland fishermen constantly intermingled in the course of their work. Unlike the inshore fishermen, who worked in isolation, or the banking crews, who worked far out to sea and never touched port until the end

31/For a brief description of the Labrador fishery, written *circa* 1908, see Grenfell, *Labrador*, pp. 282–327; for a valuable diary of a fisherman's life, see Nicholas Smith, *Fifty-two Years at the Labrador Fishery* (London, 1936).

32/Grenfell estimates the annual summer migration at approximately 20,000 persons (*ibid.*, p. 168), but this figure includes several thousand 'stationers,' i.e., whole families who travelled by steamship and spent the summer fishing from points on the Labrador coast, and 'freighters,' i.e., shore fishermen who travelled as passengers in schooners. H. A. Innis, *The Cod Fisheries: The History of an International Economy* (rev. ed., Toronto, 1954), p. 457, gives the number of schooners in 1908 as 1,432.

33/See Abraham Kean, *Old and Young Ahead* (London, 1935), p. 161. Most schooners were locally built, often by the men who sailed them. The cutting of timber for this purpose as well as the actual building were valuable sources of winter employment in the northern bays. After the turn of the century, however, many schooners were imported cheaply from Nova Scotia where the introduction of steam was rendering them obsolete. See Innis, *ibid.*, pp. 457–9.

of a voyage, the floaters joined in a great seasonal migration. Before sailing they met at merchants' wharves for the loading of supplies; while pushing their way north they often anchored in clusters to ride out a storm in a safe harbour; and once the Labrador coast was reached there were frequent rendezvous at bait depots, in sheltered creeks, and on the actual fishing grounds where dories from many schooners mingled indiscriminately.[34] In all these places the contagious union idea spread without hindrance.

A second occupational factor involved in the same process was the nature of the employment to which the fishermen of the northeast coast turned in winter: namely, logging and seal-hunting. Both of these industries were overwhelmingly dependent upon their labour, and brought them together under conditions which encouraged the spread of unionism. The pay and working conditions in the logging camps were at best inadequate and at worst indescribably poor and squalid even by the modest standards of similar camps in Canada. The industry was undergoing a period of expansion following the opening in 1909 of the Grand Falls paper mill, a paternalistic and powerfully anti-union Harmsworth enterprise that preferred to leave the cutting of pulpwood in the hands of small, often fly-by-night contractors – an effective barrier against the formation of a labour union specifically for loggers, but not against the FPU, whose roots were on the coast and which could maintain contact with its members throughout the year whatever their mode of employment.[35]

Similarly, the annual seal hunt, or 'seal fishery,'[36] must also be mentioned in connection with the union's growth. This bizarre industry was of minor economic importance[37] and was confined almost entirely to the men of the northeast coast, yet for approximately two months of each year

34/For a photograph of such a scene, see Grenfell, *Labrador*, facing p. 163.

35/In the years immediately prior to and during the First World War the loggers were more effectively organized through the FPU than they have been at any time since (for the most important beneficial results of this FPU organization, see Smallwood, *Coaker of Newfoundland*, pp. 41–2). However, with the beginning of year-round logging, made economically viable by the introduction of the 'caterpillar' diesel tractor, the industry came to be increasingly dominated by full-time loggers. The FPU lost its influence, with consequences that are still very much in evidence. Loggers' unions were later organized, but the proliferation of independent contractors remained a formidable obstacle. Since the decline of the FPU the history of labour relations in the Newfoundland forests has been characterized by trade union impotence, ineffective strikes, and periodic outbursts of violence.

36/For an account of the seal hunt by an English observer, see W. Howe Green, *Wooden Walls among the Ice Floes* (London, 1933); for the memoirs of a sealing captain, see Kean, *Old and Young Ahead*.

37/In 1906 it employed 25 steamers and 4,051 men and in 1914 20 steamers and 3,959 men (Kean, *ibid.*, p. 134). Its produce, all of which was exported, rarely accounted for more than 3 per cent of total exports.

(March and April) it gripped the imagination of the entire island. It was conducted in the North Atlantic ice floes by steamships of around 1,500 to 2,000 tons, each carrying a crew of up to 270 men.[38] These ships were for the most part second-hand steamships, purchased cheaply in Europe and refitted in the St John's dry-dock, where their bows were armour-plated with heavy steel for ice-breaking. Once under way, with their boilers at full steam, crowded with men, and carrying large stores of gun-powder and dynamite (used for blasting channels through heavy ice), they were literally floating bombs.[39] Once the seal herds were located the men took to the ice on foot, wandering miles from their ships, slaughtering as they went, taking from each animal only its pelt and a thick layer of subcutaneous fat which contained the sum total of its economic value.[40] These were stacked on ice-pans and marked with the ship's flag for later collection. The dangers of the work were notorious. Men were lost in sud-den blizzards, suffered horribly in accidents, or disappeared through great cracks in the ice that a change of wind could open up without warning. As the ship filled with seal pelts, the living quarters of the crew shrank to intolerable limits, without the slightest defence against the spread of epidemics. If the hunting was good, avaricious or foolhardy captains loaded their ships until the decks were awash.

Economically, the entire venture was a gamble. A shipowner could make large profits or equally large losses.[41] An ordinary sealer working under the share system – one-third of the value of the catch normally belonged to the owner, one-third to the captain, and the remaining third was divided among the sealing crew – could make over a hundred dollars,[42] or nothing at all, or lose his life. But in spite of the financial risk and physical peril, more men wanted berths than the ships could provide, thus enabling the owners to extract 'berth money' from each man so favoured. Little wonder, therefore, that the history of the industry was punctuated with strikes and lockouts and general discord between owners and men.[43] Before sailing, the sealers assembled in large numbers in St

38/Exhaustive statistics on all aspects of the seal hunt are contained in *Chafe's Sealing Book* (3rd ed., St John's, 1923).

39/For the horrific results of an explosion, see C. L. King, 'The Viking Disaster,' in J. R. Smallwood, ed., *The Book of Newfoundland* (St John's, 1937), I, 76–85.

40/The skins were sold mainly in the United States for use in the manufacture of fancy leather goods; the oil rendered from the fat was used in the manufacture of soap.

41/It was rare, however, for a shipowner to be dependent upon the seal hunt. Almost invariably he was also a merchant fish exporter as well, with his ships engaged for most of the year in the carrying trade to southern Europe and Latin America.

42/Kean, *Old and Young Ahead*, pp. 145–6.

43/The most serious strike occurred at St John's in 1902, but as early as 1860 three thousand sealers at Brigus had attempted to force the abolition of 'berth money'

John's and a few other eastern ports, forming a receptive audience for
agitators and union orators. As with the loggers, the seasonal nature of
their work was no barrier to the FPU, which embraced all their efforts
and accompanied them from the ice-fields to their home villages and from
thence to the Labrador coast.

Thus, it is clear that each of the labours which constituted the working
life of these men, though rugged in the extreme, was of a sort which made
the spread of a union movement possible; that is, if a union arose that was
manifestly tailored to their needs, and led by a man who understood them
and had the moral and physical strength the task required. The people of
the northeast found their union in the FPU and their leader in William
Coaker. But whether the same would be true of people in other regions,
where the economic basis of society possessed other regional characteristics, was a question the union in 1911 had yet to face. Upon the eventual
answer, however, the future of the country largely depended.

by refusing to board ship. However, all such attempts were bound to fail as long as
more men wished to 'go to the ice' than there were berths available. In fact, the
distribution of berths was rife with political patronage. First, the merchant shipowners exerted influence upon members of the House of Assembly by allowing those
who served their interests to distribute berths to their constituents. Secondly, the
merchants themselves used berths 'as a means of keeping the fishermen on the
desired terms with them.' Smallwood, *Coaker of Newfoundland*, p. 51.

8 The union in politics

Though the Fishermen's Protective Union was founded at a time of political crisis, its primary growth took place during a between-elections period of political peace. It thus escaped immediate involvement in the party struggle. At the same time, because it was a movement originating in, and largely confined to, the outports of the north, its full impact was either unfelt or unappreciated by the geographically and socially insulated merchants, journalists, and politicians of St John's.[1] Indeed, it was not until the autumn of 1911, when William Coaker's messianic appeal began to attract fishermen as far south as the Avalon district of Port de Grave, that the realization first generally dawned upon the capital that the entire north was already in the grips of a radical new social movement. And only then did it become apparent that the Union's fait accompli entailed certain disturbing political implications.

First, the area in which its main support was concentrated covered five districts which together returned eleven members to the House of Assembly,[2] a potentially crucial group in a thirty-six seat legislature. Secondly, since all five districts were predominantly Protestant,[3] the Union could drastically affect the denominational balance of the two established par-

---

1/This is not to say that Coaker and the FPU were totally ignored in St John's, since in fact there were fairly frequent press references to both; but far from being alarming, these were generally of a jocular or satirical nature. See J. R. Smallwood, *Coaker of Newfoundland* (London, 1927), pp. 15–16.

2/The districts were: Twillingate, 3; Bonavista, 3; Trinity, 3; St Barbe, 1; Fogo, 1.

3/St Barbe had the largest proportion of Catholics, 29.8 per cent. But in the five districts taken together Catholics formed only 14.3 per cent of the population. Calculated from the *Census of Newfoundland and Labrador, 1911*, vol. 1.

ties. This was particularly important to the governing People's party, which, though led by a Catholic, could nevertheless legitimately claim to represent all denominations (as well as all geographical regions) by virtue of holding six[4] of the eleven northern seats. Thirdly, if the rise of the Union could produce unwelcome results for the People's party, it could threaten the Liberal party with extinction, for the five northern seats of the latter constituted over half its total parliamentary strength (five out of nine, compared with six out of twenty-seven for the People's party).

Inevitably, therefore, as the next general election approached the Liberals faced a dilemma: they had either to fight the FPU or come to terms with it. But the autumn of 1911 found them in no condition to fight. They had been thrown into disarray by their defeat in 1909 and had not been quick to recover; indeed, disaster seemed to follow disaster, for within the Assembly, in their new rôle as official opposition, they were gravely handicapped by the uncertain state of their leader's health. Sir Robert Bond had never been physically robust, and the strain of fighting two general elections in six months, in each of which he had borne the main burden of his party's campaign, had left him exhausted and unwell – so unwell that for much of the following three years he was unable to give his party the energetic leadership to which it had become accustomed.[5] In accounting for the general inertia of the Liberal party after 1909 it is unnecessary to look beyond the simple fact of this personal misfortune. Under the deputyship of J. M. Kent the duties of a parliamentary opposition were never neglected; but, as *Hansard* reveals, the Liberal members took up the attack with force and determination only on the rare occasions when Bond appeared to inspire the debate from his place in the House.

The Liberal party's weakness, however, scarcely accounts for the strange and devious manner of its approach to the FPU. Neither Bond nor any member of his party in the House openly communicated with William Coaker; instead, they appear to have elicited his views on a possible Liberal-Union alliance through the unlikely agency of one Harry J. Crowe, a Canadian company promoter and timber speculator who held no official position in any party.[6] The exact nature of the rôle played by Crowe, and indeed how he came to be involved in the matter at all, remains obscure, but the most likely possibility is that he acted on the initia-

4/Bonavista, 3, and Trinity, 3.
5/A striking indication of the party's low morale is provided by the Burin by-election in November 1911 in which a marginal Liberal seat was allowed to fall to the People's party by default.
6/Crowe was an ardent promoter of confederation, and in some obscure way he may have been attempting to further that cause by bringing Bond and Coaker together.

tive of a group within the Liberal party and with at least the consent of Sir Robert Bond. Accordingly, in the autumn of 1911 Bond and Coaker briefly exchanged views on the question of a possible Liberal-Union alliance, but all that emerged was their fundamental disagreement over principles. Bond was willing to accept the support of the Union, but only *as a union*, not as a separate political party with its own representation in Parliament. Coaker, on the other hand, regarded the Union's direct political participation as essential. On 27 November he therefore urged the annual convention of the FPU supreme council to construct an official political platform 'from the planks we have manufactured at our previous Conventions,' and to prepare for the electoral struggle which lay ahead.[7] From that moment the Union was openly and actively in politics.

Moreover, among Coaker's convention audience there were – significantly – several Liberal members of the Assembly (including J. M. Kent, the deputy leader of the party) who had accepted invitations to attend as guests.[8] All of these members were intimately involved in day-to-day politics, and though they did not address the convention, their presence alone was enough to indicate that they entertained a higher regard for the Union's potential political power than did their more politically isolated leader. Thus, to the other afflictions of the Liberal party there was now added a latent disunity on the question of relations with the FPU.

A further attempt to negotiate the terms of a Liberal-Union alliance took place in the autumn of 1912 on the initiative of W. F. Lloyd, the editor of the *Evening Telegram*, the leading Liberal newspaper. Lloyd was a well-informed journalist, in no doubt as to the Union's political strength and the threat it posed to the Liberal party. He now added his considerable influence to the pro-Union faction in the party, but his efforts too proved fruitless. When it became clear that Bond would not be moved in his objection to the principle of separate Union representation, Lloyd's discussions with Coaker broke down. This time, however, the seriousness of the breakdown was sharply felt. With an election approaching,[9] those Liberal members who held northern seats could not help but be aware

7/W. F. Coaker, ed., *The History of the Fishermen's Protective Union of Newfoundland* (St John's, 1920), p. 29.

8/To Bond's extreme chagrin. He wrote bitterly to W. F. Lloyd: 'Did you notice what "Teddy" [Theodore Roosevelt] said in declining an invitation to attend the Great Peace Dinner? In declaring his sentiments he censured as traitors to their principles all who accepted invitations to dinner without agreeing with its purposes. I admire that. I wonder how Kent, Clift and other of my political supporters (?) who accepted invitations to the Bonavista festival regard the sentiment.' Bond Papers, Bond to Lloyd, 12 Jan. 1912.

9/The five-year statutory life of Parliament was not due to expire until May 1914, but since autumn elections were customary, the general election was expected to be held in the autumn of 1913.

of how precarious their electoral position had become: many of the electorate who had formerly voted Liberal, and even many members of district Liberal associations, had joined the FPU and could not be counted
upon to vote Liberal if Union candidates entered the field. Their leader
had taken a stand on principle: but it was their seats that were at stake.
Moreover, Bond had never consulted them on the question of relations
with the Union, apparently regarding the matter as one to be decided by
the exercise of his personal prerogative. From this point the breach between leader and followers grew steadily wider. In February 1913 Bond,
still in failing health and with his political future still uncertain, sailed for
England to consult medical specialists. He was thus absent from the crucial spring session of the Assembly, the last before the general election.
For his followers in the House and in the party outside the effect was
inevitably demoralizing.

Meanwhile, the FPU had seized the initiative in what was shaping into
a three-cornered political struggle. At the 1912 convention of the supreme
council, held at Bonavista, 12–16 December, with 160 delegates in attendance, the Union party had produced its first comprehensive statement
of policy, a catalogue of thirty-one radical demands which soon became
famous as the 'Bonavista Platform.'[10] Today, only a few of these demands
would be considered radical or even controversial; many are now commonly accepted, others have become obsolete. But in its own time and
place the Bonavista platform was rightly hailed (or calumniated) as a
revolutionary document: if carried into practice in its entirety it would undoubtedly have transformed the socio-economic structure of Newfoundland. Basically, its proposals were concentrated in three main areas –
government regulation of the fishery, administrative and constitutional
reform, and the extension of education and social welfare – and since each
of these ultimately proved of cardinal importance in the island's later
struggle to survive as an independent entity, the Union manifesto is therefore worthy of note.

First, on the subject of the fishery it contained eight specific recommendations, which may be summarized as follows: (1) the introduction of a
standardized cull of fish, to be administered in conjunction with a system
of government inspection, under the control of a permanent commission
with the power also to fix the price of fish shipped direct to market from
the coast of Labrador; (2) the appointment of trade agents abroad; (3)
the publication of weekly reports on the price of fishery produce in foreign
markets; (4) the erection and maintenance of state-owned cold storage

10/For the proceedings of the 1912 convention, including the introduction and
discussion of the Bonavista platform, see Coaker, *The History of the Fishermen's
Protective Union*, pp. 50–60.

bait depots; (5) the utilization of the government's cash reserve to assist the modernization of the fishery by the introduction of gasoline engines; (6) the closing down of the whale factories, which were held to pollute inshore waters; (7) the introduction of legislation to make fishing debts outstanding for more than two years uncollectable by process of law; and (8) the reorganization of the Fisheries Department to accommodate these innovations.

Secondly, on the subject of administrative and constitutional reform the Union manifesto demanded (1) the abolition of the existing electoral system with its multi-member districts and the creation instead of thirty-eight single-member districts; (2) the amendment of the Election Act to permit the counting of ballots by deputy returning officers;[11] (3) the raising of the sessional pay of members of the House of Assembly from $194 (for members resident in St John's) and $291 (for members resident elsewhere) to $500; (4) the introduction of legislation 'to punish any member of the Legislature who receives financial profit or gain directly or indirectly from the public Treasury'; (5) a royal commission 'to investigate public affairs'; (6) amendment of the constitution to establish the referendum and the recall; (7) retrenchment in the civil service; (8) the establishment of a transportation commission to regulate the operation of rail and steamship services by private contractors; and (9) the introduction of democratically elected school and municipal boards in all districts.

Thirdly, the Union demanded the following changes in the education of the young and the welfare of the old: (1) the provision of schools in all settlements containing twenty or more children between the ages of seven and fourteen years; (2) free and compulsory education for all children; (3) the institution of a system of outport night schools for adults, to operate during the winter months; and (4) the payment of old age pensions to all persons over seventy years of age, beginning immediately with $50 per annum and increasing to $100 as soon as public finances permitted.

Finally, the Union demanded the introduction of legislation (1) to make business combines illegal and punishable by imprisonment only; (2) to establish a commission to fix a minimum wage for labour and to make wages payable weekly and in cash; (3) to regulate the seal fishery; (4)

11/The object of this proposal is unclear and is nowhere elucidated. Under the existing law, in each electoral district all ballot boxes had to be sent unopened to the district capital, where counting took place under the surveillance of the district returning officer. This procedure, though slow, at least had the merit of preserving secrecy, which might not have been the case if ballots were counted by the deputy returning officer in each community. The advantage of the proposed amendment to the Union would be to enable it to determine the extent of its support in each community – but the same would necessarily apply to the other parties as well.

to prohibit the sale of timber areas by any means other than public auction; (5) to limit the pensions of civil servants to the same level as the old age pensions of other workers; and also (6) the establishment of a long-distance telephone system; (7) the creation of an artificial harbour on the Straight Shore; (8) the payment of a bonus for land clearing and the encouragement of stock raising; (9) the payment of a subsidy to steamships carrying coal to the outports; and (10) the reduction of tariffs on 'certain articles used by the masses, such as ready-made clothes, oil clothes, boots, tobacco, guernseys, sugar, tea, etc.'[12]

Taken as a whole, the Bonavista platform was undoubtedly the most radical political programme ever placed before a Newfoundland electorate. Its publication at once altered the whole complexion of political debate, shifting the onus onto the government to explain why the reforms demanded could not be carried out – and by implication challenging the Liberals to choose sides or make their own positions clear.

While the Liberals remained silent, the tactics of the People's party soon became clear: before resisting the Union demands it first intended to steal some of their thunder. The speech from the throne opening the 1913 session of the legislature included plans to widen the grounds on which men over seventy years of age could claim an old age pension under the scheme (revealingly entitled 'for the relief of the aged poor') introduced in 1911; to establish a system of adult education through night schools; to set up a fund to provide for the dependants of those lost at sea;[13] and to further extend the telegraph system.[14] While in his budget speech the minister of finance blandly trotted out that hoariest of pre-election stratagems – the removal of import duties from sugar, tea, salted pork, and barrelled beef. The estimated tax-loss was $385,000, nearly one-tenth of total revenue, and a ready indication of the government's fear of defeat.[15]

The main object of that fear, it was plain, was the FPU. As for the Liberals, Bond's absence from the country and the uncertainty surrounding his political future had dealt them a crippling blow. Even as an opposition they appeared less effective than the energetic Unionists, who

12/Coaker, *The History of the Fishermen's Protective Union*, p. 50.
13/This was an obvious attempt to undermine one of the Union's most appreciated benefits to its members – the FPU Disaster Fund, which was financed on a contributory basis and guaranteed a livelihood to the dependents of members lost at sea.
14/*Proceedings of the House of Assembly, Newfoundland, 1913*, p. 4.
15/It was of course not regarded as such by members of the People's party.
J. R. Bennett commented: 'We must be filled with admiration for the men who have had the courage and the character to pay back to the people one tenth of the whole of the revenue. One can hardly realize the pluck and the optimism to be found in the men who are strong enough to take a step such as this, which has never been approached in the annals of responsible government.' *Ibid.*, p. 15.

throughout the session kept up a steady barrage of well-publicized petitions and memorials to the House of Assembly. In these circumstances frustration and discontent inevitably began to proliferate within the Liberal ranks; though Bond may have been prepared to retire, there were other Liberals who were not. In their eyes the attraction of an alliance with the Union, or at least an electoral pact, multiplied the nearer the general election approached. Consequently, when Bond returned from England in April he was greeted by insistent pressure to resume negotiations with Coaker.

However, it was not until August, with the general election little more than two months away, that he finally gave in and arranged a meeting with the Union leader. It was subsequently agreed that the two parties would contest the election as a single 'Opposition' party, and that Bond as leader would incorporate fifteen points from the Bonavista platform in his manifesto.[16] But, disastrously, the vitally important question of candidacies was never satisfactorily resolved. It was only after much bickering and recrimination that the Union established its claim to seven out of the eleven northern candidacies, and also to one in Port de Grave and another in the two-member district of Bay de Verde – a total of nine out of thirty-six. Thereafter, in the few remaining weeks before polling day, behind a thin façade of co-operation, the governing spirit of the alliance was one of hearty mutual distrust.

On 3 October Bond published his manifesto, in which his references to the Union were as revealing as they were brief. His chief concern appears to have been to reconcile Liberal supporters (and perhaps himself as well) to the inevitability of Union power, however unwelcome it might be:

For the first time in the history of Newfoundland we have felt the touch of one of the *irresistible tendencies of the modern State*, namely, the disposition among its citizens themselves to form '*groups*' for the advancement or defense of particular interests. In the world around us these '*groups*' have realized that as *groups* they have no direct representative voice in the legislation by which their interests are controlled; in other words, that the Government does

16/Viz., (1) the introduction into the fishing industry of a government system of inspection, culling, and price control of the Labrador catch; (2) appointment of trade agents; (3) weekly publication of officially confirmed foreign price reports; (4) the establishment of government bait depots; (5) stricter regulation of the seal fishery; (6) reorganization of the Fisheries Department; (7) reform of the electoral system; (8) new 'corrupt practices' legislation; (9) the establishment of a transportation commission; (10) civil service retrenchment; (11) the appointment of a royal commission to investigate public affairs; (12) the sale of timber areas by public auction only; (13) the prohibition of business combines; (14) the introduction of an old age pension scheme; and (15) the reduction of tariffs on necessities.

not represent them. *The formation of the Labour Party in England is to be interpreted in that way, as must also be the formation of the Fishermen's Protective Union* in Newfoundland.[17]

Liberal collaboration with the Union was therefore to be justified in practical terms: 'I am not called upon here and now to discuss the "principle,"' Bond concluded, 'but to deal with the fact that the largest "group" of Electors in the Island demand a representative voice in the legislation by which their interests are controlled.'

At the same time, in presenting the details of his party's programme he was careful to minimize the Union's influence upon it (though, as agreed, it contained fifteen points from the Bonavista platform) and reassure Liberal voters that the traditional Liberal policies of frugal administration and low tariffs would not be subordinated to the more radical, and costly, demands of the Union. 'The waste and extravagance of the present Government,' he claimed, 'render it impossible for the finances of the Colony to respond to further demands at this time.' The Union party, however, could not allow this impression to pass unchallenged. In reply the *Advocate* pointedly devoted its centre pages to a full and uncompromising exegesis of the Bonavista platform, backed by a personal statement from William Coaker assuring Unionists that 'not a single plank will be set aside.' All Union candidates, he pointed out, were unequivocally pledged to support the full programme as formulated by the 1912 supreme council.[18]

Thus, in a final irony, the relationship between the Liberal and Union parties which had been forged only with the greatest of difficulty turned out in the end to have been scarcely worth the effort; beyond a crude constituency-sharing arrangement dictated by electoral expediency there was little else to unite the partners in a purposeful way. On policy their differences mattered far more than their areas of agreement, for, at a basic level, the former were rooted in a difference of outlook and approach rather than in disagreement over specific proposals. The main practical result was a disastrously unco-ordinated and wasteful campaign by the two opposition parties.

THE UNION AND THE PEOPLE'S PARTY

Prime Minister Sir Edward Morris and his People's party, no less than the Liberals, had good reason to fear the sudden rise of the FPU. Not only

17/*Evening Telegram*, St John's, 3 Oct. 1913 (italics in original).
18/*Fishermen's Advocate*, St John's, 6 Oct. 1913.

had they, like their Liberal counterparts, unwisely ignored it for too long; they had also positively incurred its wrath. This was no doubt partly inevitable. The Union had succeeded in stirring in the minds of thousands of fishermen a basically revolutionary idea: that they as the productive class could overthrow the conditions under which they laboured. Their spirit was militant, their language the language of class struggle, and whichever of the existing parties happened to be in office at the time it would undoubtedly have been held responsible for the status quo, condemned not only for its own acts but for the acts of all its predecessors.

Nevertheless, it was not inappropriate that the People's party should have been in power when the FPU burst onto the scene. For the People's party, though essentially opportunistic, was also essentially conservative – though not 'Tory.' The distinction is important. In some respects the change from the government of Robert Bond to that of Edward Morris may be viewed as a reflection of certain underlying socio-economic developments, for the party of the latter was preponderantly a party of 'new men' of whom Morris himself was the archetype. They were drawn not from the ranks of the old merchant Tory party, whose members had largely retired from overt politics after the annihilation of Sir James Winter's corrupt and chaotic regime in 1900, but rather from a new class of self-made men: outport merchants who had profited from the railway boom of the nineties and the generally prosperous fishery after the turn of the century; newly established lawyers whose practices owed nothing to family connection with the St John's merchant élite; and a new breed of small businessmen, unusual in that their activities were not directly related to the fishery. They were characteristically tough-minded, able, and more than a little ruthless. They were also ambitious, and, as always in Newfoundland (where business alone provided none of the outlets for talent that it did in the United States or Canada), 'ambition' turned easily into '*political* ambition.' Though for the most part nominally supporters of the Liberal party, their natural leader (for obvious reasons) was not Bond but Morris, and Morris' well-timed break with the Liberal party had opened the door for their political advancement.

Also, it was not by accident that Morris and his People's party were (to put it at a minimum) 'favourably disposed' towards the Reid railway interests, for more than any other factor the building and operation of the transinsular railway was responsible for the new climate in which the party leaders, as individuals, had flourished. With its cash purchasing power, its contracts, and its legal fees, the railway became a major source of patronage, while by opening up the long-neglected interior it brought the resources of the island to the attention of foreign capitalists – and local speculators. Of the former, the first of importance were the brothers

Harmsworth, proprietors of the London *Daily Mail*, who in 1905 formed the Anglo-Newfoundland Development (AND) Company.[19] In the next four years a large paper mill was constructed at Grand Falls, and around it a modern town – the first Newfoundland community out of sight and sound of the sea. By 1905 the railway, and the sawmills that followed it into the western interior, had already quickened the interest of timber speculators; by October 1909, when newsprint production began at Grand Falls, the greatest speculative boom in the island's history was in full swing.

This coincided with the accession to power of Sir Edward Morris and his party, with consequences that can only be described as spectacular. Newfoundland governments had rarely if ever been paragons of financial probity, but by 1909 there were opportunities for corruption on a scale hitherto undreamed of. And the 'new men' were not the sort to let opportunities slip.

Their indebtedness to the Reids was quickly and generously redeemed in the form of contracts for the building of branch lines. The throne speech in May 1909 anticipated the addition to the railway system of no less than five branches: to Bonavista, to Grates Cove, to Trepassy, to Fortune, and to Bonne Bay.[20] In October the government contracted with the Reid Newfoundland Company to provide these services at a cost per mile of line constructed of $15,000 plus an 'operating bonus' per mile of line constructed of four thousand acres of land.[21] Since the total length of the proposed new lines was approximately 250 miles, the contractor was in effect to receive around $3,750,000 in cash plus a million acres of land, including all timber and mineral rights. In the nineteenth century, governments justified the granting of such terms on the grounds that in no other way could the resources of the interior be unlocked, and that the land surrendered was worthless unless developed. The proposed branch lines, however, opened no new territories; each merely linked up a string of outlying coastal villages, all of which together were too small in population, and too easily accessible by sea, to warrant connection by rail. Even on the most optimistic estimate of their feasibility, the branch lines could not

19/See G. Harmsworth and R. Pound, *Northcliffe* (London, 1959), pp. 371, 384–5. For a comment on the *Daily Mail*–AND Company link considered as 'a notable example of vertical combination,' see C. R. Fay, *Life and Labour in Newfoundland* (Cambridge, 1956), pp. 194–5.

20/*Proceedings of the House of Assembly, Newfoundland, 1909*, pp. 24–5.

21/*Journal of the House of Assembly, Newfoundland, 1909*, p. 62. It is worth noting that the contract called for the payment of the Reid company *in gold*, rather than in government debentures, as had been the case in all previous railway contracts. This was clearly to the advantage of the contractor, for Newfoundland government debentures invariably sold at below par.

possibly have added to the government's sources of revenue or to the country's future tax potential. Indeed, the only way in which they could be financed was through further additions to the national debt, which already in 1909 stood at the burdensome level of $22,757,473.[22] Moreover, whatever may have been the case in earlier times, in 1909 it was impossible to maintain that the lands granted to the railway contractor were practically valueless. On the contrary, with the Grand Falls paper mill voraciously consuming pulp wood, timber leases alone had become readily marketable assets, with good prospects for quick capital gains. Thus, while on the one hand the branch line contracts committed the colony to the raising of new loans, on the other hand they reduced its ability to repay those loans by alienating vast tracts of revenue-producing Crown lands.

Yet even though the proposed branch lines were economically unsound, and the contracts to build them financially indefensible, there can be no doubt that the government's policy was widely and enthusiastically approved, especially by the residents of those communities that were to benefit directly. Railways were an irresistibly attractive symbol of modernity, and the desire to obtain them, without counting the cost, was a phenomenon by no means confined to Newfoundland.[23] It was perhaps this desire – and the general association of the railway with 'progress' – that enabled the government not only to commit, but to win applause for, what must in retrospect be judged a flagrant example of political 'pay off.'

Nor was the manner in which the contracts were made any more salutary than their terms: no tenders were called; work was actually begun on the Bonavista branch *before* any contract was approved by the legislature;[24] there was no preliminary survey of the country to be traversed by the lines or of their traffic possibilities. The inevitable opposition attack in the 1910 Parliament was coolly brushed aside. 'The people demanded the branch lines,' said the Hon. J. C. Crosbie, minister without portfolio,

22/*Proceedings of the House of Assembly, Newfoundland, 1909*, p. 117. Governor MacGregor's despatch on the budget speech, which indicated the necessity of raising yet another loan, provoked the following terse minute from A. B. Keith: 'Newfoundland finance is admittedly and unquestionably rotten' (co 194/276, 9 June 1909).

23/See E. J. Hobsbawm's discussion of the appeal of railway expansion in the nineteenth century in *The Age of Revolution* (London, 1962), pp. 44–7.

24/This naturally dismayed the governor, but he was assured by Morris that 'no contract with the Reid Co. would be put before [him] for signature except with the proviso that the consent of the Legislature must first be obtained before the contract became binding' (co 194/277, Williams to Crewe, 6 Oct. 1909). Lord Crewe's final minute on the financing of the railway extensions was this: 'Not satisfactory, but I don't think we can interfere' (*ibid.*, 20 Oct. 1909).

'and the people will have them. The voice of the people is the voice of God.'[25] Sir Edward Morris was more worldly:

An unusual and extraordinary condition to [sic] the country had occurred through the failure of the Labrador fishery ... and in the month of September thousands of men were coming home without the means to get wherewithal for the winter. Was it not the Government's duty to enter into this contract to enable the Contractor to employ the men immediately? *What do I care for the Audit Act when there are people in need of bread*? It is all very well to preach political economy when you have a good dinner inside of you.[26]

In that penultimate sentence is epitomized much of the history of the Morris administration. Financial impropriety was applauded in the name of 'public relief' – especially where the mode of 'relief' entailed lucrative contracts to party supporters, a flurry of handsome legal fees, and other items of patronage.

This is not necessarily to suggest that the previous administration was altogether *sans reproche*; but it *is* to say that the changing of the guard in 1909 also changed the 'tone' of public life. The new government may have been more 'dynamic'; it was certainly less principled. There was, it seems, a return to the pre-1900 norm, and of this the dubious Reid contracts were perhaps more symptom than cause, for they were soon overshadowed by other events of a not dissimilar nature.

The Reids were by no means unique in the purposeful acquisition of timber lands; they were merely more fortunate, or more astute, in obtaining outright title to them. Others who wished to hold timber rights on Crown lands could do so only under licence and subject to certain statutory conditions imposed by the Crown Lands Act of 1903.[27] The object of this measure was to deter individuals or companies from tying up timber lands for purposes of speculation rather than for development. Timber rights could be leased through the Crown Lands Department at an annual rent of $2.00 per square mile, but by stipulating that the leasee 'shall at his own expense cause the limit mentioned in his application to be surveyed by a Surveyor and the boundary lines of said limit to be cut to a width of three feet' the act in effect discriminated in favour of the bona fide mill operator, for whom such a survey was in any case a practical necessity. Moreover, the survey had to be completed within one year,

25/*Proceedings of the House of Assembly, Newfoundland, 1910*, p. 193.
26/*Ibid.*, p. 159 (italics added).
27/For the full text of the act, see *Journal of the House of Assembly, New-foundland, 1903*, pp. 61–4.

though this could be extended for a further year (but no longer) on the payment of twice the normal rent for that year. If by the end of that time a survey was not completed the lease was automatically forfeit. However, even if this condition were met, land could not be held indefinitely without further investment. The act also stipulated that leasees holding areas of more than five square miles had to provide for the erection of mills on their land of a specified capacity in board feet per day, and to do so within specified time limits, depending upon the size of the area under lease.

From 1903 to 1908 these provisions appear to have had the desired effect. Leases were granted and sawmills sprang up in areas where timber-cutting was economically feasible (which by this time included a consider-able part of western and central Newfoundland), but even there the Crown retained a large portion. According to A. B. Morine, of the initial timber rights purchased by the AND Company no less than 1,280,000 acres were purchased from the Crown, 704,000 from others, and 204,000 from the Reid Newfoundland Company.[28] Even more vitally affected by the act was the territory of Labrador, in whose southwest drainage area lay immense and practically untouched timber stands, superior in quality and many times larger in extent than those on the island of Newfoundland itself. Their remoteness, however, currently rendered them unsuitable for small-scale timber-cutting operations and hence practically worthless – yet if a pulp mill were to be established either in southern Labrador or on the west coast of Newfoundland this situation was liable to change over-night. Thus, potentially, Labrador timber lands were a highly attractive field for speculative investors – or would have been were it not for the rigorous conditions imposed by the 1903 act. Not even the infusion of Harmsworth capital at Grand Falls in 1905 (which, it seems reasonable to suppose, made other developments seem more likely) could tempt spec-ulators to disregard this barrier, as the following figures (square miles of area granted in Labrador) suggest[29]

| 1906 | 2,876 |
| 1907 | 40 |

These modest totals, however, stand in vivid contrast to the total grants issued in the years following the change of government in 1909:

| 1909 | 34,225 |
| 1910 | 58,866 |

28/ *The Railway Contract, 1898, and Afterwards* (St John's, n.d. [1933]), p. 43.
29/CO 194/285, May 1912, 'Statement showing Approximately the Areas of Timber Land for which applications were approved ... 1905 to 1911.' The area granted in 1908 appears to have been nil.

Since the law remained unchanged, the sudden boom naturally raises the question of why investors who previously had hesitated were now so willing to risk their capital. Why, in other words, did the Crown Lands Act of 1903 suddenly lose its effectiveness as a deterrent to speculation? The answer appears to be twofold. First, although it was English capital that originally awakened interest in the Newfoundland forests, an influx of American capital was mainly responsible for the 1909 'timber rush.' In this the powerful Washington lobby of the American Newspaper Publishers Association played a crucial if indirect rôle, for in the previous year that body had presented a brief (naturally well-publicized) to Congress pressing for a reciprocal arrangement with Canada for free paper and free pulp.[30] It was at least a sound bet that Newfoundland would be included in any such arrangement – hence the sudden attraction of the great and still unclaimed timber stands of Labrador. For a maximum expenditure of $6.00 per square mile land could be secured for two years that under production could rise to a value of up to $5.00 *per acre*.[31]

Secondly, the risk of forfeiture under the provisions of the Crown Lands Act was diminished, and the law compromised, by the direct personal interest of certain members of the Newfoundland government in timber companies holding large concessions in Labrador.

For more than two years this 'conflict of interests' remained hidden from public view behind a thick hedge of company regulations. The 'timber rush' had given birth to a welter of companies, some genuine, but many bogus, the latter being first registered in New York, Boston, or Montreal, with 'shadow' directors and shareholders making it virtually impossible to determine who were the true holders of lands granted, for example, to the 'Terra Nova Timber Company' or the 'Western Land Company.' Unfortunately for these new enterprises, by 1911 the anticipated pulp and paper developments still had not materialized, with the result that lands leased in 1909 were due shortly to revert to the Crown. If automatic forfeiture was to be avoided, legislation was necessary – and in this the government was only too willing to oblige.

Accordingly, in the 1911 session of Parliament the government, in the face of vehement opposition protests, forced through a series of amendments to the 1903 Crown Lands Act.[32] Section 31, which required a professional survey and the cutting of chain lines, was changed to allow

30/*Congressional Record*, vol. 42, part 3, pp. 2986–8, 60th Congress, 1st session, 10 Feb. 1908.
31/'The price at which these areas can be acquired to-day varies, according to location, from anything between one dollar and five dollars per acre. The majority of these forest lands are estimated to yield between ten and twenty cords of pulp wood to the acre.' *Standard of Empire*, London, 3 Jan. 1910.
32/*Journal of the House of Assembly, Newfoundland, 1911*, pp. 30, 39, 41–4.

boundary lines to be marked by 'blazing,' the chipping with an axe of trees in a given direction; the maximum area which could be held without the obligation to provide milling facilities was increased from five to ten square miles; on larger areas the specified time limits for the erection of mills were abolished and the matter left entirely to the discretion of the Executive Council; and, finally, the provisions of the 1903 Act which permitted land to be held without a survey for no longer than two years, and only then at a total cost of $6.00 per square mile, was changed to permit the holding of land without any obligation for three years at a total cost of $4.00 per square mile. It was further provided that those who held leases under the original act could freely exchange them for new leases under the act as amended.

Though the leader of the opposition, Sir Robert Bond, accused members of the governing party of having 'a personal interest in the timber areas, and therefore a personal interest in this legislation,'[33] the matter was pursued no further. In December, however, Coaker and the *Advocate* entered the fray with charges of corruption too blunt to be ignored: 'One grabber told us that he wanted a licence for a large slice of timber areas on the Labrador and that he met the Executive Council but one on a Sunday afternoon in a private house here, when they came to terms with him, after he had agreed to share up 49 per cent. of the proceeds of the purchase money amongst them.'[34] The members of the government sued for libel, but withdrew their charges when the *Advocate* agreed to pay costs and to publish a full retraction and apology.

But by this time the damage had been done – though it remained to another newspaper, the Liberal *Evening Telegram*, to publish the sort of concrete evidence the *Advocate* had lacked. By some undisclosed means the *Telegram* came into possession of a letter from the Hon. Donald Morison, minister of justice and attorney general, to Mr R. W. Strong, a Boston financier. It was dated some four weeks after Morison had taken office in 1909, and said in part: 'The man who holds timber abutting on a river can log and drive his timber cheapest, and until some other person locates behind him, there is nothing to prevent him from getting a good deal of timber from the adjoining Crown land.'[35] It further transpired that in August 1909 Morison became a quarter shareholder in a company formed in Boston under Strong's chairmanship, the Anglo-American Development Company Limited, which by February 1910 had acquired timber rights to no less than *13,853 square miles* of Labrador. Subse-

33/*Proceedings of the House of Assembly, Newfoundland, 1911*, p. 177.
34/*Fishermen's Advocate*, 30 Dec. 1911.
35/Morison to R. W. Strong, 6 April 1909, as published in the *Evening Telegram*, 6 April 1912.

quently, the company's original stock of $10,000 was increased to $500,000, of which Morison held $100,000.[36] Since the company conducted no survey of its lands, in November 1910, when the first of its licences fell due to expire, it sought, and received, permission from the Executive Council to hold the same area for one year more, the maximum allowed by law. Before that time could expire, the Crown Lands Act was changed in the ways indicated above. There can be no doubt that a company in which Morison was personally interested was one of the chief beneficiaries of legislation which he, in his capacity as a minister, had played a leading rôle in steering through the House of Assembly.

When it appeared that the government was determined to ride out the storm, presumably under the shelter of 'collective responsibility,' the Union took the initiative in petitioning Governor Sir Ralph Williams, calling his attention to the facts of Morison's associations with the Anglo-American Development Company and suggesting that he be dismissed from office.[37] This, as it turned out, was a tactical error, though perhaps an understandable one. For the Union took for granted the impartiality of a representative of the Crown, whereas in fact the governor was more alarmed by the alleged 'threat to society' posed by the radicalism of the FPU than by allegations of corruption in his ministry.

It is right [he wrote to the Rt. Hon. Lewis Harcourt, colonial secretary] that I should here state that my Prime Minister, Sir Edward Morris, has not only in this case but frequently contended to me that this system of licensing properties has been shewn to be the only way in which the attention of outside investors can be drawn to the timber resources of Labrador and so attract British and foreign capital ...

[Thus, he continued] I am personally satisfied that Mr. Morison did not use his influence as a Minister to obtain the licences and that they would have been equally granted had Mr. Morison not been either the Solicitor or a shareholder in it.

As for Morison's plea of forgetfulness in advising R. W. Strong that 'there is nothing to prevent a leasee from getting a good deal of timber from the adjoining Crown land,' the governor had this to say:

Personally, I believe he is speaking the absolute truth and that, strange as it may seem on the part of an undoubtedly capable lawyer holding high office,

36/These facts were confirmed by Morison himself in CO 194/285, Morison to Morris, 10 April 1912.
37/Ibid., petition to His Excellency Sir Ralph Williams, 6 May 1912.

he did forget it. To think otherwise would not only be to brand him as a rogue but also as a fool; for to deliberately place his honour and credit in the hands of another person by advising him in writing to steal (for there would be no other word for it) the property of his neighbour would be the act of a fool.[38]

The governor's sympathy with Morison, however, was most revealingly linked to his profound dislike of Morison's chief accuser, the leader of the FPU. This he made absolutely clear in his despatch of 7 May:

Mr. Coaker is an agitator of a most mischievous and dangerous type who not only poses as a champion of the fishermen but also as a second Moses arisen to relieve the fishermen (the children of Israel) from the bondage of the Merchants (the Egyptians).

[As for Morison, the governor continued] ... it would be deplorable to sacrifice him for an indiscretion at the institution of a man who will stop at nothing to accomplish his ends, which I believe to be the overthrow of law and order and the dislocation of the entire trade of the Colony.[39]

In fine, the outcome of this most unsavoury episode was that Morison, upon promising to divest himself of his shares in the Anglo-American Development Company, was publicly absolved by the governor 'of all dishonour in respect to the charges made against you.'

For the FPU this was the last straw. Indeed, it is fair to say that of all the factors precipitating its entry into politics as an ally of the Liberal party none was more decisive than the Morison case. Whatever its earlier attitude, the Union was now irrevocably committed to ousting the People's party as quickly as possible. And if this meant at the next general election, allies were essential, as Coaker seems to have realized. Thus, in this light, it is easy to see why he persisted in keeping open the possibility of a Liberal-Union alliance in the face of Liberal equivocation and in spite of Sir Robert Bond's ill-concealed hostility.

THE 1913 GENERAL ELECTION

In the election campaign of 1913 there was no shortage of issues which, in the hands of even the most inept opposition, could not help but reflect serious discredit upon the government. The hasty, ill-conceived branch

---

38/*Ibid.*, Williams to Harcourt, 7 May 1912.
39/*Ibid.*, Williams to Harcourt (another letter). This inspired A. B. Keith to append the following minute: 'It is difficult to know whether the Governor or Mr. Coaker is the more amusing.'

line contracts with the Reid company; the unclear relationship between members of the government and timber speculators; the Morison case, as well as others (not previously mentioned) such as the transfer of government shipping business to a firm largely owned and controlled by a member of the cabinet;[40] and even the light-hearted *cause célèbre* of the appointment to the magistracy of one Mr O'Toole (a poacher turned gamekeeper – O'Toole, a notorious People's party heeler was found to possess a lengthy criminal record!) were all legitimate lines of attack, and all were used.

The government could make no convincing defence, and prudently did not try. Instead, it proudly pointed to its old age pension scheme 'for the relief of the aged poor'; the incorporation into Newfoundland law of the 1906 Trade Disputes Act; the favourable result of the 1910 Hague arbitration and the rising value of newsprint exports (for neither of which could it properly claim credit, for both were in progress when the People's party first took office in 1909); the extension of the telegraph system; and the public convenience to be derived from the railway branch lines when finally completed. More potent, perhaps, were the efforts of the People's party press to identify the FPU with 'socialism and godless schools,' and then to vilify the Liberal party for its 'unholy alliance' with it.[41]

Unholy or not, it is reasonable to suppose that in the circumstances of 1913 the alliance had, potentially at least, a good opportunity to defeat the Morris government. With a concerted effort, the Liberal and Union parties might well have succeeded. But in the event, with their 'alliance' marred by an erosive mutual distrust, they were simply not equal to the occasion. In Morris, moreover, they were pitted against a master of electoral strategy, who knew well how to take advantage of their inability to work together. A combination of these factors determined the outcome of the election.

Apart from obvious differences of policy and personality which were never really submerged, the chief obstacle which kept the alliance from working effectively appears to have been Sir Robert Bond's unwillingness to abandon the north to the FPU. He either did not know, or could not bring himself to accept, that the whole of this area (which included his own constituency of Twillingate), in 1909 the securest stronghold of the

40/This was by no means without precedent, though the fact that the contract was taken away from a relatively 'non-political' firm perhaps made it more blameworthy. The minister in question was the Hon. J. C. Crosbie, minister without portfolio. For the arguments and petitions surrounding this case, see CO 194/283, governor's despatches, Jan.–Feb. 1911.

41/*Daily News*, St John's, 30 Oct. 1913.

Liberal party, was in 1913 wholly in the hands of the Union. Perhaps he feared that if the north were abandoned to the Union, without so much as an effort on the part of the Liberal party to reassert its 'sovereignty' over the area, then nowhere would the party be safe from a similar takeover. Whatever his underlying motives (and he never articulated them), the fact remains that in his personal campaign he concentrated heavily upon Union territory.[42] As an electoral tactic, this was folly. For it meant that while Bond ploughed the sands in such places as Fogo, Twillingate, and St Barbe, Morris, who apparently wrote off his party's northern seats as a permissible sacrifice, concentrated his efforts upon the marginal constituencies, located for the most part on the Avalon Peninsula. This was also an area where the Union movement had only recently begun to penetrate, so, with the exception of Bay de Verde and Port de Grave where the Union was a strong factor, the struggle was essentially between the two established parties. If there was any area in which Bond's presence could have materially altered the result it was here, where his high personal prestige and undoubted integrity might conceivably have won the confidence of informed and disinterested voters, whatever their party allegiance in 1909, when a change for its own sake might have seemed desirable after more than eight years of Liberal rule.

The other danger to the government was that the election would give a further impetus to Union expansion, and perhaps even precipitate its entry into the Catholic south. For the government, this would have been catastrophic: having abandoned the north, they had to hold the south or face defeat. Hence the rationale of their campaign: while Morris himself assiduously cultivated the marginal constituencies, simultaneously an effort was made to contain the spread of unionism. This took the form of a powerful anti-Union counterattack in the District of Trinity,[43] which in 1909 had given its three seats to the People's party, but which had since become heavily unionized. Into this particular fight the People's party threw all its formidable resources of men and money, with the primary aim of tying down William Coaker – the object, in effect, to 'localize' the disease of unionism. In this it succeeded brilliantly, though the seats themselves were lost.[44]

42/Including the last three weeks before polling day. For reports of his speaking engagements, see the *Evening Telegram*, 6–30 Oct. 1913.

43/Trinity was chosen for obvious reasons: it was large and important, and within relatively easy reach of St John's; the only local newspaper, the *Enterprise*, was hostile to the Union; and the district contained a substantial minority of Catholics.

44/In view of the importance of his subsequent career, it is worth noting that the person most responsible for the success of this holding operation was the sitting member for Trinity, Richard A. Squires, a persuasive young lawyer-politician who became, in this election at least, the Union's severest critic.

Finally, through a failure of communication, Bond, who had been campaigning in Twillingate, arrived home at Whitbourne a day too late to
reach St John's East in time for the grand eve-of-poll Liberal rally. His
message to the crowd, in a constituency where his support was sorely
needed, was read by J. M. Kent. It was an ironic touch, as was the message
itself: 'If St. John's makes no mistake,' it concluded, 'the Tory Party will
go out of power tomorrow, to remain out until God in his wisdom and
goodness shall see fit once more to chastise his people.'[45]

The results of the election, however, did not bear out these hopes. The
People's party was returned to office with its majority reduced from sixteen to six; the Liberal party fell in strength from ten members (in 1909)
to seven; while the new Union party succeeded in electing no less than
eight of its nine candidates, thus becoming the largest opposition party.

It is instructive to analyse the support for each party in terms of geographical regions. First, in the predominantly Catholic Avalon constituencies (Ferryland, Harbour Main, Placentia and St Mary's) the People's
party remained unbeatable, winning all seven seats by safe margins as it
had in 1909. In St John's East it gained one from the Liberals, increasing
its share of the city seats from three to four out of six. In the south and
southwest (Burin, Burgeo and La Poile, Fortune, and St George's) it held
all five seats. However, in the five northern districts (St Barbe, Twillingate, Fogo, Bonavista, and Trinity) the situation was reversed. There the
governing party was totally eclipsed, losing six seats. All eleven were won
by large majorities by either the Union or the Liberal parties, the former
(in accordance with their electoral agreement) securing seven, the latter
four.

The nature of the split is thus clear; the government having sixteen seats
(all in the south) and the opposition thirteen (eleven in the north), the
region which determined the outcome was Conception Bay North with its
seven marginal seats (Bay de Verde, two; Port de Grave, one; Carbonear,
one; Harbour Grace, three). Here the campaign tactics of Sir Edward
Morris paid rich dividends. In 1909 his party had captured all seven; in
1913 it needed at least three to remain in office, and succeeded in holding
five by the slimmest of margins. Port de Grave fell to a Unionist, and one
seat in Bay de Verde to a Liberal (the Union candidate – the only one
defeated – failing to win the other by ten votes). Thus, the Liberal party's
failure in Harbour Grace, where it lost by about two hundred votes, and
in Carbonear, where it lost by seventy-four, meant the return of the Morris administration. It also meant the relegation of the Liberal party to
third-party status.

45/*Evening Telegram*, 30 Oct. 1913.

For Bond the overall result was intolerable. Not only was his own party smaller than that of the upstart Coaker, it was also painfully evident that its four northern seats, including Bond's own, were held under Union auspices. Of this Bond must have been acutely aware, nor was his position made any easier by the triumphant, high spirited FPU convention in December. 'The result of the election,' declared Coaker to that cheering assembly, 'has proved without doubt the power and influence of our Union.'[46] In January, before the opening of Parliament, Bond resigned both his seat in Twillingate and his leadership of the Liberal party, retiring to the seclusion of Whitbourne. He was never again to sit in the House of Assembly.

46/Coaker, *The History of the Fishermen's Protective Union*, p. 65.

9 Politicians and the war, 1914-19

THE NEW House of Assembly elected in 1913 was destined to have a life of six full years, during which only its first session, in the spring of 1914, and its last, in the spring of 1919, were to take place in times of peace. Between the two, however, there was a world of difference. In 1914 the Union movement seemed to be the coming political force. If existing trends were projected, the next general election would inevitably give it control of the government – and its leader left no doubt but that this was 'one of the fundamental principles on which it was founded, one of the great objects of its existence.'[1] But neither the Unionists nor anyone else reckoned with a fateful coincidence of events elsewhere in the world that was profoundly to affect their – and their country's – future. By August Britain was at war with Germany, with repercussions soon to be felt in Newfoundland no less than in other parts of the Empire. Economically, socially, and politically, the consequences were immense. The exigencies of war suspended development in some spheres, accelerated it in others; and somewhere in this complex process one of the casualties was undoubtedly the Fishermen's Protective Union. The war gradually brought to a halt its previously uninterrupted expansion. Though it remained a formidable force, by 1919 the impetus was spent.

Therefore, if only for the instructive contrasts it later provides, it is worth recalling the Union's first session in the House of Assembly; for that session, though soon overshadowed by the war, appeared at the time to signal the dawn of a new era. As William Coaker succinctly put it in his maiden speech:

It is not by accident that we have come here. A revolution, though a peaceful one, has been fought in Newfoundland. The fisherman, the common man, the

1/*Fishermen's Advocate*, St John's, 15 Jan. 1914.

toiler ... has made up his mind that he is going to be represented upon the floors of this House to a larger extent than he ever was before; and the day will come, Mr. Speaker, when the fishermen of Newfoundland will have the controlling power in this House.[2]

Formal representation had of course been a fact since 1855, but the 'representatives' were almost invariably merchants or lawyers or professional politicians from St John's – the 'long-coated chaps,' as Coaker mockingly called them.[3] The Unionist members of the Assembly, however, were representative of their constituents in quite a different sense, as is immediately apparent from their occupational background: Roland Winsor (Bonavista), John Abbott (Bonavista), and Walter Jennings (Twillingate) were fishermen; John Stone (Trinity) was a boat-builder; Archibald Targett (Trinity), a tinsmith; George Grimes (Port de Grave), formerly a merchant's clerk; and William Halfyard (Fogo), headmaster of a Methodist school in Catalina. Without exception, all had risen through FPU local, district, and regional councils, or through the co-operative trading organization, or both. Each had been chosen as a candidate by the indirectly democratic procedure of election by the FPU district council in his constituency, and each was pledged to resign if called upon to do so by the district council.[4] In their political views they were by no means the 'wild men' their opponents would have them to be. Class-conscious, certainly, and filled with indignation against economic exploitation, but their speeches invariably echoed the orthodox Union policy as set out in the Bonavista platform. Not surprisingly, the only members of the party to show occasional concern for 'socialist' principles were George Grimes and William Halfyard – the clerk and the teacher. The others, including Coaker, expressed no interest in doctrine, referred to themselves as 'unionists,' rightly disclaiming any other label for themselves or their policies.

The first question the Unionists had to face in the new Assembly was necessarily that of relations with their fellow opposition members, the Liberals. The retirement of Sir Robert Bond had removed the chief obstacle in the way of their co-operation, while the surviving Liberal members were those who for the most part had been sympathetic, or at least

2/ *Proceedings of the House of Assembly, Newfoundland, 1914*, p. 37.
3/ Quoted in J. Feltham, 'The Development of the F.P.U. in Newfoundland (1908–1923),' unpublished MA thesis, Memorial University of Newfoundland, 1959, p. 129.
4/ *Mail and Advocate*, St John's, 24 Dec. 1914. (In July 1914 the Union Publishing Company acquired the plant of the St John's *Daily Mail* and began publication of a new daily, the *Mail and Advocate*. The weekly *Fishermen's Advocate* continued as before. In January 1917 the word 'Mail' was dropped from the masthead of the daily paper which until June 1917 published two editions daily, the *Morning Advocate* and the *Evening Advocate*. The latter continued publication until 1932.)

not hostile, towards the Union. They were also veteran members of the Assembly, which made them potentially valuable allies for the inexperienced Unionists. Coaker evidently recognized this, and secure in the knowledge that numerically his own party would dominate any combination, he urged the Liberals to join with them in a single opposition caucus.

The Liberals, however, differed from the Unionists both in their economic policies and in the social class of their members. They were fearful of being swallowed in an opposition merger and decided instead to preserve their political identity by sitting as a separate party in the House under their new leader, J. M. Kent. The only sign of co-operation between the two parties was that Kent – at the request of Coaker and the Unionists – agreed to serve as the official leader of the opposition. In not claiming this post for himself, though entitled to it as leader of the largest opposition party, Coaker showed impressive soundness of judgment. He may have sacrificed some small personal prestige, but his party gained the indirect benefit of Kent's parliamentary skill and experience. Yet in the public eye the aggressive and controversial Unionist was bound to overshadow the quiet Liberal parliamentarian. Moreover, Kent was a Catholic. By demonstrating their confidence in him the Unionists, all of whom represented non-Catholic districts, were also helping to combat the sectarian charge that the Union was an 'Orange' organization.[5]

It was only to be expected that a strong radical contingent in the House would considerably enliven the proceedings of that body, but no one could have anticipated the dramatic fashion in which the Unionists – and in particular Coaker – were to dominate and overwhelm it from the beginning of the session to the end. For the first time a rough northern voice had a say in the country's affairs, and it rarely stopped. 'It is too bad of me to be taking up so much of the time of the House,' Coaker once apologized, 'but I have a wonderful lot to say.'[6]

He did indeed. Beginning with the demand for democratic local government to replace the existing system of centrally controlled local patronage (which, he said, 'tends to rewards and punishments for partisan reasons and is therefore essentially corrupt'), he proceeded in the course of the session to give forceful expression to the major points of the party's basic policy document, the Bonavista manifesto. In this the government seemed strangely co-operative, producing not a single new proposal of its own, unless the proposal to study the feasibility of bringing the St George's coal

5/Coaker made no secret of this motive: 'We now look to Mr. Kent to lead us, and as the cry of the sectarian has been raised, this will have the happy result that we shall hear no more about it.' *Proceedings of the House of Assembly, Newfoundland, 1914*, p. 177.
6/*Ibid.*, p. 175.

seams into production can be counted – but this was hardly a new idea. Coaker, on the other hand, broadcast Union demands for a standardized cull of fish administered by a government inspectorate, for quality control of tinned produce, for cold storage bait depots, and for the appointment of trade agents in Latin America. He pointed to the need for timber conservation, outport hospitals, night schools for adults, and free and compulsory education for children. He declared the Union's opposition in principle to any old age pension scheme based upon a means test, or limited to men only.[7] Other Unionists put forward proposals for electoral reform (thirty-eight single member constituencies)[8] and for reform of the civil service (entrance through examination).[9]

Also, when the occasion arose, the Unionists were quick to demonstrate their feeling of solidarity with other workers. When the St John's firemen were denied a pay rise it was Coaker who took up their case in the Assembly. 'I am here to fight for the fishermen,' he said; 'I am also here to see that the working man and labouring man are treated fairly.'[10]

To stimulate public opinion and keep the government under pressure, Coaker and his colleagues availed themselves of every opportunity to introduce bills designed to put Union policies into effect. Ordinarily, attempts of this sort were easily defeated by the government majority. Unionist attempts to enact minimum wage legislation and to extend the coverage of the Workmen's Compensation Act to loggers were defeated. But in two noteworthy cases the Unionists at least had the satisfaction of a moral victory. The first was the passing of the Logging Bill, a measure introduced by Coaker with the object of regulating conditions of employment in the western forests.[11] On this matter he spoke with unique authority, for before the House opened he had toured the logging camps on foot, observing at first hand – as no other politician had ever done – the overcrowded camphouses, inadequate food, poor sanitation, and petty exploitation, such as 'blanket-rent,' prevailing at many places. The facts were indisputable; the need for regulation obvious. Hence the government, though unwilling to sponsor the bill, was apparently too embarrassed to incur the odium of defeating it, preferring instead to use its majority in the Legislative Council to emasculate it with amendments.

7/*Ibid.*, p. 162 ff.
8/To this scheme, however, the prime minister put forward the standard objection: 'In the first place,' he said, 'regards must be had to the denominational status in the various districts. You must divide up the districts in such a manner as to preserve, if possible, the relative numerical standing of the different denominations ... Take the district of Twillingate. That district calls for two Methodist representatives and one Church of England.' *Ibid.*, p. 571.
9/*Ibid.*, p. 286.   10/*Ibid.*, p. 247.   11/*Ibid.*, pp. 561–4.

Exactly the same procedure was followed with regard to the second of the Union's legislative successes, the Sealing Bill. This was designed to regulate the conditions of work and accommodation aboard sealing ships, but it too failed to survive in the Legislative Council. The Unionist reaction was predictable: 'There will be a day of reckoning for the useless Upper House,' promised Coaker in his final speech for the session, 'I shall in future do all I can ... to work for its abolition.'[12]

On the whole, the Union party's parliamentary début had been a notable success. The first 'fishermen's representatives,' and especially William Coaker, had spoken bluntly and provocatively, and their speeches undeniably quickened the pulse of the House. No longer could anyone doubt that existing economic, social, and institutional patterns were seriously challenged. Politically, the country was entering a new, uncertain, and – for the Union – distinctly promising phase. Or so it seemed in the summer of 1914.

Understandably, and indeed sensibly, Newfoundlanders had paid but little heed to the growing possibility, and possible consequences, of war; their island community was small, remote, and strategically unimportant; in the sweep of world forces it had as much influence on the great powers as a cork on the ocean. Nevertheless, like an innocent cork, it was swept willy-nilly into the whirlpool.

On 4 August, as a loyal part of the Empire, Newfoundland found itself at war – though few of its citizens could have had even the slightest comprehension of what the words meant. Not a soldier had been stationed on the island since the withdrawal of British troops and the disbandment of the St John's Volunteer Rifle Battalion in the early 1870s; the only military force was a contingent of the Royal Naval Reserve, established in 1902, with a total strength of six hundred men. The mobilization of this force (together with the imposition of press censorship!) was the government's first response – but, unfortunately, at the time all but seventy of the Reservists happened to be away at the fishery. Undaunted, the government immediately telegraphed London with a pledge to bring the active naval strength up to one thousand, and to raise five hundred troops 'for land service abroad.'[13] In September a special session of the legislature unanimously sanctioned the government's action, and made statutory provision for a 'Volunteer Force.' The terms of enlistment: 'for the duration of the war, but not exceeding one year.'[14]

12/*Ibid.*, p. 870.
13/G. W. L. Nicholson, *The Fighting Newfoundlander: A History of the Royal Newfoundland Regiment* (Ottawa, 1964), p. 102.
14/*Ibid.*, p. 106.

That Newfoundland should contribute arms was accepted without question in all quarters, the Union party included. As early as 1910, speaking of his party's general outlook, Coaker had said: 'The Union Party will act exactly as the Labour Party in England ... except that while the Labour Party in England is not of an imperialistic tone, the Union Party in this Colony will be strongly imperialistic. We stand not only for country, but for Empire as well.'[15] Though in principle his views were the same in 1914, he differed from the government on the *form* Newfoundland's contribution should take, and also on the manner in which the war effort ought to be administered. He maintained that Newfoundland ought to recruit and train seamen for the Royal Navy, a rôle for which it was naturally suited, rather than raise a separate land force of its own. Those who wished to serve on land could be encouraged to join the British or Canadian armies. At home, a coalition government ought to be formed to hold office for the duration of the war.[16] However, by the time Parliament convened a separate Newfoundland Regiment was practically a fait accompli: already several hundred recruits were encamped on a St John's sports field, enthusiastically training under the command of locally commissioned officers.

Meanwhile, in what can only be described as a bizarre abdication of responsibility, the government had in August delegated all necessary power to organize, equip, and direct this new military force to a body known as the 'Newfoundland Patriotic Committee,' comprising some fifty appointees under the chairmanship of the governor, Sir William Davidson.[17] Though no official explanation was given at the time, it is easy to see why this arrangement appealed to the government. First, it appeared to place the war effort outside the arena of party politics. (In fact, the Patriotic Committee was wholly made up of members of the St John's merchant and professional classes, but it could at least claim to be 'non-political.') This was important, for after the drastic reduction in the government's majority at the 1913 general election, it lacked the requisite moral authority to govern alone at a time of crisis. Yet the alternative of a coalition, necessarily including Unionists, was unpalatable, perhaps for fear of the influence the Unionists might exert upon domestic policies. Secondly, the Patriotic Committee could claim to be 'non-denominational' in a way

15/*Fishermen's Advocate*, 29 Oct. 1910, quoted in Feltham, 'The Development of the F.P.U.,' p. 145.
16/*Mail and Advocate*, 8 Aug. 1914. Coaker had later to defend his views on the war against charges of disloyalty; see *Proceedings of the House of Assembly, Newfoundland, 1918*, p. 168.
17/Nicholson, *The Fighting Newfoundlander*, pp. 103–7. The committee later changed its name to 'Newfoundland Patriotic Association.'

the government could not. The sectarian crows let loose during the election had unexpectedly come home to roost, with the result that the government could not be confident that Protestant areas would rally to its support. And thirdly, the need for close co-ordination with the British military authorities inevitably placed Governor Davidson, as representative of the imperial government, in a strong position to exert pressure upon the Newfoundland government. Unfortunately, it is difficult to avoid the conclusion that, in circumstances calling for great tact and constitutional integrity, he used his new powers to impose himself upon the political scene in a way that would never have been tolerated in peacetime.[18]

It was an ominous sign of things to come. No matter how improper, all was accepted, indeed applauded, in the name of war – accepted by government, by Liberals, and by Unionists, perhaps with silent qualms but without visible protest.

On 4 October 1914 the first contingent of the Newfoundland Regiment, 537 volunteers, embarked from St John's. They, and those who later joined them, were destined to see action in Gallipoli, then on the Somme and in Flanders; they were to win scores of decorations, to produce the youngest VC in the Empire, and after the battles of Ypres and Cambrai, to become the third regiment in history, and the only one in 1914–18, to be accorded the title 'Royal' in the course of war; of the Regiment's total enlistment of 6,242 no less than 1,305 became fatal casualties, 2,314 were wounded, and 180 taken prisoner. In other words, 20 per cent of those who joined the Regiment were killed. The comparable figure for the Canadian Expeditionary Force was 9.6 per cent.[19] Time after time the Newfoundland troops were committed to futile and suicidal attacks by their English staff officers, who seemed determined to prove that their men were indeed 'lions led by donkeys.' But it is not the purpose of this book to deal with the conduct of the war, except in so far as repeated disasters

18/In paying tribute to the governor upon his departure to become governor of New South Wales in late 1917, Sir Edward Morris remarked that he (the governor) had risked his prestige in 'going down into the hurly burly of ordinary departmental work' (quoted in Nicholson, *ibid.*, pp. 403–4). This was no exaggeration. So unpopular had the governor become by July 1916 that his visits to communities outside St John's very likely acted as a deterrent, rather than a stimulus, to recruitment. In the town of Argentia feeling ran so high that the parish priest, fearing violence, pleaded with the governor not to go ahead with a planned visit. The governor was indignant, but the diplomatic intervention of the archbishop of St John's eventually smoothed the matter over. Newfoundland Archives, Governor's Correspondence, 1916, Davidson to J. R. Bennett, colonial secretary, 10 July 1916; Rev. John Ashley to Davidson, 4 July 1916; Archbishop Roche to Davidson, 12 July 1916; Davidson to Roche, 13 July 1916.
19/Nicholson, *ibid.*, pp. 508–9.

in the field had inescapable political consequences at home. The most drastic and far-reaching of these was the need to impose conscription.

By 1916 heavy casualties on the western front were making it increasingly difficult to maintain the Newfoundland forces at fighting strength solely by means of voluntary recruitment. Despite the exhortations of church and state, enlistment gradually tapered off, producing for the year only 1,087 reinforcements instead of the 1,800 promised by the government;[20] while in one devastating engagement in July the first battalion of the Regiment alone suffered over seven hundred casualties. Up to this time, by far the greatest proportion of recruits had come from St John's and the surrounding area. But that supply was now virtually exhausted, which tended further to accentuate an already serious political problem: it was obvious that the fishermen of the outports were reluctant to volunteer for military service. They also happened to be Unionists.

Recruiting campaigns in the north by recuperating veterans, and William Coaker's personal appeal for Union volunteers at the 1916 FPU convention,[21] improved matters somewhat, but by the spring of 1917 the Regiment was again so seriously below strength that its separate existence was endangered. Compulsory service was the only solution, but a solution the government was in no position to impose. The war had not put an end to political hostilities; indeed, the parliamentary struggle had grown more bitter, particularly after the Legislative Council's refusal to pass the Sealing Bill in 1914 was followed by two major disasters at sea which cost the lives of 251 men,[22] 'the price,' said Coaker, 'of negligence and indifference.'[23] Thus, when in April 1917 Sir Edward Morris returned from London, where he had been attending the Imperial War Conference, to face the House of Assembly, he had also to face a mounting crisis: conscription demanded unanimity, but the Unionist opposition was understandably in no mood to co-operate. Having had their earlier offer to join a coalition refused, they were by this time looking forward to a general election, which was due in six months.

Morris, in what appeared to be an obvious move to forestall this, since

20/*Ibid.*, pp. 366–7.
21/W. F. Coaker, ed., *The History of the Fishermen's Protective Union of Newfoundland* (St John's, 1920), p. 109.
22/The *S.S. Newfoundland* lost 78 crew members who became separated from the ship by a storm while working on the ice. Charges of negligence by the *Advocate* resulted in a libel action for $20,000 damages. Judgment was for the plaintiff, but the amount awarded was only $500. See Abraham Kean, *Old and Young Ahead* (London, 1935), pp. 57–65. The *S.S. Southern Cross* disappeared at sea with a loss of 173 lives.
23/*Daily Mail*, 11 April 1914.

a 'conscription election' was practically certain to prove fatal for the government, now proposed the formation of a coalition ministry. But for the Unionists his offer came too late. As Coaker explained to the House: 'I regret that we have not been able to accept the Government's invitation to form a coalition ... If the Government had come to us in the earlier stages of the war we would have done all that lay in our power to assist them in such a crisis, but three years have gone by ... in which we have not been considered at all.'[24]

The situation radically changed, however, when it transpired that the government was making no plans for an autumn election. With its assured majority it could, if it wished, enact legislation to prolong its own life, though it had not announced its intention to do so. But the opposition, once forewarned by the lack of any provision for an election in the estimates, though it could not prevent, could at least seriously obstruct the government's legislative programme. 'We are not prepared to let the Estimates go through and then find ourselves in the position of having an extension bill forced through because of your majority,' warned W. F. Lloyd, neatly summarizing the opposition's dilemma. 'If you attempt to prolong the life of this Government,' Coaker told the prime minister, 'you will have the people rise up against you; you will turn the country upside down.'[25]

The outcome, after four weeks of parliamentary obstruction, was not an election but an all-party National government, whose formation Morris announced on 16 July.[26] Though nominally formed under his premiership, there can be little doubt that his early retirement was part of the complex bargain that made the new ministry possible. He left almost at once for London, ostensibly to rejoin the Imperial War Conference, leaving W. F. Lloyd, who had replaced J. M. Kent as Liberal leader in 1916, in effective command as acting prime minister. In fact, Edward Morris' long political career was drawing to a glorious end. He was never again to return to Newfoundland. On 31 December he resigned the premiership, and in Lloyd George's New Year's honours list of 1918 was elevated to the peerage 'for services to the Empire,' becoming Baron Morris of Waterford.[27]

One of the first acts of the new National government had been to relieve Governor Davidson and his 'Patriotic Association' of their unconstitutional powers and to replace them with a new Department of Militia under

24/*Proceedings of the House of Assembly, Newfoundland, 1917*, p. 171.
25/*Ibid.*, pp. 175–6.
26/*Ibid.*, p. 468. The size of the cabinet was increased from nine to twelve.
27/See *The Times*, London, 5 Jan. 1918.

a minister of cabinet rank. On 14 August J. R. Bennett was named to the post. Thus ended 'an organization surely unique in the history of military administration.'[28] Thereafter the administration of the Regiment was under direct government supervision. Significantly, however, though legislation was quickly enacted to prolong the life of Parliament a further year, no move was made to introduce conscription before the new department had had a chance to raise sufficient volunteers to fill the Regiment's depleted ranks. It seems reasonable to surmise that this too was part of the price exacted by the Unionists. There is no question as to how their rank and file regarded the matter: 'I was flooded with hundreds of messages from F.P.U. councils and members asking me to oppose conscription and not to consent to it,' Coaker later admitted;[29] while in justifying his action in joining the National government to the Union's annual convention in 1917, he referred to the crucial issue only in this indirect and ambiguous fashion: 'The Country desired ... protection for the people against profiteering, the possible expenditure of a large amount to purchase steamers to export fish, the importation of food and coal ... *the keeping of the Regiment intact*, the raising of a large loan for war expenditure ... the necessity of securing financial support for the treasury by placing a tax on surplus war profits.'[30]

But, it was soon made clear, not even a Department of Militia could keep the Regiment intact without some form of compulsory service. A vigorous recruiting campaign at the end of the fishing season, coupled with the opening of more recruiting stations, failed to produce the necessary numbers. Meanwhile, there was no respite for the Regiment. During late autumn it was engaged in heavy fighting against a concentrated German counter-offensive, once more suffering virtual annihilation, this time in the Battle of Cambrai. By the end of the year the shortage of reinforcements was growing desperate.

This was the situation confronting the new National government that took office on 5 January 1918 under the premiership of W. F. Lloyd. Its composition was not substantially different from that of the previous ministry, though the Unionist element was undoubtedly strengthened by the promotion of William Halfyard to the key domestic portfolio of colonial secretary. Coaker remained minister without portfolio, but in reality it was upon him that the fate of the government – and the Regiment – mainly depended. Conscription was the inescapable issue. Yet conscrip-

28/Nicholson, *The Fighting Newfoundlander*, p. 103.
29/*Proceedings of the House of Assembly, Newfoundland, 1919*, p. 5.
30/Coaker, *The History of the Fishermen's Protective Union*, p. 118 (italics added).

tion, he knew, was anathema to the vast majority of Unionists. He had not favoured the formation of a separate Newfoundland military force in the first place; now, ironically, his political future was imperiled by it.

Fortuitously, a lull in the fighting during January, and a period in reserve during February, enabled the Regiment to maintain its position in Flanders even though seriously under strength. It also enabled the government to further postpone the introduction of compulsory service; but finally its hand was forced by a message from the British Army Council on 9 April: 'Since very heavy fighting must be anticipated, at least 300 men will be required from Newfoundland as early as possible in order to bring the Battalion up to strength, and an additional sixty men per month will be required to maintain it in the field. His Majesty's Government trust that your Government will be able to supply these men.'[31] Without conscription this was impossible. Already Newfoundland had contributed more than eight thousand volunteers – 'a greater enlistment per capita of population than any other country in the British Empire, excluding only the United Kingdom.'[32] On 23 April the prime minister committed his government to the passage of a Military Service Act calling up all single men between the ages of nineteen and thirty-nine. He was well aware that resistance was likely to be great:

We need public opinion strongly behind us, he said, in addressing the House, in order that the measure may be carried out, but we are not much concerned as to how our political future may be affected ... if I am to go down to political defeat because of my action in this Conscription measure, I am prepared to accept my doom. In the meantime, however, whilst I am leading the Government, I am determined that these measures shall go through and shall be carried out faithfully, because I am convinced of their urgent and pressing necessity.[33]

Proof of his determination was forthcoming. On 27 April police raided the offices of the *Plaindealer*, a St John's weekly newspaper, confiscating an issue which was violently anti-conscription.[34]

In the outports hostility was more widespread than in St John's, and far more difficult to suppress. Were it not for the efforts of William Coaker the Military Service Act might easily have been unenforceable. But in the end, no doubt reluctantly, he had given it his full support – not only in

31/Quoted in Nicholson, *The Fighting Newfoundlander*, p. 438.
32/*Ibid.*, p. 439.
33/*Proceedings of the House of Assembly, Newfoundland, 1918*, p. 26.
34/*Ibid.*, p. 69.

the House but outside where it was needed far more. At a time when the possibility of armed resistance was very real, he was mainly responsible for lowering the temperature, especially by means of circular letters to all local councils of the FPU explaining what the bill meant in practical terms (many apparently believed that conscription would apply to married men), and why he and the other Unionists in Parliament supported it.[35] To critics in his own constituency he replied that under the FPU constitution the district council had a right to replace him if it wished.

Thus passed conscription – but not without a final irony. Though it could not be taken for granted at the time, the end of the war was drawing near. In fact, the first Newfoundland draftees were in England when the armistice was signed: not one saw service at the front.[36] Conscription had come too late to help the Regiment, but not too late to do incalculable harm, especially to the Union movement.

A sharp wedge of discord had been driven between the leader and the rank and file, producing no great or immediate split, but nevertheless weakening the Union's fibre. It might have mattered less had Coaker's personal charisma been less, but for years he could do no wrong, his every word falling with the force of gospel, which now only served to make the disillusionment all the more acute. It is not difficult to understand why, for many Unionists, Coaker's support of conscription must have seemed a betrayal of principle, as, to a lesser degree, did his participation in the suspect National government. In the exhilarating days of 1914 he had stormed into Parliament with visions of a 'peaceful revolution,' only to compromise with those the Union was supposedly dedicated to overthrowing. Nor is it difficult to understand why, during the years of war-induced crisis, his visions had been quickly – perhaps prematurely – trimmed by experience. But that is to say no more than that he became a politician. The trouble was, he had been elected as a messiah.

Moreover, the second National government, like the first, consisted of an uneasy alliance of old enemies, membership in which offered few rewards to compensate for waning popularity. Once conscription had been successfully enacted, and the House prorogued, it managed to hang together until the end of the war; but the coming of peace soon dissolved its thin cement. Smallwood attributes its breakup to Coaker's efforts to intro-

35/Even these efforts apparently aroused hostility. See *ibid.*, p. 169, for Coaker's defence of his stand. See also Coaker, *The History of the Fishermen's Protective Union*, pp. 118–27: 'I did not decide to support conscription without ... counting the cost. I expected to be misunderstood by my friends and misrepresented by my enemies, and I made up my mind to face what I considered a most critical period of my public career.'
36/Nicholson, *The Fighting Newfoundlander*, p. 439.

duce radical measures,[37] but no explanation is really necessary. With a general election in the offing it was inevitable that old personal antagonisms and clear party lines would re-emerge. Unfortunately for all concerned, the war ended too late for an election to be held that autumn, but in the spring of 1919 Prime Minister Lloyd returned from the Paris Peace Conference[38] to preside over – and indeed participate in – the disintegration of his ministry.

The exact manner of its end constitutes an episode unique in the history of parliamentary government. There were no resignations. The National government met the House in April and duly made provision for a November general election – thereby removing the last remaining reason for its existence. Not surprisingly, the coup de grâce came from the People's party which, though leaderless after the departure of Morris, still controlled a majority of seats. That they should allow Lloyd, supported by the Unionists, to obtain a dissolution in office was unthinkable: it would have been tantamount to voluntarily surrendering the spoils of office – always a valuable asset, but never more so than in an election year. Still, there were no resignations. Instead, on 20 May, without warning, the minister of finance, Sir Michael Cashin, rose from his place on the front bench and moved a vote of no confidence in the government. In the confusing scene that followed Lloyd rose to reply but was halted by the Speaker who pointed out that in the absence of a seconder there was no motion before the House. Whereupon Lloyd formally seconded the motion himself. When put to a vote the motion was unanimously carried![39]

37/J. R. Smallwood, *Coaker of Newfoundland* (London, 1927), p. 45.

38/Newfoundland was not accorded separate representation. Lloyd attended the peace conference as a member of the British Empire delegation. K. C. Wheare, 'The Empire and the Peace Treaties, 1918–21,' in *The Cambridge History of the British Empire*, III, 650.

39/*Proceedings of the House of Assembly, Newfoundland, 1919*, p. 77. Cashin's behaviour in this incident requires no explanation: as leader of the largest party, he simply wanted to break up the coalition and install himself as prime minister. Lloyd's behaviour, however, lends itself to a fascinating variety of explanations, some of which are:

(*a*) After Kent's retirement, Lloyd, as the new Liberal leader, had compromised the identity of the party by turning it into a rump of the Union. In return, Coaker had made him prime minister (there can be little doubt that his appointment was part of the price that Morris had had to pay to bring the Unionists into the coalition) but relations between the two had become increasingly strained. Thus, with no base of party support in the country, and realizing that he had outlived his usefulness to Coaker, he made the best deal with Cashin that he could – as his prompt acceptance from Cashin of the secure patronage post of registrar of the Supreme Court seems to suggest. Yet if this was his aim he could presumably have accomplished it by resigning and advising the governor to call for Cashin, without the humiliation of seconding a motion of no confidence in his own ministry.

(*b*) Lloyd must have known that either Cashin or Coaker would break up the

Thus, in a moment of farce, the parties seemingly reverted to their pre-war standing. Cashin, once Morris' lieutenant, became prime minister of another People's party government, which, however, attempted to maintain the fiction that it was a 'National Ministry'; while the Unionists, with a few Liberals, once more resumed their seats in opposition.

Yet parallels such as these may easily mislead: in many more vital respects the pre-war era was remote indeed from 1919. The impact of the war was not purely, or even primarily, political; and to concentrate exclusively upon politics at this point would be to run the risk of over-simplifying an exceedingly complex phenomenon. Moreover, without reference to at least some of the more important economic and social consequences of the war, and their interaction to a greater or lesser degree with politics, it would be difficult even to view political developments in their proper context. This of course is not to say that generalizations such as 'the war killed off a generation of leaders' (sometimes used to explain Newfoundland's subsequent decline) are worth discussing, for these, while partly obvious, are also unverifiable. It is the more immediate and measurable factors that must be given closer attention.

Economically, Newfoundland did well out of the war, just as it had done well out of European wars so often in the past.

The economic effect of the war, after the first shock of bewilderment had subsided, was to stimulate trade and industry, thus bringing about a few years of exceptional prosperity. Spain and Portugal were open markets and Italy was on the side of the Allies. Newfoundland's competitors in the dried-fish industry were unable to maintain production at pre-war levels, whereas Newfoundland's were the biggest in her history. Money was plentiful, the demand for fish rose rapidly, and prices soared to heights never attained before. The shortage of shipping was met by pressing Newfoundland sailing vessels into service. Fisherman and merchant prospered.[40]

The actual statistics are revealing. For six successive years prior to 1914 Newfoundland had suffered an adverse balance of trade; from 1914 to

coalition, but did not anticipate Cashin's introduction of a motion of no confidence while still minister of finance. Exasperated by the turn of events, and his inability to keep the warring factions in his ministry in line, he seconded the motion as an impulsive gesture – a way of saying 'a curse on both your houses.'

(c) Lloyd might not have been altogether sober at the time and agreed with Cashin to bring down the government in this way; or, taken by surprise by Cashin's motion, he made the blunder of seconding it – perhaps the automatic response of a befuddled parliamentarian.

40/R. A. MacKay, ed., *Newfoundland: Economic, Diplomatic, and Strategic Studies* (Toronto, 1946), p. 65.

1919 the balance was consistently favourable. The value of total exports for the fiscal year 1914–15 amounted to $13,136,000; by 1918–19 it had grown to $36,784,000. Meanwhile, the value of imports rose from $12,350,000 in 1914–15 to $33,297,000 in 1918–19.[41] 'Wartime prosperity was accompanied by a standard of living, or, more accurately, by a standard of spending, far above that to which the people had been accustomed, and far above what could be maintained in times of peace.'[42] This was true of government as well. After consecutive budget deficits in 1913–14 and 1914–15 the Newfoundland government was able to operate during each year of the next five years with a comfortable surplus of revenue over expenditure. In the same period annual revenue increased from $3,618,000 to $10,597,000.[43] These figures conceal the fact that Newfoundland paid for its war effort – as it paid for its pre-war railway expansion – by heavy borrowing in New York and London. War loans added no less than $13,400,000 to an already high national debt, while it was calculated in 1919 that the capitalized cost of pensions due to the war would amount approximately to $16 million, and that altogether the additional financial burden, including interest on war loans, would total $34,896,642.[44] But as long as trade remained buoyant, and revenues high, any recurring obligations could be met without serious difficulty. There were indeed clouds on the horizon, but no deluge seemed imminent.

Socially, the effects of the war – and wartime prosperity – cannot be easily analysed in concrete terms, but neither can their significance be overlooked. At one level, for example, it can be said that the war, with all that it entailed in the way of patriotic propaganda, and the deep and widespread personal involvement of the civilian population, undoubtedly strengthened the feeling of 'nationhood' among Newfoundlanders. This was particularly true vis-à-vis Canada – 'We are all very particular here that we should not be classed as Canadians,' wrote a young soldier of the Newfoundland Regiment from his camp on Salisbury Plain.[45] And it partly explains why confederation failed to become a real political issue in the critical years that lay ahead. Nor was this sense of a separate 'national identity,' which the Regiment symbolized, unrelated to the official dropping of the title 'Colony' in 1918. Thereafter, though no change in

41/J. R. Smallwood, ed., *The Book of Newfoundland* (St John's, 1937), I, 325.
42/MacKay, *Newfoundland*, p. 65.
43/Smallwood, *The Book of Newfoundland*, I, 326.
44/Newfoundland Archives, Administration of Squires, Warren, and Monroe, memorandum by F. C. Berteau, controller and auditor general, 'Obligations ... Due to War,' 3 Jan. 1919.
45/Quoted in Nicholson, *The Fighting Newfoundlander*, p. 123.

constitutional status was involved,[46] Newfoundland, asserting its equality with Canada, styled itself a 'Dominion.'

On another plane, paradoxically, at the very time when Newfoundland's ties with Britain were being loyally demonstrated on the battlefield, at home the most marked development – especially in St John's – was the growing 'Americanization' of life. Hitherto, Newfoundland had been relatively immune to American culture and mores: the social élite being orientated towards England, the mass of the population necessarily confined to simple, traditional tastes and ways of behaviour by poverty, isolation, or both. But as purchasing power increased these patterns began to break down. In St John's automobiles became a common sight, American styles of clothing replaced British, intrepid American salesmen began to appear on doorsteps in even the remotest of villages, selling everything from marine engines to 'made-to-measure' suits. Between the quinquennial periods 1911–15 and 1916–20 Britain's average share of the Newfoundland market fell from 24.5 to 10.5 per cent while that of the United States rose from 36.9 to 44.7 per cent and that of Canada from 33.5 to 40 per cent.[47] To most Newfoundlanders the wartime boom brought a first taste of material prosperity, North American style – and naturally they liked it. Habits developed in this free-spending era, and expectations were aroused, that lingered long after the means of satisfying them had vanished. This was true of the country as a whole, and of government as well. After the war few politicians dared promise, and none dared implement, a return to pre-war standards, which left only one alternative: to live hopefully on borrowed money – and borrowed time.

Finally, among the social changes which took place during the war none struck with quite so sharp an impact as prohibition. For, in 1915, in an excess of 'temperance,' which its zealots somehow managed to confuse with patriotism, Newfoundlanders voted in a national plebiscite to prohibit the sale of alcoholic beverages.[48] Thus even St John's, once known for the number and variety of its taverns, officially became 'dry.' The actual result, of course, was to initiate a virtually uncontrollable traffic in the illegal importation, manufacture, and sale of liquor; prohibition ensured that the bootlegger, rather than the publican, shared in the fruits

46/Newfoundland Archives, Administration of Morris and Lloyd, 'Memorandum,' 26 June 1918. 'The first official assumption of the title of Dominion was in the Speech from the Throne on 23rd April last, which Ministers deliberately settled.'

47/MacKay, *Newfoundland*, Appendix A, Table 13.

48/The total votes cast were: 'For,' 24,965; 'Against,' 5,348 (*Royal Gazette*, St John's, 30 Nov. 1915). More than 50 per cent of those eligible did not vote. Prohibition actually came into force on 1 Jan. 1917.

of prosperity. It also had far-reaching political consequences. Unenforceable laws are notorious causes of political corruption, especially where fortunes are to be made by their unhindered evasion. In Newfoundland, as in some microcosm of America, prohibition became a classic case – at the same time demonstrating more clearly than ever the weaknesses of a public service based on 'spoils.' Poorly paid and insecure officials, politicians with an eye to the 'rewards of office,' and those who had influence with politicians, suddenly found themselves exposed to, or able to find, temptations on a scale previously unimaginable. And the richer the rewards the more deeply entrenched and resistant to reform the system itself became.

Prohibition left few areas of politics untouched in some way, but no single element had its future more adversely affected than the Union movement. The reason was simple: among the leading prohibitionists was William Coaker. A total abstainer himself and long an active combatant in the fight against 'demon rum,' when the opportunity arose to strike it what he no doubt thought would be a mortal blow, he unhesitatingly lent his great authority – and the Union newspaper – to the 'anti' cause.[49] This did the Union little or no harm in Protestant areas, where its greatest support lay and where the strong Methodist Church already imposed what amounted to a 'de facto' prohibition; but in the Catholic south – where the Union had to expand if it was to become a governing power – Coaker's prominence in the 'temperance' campaign seemed incontrovertible proof that the Union *was* dominated by the Orange Lodge. For who else, it could be asked, would seek to deprive the Newfoundland Irish of their taverns?

No doubt there were other, perhaps more important, reasons why the Union lost momentum during the war: its entry into politics in 1913 meant that it first became known to the Catholic south as a political party, indeed as a *Protestant* party, rather than as a union or co-operative movement; after his election to Parliament Coaker had less time to devote to new organizational campaigns, and no other Union figure had his messianic appeal; and, finally, as a movement of protest the Union inevitably lost a good deal of its force as a result of the country's burgeoning wartime prosperity. Nevertheless, were it not for its open identification with prohibitionism, and hence, by implication, with militant Protestantism, these

49/Coaker had given fair warning of his intentions. In his first session as a member of the Assembly in 1914 he had declared: 'I am a temperance man and intend to do all I can to promote the temperance cause, but I am above all a total prohibitionist, and as long as I have a right to cast a vote in this House that vote shall go for total prohibition.' *Proceedings of the House of Assembly, Newfoundland, 1914*, p. 726.

other obstacles might not have proved insurmountable. After a period of marking time, the Union might still have been capable of expanding southwards when hard times returned. But its self-righteous stand in 1915 made the chances of this impossibly remote. It was a high price to pay for a misconceived moral gesture.

Thus, as the newly styled 'Dominion of Newfoundland' prepared to choose a peacetime government, contrary to the pre-war expectations of the Unionists it was by no means clear what its choice would be.

10 The post-war coalition

THE IGNOMINIOUS and generally unlamented fall of the coalition National government in May 1919 by no means signified a return to pre-war political 'normality.' For better or worse, a new era had begun. Yet superficially at least, the re-emergence in the Assembly of distinct party lines seemed to indicate a return to a two-party system. On the one side was the governing People's party, with a majority of seats; on the other was the 'Liberal-Union' opposition, dominated by the Unionists and with the few remaining Liberals apparently no longer concerned about keeping a separate parliamentary identity. The former was predominantly the party of business, supported by merchants, manufacturers, and the railway and shipping interests; the latter was predominantly the party of fishermen and loggers, of 'extra-parliamentary' origin, and strongly supported by a pre-existing social and commercial organization. One was orientated towards St John's and the south, the other towards the small outports and the north. Thus, in terms of socio-economic class, geography, and even (in the broadest sense) ideology, the split between the two was natural and easily understandable.

Yet in reality the picture was considerably more complicated, and the complicating factor was primarily religion, or rather the interaction of religion with politics. Because of it, the neat division in the Assembly was not a true reflection of party standing in the country at large. In the first place, the People's party was undoubtedly overrepresented. Under the leadership (and indeed as virtually the personal instrument) of Sir Edward Morris it had been an electorally successful, albeit historically anomalous, entity: a party with a Catholic leader and almost solid Catholic support, yet able to win considerable support in Protestant areas as well, especially in the south. Even in 1913, when it was abandoned by the north in favour of the Union, it managed to hold seats in Carbonear, Bay de Verde, Harbour Grace, Fortune, Burgeo, and Burin – all denominationally mixed constituencies with Protestant majorities. Though other elements no doubt played a part, above all, it must be concluded, the People's party owed its success to the unique personal appeal of its founder and leader. Morris was its keystone, and his removal placed the whole structure in jeopardy.

His successor, Sir Michael Cashin, was politically a substitute of sadly inferior quality. By 1918 he was a man of considerable wealth, and hence of standing in the party, but unlike Morris, who was always something of a 'renegade,' he was also closely identified with Catholicism. He was, moreover, an unappealing public figure, conspicuously lacking in the qualities of wit and charm and platform eloquence that had made Morris so beguiling a politician. He had inherited Morris' parliamentary majority – but nothing more.

On the other hand, the Union's failure to expand southwards (as noted in the previous chapter) rendered it incapable of benefiting to any significant extent from these developments. The stress of war had helped revive once more the ancient feud between Protestant and Catholic, north and south, with the result that the Union's declared ambition to form a government, seemingly so near to fulfilment in 1914, had dwindled to a remote prospect by 1918. Prohibition and conscription had done their work. St John's looked upon the former as an act imposed by the (Protestant) Union; the Union rank and file looked upon the latter as an act imposed by (Catholic) St John's. Unfortunately, there was a large element of truth in both.

The pervasive influence of the denominational struggle therefore ruled out the possibility of a fusion, or even an alliance, between the FPU and the growing ranks of organized labour in St John's. There was, it seems, no attempt whatever to establish contact between the two, which is all the more striking in view of the fact that during the war labour became more politically conscious than ever before, a tendency which appears to have been sharply accentuated by the influx of demobilized servicemen after the war ended. The outcome was the rise of a radical general union, known as the Newfoundland Industrial Workers Association (NIWA), which by 1918 was strongly organized in St John's, and was attempting to establish itself elsewhere in the island.[1] On a much smaller scale, it attempted to do for the urban workers what the FPU had done for the fishermen. It established a co-operative department store, published its own

1/See G. H. Tucker, 'The Old N.I.W.A.,' in J. R. Smallwood, ed., *The Book of Newfoundland* (St John's, 1937), I, 279 ff.

weekly newspaper, the *Industrial Worker*, and was bent upon securing labour representation in the House of Assembly. It was the only organized group which might conceivably have become a southern ally of the Union; but instead, as the general election approached, it prepared to face the electorate separately.[2]

At this juncture the political situation was marked by its extreme uncertainty. The Union was still unchallengable in the north, the People's party could still depend upon the support of the solidly Catholic constituencies, while the NIWA by itself was no more than an isolated pocket of resistance in St John's. There remained the Liberal party, or rather the ghost of the Liberal party, for after the retirement of J. M. Kent in 1916 no one could be quite certain whether it even existed; under W. F. Lloyd it had even ceased to maintain a separate caucus in the Assembly. Nevertheless, unlikely as it seemed, it was potentially the key to victory.

In the first place, the virtual eclipse of the Liberal party in Parliament was not a true reflection of feeling in the country. Though winning only three of the twenty-four seats it contested outside the north in 1913 (two in St John's East, one in Bay de Verde) it nevertheless secured approximately 45 per cent of the popular vote in this area, which clearly suggests that the distorting effect of the electoral system gave an exaggerated impression of Liberal weakness. In the second place, the bulk of its 'hidden' support was strategically concentrated in those unpredictable constituencies of the Avalon Peninsula, and in the south-coast constituencies of Burin, Fortune, and Burgeo which together returned eleven members. Moreover, it was very likely that these constituencies had been affected by the course of politics during the war and especially by the retirement of Sir Edward Morris. They had not been significantly penetrated by the Union, most were denominationally mixed, and most had returned People's party candidates by narrow majorities in 1909 and again in 1913. Now, however, they contained a potentially large 'floating' vote, composed of those Protestants who had earlier been attracted to the People's party by the personality of Morris, and those Irish Catholics who at the same time had abandoned their traditional Liberal allegiance of nearly a century in order to elect 'one of their own.' But neither group was likely to find the same attraction in the People's party of Sir Michael Cashin which suffered the double handicap of appearing to the one as a 'Catholic' party and to the other as a merchant-dominated party, 'Tory' in all but name. Finally, after the formation of the National government in July 1917,

2/'In their impatience for social reform the N.I.W.A. unwisely plunged, in the autumn of 1919, into the political arena' (*ibid.,* p. 279). Only three Labour candidates actually stood for election, all in St John's West. They were unsuccessful.

which was by no means a popular move, there existed yet another fruitful source of discontent with both existing parties.

Therefore it was not by coincidence that within a month of the National government's taking office certain unobtrusive but unmistakable signs of life began to appear in the long-dormant Liberal caucus, inspired by a percipient element in St John's who apparently foresaw the coming struggle for power and accordingly directed their first efforts towards inducing Sir Robert Bond to return to politics. Among the original proponents of this movement were H. A. Winter, the newly appointed editor of the traditionally Liberal *Evening Telegram*, and George Shea, a former Liberal cabinet minister. Bond, however, was exceedingly cautious about being drawn back into active political life, in spite of strong inducements. In his greatest electoral triumphs earlier in the century he had had the support of the Catholic hierarchy, and notably that of Archbishop Howley of St John's. Howley's successor, Archbishop Roche, had at first been much less politically inclined, but as the war progressed he had become increasingly outspoken in expressing his alarm at what he termed 'the growth of a socialistic spirit' in Newfoundland. The message was now conveyed to Bond that if he returned to politics as the leader of a revived Liberal party he could once again count upon strong archiepiscopal support.[3] Nevertheless, Bond's intentions remained undeclared as 1917 drew to a close.

Meanwhile, a younger, more ambitious politician was already manœuvring himself into position as an active contender for the Liberal leadership. He was Richard Anderson Squires, whose political career up to this time had been built entirely in the People's party.

Thirty-eight years of age, with his sights fixed firmly upon the premiership, Squires was in many respects the Edward Morris of his generation. Indeed, after taking his law degree at Dalhousie University, it was first as a clerk and then as a junior partner of Morris that he served his political apprenticeship. The pupil was evidently quick to learn, and in 1909 was elected to the Assembly as People's party member for Trinity. He lost the seat to a Unionist in 1913, but his strong campaign was credited with stopping the southward spread of Unionism, for which his reward was a seat in the Upper House and inclusion in Morris' cabinet as attorney general. Upon the formation of the National government he had become colonial secretary, still without a seat in the Assembly. Meanwhile, in 1916 he had acquired a controlling interest in a St John's newspaper, the *Daily Star*. Thus were the foundations laid. And when, at the beginning of 1918, his mentor retired to England and the House of Lords, leaving the National government to be reorganized under W. F. Lloyd, Richard Squires

3/Bond Papers, Shea to Bond, 8 Nov. 1917.

was presented with the opportunity for which his whole career had been a preparation.

Correctly perceiving that Morris' departure had left a power vacuum that in the long run neither the Union nor the People's party would be capable of filling, he took no part in Lloyd's futureless coalition ministry. Instead, he directed his efforts towards the infinitely more promising prospect of the coming struggle for power. And in this respect his prognosis was evidently similar to that of Shea and others who were actively promoting the idea of a Liberal revival, for he too saw the Liberal party as a potentially crucial force in post-war politics. The difference was, he saw himself as its leader. He also saw that party lines had become sufficiently confused during the war to make his ambition realizable. Hence, from at least the beginning of 1918 onwards, Bond's reluctance to accept the proffered leadership was more than matched by Squires's ardent pursuit of it – so much so that the move to 'draft Bond' soon became indistinguishable from the move to 'stop Squires.'

However, in the curiously oblique struggle that ensued, Squires had one inestimable advantage – unlike his rival he was in close personal touch with the political scene. As a minister in the first National government he undoubtedly saw at first hand the internal stresses that threatened it and rendered unlikely any post-war alliance between its irreconcilable elements. Bond, meanwhile, in the seclusion of Whitbourne, had grown increasingly out of touch with political reality. He placed but little faith in the reports of even his most loyal and best-informed supporters, preferring instead to judge the present by his own bitter memories of the past. In his eyes, there was nothing to distinguish Morris from Coaker: both were corrupt political adventurers. He regarded the formation of the National government as nothing more than a conspiracy to cloak 'the graft that has been rampant for eight years.' Hence, in spite of all the signs to the contrary, he thought it likely that the Union and the People's party would remain in the coalition indefinitely, because together they could always control the government. His view of the Liberal party's future was therefore extremely pessimistic. Even the retirement of Morris and the formation of a new National government under W. F. Lloyd apparently failed to kindle his hopes; for when Shea, convinced of the coalition's instability, again implored him to take a public stand, Bond coldly replied: 'we shall adopt the Asquithian advice, "Wait and see." '[4]

Richard Squires, however, was not prepared to wait for very long. Bond's inscrutability was for him a major stumbling-block, making all his

4/*Ibid.*, Bond to Shea, 29 Dec. 1917.

plans uncertain, and this eventually led him to adopt a bold, if rather transparent, strategem: 'I have professional business which calls me to New York,' he wrote to Bond, adding that he would like to stop over at Whitbourne 'if you would do me the honour of an interview.'[5] Bond's curt refusal signalled the start of an intense behind-the-scenes struggle, not so much between Squires and Bond directly as between Squires and the increasingly disheartened pro-Bond faction in St John's. Still, in what appears to have been another attempt to force Bond's hand, Henry Gear, a former Liberal MHA but now an ally of Squires, wrote to him on 2 May 1918: 'Squires came to me yesterday and stated that the [Legislative] Council were prepared to turn down the extension bill if they were assured of a leader for an election this fall. But *if you were not coming to lead, they think it better to let the matter run until the fall of 1919, and during the interval prepare, under another leader, for the fight in 1919.*'[6] To this thinly veiled ultimatum Bond scornfully replied: 'The threat contained in Mr. Squires' communication to you would be amusing were it not grossly insulting.'[7] But nevertheless, he did nothing to clarify his own position.

Such majestic ambiguity may have been justified while the war was still in progress, but increasingly it became a source of exasperation for even his most devoted supporters, and with the end of the war became completely untenable. Yet had Bond acted even then he might still have been able to defeat Squires, so great was his personal standing, and particularly in view of the fact that a new element in politics, the Returned Soldiers Association, was prepared to give him their support. The chairman of that organization had written to him in November 1918:

The 'Blue Puttees' [a smaller, but influential, veterans group, consisting of the original volunteers] have been pushing Squires, or rather he is endeavouring to get them to push him. However, the Blue Puttees are not *all* the soldiers, and they have been badly led and advised. At a pinch there are various ways in which the Soldiers may precipitate matters with the approbation of the public ... but the danger I have seen is that they might do something which was not properly thought out (more especially the Blue Puttees) and call out Squires for a leader, though I know that if he were leader the support of the country would be divided, as well as that of the Soldiers. Still, if you do not come, there are a lot of people who do not particularly favour Squires who will back him against the present aggregation. ... With your silence I have been

5/*Ibid.*, Squires to Bond, 14 March 1918.
6/*Ibid.*, Gear to Bond, 2 May 1918 (italics added).
7/*Ibid.*, Bond to Gear, 4 May 1918.

a bit nervous as regards Squires, knowing his boundless ambition and having been told that if you did not come, the Archbishop would support him against the present party, and also the fact that he is pulling a lot of strings.'[8]

Archbishop Roche's concern with the political future of Newfoundland also formed the substance of a final plea from Shea. The Liberals were by this time in desperate straits, for Bond's long equivocation had forestalled the emergence of any other leader. But now, at last, he gave them a direct answer:

While I entirely share his Grace's concern in respect to our public affairs, I feel that the present condition, and approaching conditions, must be attributed in very large measure to the Coalition of the Morris and Coaker parties, and I regret exceedingly that his Grace's powerful influence was not thrown against that most unrighteous combination, and its perpetuation ... While we may feel concern for the future, we have now to realize that the past cannot be undone, and it is the past which unfortunately, and in this case necessarily, shapes the future. It is too late. Every day simply adds to the Colony's disgrace, and hastens the debacle, and the attempt to hold back the tide now rolling in upon us would be as hopeless as Mrs Parkington's attempt to push away the Atlantic Ocean with her mop ... I have had a surfeit of Newfoundland politics lately, and I turn from the dirty business with contempt and loathing.[9]

It was the end for Bond. The path was finally clear for Richard Squires.

In May, moreover, the collapse of the wartime coalition dramatically confirmed Squires's original assumption that post-war politics would not see a continuance of the Union-People's party collaboration. But neither would the forthcoming struggle take place strictly between the two. For, as already noted, there was also an inchoate third force to be reckoned with, naturally inclined towards the Liberal party, and, if mobilized, capable of holding the balance of power. Hence, in the six-month interval before the general election which was set for 3 November, the Squires campaign was carefully mounted with the object of establishing his position as the obvious 'third' leader, along with Coaker and Cashin. In this respect, he brought to the task a number of undoubtedly valuable assets, both personal and political. In the first place, he was a Protestant, and thus able to benefit from any anti-Catholic reaction among voters in the predominantly Protestant and denominationally mixed constituencies of the south; secondly, he was in many respects the true heir of Sir Edward Mor-

8/*Ibid.*, K. M. Blair to Bond, 26 Nov. 1918.
9/*Ibid.*, Bond to Shea, 29 Nov. 1918.

ris, and for this reason alone could count on at least some Catholic support (particularly if a significant section of the Returned Veterans came out in his favour, for many of them were Catholics); thirdly, though young, he was an experienced politician and fairly well known to the country at large; and, last but not least, his control of the *Daily Star* placed at his disposal a useful vehicle of publicity and propaganda. Also, in the common New-foundland pattern, it provided him with a permanent campaign headquarters located in the capital.

Retrospectively, the most salient feature of Squires's campaign in 1919 was the almost uncanny degree to which, either consciously or unconsciously, it was modelled on that of Morris in 1908. Like his former mentor, Squires at first remained somewhat in the background – though no doubt working quietly to build support, particularly among influential Liberals – while the *Star*, like Morris' *Evening Chronicle*, set the bandwagon rolling with a gradually mounting campaign of personal publicity.[10] And, as in 1908, the predictable culmination of these efforts was a massive rally in St John's, purportedly in response to an overwhelming public desire for the services of Richard Squires, and the launching of a new political entity: the 'Liberal Reform Party.'[11] Coming at this stage, barely six weeks before the election, it was obviously designed first of all to provide its leader with an electoral machine; but secondly, it also gave notice that whatever remained operative of the old Liberal party had been effectively absorbed into the new, for among its supporters could now be numbered most of the leading 'Bondites,' including George Shea himself. Finally, such a demonstration of political strength convincingly established Squires's position – and bargaining power – vis-à-vis Cashin and Coaker. This may well have been his chief object, for the announcement of the Liberal Reform party was in fact but a portent of more momentous developments.

Barely two weeks later, on 6 September, it was suddenly announced that Squires had joined forces with Coaker, that the Liberal Reform and Union parties would fight the election as one, *and that Squires would be its leader.*[12]

There is no record of the negotiations leading up to this agreement, but there can be no doubt that for Squires the result was a brilliant coup. It

10/Its early edition was called the *Morning Post*. Like Morris' *Chronicle*, edited by P. T. McGrath, the *Star* and the *Post* were edited by an able publicist, Dr Harrison Mosdell, a physician who found political journalism more to his taste than medicine.
11/The founding rally was held in the Daily Star Building on 21 August. Squires was 'unanimously chosen' as leader. *Morning Post*, 22 Aug. 1919.
12/*Evening Advocate*, St John's, 6 Sept. 1919.

meant that before a ballot could be cast he had advanced by a series of well-timed manœuvres from 'dark horse' to 'odds-on favourite' in the race for the premiership. Obviously, he had everything to gain from such an alliance, for alone his own party had no chance whatever of winning a clear majority. Coaker, of course, was in a similar position, but nevertheless his action in placing his party effectively under the leadership of a person who previously had been among its bitterest enemies requires further explanation.

In December 1918, apparently anticipating the possibility of an alliance of some sort (though the identity of the potential ally was necessarily uncertain at this juncture), he had implored the FPU annual convention to

trust me fully and empower me to act on your behalf as discretion shall direct ... or replace me by someone to whom you will confer this power ... In the delicate matters that present themselves for arrangement and adjustment in forming our forces for the next election, I ask you to give me full power to act on your behalf, *and the strict assurance that whatever I do you will abide by.* This is asking you for greater power, but it is the only way I know to meet the circumstances. I will know the inside movements of all concerned, and will be in the best position to act for your best interests and that of the country.[13]

The assurances asked were unquestioningly given – thus constituting an interesting reversal of 'internal democracy': the annual convention was to be bound by the decision of the leader!

Coaker was thus free to negotiate, and, after the Union was driven into opposition by the fall of the National government, his political objectives naturally tended to coincide with those of Squires. Above all, they shared a common desire to oust the government of Sir Michael Cashin. Moreover, there were fewer basic policy differences between them than might have been expected. In so far as Squires had any policy, it was to diversify the island's economy by 'industrialization,'[14] though, inevitably in the circumstances, he was unable to put forward a concrete plan as to how this unobjectionable aim might be achieved. It was therefore easily compatible with Coaker's primary concern, which was reform of the fishery through increased government control of both production and marketing, as laid down in the Union's original policy statement nearly a decade before. Only by the prompt implementation of such a policy, Coaker believed,

13/W. F. Coaker, ed., *The History of the Fishermen's Protective Union of Newfoundland* (St John's, 1920), p. 133 (italics added).
14/See, e.g., the *Daily Star*, 9 Sept. 1919.

could Newfoundland be prepared for the sudden post-war slump in trade and resulting depression, which he regarded as inevitable.[15] Also, quite apart from any impending crisis, the ideal of a regulated fishery had been accepted as a basic tenet of Unionism: it stood for a new type of economy, more stable and equitable than the old. But if the Union remained in opposition it would be powerless to act. Hence, in the light of these circumstances and later events, it is not difficult to determine the general lines of the Squires-Coaker agreement: Squires was to have the premiership, Coaker a free hand to impose Union policy upon the fishery. It was transparently a *mariage de convenance*, but not at this stage a dishonourable one.

For the Cashin government, however, the formation of a united opposition spelt almost certain electoral defeat. In a three-cornered contest, with the 'Protestant' vote split between the other two parties in the denominationally mixed constituencies, they might have been able to hold on to office on the strength of their solid 'Catholic' support. But in a straight fight with Squires in these same constituencies, all the influence of sectarianism would be against them. It was this which ultimately determined the outcome of the election. The People's party tried in vain to stave off the inevitable, even changing its name to 'Liberal-Progressive Party'[16] presumably in the hope of establishing a claim to a share of the ex-Liberal vote; but since the change meant nothing in terms of policy or personnel, it merely amounted to a tacit admission of the party's desperation.

As anticipated, the voting on 3 November closely followed denominational lines: in general, Catholics voted for the Cashin government, Protestants against it. Its defeat was thus ensured, but it easily retained all but three of the fourteen 'Catholic' seats, and one of these it acquired shortly afterwards by the defection of the only successful Catholic candidate of the Liberal Reform party.[17] Only in Port de Grave, where Sir John Crosbie, minister of shipping, narrowly upset George Grimes, the left-wing Unionist, did the government win a seat in a constituency with a Protestant majority. Otherwise, the Protestant north returned a solid block of eleven Unionists, all with overwhelming majorities, while Protestant voters in the south gave their undivided support to candidates of the Liberal Reform party. This gave the latter ten seats in the denominationally mixed constituencies with Protestant majorities, and in addition it

15/J. R. Smallwood, *Coaker of Newfoundland* (London, 1927), p. 66.
16/*Evening Telegram*, St John's, 24 Sept. 1919.
17/J. McDonnell was elected as a Liberal Reform candidate for the district of St George's, but declined the portfolio of agriculture and joined his co-religionists in opposition.

won two others in St John's West, a denominationally mixed constituency with a Catholic majority.[18] Since together the Liberal and Union parties had won a clear majority of seats, Sir Michael Cashin chose to resign without waiting for defeat in the House.

On 17 November Richard Squires took office as prime minister, with William Coaker as minister of marine and fisheries. To help redress the denominational imbalance two Catholics, George Shea and Dr Alex Campbell, a defeated Liberal Reform candidate, were appointed to the cabinet as ministers without portfolio and later given seats in the Legislative Council. But this could only soften, and not conceal, the most noticeable feature of the legislature's composition: not one of the twenty-three members on the government side was a Catholic; of the thirteen opposition members only two were Protestants. It was one of these, the Hon. John R. Bennett, who expressed what must have been the regret of many: 'the last election,' he said, 'was not fought on any policy ... a man was not judged according to his ability but he was judged by the altar he worshipped at.'[19]

Unfortunately, at the very time when the country stood most in need of a period of reconciliation it also stood on the brink of economic catastrophe. There was to be no respite. Before religious tensions had time to subside the post-war depression had begun. And in this, the fact that Squires was prime minister mattered far less than that Coaker was minister of marine and fisheries; for it was the latter, with his plan for drastic reform of the fishery, who set the course which the government followed.

The ideal of a state-regulated fishery, as noted earlier, was basic to Union policy and its realization was the *sine qua non* of Union support for Squires. Therefore, with a guarantee of majority support in the House, and with European fish markets already showing signs of an impending slump, Coaker was determined to push through a comprehensive system of controls with the greatest possible speed. Before this could be done, however, he was confronted with an immediate crisis and was forced to adopt stop-gap measures. Upon taking office he had inherited a situation in which a voluntary agreement among the largest Newfoundland fish exporters to govern prices and conditions of shipment in their dealings with the Italian *Consorzio per l'importazione e la distribuzione dei merluzzi e stoccofissi* (a government marketing agency formed in September 1918) had broken down. This Coaker tried to remedy by issuing a proc-

18/This victory can be attributed to a combination of strong Liberal Reform candidates, including Squires himself, and the intervention of the Labour party (NIWA), which split the Catholic working-class vote.
19/*Proceedings of the House of Assembly, Newfoundland, 1920*, p. 90.

lamation under the Imports and Exports Restriction Act of 1918 requiring all exporters of cod to secure a government licence before shipping.[20] The exporters, who were not consulted, reacted with outraged protests and legal action which resulted in the Supreme Court ruling the proclamation *ultra vires*. But another to the same effect was quickly issued under the Emergency War Measures Act (1914), in flagrant disregard of the act's original justification, and with unfortunate effects. As a Unionist, it is doubtful if Coaker could ever have completely overcome all the exporters' suspicions, but with a more diplomatic approach he might have avoided adding a new dimension to their hostility. In the event, when detailed legislation was finally introduced into the House in the spring of 1920 the atmosphere was far from conducive to rational discussion, with the result that Coaker's far-reaching plans for the fishery – to which, ironically, the crude and hasty proclamations of the previous autumn bore small resemblance – failed to receive either the acceptance in principle or the informed criticism of detail that they so plainly deserved.

Basically, the objects of the new scheme, which Coaker explained at length to the House,[21] were fivefold, and may be summarized as follows: first, to modernize the fishery by government sponsorship of new methods of catching and curing; second, to standardize and place under government control the grading of fish, thus taking this vital function out of the hands of buyers and exporters; third, to appoint trade agents in those countries where Newfoundland produce was mainly sold; fourth, to establish a government information service for fishermen and a bureau to undertake scientific research; and fifth, to put an end to the laissez-faire conditions that had always prevailed in the marketing of fish by requiring exporters to obtain licences from a government-appointed Exportation Board, which, through negotiation with the exporters, would also fix the prices and conditions of sale to apply to the various foreign markets. On the whole, this scheme had a great deal to recommend it: it was bold, progressive, and relatively simple; its implementation would not have strained the country's financial resources; and it was capable of forming a sound basis for future planned development.

Unfortunately, by being introduced at the wrong time and in the wrong way it was doomed to failure. Had Coaker been prepared to wait for even one more year, to let fishermen and exporters alike experience the hazards of uncontrolled marketing in the chaotic and collapsing post-war econo-

20/H. A. Innis, *The Cod Fisheries: The History of an International Economy* (rev. ed., Toronto, 1954), pp. 465–6.

21/*Proceedings of the House of Assembly, Newfoundland, 1920*, pp. 138–50, 312–13, 426 ff. Already the Union press had given his plans a good deal of publicity. See, e.g., the *Evening Advocate*, 12 Jan. 1920.

mies of southern Europe, the virtues of his plan might then have been more obvious; or at least it could not have been blamed for difficulties that already existed. Moreover, since the success of the other more long-term provisions depended upon the success or failure of the export regulations, the lack of any concerted attempt by the government to obtain the co-operation of the exporters can only be judged a costly political blunder.[22] Finally, the export regulations contained a serious defect: they were too rigid to contend with a notoriously unstable market, in which conditions were much closer to perfect competition than to oligopoly. Therefore any attempt to fix prices from St John's was bound to be futile; but that was exactly what the Exportation Board tried to do. It should be emphasized, however, that this mistake need not have proved fatal. Adjustments could have been made to allow sales to be made even if the established price could not be reached, to enable the newly appointed trade agents[23] to negotiate with fish buyers on behalf of the board, and to prevent Newfoundland exporters from undercutting one another (which, in the circumstances, was the most that could have been achieved, for nothing could prevent undercutting by Canadian or Norwegian exporters). But when faced with an even more ruinous market situation in 1921,[24] the

22/There was no lack of propaganda (see, e.g., 'The F.P.U. Policy of Progress,' *Daily Star*, 2 Dec. 1920) but it was directed mainly at the fishermen. A reconciliation with the exporters was attempted only when the regulations were in imminent danger of collapse. See Newfoundland Archives, Administration of Squires, Warren, and Monroe, 'Minutes of a General Meeting of the Nfld. Fish Exporters Association, Ltd., held in the Board of Trade Rooms ... December 28th.' This meeting was addressed by the prime minister, 'after consultation with Hon. W. F. Coaker,' but his plea for co-operation to preserve the regulations went unheeded. 'It was moved by Mr. [W. S.] Monroe, seconded by Mr. Carter, that the Export Board be requested to recommend that all regulations governing the export of Labrador fish for all markets, and all regulations governing the export of Shore fish to Italy, be rescinded.' The resolution was adopted with only one dissenting vote.
23/Trade agents were appointed in Portugal, Italy, Greece, the West Indies, the United States, Liverpool, and Malaga (Innis, *The Cod Fisheries*, p. 467). These representatives were a potential source of friction with the imperial government, for their presence pointed the way to separate diplomatic negotiations. As they were soon to be withdrawn, the question never in fact arose, though a similar issue was at stake in January 1921 when Coaker visited Italy in an (unsuccessful) attempt to negotiate a trade treaty. On that occasion the governor, Sir Alexander Harris, wrote to the prime minister: 'The right of a self-governing portion of the Empire to make a special arrangement in its own interest has been somewhat reluctantly admitted; but in order to safeguard all other parts of the Empire and other treaty obligations it has been held most strongly by His Majesty's Government that they should have full knowledge of negotiations and that the actual negotiations should be in the hand of diplomatic representatives.' Newfoundland Archives, Administration of Squires, Warren, and Monroe, Governor Harris to Squires, 21 Jan. 1921.
24/The seriousness of the collapse is reflected in the trade statistics: in 1919–20 the cod fishery produced exports to the value of $23,258,666; in the following year the value amounted to only $13,495,451. Cmd 4480, *Newfoundland Royal Commission 1933 Report* (London, 1933), p. 111.

exporters, haunted by visions of their cargoes rotting unsold in Mediter-
ranean ports, directed their efforts not towards improving the regulations
for their mutual protection but towards breaking them – and Coaker.

Victory was quickly theirs. 'Serious disturbances in Portugal, Spain,
Italy, Greece, and Rumania and the sharp increases in exchange rates
between the currencies of those countries and sterling brought about a
collapse in January, 1921, and the recall of the trade commissioners.'[25]
With the entire trade paralyzed, panic-stricken exporters began to sell
without licences or below the established prices. By March Coaker's plan
lay in ruins. The regulations were withdrawn by proclamation, first for
Portugal, then for other European markets, and finally for Brazil and the
West Indies.[26]

In retrospect it can be seen that these events bore an economic and
political significance far exceeding even their immediate impact. Economically, the failure of the export regulations – and more important still,
the failure to implement any of the other farsighted provisions of Coaker's
plan – marked the end of Newfoundland's pre-eminence as a fishing country. Already in Norway and Iceland, her chief competitors, the old economic order had given way to the new, bringing government intervention
in their fisheries on a scale and in a manner not finally adopted in Newfoundland until nearly twenty years later. Meanwhile, Newfoundland did
not regress, but rather stagnated, while in these other countries a combination of centralized marketing, planned investment, and controlled production of the kind that Coaker had envisioned for Newfoundland improved both the quality of their produce and their competitive position.[27]

Politically, the effects are more difficult to assess, but no less important.
First, there was the strange alteration the defeat of the regulations produced (or was partly responsible for producing) in the behaviour of
Coaker himself. It must of course be admitted that the behaviour of a
complex individual can rarely if ever be explained in terms of simple
cause and effect, but, with all due qualifications made, it still seems to be
the case that Coaker's evident lack of political dynamism after 1921 must
be attributed largely to the collapse of those measures in which he most
deeply believed. For more than a decade fisheries reform had been a prominent part of the Union's political platform: and in the eyes of Coaker,
and indeed of Unionists generally, it had become an economic panacea.
So convinced were they of its necessity that they had entered a dubious
political alliance primarily in order to implement it – only to find that they
were powerless to deal with an economic crisis, which, though not of their

25/Innis, *The Cod Fisheries*, p. 467.
26/Announced in *The Times*, London, 9 March 1921.
27/Innis, *The Cod Fisheries*, pp. 468–9.

making, nevertheless undermined their faith in their own solutions. At the same time, it also undermined the raison d'être of their alliance with Squires; but, paradoxically, instead of weakening his position this served rather to strengthen it. He had been in Coaker's shadow from the moment his ministry took office; now, through Coaker's virtual abdication, he rapidly emerged as the dominant leader. Of even greater long-run significance was the effect upon the Union party in the Assembly. Previously, though the two groups constituting the governing coalition recognized no formal division, in practice their identities were well known, and it was the Unionists under Coaker who were unmistakably the dynamic force. But, after 1921, their leader's uncharacteristic ennui left them bewildered and rudderless, with only Squires to guide them.[28] Within the next two years the once crucial line between Unionists and Liberals became so blurred it almost ceased to matter.

28/On 1 June 1923 Coaker accepted a 'Squires knighthood' and thereafter devoted himself primarily to the management of the Union's extensive commercial operations, which he ran autocratically and increasingly in accordance with traditional mercantile principles. He was never again a radical force in politics.

11 The crisis of the twenties

A FISHERMAN is of necessity a gambler and an optimist: he must have faith in tomorrow's catch, even if today his nets are empty. And when his nets are full to overflowing, and prices, by past standards, astronomically high for year after prosperous year, his optimism becomes boundless. No debt is then too large, no expenditure too extravagant; all will be taken care of by next season's miracle. Such an attitude had been characteristic of Newfoundlanders for centuries, but never were they more strongly imbued with it than in the years during and immediately following the First World War. Hence their reaction to the sharp post-war recession in trade: it was merely another stroke of bad luck (which it was, in the sense that it was largely beyond their control), but after so much success their credit was good, loans could cover any 'temporary' loss, and all would be recouped with the next spin on the wheel of fortune – or the one after that.

Oblivious to, or preferring to ignore, the niceties of international trade, the public failed to grasp, and their political leaders failed to illuminate, the unpalatable fact that the years of plenty were over; they had now to earn a living in a more difficult, relentlessly competitive world. As R. A. MacKay and S. A. Saunders aptly put it:

The ink had scarcely dried on the Treaty of Versailles before economic nationalism had reasserted itself. Discriminatory trade agreements became more common, tariff barriers were raised, and nearly every country endeavoured to become more self-sufficient. France and Portugal resumed their policies of assisting their respective domestic fisheries. Italy and Spain endeavoured to lessen their dependence upon outside sources for their supplies of foodstuffs.

The United States, as an integral part of her protectionist policy, restricted immigration, thereby limiting one important outlet for the surplus population of Newfoundland. The production of foodstuffs in many countries had been greatly expanded during the war, and as production in European countries recovered, competition became exceptionally severe.[1]

Newfoundland was powerless to affect these external conditions, yet could not avoid being affected by them. It was therefore all the more important that, in order to improve her competitive position, she should make every effort to strengthen her domestic economy. At the very minimum this would have involved some tightening of belts while European fish markets remained depressed, but it would also have involved greater government control over production and marketing, government initiative in the search for new markets, in the sponsorship of scientific research, and in the introduction of new machinery and techniques designed to raise productivity. William Coaker, to his credit, tried. But the failure of his scheme was worse than if he had never tried at all, for it hardened resistance to reform of any sort. The ancient credit system and its counterpart, economic individualism, came back with a vengeance, and thereafter nothing could break their hold.

Instead of dealing with economic causes, throughout the twenties Newfoundland squandered her meagre resources on the treatment of symptoms. The fishery was neglected, while the government of the day recklessly ran up deficit after deficit, each covered by fresh loans, in a vain attempt to meet all the demands made upon it for immediate public relief. It was the gambler's mentality at work: politicians and public alike staked all on a change of fortune, but one that never came. Or perhaps it could be called a form of primitive, unconscious 'Keynesianism,' but indulged in without discrimination and without the resources to make it work. As the burden of the national debt grew steadily heavier, without any corresponding increase in the country's ability to bear it, interest payments swallowed up an increasingly large share of government revenue. Less was then available for 'visible' expenditure, thus further narrowing the government's scope for manœuvre, until eventually borrowing became necessary to maintain even essential services. Willing lenders were still available, particularly in the free and easy money market of New York, but a downward spiral was set in motion which could not be halted and from which there was to be no escape.

1/'The Economy of Newfoundland,' in R. A. MacKay, ed., *Newfoundland: Economic, Diplomatic, and Strategic Studies* (Toronto, 1946), p. 67.

'SQUIRES AND CLEAN GOVERNMENT'[2]

The campaign for the premiership so successfully waged by Richard Squires in 1919 was in many respects an exercise in smooth professional politics on the American model – even the word 'Reform' in his party's name was drawn from the American rather than the English political vocabulary – and was followed by the usual consequences. Sweeping to power on a string of generalities, pledging, for example, to 'Make Newfoundland Safe for Democracy' and to 'Rid Newfoundland of Her Grafters' (the alleged grafters being of course the government of Sir Michael Cashin – or 'Cash In' as the *Morning Post* maliciously called him), Squires avoided committing himself to any specific reforms in the conduct or the structure of government. Indeed, 'reform' in practice turned out to mean nothing more than a change of personnel wherever personnel could be changed; that is to say, the victorious party paid its political debts in the traditional way.

Beyond this, the new prime minister appeared to have no certain idea of how to use the power he had so skilfully and energetically pursued; but even if he had, he could scarcely have taken office under less auspicious circumstances. As noted earlier, he had begun his premiership under the shadow of William Coaker, emerging in his own right only after the collapse of Coaker's momentous dream for the fishery and subsequent political decline. In 1919 he had sought the highest office in what was then a prosperous self-governing Dominion; after 1921 he found himself securely in the premiership of a country in dire economic trouble. The 'glittering prize,' if such it was, had turned to dust by the time he was able to grasp it.

After five successive years of rising government revenue and balanced budgets, for the fiscal year 1920–1 the financial returns disclosed an unprecedented deficit of $4,271,474 – a vast figure in proportion to total revenue, which amounted to only $8,438,039. Revenue had fallen by over $2 million; expenditure had increased by approximately the same amount. It was thus an unenviable task that faced the Squires government in the 1921 session of Parliament: the fisheries regulations had ended in collapse, a financial crisis was imminent, and, to make matters still worse, the political atmosphere in St John's was tense with the threat of violence. The Assembly met to the accompaniment of hostile street demonstrations by unemployed workers, and on two occasions demonstrations and fight-

2/Headline in the *Morning Post*, St John's, 23 Aug. 1919.

ing in the public galleries forced the Speaker to suspend the sitting of the House. Scenes such as these were not conducive to governmental frugality. Though the deficit on current account was reduced in the following year to $1,811,299 and in 1922–3 to $1,268,808, these figures do not reveal the substantial expenditure on capital account, much of which was expended on projects frankly designed to provide relief, and all of which was financed through borrowing. The resulting increase in the national debt due to government loans was staggering:[3]

When raised	Amount	Interest rate	Interest payable in	Maturity (years)
1921	$6,000,000	6½%	sterling	25
1922	6,000,000	6	gold	20
1923	2,061,033	5½	sterling	20
1923	3,500,000	5	gold	20

At $43,032,785 the national debt in 1920 was already high for a small, relatively poor community. These additional loans raised it to $60,451,754.

Government expenditure, however, was not only large – serious as that was, it is at least arguable that its size could not have been reduced under the circumstances – but it was also accompanied in certain of the key departments of state by what can only be described as at best culpable incompetence and at worst graft and corruption of unparalleled magnitude. In this, it transpired, the prime minister and at least one other cabinet minister were deeply implicated, as were some members of the Assembly and a number of public officials. Expenditure was commonly authorized by order-in-council and made with a cavalier disregard for every tenet of financial propriety. Positions of public trust and responsibility were exploited for private gain. Eventually a reckoning had to come. In certain particularly flagrant instances the sums of money which changed hands, or were bargained for, were too large – and the persons involved too distrustful of one another – for easy concealment. In 1923 the lid suddenly blew off, releasing a malodorous scandal, bringing down the government, and initiating a period of political confusion without precedent in the island's history. It also formed the subject of a remarkable royal commission of inquiry by T. Hollis Walker, whose investigations cast a unique light into the dark corners of Newfoundland politics. But

3/Compiled from statistical data contained in Cmd 4480, *Newfoundland Royal Commission 1933 Report* (London, 1933).

these developments are examined more thoroughly in the next section of this chapter. For present purposes it is sufficient to call attention to them, for they bring into focus the background of reckless rapacity against which the 'reform' administration of Richard Squires ran its course. However, it would be myopic to suggest that one administration could have been wholly or even mainly responsible for what was in fact a widespread social disease. There were many contributing causes – the revival of sectarian strife, the generally unsettling effects of the war, prohibition with its attendent lawlessness and hypocrisy, an already entrenched patronage system, sudden prosperity followed by even more sudden depression – all tending in a complex way to produce a climate of cynicism and laissez faire which left no part of the community untouched. But it can fairly be said that it was the responsibility of those in high office to combat, or at least to refrain from exploiting, these destructive tendencies. By failing to do either they undoubtedly compounded the dangers already threatening their country's future.

Inevitably, in a period of financial strain, one of the most pressing issues facing the government was that of its peculiar relationship with the Reid Newfoundland Company, a huge and multifarious concern which numbered among its enterprises the operation of the national railway. In surrendering its title to the railway in 1901 the company had contracted to operate it for a period of fifty years.[4] Before the war, lucrative contracts for the construction of branch lines, undertaken by the company and paid for by the government, more than made up for any operating deficit; during the war, greatly increased traffic made the operation of the railway a profitable venture, very likely for the only time in its history. But immediately after the war its fortunes suffered a sharp reversal. Burdened by high operating costs, in need of repair, and with its branch lines exposed for the economic folly they undoubtedly were, it became a heavy liability on the company, which turned to the government for help. According to A. B. Morine:

Early in the summer of 1920 the Reid Company notified the government that they were unable to continue the operation of the railway. The track was unsafe, locomotives were worn out, the fastenings of the railway were insufficient. There were not sufficient box and flat cars to provide for traffic. Freight terminals were required. The Company had not money enough to remedy these deficiencies.[5]

4/See above, p. 34.
5/*The Railway Contract, 1898, and Afterwards* (St John's, n.d. [1933]), p. 47.

Since the company was responsible for the supply and maintenance of rolling stock and other equipment, including the rail lines, its difficulties were at least partly of its own making – either through bad management or through a deliberate policy to maximize profits in the short run by making insufficient allowance for the depreciation of capital equipment. In either case, the company was proposing to default some thirty years before its contract was due to expire.

To avoid this, the government, with astonishing magnanimity, agreed to establish a joint commission with the company, each appointing three members, to operate the railway for one year from 1 July 1920. The parties also agreed to share responsibility for any operating deficit, the company being liable for the first $100,000 and the government for the remainder – which amounted to $1,758,025.[6] Meanwhile, the government had sought the advice of Sir George Bury, a former vice-president of the Canadian Pacific Railway, who duly warned against the 'unfortunate results' of government operation of railways in other countries and advised yet another operating contract with the Reid company. Under it, he suggested, the company should be required 'to operate the railway with the utmost economy, consistent with safety and reasonable service' and that 'the Government agree to pay the actual loss from operating the railway during the coming year, but that, should the loss exceed 1½ million dollars, such excess should be borne by the Reid Nfld. Co.'[7]

On the basis of Bury's report the government entered a new agreement with the company, but not without encountering strong opposition. Even Governor Sir Alexander Harris felt compelled to point out to his prime minister the seemingly obvious advantages of an alternate course. With charming naïveté, he wrote:

I have every feeling of kindness and courtesy towards the Company but clearly the first point of view of the Governor and his Administration must be the interest of the Colony which owns the Railway ...

In other words, whatever Sir George Bury says, I think you will make a mistake if you come to an arrangement with the Company whereby the Government undertakes any serious loss until you have put them in a position of making a default even for 24 hours, so that you can bring to bear the whole of the Government's rights under the contract and establish your lien upon all their undertakings ...

It seems to me that it would not do for the Company to throw the loss of

6/Cmd 4480, *Report*, p. 63.
7/As quoted in Anon., 'The Newfoundland Railway,' in J. R. Smallwood, ed., *The Book of Newfoundland* (St John's, 1937), II, 413–14.

the Railway on the Government and yet get profits from their other concessions. That they will attempt to do so is natural but it seems to me better to
fight the question up to the House of Lords rather than give away any rights
in law.[8]

His words went unheeded. For the year 1921–2 the government was obliged to meet the railway's operating deficit of $953,367.

As the company was no doubt well aware, its good fortune in dealing
with an accommodating government could not be expected to last indefinitely – and indeed could disappear overnight. Therefore, from the
company's point of view, the ideal solution was one which permanently
relieved it of its burdensome obligations, for there was no foreseeable
prospect of the railway business ever recovering. Hence, in April 1922,
even before the 'Bury' agreement had expired, the company announced
that it was unwilling to continue and offered to surrender the whole of its
railway operations to the government. In May for eight days the trains
ceased to run. Employees were notified that wages would not be paid. The
company was technically in default. But once again, instead of instituting
legal proceedings, the government responded with additional financial support and the company was persuaded to resume its services.[9]

This, however, was but a temporary arrangement, for in the meantime –
in a different but not unrelated sphere – highly significant developments
were taking place which cast the whole matter in a new light.

Around this time, certain British financiers and industrialists were looking closely at the potential of the Newfoundland forests. The shortage of
newsprint during the war pointed to the advisability of 'Empire' sources,
and the notable success of the Harmsworth paper mill at Grand Falls,
together with large timber resources and direct ocean transport to Britain,
pointed straight to Newfoundland. Two undeveloped sites in the island
were geographically favourable for the economic production of paper: the
Gander Valley and the watershed of the Humber River. In both these areas
the property and power rights were largely owned by the Reid Newfoundland Company.[10] Without their co-operation no development was possible.

A Reid subsidiary, the Newfoundland Products Corporation, which had
been seeking to interest outside capital in the Humber property since 1915

8/Newfoundland Archives, Governor's Correspondence, carton 6, folder 12,
Harris to Squires, 6 July 1921.
9/Morine, *The Railway Contract*, pp. 47–8.
10/The Reid company was still acquiring lands in the Humber area, as an
operating subsidy for the branch lines it had constructed for the government, as late
as 1915 (*ibid.*, p. 44). Its total holdings in the area extended to some 7,200 square
miles (Cmd 4480, *Report*, p. 150).

without success, after the war found its prospects greatly improved. It soon found a willing client in the firm of Sir W. G. Armstrong, Whitworth and Company, armament manufacturers of Newcastle-upon-Tyne who apparently had a surplus of capital for which they were seeking a peacetime use. Early in 1923 the two parties agreed to set up a new company, the Newfoundland Power and Paper Company, to construct a paper mill in western Newfoundland and harness the Humber as its source of hydro-electric power. The estimated cost of the project was $20 million or about £4 million, to be raised through an issue of debenture stock in two series of £2 million each. The British government, under the provisions of the Trade Facilities Act, 1921, agreed to guarantee the interest and principal on the first series, and the Newfoundland government agreed to provide an equal guarantee for the second series.[11]

For Sir Richard Squires, the 'Humber deal' was a godsend: it gave him an unbeatable issue on which to fight the next general election. 'Industrialization' had been one of his party's slogans in 1919; now he could proudly point to a development that promised 'employment for 2,500 men' and a '$5,000,000 annual wage bill.'[12] An election fought mainly on the railway issue would undoubtedly have been dangerous for the government; now the railway issue faded out of view. The new slogan became: 'A vote against Squires is a vote against Humber industry.'[13]

Less obviously, the Humber proposal appears to have helped Squires to overcome growing discontent within his ministry. The exact causes are obscure, but there can be no doubt that the discontent was of a serious nature. In January William Coaker had publicly declared his intention to retire from the cabinet at the end of the current Parliament 'to carry out our plans for reorganizing the F.P.U.,'[14] ominously omitting to state whether he would continue to support Squires or not. But the proposed developments on the Humber, which he strongly favoured, ensured Squires of his renewed support. Consequently, in April the prime minister was able to purge his cabinet of the dissident element without difficulty.[15]

Though a general election was not due until November, Squires obtained an early dissolution of the House, with the election set for 3 May,

11/For a detailed account of the capitalization of the project, see Cmd 4480, *Report*, p. 145 ff.

12/*Daily Mail*, St John's, 24 March 1923. (The *Daily Mail* was the *Daily Star* under a new name. The change came about in February 1923 after the *Daily Star* absorbed the *Evening Herald*.)

13/*Ibid.*, 28 March 1923.

14/*Evening Advocate*, St John's, 2 Jan. 1923.

15/Coaker's support was obviously crucial, for one of those at odds with the prime minister was Walter Jennings, a Unionist, who resigned as minister of public works on 3 April. For other changes in Squires's ministry, see Appendix A.

in order to place 'the one great issue' before the country without delay. That the campaign would be a ludicrous affair was practically inevitable, for no one opposed the Humber guarantees in principle. Also, the government had the additional good fortune to face a weak and undistinguished 'Liberal Progressive' opposition party, containing not a single leader of national stature. Once they had lost the initiative to Squires, their position became hopeless. In a shuffle obviously designed to broaden the party's appeal outside the Catholic south, J. R. Bennett, a Protestant, in February replaced Sir Michael Cashin as leader.[16] For good measure, the party also changed its name to 'Liberal-Labour-Progressive' – a title wonderfully at variance with its general merchant-conservative composition, but hopefully based upon the support given it by a small, mainly Irish Catholic, section of St John's labour, including W. J. Linegar, a Labour candidate in 1919. However, by selecting the alleged iniquities of the defunct 'Coaker regulations' as the major element in its campaign, the opposition left no doubt as to its true mercantile nature. Finally, though a certain amount of government 'pump-priming' was by no means uncommon in past election years, in the spring of 1923 the pump was primed as it had never been primed before. Public funds flowed freely; the first object of government became the re-election of the party in office.

In this it was successful. The results produced no change whatever in party standings in the Assembly: the government held twenty-three seats, the opposition thirteen. As in 1919 the latter's support was mainly concentrated in predominantly Catholic constituencies, but its share of the vote in the country as a whole increased from 35.5 per cent to 48.6 per cent. And though the relative strength of the parties remained the same, six seats changed hands. The Liberal Reform party gained seats in Port de Grave, Harbour Main, and St George's (the successful candidates in the latter two being Catholics), but lost seats to the opposition in Burin, Carboncar, and St John's West. The prime minister held his seat in St John's West by a mere four votes. J. R. Bennett was defeated in Harbour Grace by sixty-three. The Union again elected eleven members, including the minister of education, Dr Arthur Barnes, who, though not a Unionist, was given a safe Union seat in Twillingate.

'The election,' reported *The Times*, 'may be taken as an endorsement of the projected paper mills on the West Coast, which was the chief issue of the campaign.'[17] It was that, and much more – at least in the eyes of the government and the Reid Newfoundland Company. With Squires seemingly secure in the premiership for another term of office, negotiations

16/ *Daily News*, St John's, 28 Feb. 1923.
17/ London, 6 May 1923.

were reopened on the financing of the railway, and this time the question was finally settled: the government agreed to cancel the company's operating contract, and, moreover, to pay it the sum of $2 million in return for the surrender of its assets.[18] 'No part of the lands granted as subsidy for operation were taken from the Reid Company, although only half of the operating period originally contracted for had expired.'[19]

On 1 July 1923 the operation of the railway became the responsibility of the Newfoundland government. For the Reid company it was a final stroke of fortune. On 23 July Richard Squires was removed from the premiership by a cabinet revolt.

THE HOLLIS WALKER REPORT

In the 1923 general election two cabinet ministers failed to secure seats. Captain Thomas Bonia, newly appointed minister of finance, was unsuccessful in Placentia–St Mary's and Dr Alex Campbell, minister of agriculture and mines, in St John's West. The former was subsequently demoted to the ministry of posts and telegraphs and appointed to the Legislative Council. Campbell, however, was in a more invidious position: he had held office since 1919, yet had now been rejected by the electorate for the second time running. In spite of this disability, he retained the prime minister's confidence and continued in his cabinet post, once more through the convenience of a seat in the Upper House. But with his reappointment, though not simply *because* of it, the future of the Squires government was placed in jeopardy. Thereafter, with Campbell as its focus, dissension within the ranks began to mount.

As minister of agriculture and mines, Campbell was responsible for one of the government's major 'spending' departments. Not inappropriately, he also served, it appears, as his party's unofficial 'patronage secretary.' His department was ideal for this purpose, for it was continuously involved in the administration of various costly 'relief' projects – such as the purchasing of cut timber, supposedly to be exported for use as pit-props in European coal mines, and the free distribution of 'seed' potatoes and other (edible) aids to agriculture – which gave almost unlimited scope for the political use of public funds. Expenditure on the government's 'pit-props' account in particular increased spectacularly during the 1923 election campaign – even in forestless St John's West. This in itself could hardly be regarded as untypical or scandalous, except perhaps for its lavishness, since public morality was notoriously flexible about such matters. But in the past, dispensers of bounty generally made at least a customary obeis-

18/Anon., 'The Newfoundland Railway,' p. 414.
19/Morine, *The Railway Contract*, p. 48.

ance in the direction of the auditor general by taking some pains to conceal or 'legitimize' their political expenditures. Victory and post-election apathy could be counted upon to take care of the rest, or, if the government suffered defeat, the incoming party's 'revelations' could easily be dismissed as a pretext invented to justify wholesale dismissals and the distribution of spoils to their own supporters. What made Dr Campbell's behaviour extraordinary, therefore, was not his zealous use of public funds on behalf of his party; it was rather his inability to control their outflow or disguise their purpose.

Consequently, once the wild election binge was over, and detailed returns of expenditure by the Department of Agriculture and Mines began to be tabled in the House, it became apparent that the government had left itself open to serious charges of corruption and that the unvarnished public accounts were a source of much embarrassing evidence. Aided by the skilful probing of W. J. Higgins, the new leader of the opposition, throughout the early summer the chief opposition newspaper published with great relish lengthy columns of payments made by the department to individuals in the period prior to the election – usually for obviously political purposes, including cab and motor car hire in St John's West – and all charged to the 'pit-props' account.[20] Meanwhile, apparently determined to ride out the storm, Prime Minister Squires unobtrusively carried on with his main work of negotiating a railway settlement with the Reid Newfoundland Company. However, other ministers were less sanguine, and when the opposition's assault gathered momentum instead of losing steam as time went on, the bonds of cabinet solidarity and personal loyalty began to crack. In July, with the controversial railway deal a fait accompli, with fresh fuel added to the critics' fire by a condemnatory auditor general's report, and with the air thickened by scandalous rumours of every sort, the breaking point was finally reached. When efforts within the cabinet to secure Campbell's 'retirement' proved fruitless, a group of four ministers, headed by William Warren, minister of justice, determined to force the issue. On the morning of 23 July the four confronted Squires with a demand for Campbell's dismissal.[21] When their demand was refused they submitted their resignations. Some three hours later Squires called upon the governor, resigned, and advised him to send for Warren.

Though simple in outline, these events leave a number of unanswered questions. First, it has never been made clear why Squires, an undoubtedly

20/See below, pp. 167–9.
21/'When asked by reporters why ministers had taken this most unusual course, the Hon. Mr. Warren replied that they were influenced by personal reasons. The Hon. Mr. Halfyard when asked the same question admitted that they were up against [sic] an "intolerable position." But just what that intolerable position was he refused to say.' Daily News, 24 July 1923.

ruthless politician, persisted in shielding Campbell.[22] On tactical grounds he may well have maintained that one sacrifice would merely have whetted the opposition's appetite for more; but the *identity* of the dissident ministers should have been enough to warn him that *their* resignations would make his own inevitable: Warren was the party's deputy leader; Dr Arthur Barnes, a distinguished teacher, was widely respected as a 'non-political' minister; and, most important of all, William Halfyard was the leading Unionist in the cabinet.[23] It is of course possible that Squires misjudged the strength of their objections and was taken by surprise. It seems more likely, however, that he was fully aware of what the consequences would be, and knowing privately that other scandals were about to explode nearer home which would make his survival impossible in any case, preferred to go down defending Campbell rather than wait until he himself became the main target.[24]

A second question which arises is whether Squires was 'the victim of a conspiracy,' as his supporters later alleged. The allegation is indeed true in the sense that the four ministers acted in concert, but the implication that they did so with the *direct intention* of removing Squires has never been substantiated. The idea that he *might* resign must have occurred to

22/It is impossible to assess, but perhaps wrong to ignore, the personal factors that seem to have been involved. Squires was a solitary sort of person of whom William Halfyard once wrote: 'he is not in the habit of consulting other people as to his actions and has prided himself on carving out his own fortunes' (Newfoundland Archives, Warren Papers, Halfyard to Warren, 12 Oct. 1923). Campbell was one of his few personal confidants. The doctor was an urbane, slightly flamboyant, rather mysterious character. A Prince Edward Islander by birth, and possessor of a distinguished medical education, he was a passionate if unsuccessful politician throughout most of his life. His other passion was the breeding of racehorses – which presumably qualified him for the ministry of agriculture.

23/William Coaker, as he had promised, did not rejoin the cabinet after the election but remained a backbench MHA. He was curiously absent from the scene of these struggles but later correspondence makes clear that Halfyard, and by implication Warren, acted with his knowledge and support. Warren Papers, Warren to Halfyard, 28 Sept. 1923; also Newfoundland Archives, Administration of Squires, Warren, and Monroe, c. 2, f. 6, Warren to R. M. Wolvin, 28 Dec. 1923.

24/Squires, in his capacity as colonial (i.e., home) secretary, had before him at the time a police report on a burglary at the Liquor Control Department in which a safe had been forced open and papers stolen. 'Those stolen,' the report stated, 'were in an envelope marked R.A.S. [Richard Anderson Squires]. There were also some other papers taken from the filing cabinet marked Prime Minister.' The report also recorded a remark alleged to have been made to the head constable investigating the incident by the acting liquor controller (who later denied making it) that 'the Prime Minister was on the back of it' (Newfoundland Archives, Administration of Squires, Warren, and Monroe, c. 2, f. 6, 'Report of Head Constable Byrne,' 19 June 1923). Squires must have known that a copy of the report would eventually reach the hands of the minister of justice, Mr Warren, if it had not already done so. It was later established that there were huge shortages in the Liquor Control Department and that the acting controller had been making 'loans' to Sir Richard from public funds.

them, but there is nothing to suggest that this was their real aim, rather than the dismissal of Campbell. To say this is not necessarily to accept at face value their expressions of wounded innocence. With the exception of Halfyard, they had all been cabinet ministers for several years, and while it is possible, it is extremely unlikely that they were unaware of the way in which Campbell was operating his department. Rather, it would seem, Campbell was chosen as a scapegoat not because of what he did but because he was caught doing it.

After being called upon to form a ministry, Warren, with the strong support of William Coaker, was unanimously elected leader by the governing party.[25] Squires had failed to take a single supporter with him. Warren's next move was to announce that he would 'attempt to form an administration of strength and stability that would command the confidence of not only both sides of the House of Assembly, but of the community as well.'[26] However, when negotiations with the opposition to form a coalition broke down, apparently when no agreement could be reached on the terms of reference for an inquiry into public expenditure,[27] the new ministry turned out to be much the same as its predecessor. Of its ten members, seven had held office in the previous cabinet and one of the 'new' members was William Coaker.[28]

It was immediately clear, however, that their first responsibility would be to institute 'a thorough and complete enquiry, which will either exonerate or condemn.'[29] It was also clear that such an enquiry would have to be conducted by someone whose impartiality was beyond question, and not by any member of the new government. The only truly contentious question was whether the terms of the enquiry should extend to the affairs of *all* government departments or be confined to those matters in which Campbell and Squires were known to have been involved. Warren had at first promised 'a complete investigation by a Commission with absolute freedom of action,'[30] but preliminary investigations by the government, with the aid of a firm of chartered accountants, were limited to the accounts of the Department of Agriculture, while Warren himself, in his capacity as attorney general, undertook the preparation of evidence against Squires.[31]

The government evidently intended from the start to opt for the narrower terms of reference; for in spite of their victory over Squires, they were not so politically secure that they could run the risk of having for-

25/*Evening Advocate*, 24 July 1923.   26/*Daily News*, 25 July 1923.
27/*Ibid.*, 30 July 1923.   28/For the full ministry, see Appendix A
29/*Evening Advocate*, 28 July 1923.   30/*Daily News*, 30 July 1923.
31/Newfoundland Archives, Administration of Squires, Warren, and Monroe, 'Report of G. N. Read, Son & Watson, Chartered Accountants,' 10 Dec. 1923.

gotten skeletons exhumed from their own departmental closets. Fresh accusations of this sort could split the party and perhaps even permit the return of Squires – who, meanwhile, had by no means faded out of the picture:

Squires is here [wrote Warren from London, where he was attending the Imperial Conference] and is doing everything he can to embarrass me and intimidate me into calling off the investigation, but I am holding my own, and after my interview with him today I have no fear of any trouble. He has been circulating several stories about me, and, in particular, he poses as Leader of the Liberal Party, says that while he resigned his official positions he [is] still the Leader of the Liberal Party, has told this to officials in the Colonial Office (who do not believe him) and he states that you [Halfyard] and Barnes deliberately left St. John's so that you would not sit at Council meeting [sic] with me at my final meeting before coming to the Conference, because you were so disgusted with the way in which I was mismanaging matters.[32]

But these curious off-stage struggles failed to have any visible effect.

Since it was impossible, in a community as small and as saturated with politics as Newfoundland, to appoint a commissioner whose impartiality would not be open to doubt, Warren sensibly approached the British government with a request that they recommend a suitable person. Accordingly, on 22 December Mr Thomas Hollis Walker, KC, recorder of Derby, was commissioned and given all necessary authority to enquire into the following five specific allegations:

[1] ... that amounts paid to the Department of the Liquor Controller were not paid into the Treasury but were paid over to private individuals.
[2] ... that while negotiations were in progress between the Government ... and the Dominion Iron and Steel Company Ltd., and the Nova Scotia Steel and Coal Company Ltd., respectively, concerning the obligations of the said Companies to the Government, certain monies were paid to the then Prime Minister by the said Companies.
[3] ... of wrong-doing in the Department of Agriculture and Mines during the years 1922 and 1923 in relation to the expenditure made for the relief of destitution and known as 'Pit-Prop Account,' and also in relation to the expenditure upon the Model Farm.
[4] ... respecting the expenditure upon able-bodied poor relief by the Department of Public Charities during the years 1922 and 1923.

32/Warren Papers, Warren to Halfyard, 28 Sept. 1923.

[5] ... respecting expenditure by the Department of Public Works known as 'Relief Account No. 1' and 'Relief Account No. 2.'[33]

Within these terms of reference the commissioner was to find ample scope for a profound and far-reaching enquiry. The choice of Hollis Walker, moreover, turned out to be an extremely fortunate one; he brought to the task not only his remarkable skill as a cross-examiner but also qualities of painstaking thoroughness, courtesy, and at times a wry wit. Throughout the lengthy, involved, and often sensational public hearings which were held in St John's between January and March 1924,[34] his authority and impartiality were never challenged. His report, which was submitted to the cabinet on 20 March and published in full on the following day,[35] remains a classic document of the times, setting out in some twenty-five thousand words a damning indictment not only of the persons involved but of the political system under which they were able to flourish.

The commissioner's technique was simple: taking each of the five stated allegations in turn, he would probe relentlessly until the facts of the matter emerged. It is not possible here, nor would it serve any useful purpose, to review the immense volume of evidence upon which his report is based, but certain of his more important findings must be mentioned for the light they throw upon the politics of the period.

On the first allegation, that of graft in the Liquor Control Department, the commissioner's findings revealed above all the corrupting influence of prohibition. The department itself, he found, was little more than a legal 'front' for a large-scale bootlegging operation directed by the acting controller, J. T. Meaney, an ex-journalist of the *Daily Star* and appointee of Squires:

According to his own evidence, Mr. Meaney supplied liquors (*a*) against certificates of medical practitioners known as scripts, and (*b*) without scripts to any one who in his judgement needed (or wanted) it. He professed to regard

33/Newfoundland Archives, Administration of Squires, Warren, and Monroe, c. 1, f. 2, 'Commission to T. Hollis Walker, Esquire, κ.c.,' 22 Dec. 1923.

34/The hearings were held in the Chamber of the Legislative Council. Verbatim reports of all the proceedings were published in the St John's press (see, e.g., the *Daily News*, 7 Jan.–12 March 1923). Excellent comprehensive reports were also published in *The Times*.

35/Curiously, the *original* of the report is not to be found in the public records, nor in the Warren Papers. All quotations from the report are therefore taken from the copy which appeared in the St John's press, 22–3 March 1923. Though the disappearance of the original is to be regretted, there is absolutely no doubt that it was published accurately and in its entirety. It was divided into five sections, corresponding to the stated allegations. These are referred to here as Hollis Walker Report 1, Hollis Walker Report 2, etc.

sales without scripts as within his powers, but he was unable to show me, and I was unable to find, any provision which afforded any justification for the practice. It was further elicited from him that he was in the habit of making considerable presents of liquor from the stores in his charge without payment or promise or expectation of payment, and of receiving large sums by way of gratuity or secret commission from those who supplied liquor to the Department.[36]

The next question concerned the disposition of money received for sales made without scripts, for 'these sales ... were usually for cash, a small proportion only being credit transactions, and brought considerable sums of money into Mr. Meaney's hands.' Already the auditor general had pointed to 'a shortage for the two-year period (1921–22, 1922–23) of $200,366.15' and further noted that 'the Department was for the two years a cash charge upon the Revenue of the Dominion of $56,512.63.'[37] A chartered accountant employed to assist the investigation found that 'the absence of any stocktaking made it impossible ... to give precise figures' but the shortage 'was not less than 100,000 dollars, or dollars worth, and that it might be twice as much.' Whatever its exact amount, a large part of the missing money was never accounted for; but a significant portion of it Meaney admitted handing over to Miss Jean Miller, a young lady employed by Sir Richard Squires as his office accountant and with whom he shared a 'close and confidential business relationship.' The commissioner reported:

The total payments made by Mr. Meaney to Miss Miller were:
    (1) Against cheques ... $6,905.00
    (2) Against I.O.U.'s ... 19,325.76
    (3) Against deposit slip ... 500.00
Of this $3,100 may have been provided by Mr. Meaney himself, but I find that the balance of $23,630.76 was improperly paid by him out of the funds of the Department which ought to have been paid into the Treasury. A sum of $1,000 may have been returned to the Department after some months or weeks use, but more than $22,500.00 are still outstanding.

    I find that Miss Miller, though nothing was said as to the source from which the earliest payments came, was fully aware that the bulk of the money was taken from the funds of the Department.

    I find further that the whole of the money paid by Mr. Meaney to Miss

36/Hollis Walker Report 1.
37/Newfoundland Archives, Administration of Squires, Warren, and Monroe, c. 1, 'Report on the Department of the Controller,' July 1923, p. 4.

Miller was applied by her to the purpose of Sir Richard Squires and for his benefit.[38]

The only question that remained was whether Sir Richard was aware that the contributions and 'loans' supplied to Miss Miller on his behalf by Meaney came in fact from the funds of the Liquor Control Department. On this point the commissioner concluded:

Miss Miller did not say that she had ever told Sir Richard in so many words that the money was coming from the Liquor Control Department. According to her it was understood.

I find that it was. There was no need to tell him. It was obvious Sir Richard knew all about Mr. Meaney, his aggressive politics, his fluent pen and his slender purse.

Mr. Meaney had followed many callings. Immediately before he went to the Liquor Control he held a post on the Daily Star at $35.00 a week, and his income was supplemented by other journalistic work ... and occasional participation in lumber ventures; he was a poor man, and as Sir Richard intimated, he had to be fed and clothed by some one ... Sir Richard himself told me that no one could take large sums from Mr. Meaney ... without the strongest suspicion that public funds were being used, and that he would regard $4000 as a large sum. Yet in December, 1921, no less than $9000 was received for him from this source. I do not believe that he was ignorant of it, and I find:— That Sir Richard Squires realized in August, 1920, that money might be obtained for him through Mr. Meaney from the funds of the Liquor Department, and that after his return [Squires had been in England when the first payment was made into his account] he realized that it had been so obtained, and was being so obtained; that he accepted the use and benefit of over $20,000.00 so obtained with knowledge of their tainted history, and made himself a receiver and an accomplice in Mr. Meaney's wrong.[39]

The second allegation – that while negotiations were in progress with certain mining companies concerning their obligations to the government, certain monies were paid by them to the prime minister, Sir Richard Squires – was perhaps the most serious of all, and occupied the largest portion of the report. The origin of the charge may be traced to the expiry on 31 December 1919 of a ten-year agreement relating to taxation, safety standards in the mines and other conditions of work, and the provision of housing and other facilities for employees and their families, between the government and the two companies, Dominion Iron and Steel and Nova

38/Hollis Walker Report 1.   39/*Ibid.*

Scotia Steel and Coal,[40] which owned and operated iron mines at Wabana on Bell Island, about nine miles from St John's. Negotiations followed between the companies and the government on the terms of a new agreement, and continued intermittently until November 1920 when all the details were settled and a new contract signed, which relieved the companies of their more costly obligations to the miners and to the community.[41] Meanwhile,

the financial position of Sir Richard in the summer of 1920 was not satisfactory ... His office books were badly kept, and his banking accounts were confused. He was in sole control of the campaign funds of his party, but he kept no record of them or separate account for them. They were mixed up with his private affairs and the affairs of the Daily Star, an unsuccessful newspaper which he was financing; they had been depleted by a general election in 1919 ... and the only thing that is certain in this regard is that he was being called upon to pay out a great deal more than was being paid in.

At the time, two Canadian officials of the companies, Messrs McInnes and McDougall, were in St John's for the negotiations:

... it is clear that some information as to his [Squires's] financial position was conveyed to both Mr. McInnes and Mr. McDougall when they were in St. John's. Mr. McDougall at any rate desired to help him, and borrowed from Mr. McInnes for the purpose; early in June, 1920, the latter drew a cheque for $4000 on the Bank of Nova Scotia, and this having been cashed and a further $1000 added, a parcel containing $5000 was handed to Sir Richard Squires.

   In August the prime minister left for an extended visit to Europe, leaving his financial affairs in the hands of Miss Miller, whom, the report noted, he had 'armed with a wide power of attorney which enabled her to sign negotiable instruments on his behalf.' Also, by a remarkable coinci-

40/The report stated: 'It was also in contemplation that the two companies would shortly be federated or fused, their interests were identical and the agreement did not draw the slightest difference between them.' One of the directors of the Dominion Iron and Steel Company was Sir W. D. Reid, co-owner with his brother of the Reid Newfoundland Company, operators of the railway. Reid was unquestionably involved in the matter under the commissioner's terms of reference, but officials of the Bank of Nova Scotia, the only persons who could have illuminated his part in the affair, had been recalled to Canada, refused to return to testify, and could not be compelled to do so. No connection was established between the two aspects of Reid's relationship with Squires: railway matters were outside the scope of the inquiry.
41/Hollis Walker Report 2.

dence, Miss Miller's brother, J. J. Miller, happened to be a responsible local official of the Dominion company, and, 'During Sir Richard's absence Mr. Miller engaged in a series of transactions with the object and effect of relieving the financial pressure upon him, and the Bank of Nova Scotia in consequence transferred considerable sums of money, amounting in all to more than $43,000, from the account of the Dominion Company to that of Sir Richard Squires.' These were endorsed for deposit by Miss Miller, who gave her brother as receipts cheques drawn upon her employer's personal account; but upon his return Squires 'complained that the transaction should have been vouched for by a Daily Star cheque.' He subsequently took back his personal cheques and

handed to [Mr.] Miller what purported to be a Daily Star cheque for the agreed total of $46,065.05 dated 28th March, 1921. As a cheque, this document was worthless; it was insufficiently signed, it was on a bank where the Daily Star had no account and in fact the Daily Star had not at that time any funds in any bank. Sir Richard excused this transaction by telling me that the document was not intended to be used as a cheque, it was a mere receipt or voucher given to satisfy Mr. Miller's principals, that is to say, his company.

There was therefore no doubt as to Squires's complicity. The commissioner summarized his findings in these words:

The total sum was large; no other company had ever contributed more than $5000 to his campaign funds. It did not come from the pockets of individual officials whose political opinions might have coincided with his own, but from the resources owned by the Dominion Company in its corporate capacity; in reality it was the money of the shareholders of a Canadian corporation carrying on a very large undertaking of whose operations the works in Newfoundland were but a comparatively small portion. The Company as such had nothing to do with politics except in so far as its own business interests were affected, and the great if sole concern in this regard was to secure good terms in its contracts with the Government. In my view the handing over of the Company's money to the Prime Minister of Newfoundland at any time material to this issue could only have been with the hope and object of furthering the prospects of the Company by securing his favour, and that the recipient could not fail to realise it.

The third subject of the inquiry concerned 'wrongdoing in the Department of Agriculture and Mines,' and there investigations disclosed an almost unimaginable state of chaos and corruption. One notorious source of both was the 'pit-prop account,' the origin of which the commissioner traced to an order-in-council of 21 January 1921 relaxing the prohibition against the export of unmanufactured timber and authorizing, as an emergency relief measure to deal with the severe post-war depression, 'the purchase of timber cut upon ungranted Crown lands by any persons as may be approved by the Governor-in-Council.'

The administration of this order was entrusted to the Department of Agriculture and Mines (of which Dr. Campbell was the head) and kept in that Department under the title 'Pit Prop Account.' As time went on the relief work of the Department increased both in volume and variety. The Department itself conducted cutting operations, made contracts for rossing [that is, rinding] or selling wood ... provided work on unremunerative undertakings such as roads and bridges, and sought to increase food supplies by distributing seed potatoes.

The results from a financial point of view were disastrous. There are items still awaiting adjustment, and there are claims outstanding by and against the Department, but the total loss to the Colony up to the end of 1923 cannot be less than $1,200,000.[42]

One cause of the loss the commissioner attributed not so much to those who administered the funds as to those who received them. He referred to 'a deplorable public spirit shown by the people themselves; relief meant to them payments or supplies without work and men would secure supplies, work a few days and disappear; pilfering went on everywhere and always, and there were instances of schooners sailing into some quiet bay and taking away whole cargoes of wood ...' On the other hand there were serious abuses for which the minister of agriculture and mines was directly responsible. One of these concerned the purchasing of supplies for government-maintained logging camps:

... these were arranged and forwarded by the Minister himself and he distributed the patronage among a number of people in St. John's, many of them retail tradesmen in a small way of business and some of them not tradesmen at all. My attention was called to many of their prices which I found to be very much in excess of those ruling at the time among the bigger houses along Water Street ... and in my view much public money was thus wantonly wasted.

On other relief projects of a 'public works' nature, the commissioner did not criticize the minister's distribution of funds for such purposes through members of the Assembly, for this was in accordance with a well-established practice. However, he did point out that

42/Hollis Walker Report 3.

much of the $289,804 spent on this form of relief produced no return whatever. Many of those who received portions of this money have certainly failed to make the returns demanded of them, and it is impossible now to trace how much has been spent in direct relief and how much in work, and whether the whole ever reached those for whom it was intended. That it was possible to keep account of it was shown by the careful conduct of some of the members who at once paid the amounts received into a special account at a bank and were prepared with cheques and vouchers; but no such system was enjoined, and other recipients simply mixed the money up with their own, and there is nothing but their word to show how it was disbursed.

On the alleged misappropriation of funds by the minister himself the commissioner stated: 'I find that the allegation that Dr. Campbell paid his own private cab fares to a very substantial amount out of the public funds under his control is fully proved.' But even more remarkable was the minister's habit of bestowing gratuities upon the official from the auditor general's department who was sent to audit the books of his department:

In each of these cases the official from the audit department who actually conducted the audit was among the recipients of the minister's bounty. I do not say that he did not deserve it, but a practice under which a minister distributes among his staff at his own discretion presents from the public funds and adds a similar gift to the only person whose duty it is to check his actions seems to be fraught with mischievous possibilities and not to be in accordance with the law of the land.

The remaining subjects of the inquiry both related to expenditure on direct relief, particularly by the Department of Public Charities. The commissioner reported that

as the year 1923 advanced the work of the Department got completely out of hand ... the greatest distress was in January, February and March, but the demands were greatest in respect of April, the month before the Election; after that event the pressure was relaxed, and in a month or two the work was within bounds again. I have no doubt that a great deal of money did not go in necessary relief; it was not reserved for proper cases after due and searching enquiry; it was lavishly scattered broadcast with both hands for political purposes.[43]

Certain of his general remarks on the facts his investigations had revealed are also worthy of note:

43/Hollis Walker Report 5.

A candid witness had reminded me that I did not understand Newfoundland politics. At the outset of the enquiry this was undoubtedly true, but as time went on I came more and more to realize the great part played by politics in many of the matters which came up for discussion. The key to many of the problems with which I was confronted, the mainspring of many of the actions which I questioned was to be found in the word 'politics.'[44]

His report concluded: 'Nor is it enough to say that the accusations out of which this enquiry arose were raked up by political rivals or malcontents. By whatever means the evils which have tainted the past and are threatening the future of Newfoundland have been brought to light, the light has shown that they exist.'

Coming after so much sensational testimony, the report attracted wide attention even outside the island. 'It makes singularly unpleasant reading,' commented *The Times*, 'and not even the best friends of Newfoundland will attempt to minimize the extreme gravity of all that it has revealed.' With this there could be no quarrel, nor with its comments on the case of Sir Richard Squires: 'That it should have been possible to level such accusations against the Prime Minister of a great Dominion of the Crown seems incredible; that it should have been possible to prove them is nothing short of a tragedy.'[45] But if tragedy it was, the last act had yet to be played.

1924: 'NEWFOUNDLAND'S OPPORTUNITY'[46]

'Our civil service,' commented an anonymous wag on the royal commission's findings, 'resembled the military service of Mexico – little pay but unbounded licence to plunder.'[47] This pardonable exaggeration was not untypical of the public's reaction: politics had long been regarded as 'a dirty game'; now it was proved. The only questions remaining were whether the sordid revelations of the inquiry could arouse a strong and genuine desire for reform, and if they could, who would be entrusted with the task?

The likeliest candidate was the prime minister, William Warren. His political position, it seemed, could only have been strengthened by the outcome of the inquiry. In precipitating the whole affair, he and his three

44/Hollis Walker Report 3.
45/*The Times*, 22 March 1924.
46/Leading article in *The Times*, 29 April 1924.
47/Letter to the editor of the *Evening Telegram*, St John's, 24 March 1924.

colleagues, Halfyard, Barnes, and Foote, had risked their political careers; but, as they had no doubt hoped, the commissioner's report provided more than ample vindication of all that they had done. Warren therefore seemed to be adopting a politically safe, necessary, and practically unavoidable policy when he announced on 8 April that the government had decided 'to continue the work of investigations into the various departments of the Civil Service.'[48] Many new lines of inquiry had been suggested during the commission hearings which, because they lay outside its terms of reference, had not been followed up. The Department of the Auditor General and the Posts and Telegraphs Department, among others, had shown up badly and were mentioned by the prime minister as subjects for a new inquiry. The prime minister also indicated that there would be criminal prosecutions arising out of the royal commission report, and that these would most likely be instituted after the new investigations had been concluded.[49]

Public opinion, the government could reasonably expect, would be behind it; Squires, despite his angry protests that the royal commission's findings 'were absolutely absurd and contrary to the evidence' and that 'from the beginning to end it was a purely political affair,'[50] was under threat of arrest and hardly seemed capable of rallying widespread support, even if he had the audacity to try; and the Liberal Reform and Unionist members of the Assembly, who had unanimously supported Warren *before* the inquiry, in the light of its findings could hardly desert him *after* it. Thus, to all appearances, Warren seemed assured of parliamentary support. But appearances were deceptive. His ministry fell on the day the legislature opened.

Its fall resulted from a bizarre series of events which is perhaps unique in the history of parliamentary government. On 22 April, two days before the legislature was due to open, a rumour reached the prime minister to the effect that certain members of his party were contemplating defection in order to bring down the government and stifle the impending prosecutions. Apparently to forestall such a move, Warren authorized the immediate arrest of Sir Richard Squires, Dr Campbell, and several civil servants, all of whom were charged with larceny.[51] Squires, however, was released on $40,000 bail. Meanwhile, at a meeting of the government caucus on the same night (22 April) two members were unaccountably absent. They were Richard Cramm, a Liberal Reform member, and

48/*Evening Advocate*, 8 April 1924.
49/*Evening Telegram*, 9 April 1924.
50/*Ibid.*, 21 April 1924.
51/*Ibid.*, 22 April 1924; *The Times*, 23 April 1924. Squires was charged with the larceny of $20,000.

George Jones, a Unionist, both of whom on the following day announced that they intended to support Squires.[52] On the next day, when the House opened, it was discovered that two other Liberal Reform members, E. Simmons and A. M. Calpin, both of whom had pledged to support the government at the caucus meeting, had also defected. When Cramm moved, and Calpin seconded, a motion of want of confidence it was carried by one vote – the marginal vote being supplied by Squires himself![53]

Neither the action of the four members who crossed the floor of the House to support Squires, nor the action of the opposition in co-operating with them to bring down the government, have ever been adequately explained. Predictably, the defectors were vehemently denounced by a section of the press, with the *Evening Advocate* going so far as to claim that 'Mr. Cramm has shown himself of the same calibre as Mr. Calpin and Mr. Simmons, who at Tuesday night's party meeting (when they pledged themselves to support the Government) intimated that all they wanted was cash, and if the Government was prepared to pay for their support the Government would have it.'[54]

Whatever the truth of this libellous allegation, it was never contradicted; but not even the *Advocate* would venture to explain the behaviour of the opposition. There was no hint of bribery in their case, and still less of personal regard for Squires. Why then did they support, or appear to support, him? A tentative explanation – though no more than that, in the absence of any clear statement from the opposition itself – can be found in the general twist of political fortune after the Hollis Walker inquiry. From the opposition's point of view, the results could not have been entirely satisfactory: they had performed the duties of an opposition with great effectiveness, the struggle against Squires had been initiated by them, yet it was not their leader, W. J. Higgins, but William Warren, a former associate of Squires, who had somehow emerged with the politically valuable image of 'the honest reformer.' Thus, in the face of Warren's growing stature as prime minister, the opposition – unexpectedly confronted with a chance to force an early election – decided that it would be to their advantage to do so.[55]

52/*Evening Telegram*, 24 April 1924.
53/*Proceedings of the House of Assembly, Newfoundland, 1924*, p. 16; *Evening Telegram*, 25 April 1924. Two members from each side of the House were absent. Those voting in the division were, *for*: Cramm, Calpin, Simmons, Jones (all defectors from the government side) and the following members of the opposition, Higgins, Sir M. Cashin, P. J. Cashin, Walsh, Sullivan, Sinnott, P. F. Moore, J. Moore, Harris, Vinnicombe, Woodford – and Squires; *against*: Warren, Coaker, Halfyard, Barnes, Cave, Hawco, Downey, Foote, Grimes, Hibbs, Brown, Scammell, Winsor, Abbott, Randell.
54/25 April 1924.
55/They could hardly have hoped to take office. The constitutional case for a

Warren was immediately granted a dissolution, with the date of the general election being set for 2 June. In the interval, however, the election campaign was practically forgotten; instead, politicians of all parties engaged in a wild scramble for office, scarcely moving outside the capital for fear of missing their place in the game of musical chairs. The scene was one of unprecedented confusion. Factions mysteriously took shape, and just as mysteriously evaporated; the puzzling combinations of one day became the bitter feuds of the next, and vice versa. Party politics became meaningless; the party system, such as it was, had disintegrated.

For this William Warren must bear a large share of the responsibility. His humiliating defeat seems to have had an unnerving effect upon him, for thereafter, in contrast to his earlier steadiness, his conduct was marked by political ineptitude. Admittedly, he faced a difficult situation. The desertions to Squires had, in effect, split the Liberal wing of the Liberal-Union alliance, leaving Warren with only seven Liberal supporters, one of whom, Dr Arthur Barnes, held a Union seat. But instead of hanging on with minority, and mainly Union, support, while trusting the electorate to punish the deserters, he instead began to cast about for new allies both within and without the Assembly. Among those he approached were Higgins, the opposition leader,[56] and, more obviously, an extra-parliamentary group composed of prominent St John's merchants and exporters, and some ex-ministers of the Cashin government, including J. R. Bennett, the defeated opposition leader in 1923. The effective leader of this group was Walter Monroe, a wealthy merchant and manufacturer who had never held a seat in Parliament.[57]

By attempting to reconcile this element with the Unionists, whose support he already had, Warren committed a politically fatal error. The two were irreconcilable, and he could not placate the one without antagonizing the other. Nothing more vividly conveys the difficulties with which he was faced, or the general atmosphere of intrigue, than his personal diary of events as he sought to form a new cabinet:

dissolution was beyond dispute, and there was no reason why Warren should not have asked for one.

56/This would seem to indicate that he regarded Squires, not the opposition, as the chief threat against which he had to guard, though both had been responsible for his defeat. *The Times* (29 April 1924) was understandably puzzled: 'For those who view Newfoundland politics from this distance the latest news from St. John's does not make things easier to understand. Mr. Higgins, having accepted Sir Richard Squires's help in defeating Mr. Warren's Government, is apparently now negotiating with Mr. Warren in the formation of a union against Sir Richard Squires.'

57/In the 1923 general election he had been an unsuccessful Liberal-Labour-Progressive (i.e., Conservative) candidate in Bonavista. He was minister without portfolio (without a seat in either House) in Warren's 'four day' cabinet in May 1924.

Tuesday Morning – Apl. 29.

Monroe dropped out and then Higgins assured me he wd join with Coaker & self and I was to endeavour to get Water St. support as Monroe had dropped out. After Council meeting I told this to Coaker, Cave & Foote at Coaker's house & thought the matter was settled.

Wednesday Morning – Apl. 30.

I neither saw nor heard from Higgins or Coaker until one o'clock. In the meantime I saw Mr. Ayre & Mr. Outerbridge [two merchants] both of whom promised their support. Mr. Ayre said he wd like to see Mr. Monroe again and persuade him to come in. At one p.m. I was asked by Sir M. P. Cashin to come to his house. I found Sir Wm. Coaker, Higgins & Cashin there, Monroe was invited to come & express his views which he did – refusing to have anything to do with the F.P.U. Without knowing what had taken place between Coaker, Higgins & Cashin & without any intimation from either Higgins or Coaker, Higgins informed me that the Opposition wd not have anything to do with any Coaker candidate and they wd side with Monroe. Coaker on the advice of Cashin said he wd call his crowd together & advise them to keep out of it. Although I argued with Monroe against the course he was taking I was not consulted at all. I rang up Monroe [later, obviously] and asked him not to commit himself. Later Scammell [a Unionist MHA] rang me up & told me that Sir Wm. Coaker had asked him to tell me that they had had a meeting but had come to no decision. I did not know what was going on.[58]

The outcome was finally made clear on 3 May. Warren broke with the Union and formed a new ministry including both Higgins and Monroe. Apart from the prime minister, the only member of the previous cabinet to retain office was Matthew Hawco, who continued as minister of posts and telegraphs.

Warren, it turned out, had not only antagonized the Unionists – he had also abandoned, or been abandoned by, his own supporters in the Liberal party, including W. H. Cave and Dr Barnes. These two factions now found it expedient to reunite under a new leader and call themselves the 'Liberal-Progressive Party.'[59] However, their new leader was neither a Unionist nor a Liberal – and still less a 'progressive'; he was Albert Hickman, one of the merchant group whom Warren had neglected to include in the cabinet![60]

58/Warren Papers, vol. I, notes, 29 April–3 May 1924.
59/*Evening Advocate*, 3 May 1924.
60/Hickman had had a chequered political career. In 1919 he had contested the district of Bay de Verde as an 'anti-Squires' candidate. There were irregularities in the voting, and in a case decided before the Supreme Court in May 1920 he was found guilty of corrupt practices. In 1923 he had unsuccessfully contested the district of Harbour Grace as an 'anti-Coaker' candidate.

William Coaker, meanwhile, had announced his retirement from politics, but publicly gave Hickman his 'warmest support,' and presumably the whole of the Union's electoral machine. The campaign appeared to be on:

Last evening [reported *The Times* correspondent in a despatch dated 4 May] Mr. Warren seemed assured of an almost unopposed victory at the elections; now he faces a combination which may be really formidable. Mr. Warren has the advantage of enjoying the possession of the control of the election machinery, which is a valuable asset in this country, but the opposition is making the most of the sectional aspect of the campaign and concentrating its efforts on the capture of the northern districts. Newfoundland somewhat resembles Ireland in regard to its racial and political problems; hence the original issues arising out of the Governmental scandals are rapidly being obscured by others which are entirely different and are the outcome of the partisan and personal animosities engendered by the present struggle.[61]

Yet on the very day the above despatch was filed another political upheaval was in the making.

The government, and Warren personally, had come under blistering attack by both the Union and the pro-Squires newspapers, and, more seriously, because of its alleged 'Catholic domination' it was having difficulty even in finding candidates to contest seats in solidly Protestant areas. Its position thus grew increasingly precarious, until Matthew Hawco's sudden resignation on the morning of 7 May brought it toppling down – just four days after it had been sworn in.[62]

'The position now,' stated the *Advocate* with satisfaction but not inaccurately, 'is that the Hon. W. R. Warren has gone alone to the enemy's side, is unsupported by a single elected member of his old Executive, and has been utterly disavowed by the whole rank and file of his former party following in the House of Assembly.'[63]

Warren's eventful premiership had come to its end, but it was by no means clear who would succeed him. In a remarkable admission of political bankruptcy, the first call, like an echo from the past, went out to Sir Robert Bond, the ageing recluse of Whitbourne. When he declined,

61/ *The Times*, 5 May 1924.
62/ Hawco explained his resignation in these words: 'I was not fully cognizant of the political shuffling taking place in connection with the formation of your Ministry, and it is [sic] only when I arrived at Government House for the purpose of taking the oath of office, that I discovered that your Cabinet and Party were not of the political faction that I expected it would be.' Hawco to Warren, as published in the *Daily Mail*, 7 May 1924.
63/ 7 May 1924.

Warren advised the governor to send for Coaker; he too declined but advised the governor to send for Hickman, who was duly commissioned to form a government. It was widely reported, however, that in commissioning Hickman Governor Sir William Allardyce had 'stipulated that the prosecutions arising out of Mr. Hollis Walker's report should be unflinchingly carried out,'[64] and the eventual composition of the Hickman cabinet suggests that some such undertaking was in fact given. Of its nine members (besides Hickman) four were known supporters of Squires; three, Halfyard, Barnes, and Cave, were former ministers in Squires's cabinet who had supported Warren in the previous July and were now of unknown or uncertain allegiance; but, significantly, the other two were Sir William Lloyd, an ex-premier, and L. E. Emerson, a lawyer not previously involved in politics who had earlier been engaged as government counsel to conduct the pending prosecution of Squires. Their inclusion was obviously intended to allay the Governor's fears that the prosecutions might not be pressed.

The opponents of the new government rallied not to Warren, who later stood as an 'Independent' candidate, but to Walter Monroe, and at a public meeting in St John's elected him leader of the 'Liberal-Conservative Party.'[65] It was, in fact, a true merchant party of the nineteenth century type, an *ad hoc* group created, dominated, and financed by the Water Street interests, whose preoccupations it unmistakably reflected in its policies.

Monroe's manifesto contained the almost mandatory pledge that 'the Public Enquiry whose work has been so well begun ... shall be promptly and vigourously continued to the end,' but in his view 'the really acute issue' was none other than this: 'Shall Coakerism, naked and unashamed, be permitted to continue and to increase its control over our public affairs, or shall a change be wrought for the people?' The candidates of the government, he maintained, 'are put forward in the name of Hickman, but are the chosen tools of Coaker.' Finally, in his remarks on the fishery he laid bare the gist of his political beliefs, a rosy merchant-conservative view of society: 'They [the fishermen] and I are in business together; they to catch, I to export. If they prosper, I prosper. If their energies and rewards decrease, so will mine. We have a common interest and a common cause, and should work together for the common good. This is a fisherman's paradise, and we should work together for the good of each other.' But even in paradise there were dangers, especially if a government were returned 'whose master and chief members, by the infamous Fishery Regu-

64/ *The Times*, 10 May 1924.
65/ *Daily News*, 11 May 1924.

lations of 1920, struck a most deadly blow to the prosperity of our country.'[66]

However, it would be impossible to maintain that the election was fought on this or any other clear issue. In a campaign marked by extraordinary confusion and uncertainty, and following upon so many unexplained or outrageous shifts in the centre of power, many of the electorate either turned away from politics or were intensely moved by irrelevant passions. Sectarianism and – towards the end – the re-emergence of Richard Squires as a political force, became the most salient and significant features.

The former played a curious part. The government at first appeared to have the advantage of being the 'Protestant' party, while the opposition seemed likely to suffer from a 'pro-Catholic' image, however unjustified – Monroe was a Protestant, as were the other leading figures in the party, with the notable exception of Higgins. But in forming his cabinet Hickman had made one omission that proved to be disastrous. Like every premier, he was faced with more 'dangerous men' than there were cabinet posts: the key to success was to strike the right combination. On 13 May the grand master of the Orange Lodge, F. Gordon Bradley, a supporter of Squires and government candidate for Port de Grave, left the party and announced that he would instead contest the seat for the opposition on the grounds that he had not been 'consulted' (that is, included) when the cabinet was formed.[67] With this one stroke the opposition's greatest electoral disability was removed.

On the other hand, Bradley's support was not an unmixed blessing, for it also signalled the introduction of a new element into the campaign – the open and energetic intervention of Richard Squires.

'Party Lines Hopelessly Confused' ran the headline in Squires's newspaper, the *Daily Mail*, on 16 May. 'For the Liberals of Newfoundland there is one course, and one course only, open,' claimed the *Mail*, 'and that is to support Liberal candidates [that is, supporters of Squires] ... In the Hickman Party there are some strong Liberals; likewise in the Monroe Party.' Nine of these were named,[68] and, with their implicit acknowledgment, or at least without their repudiation, Squires publicly campaigned on their behalf. Another tactic employed by the Squires forces as polling day approached was to discredit the Hollis Walker Report by denigrating

66/'Manifesto of W. S. Monroe,' *Evening Telegram*, 15 May 1924.
67/*Daily Mail*, 13 May 1924.
68/They were F. Gordon Bradley, R. Cramm (Monroe party), C. A. Forbes, T. Ashbourne, J. F. Downey, A. M. Calpin, J. Fitzgibbon, R. Dowden, A. V. Duffy (Hickman party).

the governor, charging that he had acted unconstitutionally in giving a dissolution to Warren, and that:

The attitude of His Excellency is not surprising, in view of what is now public knowledge, namely, that in September he refused a broad Commission of Enquiry and issued a narrow one; in December he cancelled the narrow Commission ... and issued a still narrower one, so deliberately worded and planned that, to quote Mr. Cramm's remark ... 'It was a Commission designed by Mr. Warren to "get" his former leader.'[69]

The allegation was utterly baseless, but served its purpose. In the ceaseless and cynical shuffling to and fro of politicians after the fall of Warren's first ministry, the judicial impartiality of the Hollis Walker Report was gradually obscured. The political process itself fell into disrepute, and to many Squires seemed no more reprehensible that any other politician: if the governor too was part of the conspiracy against him, might it not also be true, as the *Mail* claimed, that 'the only attempt to clean up a political mess was done by Sir Richard Squires, who, rather than surrender to sinister influences resigned the Premiership of Newfoundland?'[70]

The campaign, such as it was, ended in farce and violence; the election took place amid police preparations to deal with rioting. The cause of the disturbance was a ludicrous sectarian circular of dubious origin, charging, among other things, that 'a mob of drunken Sinn Feiners' were responsible for breaking up an election meeting of the Hickman party. When the circular was read at a meeting of the Monroe candidates in St John's, to refute it a mob of drunken 'Sinn Feiners' actually did attack the offices of the *Advocate*.[71]

The election itself was mainly remarkable for the apathy shown by the electorate. In a country where normally 80 to 90 per cent of those eligible exercised their franchise, only 67 per cent went to the polls. The opposition party secured twenty-five seats, the government ten, and William Warren was returned as an Independent. The government conspicuously failed to win a single 'Catholic' seat; all but two of its successful candidates represented the Union north. Even there, the opposition made significant gains; Bonavista, a Union stronghold since 1913 fell to Monroe by a substantial margin.[72]

For Sir Richard Squires the results were ambiguous. Of the nine 'true

69/ *Daily Mail*, 23 May 1924.
70/31 May 1924.
71/ *Evening Telegram*, 1 June 1924; *The Times*, 2 June 1924.
72/ However, the three government candidates, C. A. Forbes, A. Barnes, and L. T. Stick, were not Unionists, and William Coaker played no part in the campaign.

Liberals' he had endorsed only three were successful, but two of these, Richard Cramm and F. Gordon Bradley, were his most powerful supporters, and both were elected for the Monroe party, with strong claim to be included in the next ministry.

1925-8: A CONSERVATIVE INTERLUDE

I am no plausible, professional politician, no writer of pleasing promises intended to corrupt an electorate, but a plain man of business ...

The Manifesto of W. S. Monroe, 15 May 1924

The new government which took office in June 1924 possessed a clear majority of fourteen and a clear mandate 'to clean up, keep clean, and to give stable government.' The new prime minister, who was in the unusual position of entering Parliament for the first time, was not well known; but in seeking election he had promised, if successful, to form a ministry 'filled with reforming zeal and energy' and pledged to 'a policy of wise economy and retrenchment.'[73] It is therefore in the light of such statements that the composition of his cabinet must be viewed.

Were it not for the presence of Monroe himself – of whom it can be said that lack of political experience was no handicap but rather a mark of virtue – it would be difficult to imagine a more unconvincing group of 'reformers.' They were an anomalous mixture, comprising a Catholic element led by W. J. Higgins, minister of justice; two followers of Squires, Cramm and Bradley, ministers without portfolio; and a dominating group of nouveau riche or first-generation St John's 'Torics,' the most prominent of whom – Sir John Crosbie, minister of finance, and J. R. Bennett, colonial secretary – had their political origins in the People's party of Edward Morris where, even by the standards of that régime, they had been among the more unsavoury elements. Yet they were powerful, financially, socially, and politically; Monroe could not have excluded them, nor is there any suggestion that he wished to do so. On the contrary, they were his most trusted advisers, his 'inner cabinet.' And finally, as if to emphasize his ministry's political heritage, Monroe appointed as legislative councillor and minister without portfolio the ageing A. B. Morine, a durable survivor of the last purely 'merchant' government, that of Sir James Winter in 1897–1900.

For any radical reform of the existing political order to have emerged

73/*Evening Telegram*, 15 May 1924.

from an aggregation such as this would have been little short of miraculous. So far from being enemies of the old system, they were its quintessential products; their habits of political thought and behaviour had been moulded by it; under it, and indeed to a large degree *because* of it, they had materially prospered and risen to positions of political power. It is hardly surprising, therefore, that they should have shown neither the will nor the imagination to carry out substantial alterations.[74]

To say this is not to suggest that the whole record of the Monroe administration, which continued until 1928, contained no useful or beneficial measures. But it *is* to suggest that these were mainly peripheral, or else – like the extension of the franchise to women[75] – important in their own right though largely irrelevant to the problems at hand. The one exception, perhaps, was the repeal of prohibition, a campaign promise Monroe promptly carried out at his first legislative session.[76] This, however, was a reform that would probably have been made no matter who had formed the government. Hickman had also come out in favour of repeal, but held that another plebiscite would be necessary to determine whether the electorate wished to reverse their decision of 1915. The abuses arising from the 'noble experiment' had helped bring the law, politics, and even, because of their indiscriminate sale of 'prescriptions,' the medical profession into disrepute; after the Hollis Walker inquiry, in particular, with its revelations of how far the corruption had spread, there arose an overwhelming consensus in favour of repeal.

In another area, too, the Monroe administration was the instrument of a change that would most likely have taken place in any event – the redistribution of seats in the Assembly. This necessary enactment brought parliamentary representation closer in line with the actual distribution of population as indicated by the decennial census of 1921, increased the number of seats to forty, and eliminated all three-member constituencies (of which there had previously been seven), and reduced the number of two-member constituencies from four to two.[77]

74/The government was, however, an uncompromising defender of the sanctity of private property: in 1927 Sir Robert Bond died, leaving his Whitbourne estate to the people of Newfoundland for recreation and agricultural research. The government refused to accept the bequest for fear it would set a 'dangerous precedent.'
75/The measure did not give women the same voting rights as men; only those over twenty-five years of age were enfranchised.
76/*Proceedings of the House of Assembly, Newfoundland, 1924*, pp. 31–5. It is worth noting, however, that the minister responsible for the act, J. R. Bennett, colonial secretary, was also co-owner of the largest brewery in St John's – which had been idle since 1917 except for the production of a beverage called 'near-beer.'
77/However, because of the importance attached to religious denominations, representation was not strictly in accordance with population. See G. O. Rothney,

But neither the legal sale of liquor nor legislative redistribution, however valuable and long overdue, were capable of effecting the sweeping reforms in the conduct of public administration which had been so widely advocated after the Hollis Walker Report. It was soon clear that not even these were typical measures. The new government's idea of 'reform' turned out in practice to be as euphemistic as that of its predecessors; its accession to office was attended by widespread dismissals from the public service of allegedly corrupt or incompetent officials, very few of which were ever brought to trial. Their replacements were political appointees, with nothing to show that they were in any way better qualified. It all looked like the usual distribution of spoils. Civil service reform was duly debated in both Houses of the legislature – and promptly forgotten.

Nor was any halt put to the practice whereby members of the executive and the governing party in effect rewarded themselves with extra 'fees' in addition to their salaries for the performance of services to the government, usually of a legal or business nature. Even the 'reformed' office of the liquor commissioner, a civil service post to which N. J. Vinnicombe had been appointed, thus causing him to vacate his seat in St John's East where he had been elected as a Monroe candidate, turned out to be little different from its predecessor. No 'loans' were made to members of the government, but bulk purchases of liquor were made not directly from the manufacturers but indirectly through various newly established 'commission agents' – one of whom happened to be a member of the executive, others were members of the governing party in the Assembly, or well-known party supporters.[78]

There was, however, one very important field – that of taxation and tariffs – in which clear ideas of reform were allowed to prevail and were vigorously and uncompromisingly carried through. It was obvious that Newfoundland's tax structure, which resulted in 80 to 90 per cent of government revenue being derived from customs duties and other forms of indirect taxation, was a dangerously unbalanced and unstable means of public finance, quite apart from its internal anomalies and its basically regressive nature. 'The Customs Tariff requires rearrangement,' Monroe had ambiguously asserted in his election manifesto, and 'if given power, I shall cause a careful investigation to be made into the way in which improvement can best be made in the financial methods of the country.'[79]

'The Denominational Basis of Representation in the Newfoundland Assembly, 1919–1962,' *Canadian Journal of Economics and Political Science*, vol. 28, no. 4 (Nov. 1962), pp. 557–70.

78/The minister involved was M. S. Sullivan, minister without portfolio. See the *Globe*, St John's, 14 May 1925.

79/*Evening Telegram*, 15 May 1924.

Accordingly, in February 1925 the government introduced its proposal for financial reform. The most burdensome tax, it had evidently decided, was the *income tax*, in fact an extremely modest measure originally introduced in 1918. This it proposed to abolish altogether. Another proposed reform was a sharp reduction in the tax on banks. Thus, the general effect was to reduce still further the government's meagre revenue from direct taxation. To compensate for the reduction it was proposed to fulfil Monroe's promise to 're-arrange' the tariff.

Total revenue from this traditional source was to be increased by an estimated $1,500,000, but even more significant were the particular changes made, for tariffs necessarily have a double effect: besides raising revenue, they also give protection to domestic manufacturers where these exist. It is noteworthy, therefore, that among the items on which import duties were raised were cigarettes and tobacco; rope, twines, and fishing nets; and butter and margarine.[80]

For it then became apparent that in the process of enacting 'financial reforms' not only had a cabinet containing some of the country's wealthiest men abolished the income tax, but they had also increased tariffs to the direct benefit of manufacturing concerns in which the prime minister himself was largely interested. It was no secret that W. S. Monroe held a substantial interest in the Imperial Tobacco Company of St John's; he was also the major shareholder in the Colonial Cordage Company, the country's only manufacturer of rope, twines, and fishing nets. Finally, shortly after the increase in tariffs became effective the minister of finance, Sir John Crosbie, invested heavily in the construction of a margarine factory.[81]

Predictably, and understandably, the government's newly revealed notion of reform provoked strong opposition protests, particularly from the Unionist members; but more politically ominous was the reaction of one of the governments own backbench supporters, Major Peter Cashin, MHA for Ferryland. He refused to support a measure which he regarded as being 'in direct contradiction of the policy I championed before my constituents, and on which I was sent to this House only a year ago,' and accused the prime minister of enacting 'class legislation of the rankest kind.'

The Income Tax had been expunged, and in its place we have a new tariff that will bleed the people white ... The Prime Minister is here with a tariff policy that gives the Ropewalk [Colonial Cordage Company] and Imperial Tobacco

80/*Proceedings of the House of Assembly, Newfoundland, 1925*, p. 9 ff.
81/Smallwood, *The Book of Newfoundland*, II, 377.

Company a protection which amounts to monopoly ... Mr. Monroe is a large shareholder in both these concerns, who [sic] are already making tremendous profits out of the fishermen and labouring classes.[82]

The prime minister testily replied that he 'felt the honourable member was opposed to the Government and thought the best place for the member was on the opposite side of the House.'[83] Cashin promptly obliged.

The government had suffered its first defection but not its last. By refusing to 'compromise its principles' on the tariff issue it had destroyed the last small illusion there may have been that it really intended to reform anything of consequence. Monroe's image was shattered. Less than a year after taking power he and his ministry stood revealed as another merchant junta, zealously dedicated to their own financial self-interest and the interests of their class. Public confidence in the government waned and as it waned opposition grew stronger, not only in the north where the Union movement was showing signs of resurgence, but also in the south and even in St John's. This soon produced results in the Assembly, where weak party lines were notoriously apt to crack under political pressure from outside. In the spring of 1926 the tenuous stability restored by the 1924 general election suddenly disintegrated: overnight the government's safe majority totally vanished with the defection of five members, one of whom was F. Gordon Bradley, minister without portfolio.[84]

With the Speaker in the chair, seventeen members now sat on either side of the House, but with the support of William Warren (Independent, Fortune) the government was able to survive. A month later, on 29 June, it managed to acquire a slim majority once more by inducing an opposition member, R. Duff of Carbonear, to cross the floor and fill the cabinet seat vacated by Bradley. Finally, the government decided to run the calculated risk of holding a by-election in St John's East, where in 1924 the Liberal-Conservative candidate with the lowest vote possessed a clear majority of 2,287. If any seat in the country was safe for the government, this was

82/Proceedings of the House of Assembly, Newfoundland, 1925, pp. 40–1.
83/Ibid.
84/The circumstances surrounding the split are obscure. Bradley and C. E. Russell, minister of public works (without cabinet rank), appear to have been engaged in a movement to overthrow Monroe, who became aware of their efforts and demanded their resignations. In resigning, both alleged that the government was in the hands of a 'small coterie' of which they were not a part (the Globe, 22 May 1926). They were followed into opposition by three others: P. F. Moore (Ferryland), J. L. Little (Bonavista), and H. B. C. Lake (Burin). Little's letter to the prime minister casts some light on earlier events: he charged that the alleged conspiracy was nothing more than 'a meeting of some of your supporters to discuss public affairs' (quoted in the Globe, 25 May 1926).

likely to be the one. But even here the government had suffered a humiliating loss of support; the seat fell to the opposition.[85] It was clearly a vote of non-confidence in Monroe and presaged the end of his premiership. He managed to hold on to office for another year, but as the government drifted towards the end of its term he announced his intention to withdraw from public life. In August 1928 the 'plain man of business' quietly handed over the premiership to a successor of his own choosing, who was, not unfittingly, his nephew and business associate, Frederick C. Alderdice.[86] After four years in power, Monroe left behind a state of affairs remarkably unchanged from that which he had inherited. Patronage remained the basis of public administration; the conflict of interests on matters affecting members of the cabinet was as ignored as at any time in the past; expenditure on relief projects, with highway construction taking the place of pit-prop cutting, was again on the rise; the budget remained unbalanced; and the public debt continued to mount. On average, new loans were raised during the period 1924–8 at the rate of approximately $4 million per year. By the fiscal year 1927–8 more than 40 per cent of total revenue was required to meet interest payments on the accumulated debt.[87]

Meanwhile, the public's disillusionment and growing hostility towards the government created ideal conditions for the rise of a new leader who could channel these feelings to his own political advantage. But as time went on it became increasingly apparent that the likely beneficiary was going to be no 'new' man but rather the familiar figure of Richard Squires.

After his arrest in 1924, Squires had successfully fought against being committed to stand trial. In preliminary hearings, a grand jury at St John's refused to indict him on the charge of larceny on the grounds of insufficient evidence, a decision the Supreme Court later upheld.[88] And though subsequently convicted and fined on the much less serious charge of income tax evasion,[89] he was otherwise cleared and free to resume a political career. In December 1924 a new political newspaper called the *Globe*, a successor of the *Daily Star* and the *Daily Mail*, began to appear, not overtly supporting Squires, but declaring itself to be 'opposed, politically,

85/W. E. Brophy (opposition), 5,034; J. C. Barter (government), 4,483. St John's East was described by *The Times* (22 April 1927) as 'the largest, most representative and most influential district in the Island. Within it are several fishing villages and most of the manufacturing centres. It is also the headquarters of most of the mercantile companies and the home of the professional and leisured classes.'

86/*Evening Telegram*, 22 July 1928.

87/Interest of $3,841,922 was paid out of a total revenue of $9,466,005. Cmd 4480, *Report*, pp. 57, 63.

88/*Evening Telegram*, 9, 13 Oct. 1924. Dr Campbell was later committed to trial but a jury returned a verdict of not guilty.

89/*Ibid.*, 30, 31 Nov. 1925.

from the first page of this and every subsequent issue to the last, to the Monroe Administration.'[90] By July 1925 Squires had succeeded in being elected grand master of the Orange Lodge; and by the end of the year his former ally, William Coaker, was preparing the ground for a new combination with appeals to 'those opposed to the Government to get together and produce a new party.'[91] And though absent from the Assembly, Squires was undoubtedly able to make his influence felt within it. He may not in fact have engineered the split in the government ranks in 1926, but neither was he unconnected with it. The most prominent rebel, F. Gordon Bradley, was his close associate, and with several of the others who crossed the floor, including Peter Cashin, later formed the nucleus of a new Squires party.

But before this could take shape, one last stumbling block had to be removed: that was the official leader of the opposition, Albert Hickman. However, since he held this position only by virtue of the support given him by the Unionists, it followed that if Squires were reunited with Coaker the leadership could be taken from Hickman whenever Coaker determined. This was in fact the pattern of events. In May 1928 nine members of the opposition, seven of them Unionists or holders of Union seats, deserted Hickman and notified the Speaker of the House that they had formed a new party under the nominal leadership of the Unionist William Halfyard but supporting Richard Squires.[92] The 1928 election campaign had begun, with Squires as a principal contender.

90/16 Dec. 1924.
91/*Fishermen's Advocate*, St John's, 26 Nov. 1926 (report on proceedings of the FPU convention).
92/*Proceedings of the House of Assembly, Newfoundland, 1928*, pp. 203–10. The original members of this group were W. W. Halfyard, I. R. Randell, E. J. Godden, J. H. Scammell, K. M. Brown, G. F. Grimes, R. Hibbs, F. G. Bradley, and H. M. Mosdell.

12 The collapse of responsible government

IN 1928 the newly enlarged Newfoundland electorate was faced with a choice between Frederick C. Alderdice, another 'plain man of business' in so far as he was known at all, and Richard Squires, a familiar 'man of politics.' Their preference was clearly for the latter, whose party was returned with a majority of sixteen in the new forty-seat Assembly.[1] It was a personal triumph for Squires in a way that even his 1919 victory was not, for this time he was not overshadowed by William Coaker nor was his party dependent upon Union support to nearly the same extent. Though the two groups were once again allied with one another, in the election campaign their alliance had been discreetly underplayed; each fought as a separate party, but with the Union strictly confined to the north. In Squires's new campaign organ, the *Liberal Press*, Coaker's name was scarcely mentioned until after the election, when he was fulsomely acclaimed as a member of Squires's cabinet.[2] Of the twenty-eight seats won by the victorious combination, only nine were held by Unionists.[3]

It was thus a remarkable twist of fortune that saw a prime minister, who a mere four years before had seemed utterly discredited, come sweeping back into power with increased, and indeed almost overwhelming, popular support. Explanations of his success may vary: the judgment of the electorate may be taken to imply simply their preference for 'the devil they knew over the devil they did not'; or the choice offered them may be

1/Squires led a party of 28, Alderdice of 12, but in December 1928 the former's majority was increased to 18 following a by-election victory in Burgeo.

2/See the *Liberal Press*, St John's, 17 Nov. 1928.

3/The smaller proportion of Unionists cannot be attributed to the Redistribution Act, 1925. After the act there were 13 northern seats, but one of these returned an Alderdice Conservative and in three others Union support was given to Squires Liberals, one of whom was F. Gordon Bradley.

taken as reflecting 'the ultimate bankruptcy of public life' that Sir Robert Bond had been so fond of predicting; but above all it is clear that the return of Squires was not merely a victory for him and a defeat for Alderdice; it was also the most damning verdict that could have been given on the record of Monroe's administration.

After four years of aggressively self-interested merchant rule, to many voters even Squires's gravest misdemeanours must have seemed like mere peccadilloes. Under Monroe there may have been less corruption (though even this is not beyond question), but positive achievements, such as the Humber development, were conspicuously lacking. Alderdice, as the heir of Monroe, stood only for the status quo of economic stagnation and dependence on the fisheries. Squires, on the other hand, stood for exciting new developments; he believed the island's economic salvation lay in industrialization – and the prosperous paper-making towns of the western interior seemed to prove him right. 'Who put the Hum on the Humber?' asked the Liberal election slogan, and the electorate answered 'Squires.'

Squires, however, was destined to have the misfortune of again assuming office at a time of impending economic crisis. For just as in 1919 his government had soon to face the post-war collapse of Newfoundland's vital European markets, so in 1928 his new government was soon to suffer the repercussions of a world depression.

But at the time, ironically, economic conditions seemed better than at any time since the end of the war. The period 1920 to 1928 had been one of general stagnation or only marginal improvement in the markets for Newfoundland's fishery products, but towards the end of the period increased exports of paper and minerals gradually raised the value of total exports back to near wartime levels, exceeding $30 million in 1926–7 for the first time since 1919–20.[4] During the next two years Newfoundland began to enjoy once more a modest degree of prosperity, and by 1928 the long anticipated economic upsurge seemed about to begin. Nor was such a view altogether groundless: a new lead and zinc mine, financed by American capital, was under construction at Buchans in the western interior, thus encouraging hopes of further development of mineral resources; in the previous year a decision of the Judicial Committee of the Privy Council had settled the protracted dispute over the location of the boundary separating Labrador from Canada by confirming Newfoundland's sovereignty over a vast territory nearly three times the size of the island itself and known to be endowed with valuable resources of timber, minerals, and water power. Moreover, even the fishery seemed well on the

4/See J. R. Smallwood, ed., *The Book of Newfoundland* (St John's, 1937), I, 325.

way to recovery. Prices were rising; Brazil had suddenly become a major customer, as it had been up to the end of the war, after which its market had drastically shrunk; and there were hopes of other new or revived markets in South America. All these various signs, which in retrospect seem no more than moderately promising, nevertheless (and perhaps characteristically) laid the foundations for another of Newfoundland's periodic outbursts of financial and economic self-confidence. 'It was felt,' the Amulree Report remarked of this period, 'that the old bogey of dependence on the fishery had been expelled for ever.'[5]

It was in such an atmosphere that the new Liberal ministry of Richard Squires took office in the autumn of 1928; once more the seriousness of the country's financial position could be evaded; the coming industrial miracle was expected to take care of all. Yet it could easily be seen, if anyone cared to look, that the government was operating on a continuous budget deficit, which it was managing to meet from year to year only by fresh borrowing, and that the national debt had grown so large that the annual interest upon it absorbed so high and increasing a proportion of current revenue as to render the prospect of a surplus extremely remote, if not impossible. Furthermore, since no administration after that of Sir Robert Bond had made provision for a sinking fund, the only way in which matured loans could be redeemed was by additional borrowing. The government, in fact, was caught in a vicious circle from which there could be no escape, barring an economic miracle that would inflate revenue without adding to expenditure. But, in spite of this, there was no shortage of willing lenders.[6] In 1928 Newfoundland was able to borrow without difficulty (and at an interest rate of 5 per cent) over $10 million in order to retire a war loan of approximately $7.5 million, the remainder being used to cover the current deficit and also for certain items of capital expenditure. In 1929 new loans amounted to just under $6 million, of which $2,885,000 was required to redeem a loan of 1905. Even after the stock market crash of 1929 Newfoundland's credit remained good. In 1930 another loan of $5 million was raised on favourable terms.[7]

Meanwhile, however, Newfoundland had begun to feel the effects of the depression in international trade. Fish prices dropped in 1930 to their

5/Cmd 4480, *Newfoundland Royal Commission 1933 Report* (London, 1933), p. 49. The chairman of the commission was Lord Amulree.
6/The situation was very similar to that described by J. K. Galbraith with reference to the willingness of New York bankers to make dubious loans to Central and South America: 'The underwriters' margins in handling these loans were generous; the public took them up with enthusiasm; competition for the business was keen.' *The Great Crash, 1929* (Penguin ed., London, 1961), pp. 197–9.
7/Five per cent interest, issued at 99. Cmd 4480, *Report*, pp. 51, 251.

lowest level since 1913[8] thus reducing incomes in general, and as incomes fell government revenue also fell, for incomes were largely spent on imported goods, on which *ad valorem* tariffs formed the main source of revenue. At the same time, government expenditure was growing under pressure to provide 'able-bodied relief' to the unemployed and the destitute. For the year 1930–1 it was anticipated that the budget deficit would amount to some $4 million.[9] In addition, $3 million would be needed to redeem loans that were due to mature and $1 million for the city of St John's. Accordingly, the government had no choice but to invite tenders for a further loan of $8 million. But the stream of willing lenders had at last dried up. No tenders were received.[10]

For Newfoundland the blind financial course pursued by successive governments over many years ended where it almost certainly had to end: on the rocks of financial ruin. In the chilling words of the Amulree Report, written two years later:

The onset of the world depression found the Island with no reserves, its primary industry neglected and its credit exhausted. At the first wind of adversity, its elaborate pretensions collapsed like a house of cards. The glowing visions of a new Utopia were dispelled with cruel suddenness by the cold realities of national insolvency, and to-day a disillusioned and bewildered people, deprived in many parts of the country of all hope of earning a livelihood, are haunted by the grim spectres of pauperism and starvation.[11]

It would, of course, be wholly wrong to suggest that the government in power was responsible for this state of affairs. They were but the hapless victims of a trap constructed by preceding governments, one of which had been Squires's own, and devastatingly sprung by economic forces beyond their control.

Yet nevertheless they were caught, and had to do something. Had Newfoundland been a Latin American republic (a number of which were in similar straits for not altogether dissimilar reasons) the most likely or even unavoidable expedient would have been default on the national debt. Since the sum total of indebtedness had by this time climbed to nearly $100 million, interest payments alone were demanding some 65 per cent of the government's depleted current revenue.[12] Thus, by defaulting on these payments the government would have been able to meet all its current obligations without difficulty. Indeed, were it not for the burden of

8/Smallwood, *The Book of Newfoundland*, I, 325.
9/Cmd 4480, *Report*, p. 51.   10/*The Times*, London, 25 May 1931.
11/Cmd 4480, *Report*, pp. 43–4.   12/*Ibid.*, p. 46.

the national debt Newfoundland would have been able to survive the depression if not in comfort at least in a more tolerable state of poverty than many other countries, and much better than such hard-hit areas as western Canada. But Newfoundland's position, perhaps unfortunately in this case, was not that of Peru or Chile. As a self-governing Dominion, whose constitutional status had been confirmed by the Statute of Westminster as equal to that of Canada and the other sovereign dominions, Newfoundland was subject to additional pressures that were as much political as economic or financial, and for the same reason also had access to more potential sources of aid. For the question was bound to be asked, especially in Britain and Canada, whether default by Newfoundland might not have wider ramifications affecting other parts of the Empire and Commonwealth, and, more specifically, themselves.

Though by May 1931 Newfoundland's international credit was exhausted, the government was not immediately bankrupt nor would it become so until the half-yearly interest payments on the national debt fell due on 30 June. This allowed the government approximately six weeks in which to raise the $2 million required. In that desperate interval the most readily available sources of at least temporary relief were the four Canadian banks (Bank of Montreal, Bank of Nova Scotia, Royal Bank of Canada, and Canadian Bank of Commerce) operating on the island. Of these the most important was the Bank of Montreal which had held the government's account ever since the crash of Newfoundland's domestic banks in 1894. That the other banks would act independently was almost out of the question; but the government was already in difficulty with the Bank of Montreal over a temporary loan of $1 million agreed to in October 1930, half of which the bank – by means of a legal loophole – subsequently refused to pay, presumably for fear that Newfoundland would default.[13] It was therefore unlikely to look favourably upon a new request, nor did it. When no loan was forthcoming, Squires, with less than two weeks remaining before the date of automatic default, visited Ottawa to press the seriousness of Newfoundland's situation upon the Canadian government. Here, at last, he met with success. The Conservative prime minister, R. B. Bennett, was held in high regard in banking circles, and his intervention proved decisive. He wrote to the general manager of the Bank of Montreal:

My colleagues and myself have had an interview with Sir Richard Squires ... who has indicated to us that, unless the Banks come to the assistance of the Government, there is a probability of default being made in respect of the half

13/Newfoundland Archives, Administration of Squires and Alderdice, minister of finance to A. A. Werlich (manager, Bank of Montreal, St John's), 3 Sept. 1931.

year's interest on the bonded indebtedness of that Dominion ... It is the opinion of this Government that it would be very injurious to Canada if Newfoundland should make default at this time, and therefore we would appreciate the banks taking such action as would make this event impossible.[14]

Consequently, the four banks agreed to act as a syndicate for the purpose of advancing the Newfoundland government a further temporary loan of $2 million.[15]

Default was thus narrowly avoided, and in a jointly signed letter sent to each of the banks formally requesting the loan, the prime minister and the minister of finance, Peter Cashin, set out the conditions their government would seek to fulfil if their request were granted. They pledged faithfully to implement a policy of tariff revision and strict retrenchment, but more significant was their indication that

it is deemed desirable, in view of the complexity of the matters involved, that expert advice and assistance should be sought. It is therefore our purpose to request immediately His Majesty's Government in Great Britain to nominate a Commissioner who, in collaboration with His Majesty's Government in Newfoundland, will:

(a) investigate the whole financial structure of our Dominion;

(b) revise and reconstruct our Customs tariff, including the revision of other sources of national revenue, on a basis designed to afford the Dominion a more substantial and certain income;

(c) advise on the reorganization and coordination of our various public services, and

(d) generally make recommendations with a view to the strengthening of our finances; the positive assuring of a continued balancing of our Budget; the creation of a sinking fund for outstanding and future bond issues; and the bringing into effect of a plan of long term financing of short term indebtedness.

We agree, if our present application for the loan above-mentioned is acceded to by you, immediately to advise the issuance of a Commission to the person nominated ... and upon the presentation of such Commissioner's report ... to proclaim a session of the Legislature at which, in addition to the general business of the Dominion, the said report would be considered and legislative effect given the recommendations of the said Commissioner, *provided they meet with your approval*.[16]

14/Bonar Law–Bennett Library, University of New Brunswick, Bennett Papers, N452, Bennett to Jackson Dodds, 19 June 1931.
15/*Ibid.*, Dodds to Bennett, 20 June 1931.
16/Newfoundland Archives, Administration of Squires and Alderdice, Squires and Cashin to [the four banks], 20 June 1931 (italics added).

Accordingly, in August arrangements were made with the British government to secure as 'financial adviser,' Sir Percy Thompson, deputy chairman of the Board of Inland Revenue. At the same time, Robert J. Magor, a Montreal business man, was appointed to advise on the more economical reorganization of the railway, dry dock, telegraph system, and other public utilities.[17]

Having gained, in effect, a six-month respite before the crisis of interest payments would again be upon it, the government strenuously attempted to reduce expenditure, but their efforts were largely in vain; as the depression deepened, revenue fell even more sharply. Unemployment had begun to strike the paper-making and mining towns. Prices in the fishery had sunk to a par with those of the notorious 'black autumn' of 1908, and to add to the misery the total catch was the smallest since the nineteenth century.[18]

By November, Sir Percy Thompson's interim report was ready, but while his organizational recommendations were far-reaching, it was also apparent that not even he had been able to find a means of avoiding ultimate disaster. He could suggest various administrative economies that might be effected, but there were no new or unused sources of revenue to be tapped beyond further tariff increases and the imposition of a higher and more 'scientific' income tax.

However, he did find much that was basically wrong with Newfoundland's financial and administrative system, whose more glaring flaw, on his analysis, was the virtual absence of any system of treasury control: 'The present system, or rather lack of system, which has been followed ever since Newfoundland attained responsible Government, has given rise to many irregularities and abuses and it may be said with truth that much of the difficulty in which the Government now finds itself can be traced to this cause.'[19] He therefore set out in an appendix to his report a detailed yet simple plan for a reorganized Department of Finance and the operation of a practically water-tight system, modelled on that of the British Treasury, for the financial control of expenditure. It was an admirable plan, and long overdue, but contained nothing that was not already known. There had been talk of treasury control before, but, as the Amulree Report was to point out, control over public finance had always remained 'wholly in the hands of the political party in power at the time.'[20] It had

17/See *The Times*, 24 Aug. 1931.
18/Smallwood, *The Book of Newfoundland*, I, 325.
19/Newfoundland Archives, Administration of Squires and Alderdice, memorandum by Sir Percy Thompson, 'Financial Position of the Newfoundland Government,' p. 6.
20/Cmd 4480, *Report*, p. 53.

remained there because the parties found it to their advantage. Now, when extreme circumstances, and the government's undertaking to the Canadian bankers, made reform unavoidable, it was unfortunately many years too late.

At the time Sir Percy Thompson's interim report was presented, another financial crisis was already in the making. Revenue was continuing to contract more rapidly than expenditure, and even more alarming was the growing drain from the reserves of the Newfoundland Savings Bank. Since by law the government was liable for all deposits in the bank, it had no choice but to use exchequer funds to meet withdrawals. 'I am convinced,' wrote Sir Percy, 'that the only sound policy is to support the Savings Bank as long as public funds hold out; to let the Savings Bank go would be disastrous and would render the Government of this Dominion very difficult.'[21]

Meanwhile, Sir Richard Squires was making another desperate effort to secure help from the Canadian banks. On 7 October Jackson Dodds, general manager of the Bank of Montreal, wrote to the prime minister of Canada:

Sir Richard said the imperative need of the Government was $1,500,000 for relief purposes and that if this was not forthcoming many people would die ... While expressing sympathy we made no promise whatever that we would make any loan. Sir Richard said such a gesture as making a loan at this time would affect public opinion favourably if the question of confederation with Canada came up and a refusal would be an adverse factor.[22]

The only concession the bank was willing to make was to give Newfoundland one additional month in which to repay the $2 million advance made in the previous June[23] – which the state of government finances clearly made impossible in any event.

With further payments falling due at the end of the year, default was again imminent. But again there were other governments who could not altogether ignore Newfoundland's plight. In November, in a secret memorandum to the Canadian prime minister, the British government expressed its anxiety over Newfoundland's financial difficulties, and particularly over the position of the faltering Newfoundland Savings Bank. 'If the

21/Newfoundland Archives, Administration of Squires and Alderdice, memorandum by Sir Percy Thompson, 'Financial Position of the Newfoundland Government,' p. 2.
22/Bennett Papers, N452, Dodds to Bennett, 7 Oct. 1931.
23/Ibid., Dodds to Sir George Perley (acting prime minister of Canada), 24 Nov. 1931.

Savings Bank is unable to meet withdrawals,' the memorandum stated, 'the credit of His Majesty's Government in Newfoundland goes with it and thereafter commercial disaster must follow with far-reaching consequences which cannot be predicted.'[24]

Nevertheless, when in December the Newfoundland government applied to the Canadian banking syndicate for another $2 million advance,[25] the bankers flatly refused:

I have now to inform you [wrote Jackson Dodds to R. B. Bennett] that the four banks represented in Newfoundland, to whom the Government of Newfoundland applied for an immediate loan of $2,000,000 and a further loan of $1,600,000 in July next, have reached the decision not to grant the application. The result will be that, failing assistance being received from some other source, the Dominion of Newfoundland will default in their Bond interest of 1st January.[26]

But within three days of the date of default, and under renewed pressure from Bennett, the bankers suddenly changed their minds. In a letter apparently written 'for the record' Dodds informed Bennett that

at your urgent request and on your assurance that you will take a convenient opportunity to bring before your Cabinet, and, if necessary, before Parliament, the matter of having urged the Canadian Banks, in view of the Empire and international importance of the matter, to advance the money necessary to pay the interest due on the 31st December and the 1st January thus preventing a default on the part of Newfoundland, our Board agreed to the advance being made.[27]

The loan, however, was to be made only under the most stringent conditions. These were not initially the product of negotiation; they were laid down by the banking syndicate and the Newfoundland government was given twenty-four hours in which to accept.

'This is the first and only communication or indication of conditions or

24/*Ibid.*, F217, memorandum from the Office of the High Commissioner for the United Kingdom, 'Financial Difficulties in Newfoundland,' marked 'Most Secret,' 20 Nov. 1931.

25/The government was hopefully looking forward to a balanced budget for 1932–3 and a revival of trade that together with the economies proposed by Sir Percy Thompson 'will have the effect of creating a substantial surplus which can be utilized for the repayment of Debt.' Newfoundland Archives, Administration of Squires and Alderdice, A. Barnes (secretary of state in the Newfoundland government) to Bank of Montreal, 1 Dec. 1931.

26/Bennett Papers, F217, Dodds to Bennett, 18 Dec. 1931.

27/*Ibid.*, F217, Dodds to Bennett, 28 Dec. 1931.

terms submitted by the banks to me directly or indirectly,' Squires protested in a telegram to R. B. Bennett, expressing his cabinet's 'unanimous resentment' at the banks' 'ultimatum procedure.'[28] But caught unawares, without bargaining power, and with time running out, the government was in no position to stand on its dignity. With the hurried assistance of J. H. Penson, a British Treasury official who had been seconded to the Newfoundland government first as an assistant to Percy Thompson and later as acting deputy minister of finance, certain minor modifications in the conditions were agreed to by the banks on the night of 29 December.[29] On the next day the government accepted.

Newfoundland was thus committed to a financial policy directed towards the fulfilment of the bankers' conditions, which were thirteen in number. The first two demanded legislation to prevent the export of gold, to make the notes of the syndicate banks legal tender, and to relieve the banks of any obligation to pay these notes in gold. The third consisted of a (rather gratuitous) exhortation to the government to balance its budget and make provision for a sinking fund. But the fourth stated:

The Government will pay the whole of the proceeds of the customs duties day by day into a special account at some bank to be nominated by the four Banks. The special account is to be carried in the joint names of Sir Percy Thompson and the Controller of the Treasury with provision for a deputy in each case. This procedure should be put into force at the earliest possible date after 1st January.

And the fifth added:

(a) Until the 30th June the persons named in the preceding section shall set aside each week and pay over to the consolidated revenue fund such amount as will be sufficient for the maintenance of the public services upon the minimum scale necessary for their continued functioning ... and shall retain the balance for the purpose of the payment of interest on the whole of the public debt.

Thereafter, however, the order of priority was to be reversed:

(b) As from the 1st July 1932 and until the end of the first year in which the Newfoundland budget is shown to have balanced the persons named in the preceding section shall retain each week out of the funds standing to the credit

28/*Ibid.*, F217, Squires to Bennett, 29 Dec. 1931.
29/*Ibid.*, N450, Dodds to Werlich for transmission to the government of Newfoundland, 30 Dec. 1931.

of the Special Account a sum ascertained on a basis to be agreed upon such
that over each six monthly period an amount will be accumulated sufficient to
pay the interest on the public debt and the balance shall be paid over to the
exchequer.[30]

The sixth and seventh conditions related to the passage of legislation
to implement the recommendations of Sir Percy Thompson and Mr
Magor; and the eighth required the government to appoint an adviser
nominated by either the imperial or Canadian governments and 'authorized to furnish the Syndicate Banks with reports in writing of any matters
which come to his attention of which, in his opinion, the Banks should be
informed.' The ninth required legislation to permit the repayment of temporary loans by new temporary loans; the tenth demanded that the government endeavour to raise an internal loan; the eleventh that the government
float a bond issue as early as possible in order to repay the syndicate banks
their temporary loans; and the twelfth that so long as the temporary loans
remained outstanding the government would not 'alienate by lease or sale'
the Labrador territory or its timber, water power, or other natural resources without the consent of the banks. And, finally, the thirteenth condition succinctly warned the government not to apply for further credit:
'The Syndicate Banks do not expect to be asked to loan any further
amounts to help meet interest payments due next July and January 1933,
it being understood that the Government will be able to provide these
themselves.'[31]
   It was, of course, anything but 'understood,' least of all by the harassed
government of Newfoundland. But the meaning was none the less clear:
the last door of orthodox finance, forcibly held ajar for more than a year,
had now been shut. Unless some other source of aid could be found, and
there were none in sight, it was but a matter of time before the unfortunate
ministry of Sir Richard Squires would find its position completely untenable. There was no possibility that sufficient loans could be raised internally to meet the interest payments due at the end of June; instead of a
surplus, a deficit on the fiscal year 1931–2 was likely, and in fact eventually turned out to be the largest in Newfoundland's history.[32]
   Apart from the question of default, there was also the question of
whether the ministry could survive to the end of its term. For it would have
been extraordinary had the severe financial strain upon the country not
had political repercussions. Every cut the government made, every train

30/Newfoundland Archives, Administration of Squires and Alderdice, Werlich
to Squires, 28 Dec. 1931.
31/*Ibid.*
32/It amounted to $4,368,371. Cmd 4480, *Report*, p. 47.

that ceased to run, every post office that closed, directly affected the livelihood of individuals. Some were placed on the 'dole,' a payment, generally made in kind, to the value of six cents per person per day,[33] but perhaps as politically potent was the general uncertainty and *fear* of the dole that such cuts aroused. While bankers, businessmen, and expert financial advisers could press for and demand drastic economies, it was not they who had to deal with a bewildered and largely distressed community. Because the government did, it was inevitably subject to conflicting pressures; the confidence of bankers was vital, yet always in the background was the growing mob of the unemployed marching in the streets. These could not be ignored, and as the winter of 1931–2 wore on their demands grew louder and more insistent.

St John's was suffering from the depression even more than most outports, for as the country's foreign trade declined traffic through the port of St John's was reduced to a trickle, and, as the level of domestic incomes fell, the small protected market on which St John's manufacturers depended shrank to miniscule proportions. The result was urban unemployment, which left workers and their families with only a slightly supplemented dole on which to subsist, whereas there were few outports in which the inhabitants could not improve their lot by growing vegetables or even, if fortunate, by keeping livestock or poultry.

But in spite of hardships, public order in the city was not seriously threatened until early in February 1932. The month of February is always the winter's nadir in Newfoundland, and in 1932 it was for many people a month of unendurable cold and hunger. Even among the destitute, however, public combustion is not normally spontaneous; a spark is needed, and in St John's the opening of the legislature on 4 February promised to provide one.

Three days previously the minister of finance, Major Peter Cashin, had resigned, giving no reasons for his action and refusing to make any public comment.[34] His first speech in the new session was therefore the subject of much speculation. The last thing the government (and particularly a government led by Sir Richard Squires) could stand in the existing crisis was a political scandal, or even a threat of scandal. Thus, when on the opening day of the session Cashin rose to speak, the future of the government lay very largely in his hands, and he did not fail the occasion. He had resigned, he stated, because the prime minister was guilty of deliberately falsifying the minutes of the Executive Council in order to deceive the governor and some of his cabinet by covering up certain fees he had

33/*Ibid.*, pp. 50–1. Approximately 25 per cent of the population were receiving relief of this sort.
34/*Evening Telegram*, St John's, 2 Feb. 1932.

been paying to himself out of public funds. Other members of the cabinet, he charged, were similarly guilty of corrupt practices, and one (unnamed) had even failed to file income tax returns.[35]

These charges, coming after so much government talk of the need for 'economy,' could scarcely have been more damaging. In the days that followed the street gatherings of the unemployed, once passive, became increasingly menacing. On 11 February the inevitable outburst occurred. A mob of several hundred gathered outside the Court House, in which, at the time, the prime minister had his office. After hours of standing in the cold without receiving the interview they sought, the mob grew restless, surged forward, brushed aside police, and forced the door to the prime minister's chamber. In the struggle Squires was roughly jostled by the crowd; but worse violence was averted, and an uneasy peace restored, by an immediate distribution of dole orders.[36] It was, however, a frightening harbinger of things to come.

The legislature, adjourned in confusion after its sensational opening, reconvened on 16 February. Again the scene was dominated by Cashin, who was now prepared to elaborate his charges. Dramatically rising from his seat, in his hand an ominous but unidentified manuscript, he reiterated his reasons for resigning:

I charged that minutes of Council had been falsified, bank accounts had been manipulated, and a member of the Executive Council had failed to pay his income tax. These charges were ignored by the men in question but silence on the part of those who have already wandered in the shadow of the gaol does not convey an expression of innocence. Rather does it smack of guilt and revive in this Assembly the odour of the police court from which the country thought that the Walker inquiry had purged it; but the incorrigibles are up again – men brazen, persistent, wily, crooked and criminal.

Pointing an accusing finger, he named Dr Alex Campbell as the minister who had evaded the payment of income tax. The Unionist member for St Barbe, Walter Skeans, he accused of forgery for signing another's name on a cheque issued by the Department of Marine and Fisheries. But the accusation with the greatest emotional impact he reserved for the prime minister himself, who, he claimed, had personally taken $5,000 per year from the funds of the War Reparations Commission. Coming from a distinguished veteran of the war, these words were doubly sharp: 'Those who fought for their country and the relations of those who died will no doubt feel aggrieved that no mean portion of their small material recompense

35/*Proceedings of the House of Assembly, Newfoundland, 1932*, pp. 20–4.
36/*Evening Telegram*, 11–12 Feb. 1932.

falls into the hands of slackers under the pitiful guise of payment for services rendered.' Cashin then concluded: 'In view of the statements I have made, which are, so help me God, to the best of my knowledge true, one is forced to the dreadful conclusion that what we won by honour and in death is falling into dishonour and decay.'[37]

The government's position was now desperate, the danger of civil commotion great. Cashin's indictment could not be ignored, and certain of his specific charges at least were undeniably true. Yet if the prime minister could maintain a majority his survival was still possible, even though an inquiry of some sort was now unavoidable. It was the crisis of 1923 repeating itself. But this time Squires had greater success in rallying his supporters, and when on 18 February the opposition moved the charges be investigated by a select committee of the House, he was ready with an amendment to the effect that the inquiry should be conducted by the governor, Sir John Middleton, and should cover only the charges made against himself. The motion as amended was carried and again the House adjourned.[38]

Squires had out-manœuvred his opponents and won a breathing space, at least until the governor replied to the address from the House of Assembly. Moreover, the peculiar terms of the address held out every prospect that the reply would be favourable to the ministry. For, after listing nine specific charges, it concluded as follows:

The House of Assembly humbly prays that Your Excellency will be pleased to enquire fully into the charges and any matter or matters connected therewith and to take such action as may be meet in the premises, and to inform the House as to whether or not there has been any falsification of the said Minutes, and whether or not Your Excellency was deceived or induced by such deception to sign the Minutes in question.[39]

In other words, the governor was being asked whether or not he had been duped.

It was hardly surprising, therefore, when his formal reply repudiated the Assembly's request as unconstitutional:

The accuracy of these records [minutes of council] is impugned in your Address. There can be no question whatsoever as to your undoubted right to discuss and to express approval of the policy which the records enforce. But, having regard to the origin and constitution of the Executive Council ... I am

37/*Proceedings of the House of Assembly, Newfoundland, 1932*, pp. 36–7.
38/*Ibid.*, pp. 78–81.
39/Newfoundland Archives, Correspondence of Governor Middleton, 'Address from the House of Assembly,' 23 Feb. 1932.

unable to admit that you have any constitutional or statutory power to question the accuracy of those records. On the contrary, it would appear that in questioning the accuracy of the records ... you have essayed, without doubt unwittingly, to assume a function which has been entrusted by the Royal Instructions to another body and to exercise a power which has not been conferred upon you by the Constitution or by Law. The Executive Council alone is empowered ... to pass judgement on the accuracy of its own records ...

At the same time, however, he was anxious to afford the Assembly 'all information which, in my opinion, may be properly communicated to you without detriment to the conduct of the business of the State.'

The latter phrase, as it turned out, was crucial. For after an involved explanation of the formal procedure followed in the recording and authorization of minutes of council, the governor stated that such procedure had been invariably followed, and concluded: 'I have the honour to inform you that there has not been any falsification of the said Minutes and that I have not been deceived or been induced by deception to sign the said Minutes.'[40] But, from the documents before him at the time, it is clear that his reply was true only in a very narrow technical sense. There was much else that the governor evidently felt he could not communicate. In particular, though all the minutes were properly presented to him, there were unexplained discrepancies between these minutes and the decisions recorded on the cabinet agenda from which the minutes were compiled. There were entries on the agenda which gave no record of members present and recorded decisions in this manner:

No. 838. Balance of Humber Account – Get transfer.
        Sir Richard will draft Minute.[41]

The formal minute of the Executive Council then ordered that a balance to the credit of Sir Richard's constituency (Humber) in the Department of Marine and Fisheries not be returned to the general fund of the Dominion but instead 'be deposited to the credit of the Minister of Marine and Fisheries ... for Humber Constituency marine expenditure as and when he may decide.'[42] In another instance the agenda recorded only this cryptic notation:

No. 535. $5,000.00 German Reparation Account.
        Agreed.[43]

40/*Ibid.*, 'Reply of His Excellency the Governor,' 22 March 1932.
41/*Ibid.*, 'Copy of Agenda,' 12 Nov. 1929.
42/*Ibid.*, 'Copy of Minute of the Executive Council,' 3 Dec. 1929.
43/*Ibid.*, 'Extract from Agenda,' 3 Dec. 1931.

The resulting minute ordered that that sum be paid 'to the German Reparations Commissioner, Sir Richard Squires.'[44] On these matters the governor remained silent. As a representative of the Crown in a self-governing Dominion he could scarcely have done otherwise without incurring a heavy responsibility for public safety.

In the event, his reply misled no one. Whether the minutes of the Executive Council were in order or not was already largely irrelevant. Enough previously unknown facts had emerged to undermine any confidence that may have remained in the government. On 18 March Sir Richard Squires and Dr Campbell (who, it was discovered, had also been receiving a salary as 'Immigration Officer' – in a country with no immigration) were issued with writs under the Legislative Disabilities Act, both brought by L. E. Emerson, a member of the opposition.[45]

While these were pending the government faced a new emergency: in accordance with the undertaking given the Canadian banks, efforts would have to be made to implement the economies recommended by Sir Percy Thompson. These were severe. The House met on 23 March to pass further increases in the tariff, including charges on basic foodstuffs, and to impose a reduction in the pensions of ex-servicemen.[46] The contrast with the prime minister's own financial transactions was only too obvious. For the government the breaking-point had been reached. One cabinet minister, H. M. Mosdell, minister without portfolio, and two members of the governing party chose this occasion to resign.[47] The House adjourned until 5 April, with the stage set for the final débâcle.

On that day, what began as an orderly demonstration demanding a 'proper investigation' into the charges against ministers turned into a seething mob of ten thousand people massed outside the legislature where the House was in session. When a deputation failed to secure entrance, the mob began to stone the building. Inside, debate was drowned by the noise of breaking glass. Outside, the public explosion had begun.[48]

At some point in the outburst, mounted police began to push the crowd back, but their efforts were more provocative than effective. The demonstrators turned their stones upon them, knocking them from their horses, and surged unhindered up the steps of the legislature. As they reached the doors they were met by more police, who charged with batons flailing. The mob fell back under this unexpected assault, but a second wave of at-

44/*Ibid.*, 'Copy of Minute of the Executive Council,' 5 Dec. 1931.
45/*Evening Telegram*, 18 March 1932.
46/*Proceedings of the House of Assembly, Newfoundland, 1932*, pp. 149–60.
47/*Evening Telegram*, 24 March 1932.
48/The account which follows is based upon reports in the *Evening Telegram* and *Daily News*, 5–12 April 1932, and the Montreal *Gazette*, 6 April 1932.

tackers, some armed with clubs, could not be stopped. The police were forced to retreat, the doors gave way, and the battle moved inside. There, while the police successfully defended the Assembly chamber, the mob took possession of the basement, looting government offices and destroying files and records.

Meanwhile, Squires, with a police escort, made a dash through a side exit in the hope of reaching a waiting car. But before he could get away the mob closed in. Just as the police were losing the struggle to defend him, a party of rescuers, including several clergymen, arrived and pleaded with the mob to let him through. Their intervention was partly successful, but the streets were too crowded for the prime minister's car to pass, and before he could get more than fifty yards on foot another section of the mob attacked. In the ensuing mêlée he was struck a blow on the face, but his police guard managed to clear a path to a private residence on Colonial Street where he took refuge. From there he later escaped from the city by car and went into hiding.

The Dominion's crisis had reached its bitter climax. There was no further violence, apart from the looting of government liquor stores; a militia of ex-servicemen was hastily sworn in to help preserve order, and during the night the rioters gradually dispersed. They left behind streets littered with debris, broken furniture, smashed office equipment, and the contents of countless government files. Guarded by a police cordon, the empty House of Assembly with its shattered windows foreshadowed the end of parliamentary government.

On the following day Major Peter Cashin announced that during the riot the prime minister, who was still in hiding, had promised in his and Sir William Coaker's presence to resign at once.[49] But twenty-four hours later a defiant communiqué was issued from Squires's office stating that he had 'no intention whatever of tendering his resignation.'[50] Instead, it was apparently his intention to seek a dissolution. Meanwhile the city remained quiet, and on 12 April a British cruiser, *H.M.S. Dragon*, arrived in port. On the next day, at a caucus of the governing party it was resolved that a general election should be held as quickly as possible. Squires, it was clear, would have to fight almost alone. Many, including Coaker, Halfyard, and Barnes, were quitting politics; of the 1928 ministry of ten only three, Campbell, F. Gordon Bradley, and Tasker Cook, remained with him.[51] The date of the election was subsequently set for 11 June.

The campaign was predictably rancorous, and offered small consolation to a largely bewildered and poverty-stricken electorate. Squires could pro-

49/*Evening Telegram*, 6 April 1932.   50/*Ibid.*, 7 April 1932.
51/*Ibid.*, 13 April 1932.

duce nothing better than a hollow parody of his successful appeal in 1928, promising bonuses for fisheries and agriculture, industrial development – and a balanced budget.[52] Alderdice, the heir of Walter Monroe, had gathered about him a formidable collection of merchants calling themselves the 'United Newfoundland Party' and adopted the stance of a plain man of business. It was not his purpose, he said, 'to make any promise impossible of fulfillment.' His manifesto, however, contained the single issue of the election in these words:

Let me repeat the pledge recently made through the daily press that one of my first acts will be the appointment of a committee, the members of which will serve without remuneration, to enquire into the desirability and feasibility of placing the country under a form of commission government for a period of years. In case the proposal is favourably reported upon, it will be submitted to the electorate for their approval. No action will be taken that does not first have the consent of the people.[53]

This was a policy that even William Coaker wholeheartedly endorsed. Physical disabilities kept him from campaigning, he stated, 'otherwise I would be actively associated with the policy of government by Commission ... The people are disinclined to vote any longer for what is nothing more or less to them than a struggle between the 'ins and outs,' for in their opinion each administration has gone from bad to worse.'[54] If the electorate voted in the 'outs' who promised to give consideration to constitutional changes, it might be taken as a sign that they favoured such changes. That, in the event, was the assumption later made, for Alderdice never fulfilled his pledge to consult the people.

The election resulted in a landslide victory for the United Newfoundland party, which won all but two of the seats in the new Assembly.[55] Sir Richard Squires was not among the successful Liberals; fourteen years after the career of his political mentor, Sir Edward Morris, had been crowned with a British peerage, his own ended with personal defeat in the district of Trinity South. For Alderdice victory was hardly a cause for celebration. His country was on the verge of bankruptcy and in danger of civil collapse.

52/ *Liberal Press*, May 1932 (a campaign sheet).
53/ 'Manifesto of F. C. Alderdice,' *Evening Telegram*, 23 May 1932.
54/ *Fishermen's Advocate*, St John's, 30 May 1932.
55/ The two districts which returned Liberals were Humber and Green Bay, both of which were economically dependent upon the relatively prosperous forest and paper-making industries. Prior to the election the Assembly was reduced in size from 40 to 27 as an economy measure, but the resulting redistribution had no appreciable effect upon the outcome.

13 Unconditional surrender

ALDERDICE was fortunate in only one respect: his government would not have to face financial catastrophe at the end of June, but rather at the end of December, which allowed him six months in which to find some avenue of escape. This could not be by way of further bank advances, for the bankers had made it absolutely clear that Newfoundland's credit had run out; it could not be by way of internally floated bond issues, for that source too had been exhausted.

In March, in accordance with the recommendations of Sir Percy Thompson, the Squires government had attempted to raise an internal issue of $2.5 million (called, ironically, a 'Prosperity Loan'), but in spite of urgent appeals less than $350,000 was subscribed by the public. To avoid failure the government was forced to adopt the unusual and controversial expedient of persuading the Imperial Oil Company to take bonds to the value of $1,750,000, and to pay the government a minimum annual royalty of $300,000, in return for a monopoly on the importation, manufacture, and sale of all petroleum products, including gasoline, kerosene, and lubricating oils.[1] With a loan so raised, in June the Alderdice government was able to meet the half-yearly interest on the national debt, thus emptying the treasury once more.

Since there was now absolutely nowhere that Newfoundland could turn for further loans, the time had come to dispose of the country's assets; but of these the only one that was even remotely disposable, it being inconceivable that purchasers or lessees could be found for the railway or any of the other run-down public utilities, was the territory of Labrador. Though rich in resources, this vast territory lay idle through lack of capital

1/See Cmd 4480, *Newfoundland Royal Commission 1933 Report* (London, 1933), pp. 52–3.

development, its administration a positive liability on the state. The island could no longer wait for its northern 'El Dorado' to produce, and in the summer of 1932 the government's main preoccupation was to obtain some immediate benefit from it, either through sale or lease.

This, however, was far from a new idea. In the previous year the Squires ministry had made some strenuous efforts to sell the territory to Canada, but without success.[2] Alderdice turned to Britain and by August 1932 had interested a group of highly reputable financiers, under the chairmanship of E. W. Sutphen,[3] in the formation of a development syndicate to lease the territory for a period of ninety-nine years. At a secret meeting in Ottawa on 18 August Alderdice and Sutphen signed a memorandum to the effect that, subject to a conference in St John's to arrange details, and the approval of Parliament, the syndicate would 'progressively develop the natural resources of Labrador and provide the Treasury of Newfoundland, through rentals, royalties, export duties and/or otherwise, with an annual income which, in the aggregate, shall be sufficient for the payment of the interest on and maturities of the bonded indebtedness of Newfoundland.'[4] But thereafter the syndicate appears to have run into difficulties, for despite this promising beginning there was no further progress for several months, after which the proposal fell through.

Meanwhile, the government had encountered (or created for itself) difficulties of another sort. Relations between Alderdice and the British officials on loan to his government, whom he regarded with suspicion as appointees of Squires,[5] had deteriorated to the point where the officials' usefulness was being undermined. The senior of these, Sir Percy Thompson, was shortly to be recalled to England, but before leaving St John's he revealingly wrote:

I believe that the Alderdice Government is as honest and well-intentioned as any Government which is likely to be returned to power in this Dominion, *but I am rapidly reaching the conclusion that no elected Government can really*

2/There is a voluminous correspondence on this subject in both the Newfoundland Archives and the Bennett Papers. The attempt failed for a number of reasons, not the least of which, it would appear, was Bennett's deep suspicion of the Newfoundland government's insistence that the sale be made through a Montreal agent of dubious reputation who would receive a commission of $10 million. The price asked for the territory was $110 million.

3/One of his associates in the consortium was the Rt. Hon. L. S. Amery, a leading member of the Conservative party in Britain.

4/Newfoundland Archives, Labrador, 'Outline of a Plan for the Development of Labrador,' confidential memorandum, 18 Aug. 1932.

5/Bonar Law–Bennett Library, University of New Brunswick, Bennett Papers, F217, Alderdice to Jackson Dodds, 27 Sept. 1932.

govern successfully; it is much too closely in touch with the governed, is constantly amenable to irresistible pressure from vested interests and moreover politics here has reached such a state of degradation that most decent people refuse to take a hand in the game ... I hesitate to put my recommendations in any document which may be made public.[6]

He was not alone in his growing despair with the machinery of democracy, as was later to become apparent.

Financially, the government's dilemma was simple. As Alderdice expressed it in a letter to Jackson Dodds of the Bank of Montreal: 'Without provoking an absolute revolt I do not see how we can further economize, and, on the other hand, without further retrenchment, I do not see hope [*sic*] to balance our budget by the end of the financial year.'[7] Newfoundland, he said, would therefore have to seek 'temporary postponement of the payment of interest due December 31st next.'

In October Sir Percy Thompson's final report, submitted shortly before he returned to London, gave authoritative confirmation of this view:

To attempt to reduce the general expenditure of the Dominion by a further sum of say one million dollars would impair the whole fabric of governmental functions. It would involve the almost complete withdrawal of educational facilities, the cancellation of Public Health and Welfare Services, and the virtual abolition of War and Civil Pensions. I should not be disposed to advocate such a course, which would be manifestly detrimental to the future interests of the Dominion.

Furthermore, he now believed the consequences of default would be 'less disastrous' than if it had occurred previously: 'In the first place the default need only be partial, and secondly the determined effort which has been made to avoid default by drastically cutting down expenditure must command general appreciation and sympathy and in the main criticism would be directed more to the past than the present.'[8]

Upon receiving copies of the report, the Canadian bankers, anticipating default, were concerned to secure repayment at full interest of the temporary advances they had made, and accordingly applied further pressure upon both Alderdice and the Canadian prime minister, R. B. Bennett.[9]

6/*Ibid.*, Thompson to Dodds, 11 Sept. 1932 (italics added).
7/*Ibid.*, Alderdice to Dodds, 27 Sept. 1932.
8/*Ibid.*, N450, 'Report by Sir Percy Thompson on the Financial Circumstances of Newfoundland,' Oct. 1932.
9/*Ibid.*, Dodds to A. A. Werlich for transmission to the government of Newfoundland, 12 Oct. 1932; and Dodds to Bennett, 12 Oct. 1932.

The next initiative, however, came not from Ottawa but from London, where Sir Percy Thompson's report had also been received with misgivings. In a 'Personal and Secret' despatch to Bennett, the secretary of state for the dominions cabled:

Chancellor of Exchequer and I are very much concerned at financial situation developing in Newfoundland ... Default on the part of Newfoundland would be viewed here with profound regret not only on its own account but also because no part of the Empire has so far failed to meet its obligations on an external loan. Only one quarter, however, of Newfoundland's debt liabilities are in sterling, and owing to geographical considerations and her trade associations Newfoundland is in the minds of many people, especially in the United States, regarded as closely associated with Canada ... Hence we cannot help feeling apprehensive lest default on the part of Newfoundland might appreciably impair credit of Canada in New York. We have therefore thought it essential to bring the facts of the case to your notice, *and to ask whether you would feel disposed to take any action to prevent a situation arising which is likely to have such serious repercussions.* This telegram is being sent entirely on our own initiative and Alderdice has no knowledge that we are in communication with you on the subject.[10]

The Alderdice ministry thus began its preparations for default without knowing that the first step to prevent it from doing so had already been taken. On 15 November it sent to the British government details of a plan for a unilateral declaration to bondholders reducing interest payments to one-quarter of the normal rate for a period of four years.[11] 'We have economized and are economizing,' Alderdice explained to the secretary of state for the dominions, 'but must avoid starvation.'[12] Unimpressed, the British government responded with a stern warning.

We are greatly disturbed by your telegram of yesterday ... As regards your proposal for unilateral declarations to bondholders ... we cannot too strongly emphasize our view that the action proposed would be regarded as unacceptable by holders of debt in United States, Canada and United Kingdom. There is no ground on which Newfoundland Government could claim to make continued payment of partial dividends dependent on acceptance by individual bondholders of conditions on which they have never been consulted. Good

10/*Ibid.*, secretary of state for the dominions to Bennett, n.d. [Oct. 1932] (italics added).
11/*Ibid.*, revised draft, 'Leaflet to Bondholders,' Nov. 1932.
12/*Ibid.*, Alderdice to secretary of state for the dominions, 15 Nov. 1932.

faith requires that Newfoundland Government should make and continue to make to everyone the maximum payment its financial circumstances actually permit.[13]

Alderdice, however, would not be moved, nor would he agree to a suggestion that he first consult Canada.

At this time, the Canadian prime minister had evaded the issue of the British government's initial enquiry regarding Newfoundland's default, replying only that 'my colleagues do not now favourably consider the idea of assistance.'[14] But on 24 November the secretary of state for the dominions again pressed upon him the case for joint aid:

We are not prepared to meet Newfoundland's obligations by ourselves and without considerations. We are unwilling on the other hand to risk damage to the prestige of the Empire which default might cause.

Two alternatives present themselves if this is to be avoided; either Newfoundland must accept some form of non–Responsible Government involving in effect administrative control from this country with all its implications ... or, what we ourselves would prefer, some joint action must be taken by the Government of Canada and ourselves.

He then proposed that the two governments each lend Newfoundland half the sum needed to meet the interest on the national debt due on 31 December, and in return Newfoundland be required to raise an internal loan to repay these advances, and also 'undertake to accept a Mixed Commission of United Kingdom, Canadian and Newfoundland personnel to examine into the future of the Dominion with a view to reaching decisions and making appropriate arrangements before debt interest due on 1st July, 1933 matures.'[15]

However, Sir William Stavert, a Canadian banker who had replaced Sir Percy Thompson as the Newfoundland government's financial adviser, had other ideas. Without consulting or even informing Alderdice, he telegraphed Jackson Dodds advising him to contact Prime Minister Bennett and arrange for the offer of a loan to Newfoundland 'on the understanding that an Order-in-Council should pass committing [the Newfoundland] Government to negotiations looking to confederation during the ensuing six months.'[16] On 29 November Stavert telegraphed again to suggest that

13/*Ibid.*, secretary of state for the dominions to Alderdice, 17 Nov. 1932.
14/*Ibid.*, Bennett to secretary of state for the dominions, 21 Nov. 1932.
15/*Ibid.*, F217, secretary of state for the dominions to the secretary of state for external affairs (Canada), 24 Nov. 1932.
16/*Ibid.*, N450, Stavert to Dodds, 25 Nov. 1932.

Canada was now at least in a position to obtain favourable terms in negotiations with Newfoundland for the sale of Labrador,[17] and again on 30
November to ask that, in view of the likelihood of default, 'if influence
even amounting to coercion is possible by England and Canada it be
exercised,'[18] presumably in order to compel the adoption of some other
remedy, such as those he had suggested.

There would, however, be no default. On 15 December Bennett conferred in London with the British chancellor of the Exchequer, Neville
Chamberlain, and came away convinced that Newfoundland would have
to be supported.[19] Originally, his agreement with the chancellor was to the
effect that Newfoundland would provide for one-third of the interest on
its national debt, the British Treasury one-third, and the Canadian banks
would be asked to provide the remaining third. But when the latter, in
spite of pressure from the Canadian cabinet, adamantly refused,[20] Bennett
finally agreed, in the face of strong objections from his leading ministers,[21]
to provide a loan from the Canadian Treasury equal to that provided by
Britain. The Newfoundland government was then offered a joint loan of
$1,250,000, subject to the conditions previously outlined to Bennett by
the British government; namely, that Newfoundland accept a Commission

consisting either (i) of two members nominated by His Majesty's Government
in the United Kingdom, and one by His Majesty's Government in Newfoundland, or (ii) of three members nominated by His Majesty's Government in
[the] United Kingdom, whichever alternative shall be more acceptable to you.
We should reserve in either case the right, in consultation with His Majesty's
Government in Canada, to invite a Canadian to act as one of our nominees.

The purpose of the Commission would be to examine into the future of
Newfoundland and in particular to report on the financial situation and prospects of the Dominion and what measures may be necessary to secure its
financial stability with a view to decisions being reached and appropriate
arrangements made before the debt interest due on July 1st, 1933, matures.

We assume, of course, in view of the wide terms of reference suggested
above, that pending the report of the Commission Newfoundland would not
alienate any substantial assets by sale or long lease without prior consultation
with us, but we should like to have this confirmed.

It is recognised that you may not be in a position to commit Newfoundland

17/*Ibid.*, Stavert to Dodds, 29 Nov. 1932.
18/*Ibid.*, Stavert to Dodds, 30 Nov. 1932 (italics added).
19/*Ibid.*, N452, Bennett to Sir George Perley (acting prime minister of Canada),
15 Dec. 1932.
20/*Ibid.*, Perley to Bennett, 16 Dec. 1932.
21/*Ibid.*, memorandum by Perley, 19 Dec. 1932.

to acceptance of these proposals, but you will realise that we could not provide money unless we were in a position to give Parliament assurance that His Majesty's Government in Newfoundland were ready to recommend such a scheme at once to their Legislature and ask for necessary powers, or that if these were for any reason not obtainable at once you would forthwith appeal to the Electorate for their support of [the] plan.

You will recognize that in the event of your being unable to give assurance in the above sense and default occurring at once we should have no alternative but to make our position clear by public statement to the effect that financial assistance had been offered to Newfoundland by His Majesty's Government in the United Kingdom on these conditions and had been refused by Newfoundland.[22]

The terms of the offer thus contained a classic combination of diplomatic pressures in the form of a small but adequate 'carrot' and an implied 'stick.'

Newfoundland had no counter-proposals, nor was there time to make any. Alderdice replied at once accepting the first alternative for the constitution of a Commission which, he said, 'in view of the severe prospective financial stringency we would welcome at the earliest possible date.'[23]

On 17 February 1933 a Royal Warrant was issued from London appointing a Commission of three with the broadest possible terms of reference – 'to examine into the future of Newfoundland and in particular to report on the financial situation and prospects therein.'[24] Britain's first nominee was a Labour peer, William Warrender Mackenzie, Baron Amulree, a Scottish lawyer who had briefly held office as minister of aviation in the 1929 Labour government. Britain's second nominee, in consultation with Canada, was Charles Alexander Magrath, a Canadian banker and financier.[25] Newfoundland's nominee was the government's financial adviser, Sir William Stavert, another Canadian banker. There is no evidence to suggest that Alderdice was forced into making this nomination by pressure from the British government. Presumably, therefore, he was prepared to trust Stavert to represent Newfoundland's interests on the Commission – which suggests that he was unaware of the latter's double rôle as financial adviser to the Newfoundland government *and* confidential agent of the Bank of Montreal and, indirectly, R. B. Bennett!

During the following months the Commission, under Amulree's chair-

22/*Ibid.*, draft telegram, secretary of state for the dominions to the governor of Newfoundland, 23 Dec. 1932.

23/*Ibid.*, government of Newfoundland to the secretary of state for the dominions, 24 Dec. 1932.

24/Cmd 4480, *Report*, p. ii.

25/See *Who's Who in Canada, 1930–1*, p. 809.

manship, conducted hearings in St John's and various other parts of the country, and also in Ottawa and Montreal. 'In all,' the Commission later reported, 'we held about 100 formal sittings, and 260 witnesses, nearly half of whom came from outlying settlements, were heard and examined.' However, none of this evidence was ever published, nor does the Commission's report indicate from whom the testimony came: 'After full consideration, we decided to hold our sittings *in camera* in order that all those who wished to give evidence might speak their minds freely with the assurance that their confidence would be respected ... The wisdom of this decision was fully confirmed as our hearings progressed.'[26] But without some record of the evidence there is no way of judging the wisdom or otherwise of their choice. Their report, therefore, can only be judged by the assumptions upon which it appears to have been based, and, inevitably, by the concrete results it produced. Both these criteria leave room for serious doubts. Moreover, it cannot be overlooked that the two Canadian members of the Commission were strongly desirous of bringing Newfoundland into confederation, either then or at some later date, and that this may well have affected their contributions to the report.

On 6 February Stavert, knowing he was to be appointed a commissioner, had written to Jackson Dodds suggesting that press reports in Canada were exaggerating the extent to which Newfoundland would welcome confederation, 'but I should like very much to have a personal opinion from you as to the extent to which Canada would be interested in such a proposal if it should be thought desirable by the projected Royal Commission.' In view of his connection with the Newfoundland government, he had added: 'I consider it better that I should not personally approach the Government of Canada on the subject, preferring that ... I should maintain my present position of not having debated the situation with representatives of the Canadian Government.'[27]

His fellow Canadian, C. A. Magrath, was under no such inhibition. In April, while the Commission was in session in St John's, he wrote privately to R. B. Bennett expressing the view that 'Newfoundland must become in time part of our Dominion,' and urging 'generosity on the part of Canada.' He continued: 'By treating them generously, taking a proper interest in their affairs, and giving them the benefit of our public services, it would only be a question of a few years until they would seek entry into our confederation, meanwhile aiding them to bring their public services up to a much higher level of efficiency.'[28]

It is interesting to note, however, that Magrath later felt uneasy about

26/Cmd 4480, *Report*, p. 1.
27/Bennett Papers, N453, Stavert to Dodds, 6 Feb. 1933.
28/*Ibid.*, Magrath to Bennett, 13 April 1933.

the rôle he had played on the Commission. More than a year after its report had been submitted he sent Bennett a lengthy memorandum designed to show how Newfoundland would benefit from confederation. He did so, he wrote, 'in order that no misunderstanding could exist at a later date as to my attitude towards the people and their problems.' But in the memorandum itself he makes the striking admission that in urging confederation on the island *'I was thinking only of Canada's appearance on the map.* Now I am thinking of the people ...'[29]

But in spite of the Canadian commissioners' advocacy of confederation, by mid-1933 Canada's own deteriorating economy had made a generous Canadian gesture towards Newfoundland politically unattractive to the party in power. In June the interest on the Newfoundland national debt was again about to fall due, and this time the Canadian government refused to help. The whole sum required, $1,850,000, was therefore advanced by the British government. 'I explained our case to them,' Bennett wrote to C. A. Magrath, 'and I think they quite appreciate the fact that we are not in a position to render the assistance we did last January.'[30] Still less, it went without saying, did he believe that his government could now actively encourage a move for confederation.

On 4 October 1933 the report of the royal commission was submitted to the British House of Commons. Its recommendations, it was then clear, were of a most sweeping and uncompromising character. Various financial proposals that had been canvassed from time to time – default, devaluation, the sale of Labrador – were perfunctorily discussed and dismissed. Newfoundland's ills, the report implied, were more than financial; they were also political and even moral. For financial rehabilitation to be effective, it stated, the country would have to be freed 'from the malign influences which, developing from a prolonged period of misgovernment, have demoralised the people and warped their outlook.'[31]

It is in the light of this attitude that the recommendations of the Commission must be viewed. For if the existing political system was held to be irredeemably corrupt, and to form an insuperable barrier to financial improvement, then one conclusion inexorably followed: 'After much anxious consideration, therefore, and in spite of a strong pre-disposition in favour of the maintenance of established representative institutions and of responsible government, we have been forced to the conclusion that only by a radical change of regime for a limited period of years can the Island be

29/*Ibid.*, Magrath to Bennett, 8 Dec. 1934 (italics added). The attached memorandum is dated May 1934.
30/*Ibid.*, Bennett to Magrath, 20 July 1933.
31/Cmd 4480, *Report*, p. 193.

assisted to effective recovery.' It was essential, the report asserted, that the country should be given 'a rest from politics.' By this it presumably meant that democratic political institutions, having failed, should be replaced by non-democratic ones, for its basic constitutional recommendation was as follows:

that, until such time as Newfoundland may become self-supporting again, there should be substituted for this [the existing system] a form of Government under which full legislative and executive power would be vested in the Governor acting on the advice of a specially created Commission of Government over which His Excellency would preside. The existing Legislature and Executive Council would for the time being be suspended.

Responsibility under this new form would be to the British government with general supervision exercised through the secretary of state for dominion affairs. The Commission would be composed of six members exclusive of the governor: 'The members of the Commission would be appointed by Your Majesty, on the advice of your Ministers in the United Kingdom. Three members of the Commission would be chosen from New-foundland, and three from the United Kingdom.'[32] For a people who had lived under some form of representative government, however imperfect, however turbulent, for more than a century, the Commission thus recom-mended nothing less than the sweeping away of their entire political heri-tage.

It might be thought that a proposal of such magnitude would have stirred acute controversy, if not in Britain then certainly in New-foundland itself. Instead, it was greeted calmly, almost apathetically. There were no leaders to rally opposition. Squires was silent, and in any case widely discredited; Coaker had long ceased to be a dynamic force; which left Alderdice, who had campaigned in the 1932 general election on a promise to consider some form of constitutional change. Nothing had come of that promise, but now he was presented with a fully developed scheme for what was called, in the very words he had used, 'Government by Commission,' and may even have been along the lines he had originally envisaged.

Within the Assembly there was no effective opposition. The two Lib-erals returned in 1932, F. Gordon Bradley and R. G. Starkes, raised certain objections, but they had been closely identified with Squires and lacked standing in the country. Opposite them, at a brief session of the legislature convened in November, sat the solid ranks of Alderdice's party of merch-

32/*Ibid.*, pp. 195–7.

ants, the United Newfoundland party, who without demur adopted the necessary address to the King requesting that the constitution be suspended.[33] In Britain, the Labour party briefly fought the adoption of the report, but the vote was easily carried by the National government.

On 16 February 1934, in a ceremony held, incongruously, in a hotel ballroom, the last prime minister of Newfoundland, Frederick C. Alderdice, placed his signature on the paper that surrendered dominion status.

33/*Proceedings of the House of Assembly, Newfoundland, 1933*, pp. 157–60.

14 The Dominion of Newfoundland: a retrospect

If only I had the strength how the fetters would fly! My poor country. The
last phase.

Sir Robert Bond in 1923

For Newfoundland the opening years of the twentieth century seemed
bright with promise; where, it must be asked, did the decline set in that
ended with the débâcle of 1932 and the surrender of dominion status?

The eight years of the Bond administration, with which the century
began, may be seen in retrospect as Newfoundland's 'gilded age,' not only
for the substantial economic progress made, but because in these years –
through conflicts with the French and later the Americans – it also played
a rôle on the world stage and in the councils of Empire which its size would
not otherwise have warranted. In all these affairs it was represented by a
prime minister who was in another sense a most 'unrepresentative' figure;
indeed, Robert Bond's urbane presence at gatherings of Empire statesmen,
or at negotiations in Washington, must have conveyed an oddly misleading
impression of what political life was really like in a poor and backward
colony.

After Bond, no Newfoundland premier played a rôle of any significance
at the imperial conferences. Once the issue of reciprocity with the United
States was dead, in all other matters Newfoundland was quite content to
follow Britain's lead. And, as the usage of the word 'Dominion' evolved
from 1907 to 1931, Newfoundland's constitution was, in effect, carried
along *pari passu* with the others. Dominion status did not broaden the

island's political horizons in the way the French Shore dispute had done; once her territory was secure, Newfoundland had no more ambitions which could have been served by her own diplomacy. Dominion status was, however, a matter of national pride, and as such contributed in no small way to the harmful myth that Newfoundland was really the 'equal' of Canada. In the beginning this may not have been altogether absurd; by 1919 it most assuredly was.

In the conduct of home affairs, Bond's administration set new standards of probity and effectiveness. It is not by accident that he alone of the island's prime ministers saw fit to preserve his private papers to the last detail; for he alone could rest assured that no matter how future historians might judge his political acts, his personal integrity would never be open to question. In the overheated politics of St John's such conduct was bound to make more enemies than friends, and, moreover, Bond had a nemesis he could not escape, in the person of Edward Morris.

There was nothing Bond could have done to avoid splitting with Morris, short of surrendering the premiership. The ambitious favourite of the local Irish had not climbed out of Lime Street to let an artistocratic Liberal block his path to the highest office. By 1909, with a timely assist from a governor who was something less than a credit to his office, Morris and his People's party were firmly in control. Thereafter the hopeful examples of prudent finance and scrupulous administration that Bond had set were swept away by as rapacious a group of ministers as the country had ever known. It was they who in large measure planted the seed that came to fruition in 1932, for it was they who first sent the national debt soaring on its giddy course by building useless branch railways for political purposes.

Still, unmitigated disaster need not have followed. The Union movement, with its wonderful promise of a more just and equitable economic system, very nearly transformed the whole basis of the island's politics. But, for reasons that have already been discussed, the movement became in a real sense a 'casualty' of the First World War. The heroic early struggles of William Coaker ended in a post-war alliance with Richard Squires and a sad and puzzling personal decline.

In 1924 the Hollis Walker Report came as a sombre warning to the people that drastic reforms were necessary in the conduct of their public affairs. That warning went unheeded. The 'new broom' of Walter Monroe filled more dark places than it swept clean, and the public debt continued its upward spiral. By 1928 the 'incorrigibles' were back in power, but their presence was incidental: it was already too late. When the storm of the depression struck it mattered little whose hand was on the tiller.

II

For those who believe in democracy the prestige of the British Empire must have suffered a blow with the destruction of its fundamental basis in the oldest colony. We cannot base our argument on the importance of the British Empire to the maintenance of democracy when we calmly allow the light to go out in Newfoundland.

H. A. Innis in 1940

The members of the Amulree royal commission were, inevitably, men whose political values and assumptions were shaped by the forces of their own times; and in the early 1930s in no country were conditions such as to inspire men's faith in the efficacy or permanence of democratic institutions. Democracies, it seemed, were generally less capable than dictatorships of ensuring the maintenance of social order in the midst of a world economic depression. Open competitive politics in particular were widely regarded as socially disruptive and economically harmful. It is therefore not surprising that in 1933 a royal commission composed of a British peer and two Canadian bankers should have recommended the suspension of Newfoundland's broken-down system of democracy and its replacement by an essentially dictatorial form of government.

Yet, however understandable their thinking, it may still be asked whether their diagnosis of Newfoundland's ills was correct, and even if it was, whether the treatment they prescribed was the right one.

First, from the emphasis their report placed on the evils of the 'spoils' system it could easily be concluded that St John's in the twenties and thirties was politically on a plane with Sodom and Gomorrah. But in retrospect, can this be considered a fair judgment? Were the commissioners right to decide that there was not even *one* aspect of the old political order worth saving – before calling down 'fire and brimstone' upon all the rest? Or were they perhaps unduly influenced by the testimony of bitter, panic-stricken men who, not understanding the economic nature of their troubles, blamed everything on the 'dirty game' of politics?

That there was, in fact, political corruption on no small scale is beyond doubt; indeed, considerable attention is devoted to it elsewhere in this book. There can also be no doubt that the Newfoundland government was on the verge of financial collapse, and that in the long run the weaknesses and abuses of the political system were in large measure responsible. But it is equally clear that the *immediate* financial crisis, the inability of the

Newfoundland government to meet the interest payments on its foreign debts, was caused not by corrupt politics but rather by the severe depression in world trade, and the consequent fall in the value of Newfoundland's exports. The Commission, however, could scarcely have maintained that this alone was sufficient reason to justify the indefinite suspension of representative government. Newfoundland, after all, was not unique in being unable to meet all its financial obligations. Other countries – including Britain! – were in a similar position. The extreme remedy proposed in Newfoundland's case had therefore to be justified on the grounds that the island's political system was corrupt beyond all hope of redemption.

But the validity of such a judgment depends upon more than the accurate observation of facts; it depends also upon the *standards* by which those facts are evaluated. By what standards, it may be asked, did the Commission evaluate what they found in Newfoundland? Though their report offers no explicit guidance on this matter, its whole approach suggests that they had in mind an inflexible and possibly somewhat idealized 'Westminster Model.' Thus, when they found themselves convinced that corruption and inefficiency were endemic in Newfoundland's political system, they evidently saw nothing anomalous in judging it according to the highest standards of a politically mature, economically developed state such as Britain itself – rather than by the standards of, or in comparison with, for example, some of the more backward and underdeveloped parts of Canada, such as New Brunswick or Quebec, where graft, jobbery, administrative chaos, and all the rest were not exactly unknown. Since two of the commissioners were Canadians it is not unreasonable to assume that they at least were aware that few if any of the Canadian provincial governments at the time could have passed as paragons of financial rectitude.

They might, of course, have argued that because Newfoundland was one of the British dominions, nothing less than the strictest Westminster standards would have been in keeping with its constitutional status. But even if this is granted, and the Commission's analysis accepted, does its conclusion that Newfoundland needed to be stripped of every last vestige of representative government *necessarily* follow? Though such an extreme remedy may have been a cure for political corruption, in the eyes of those who cherished democracy it was to cure the disease by killing the patient.

Yet in the existing circumstances, was there any practical alternative? If the question is put in this form, the answer must be that there probably was not. It is impossible now to say with certainty what the consequences of default would have been. To bankers everywhere the very word was anathema, and commissioners Magrath and Stavert were no exceptions. The brief and unfavourable pronouncement on this subject in the royal commission report must therefore be viewed with suspicion. But, leaving aside such spurious concerns as the possible effect of default on the 'prestige' of the British Empire, and assuming that Newfoundland's default would not have been 'the pebble that let loose the avalanche' (just as the default of New South Wales in 1932 was not), it is at least possible that with the burden of interest payments temporarily reduced, or with the *rate* of interest realistically adjusted to a level commensurate with other prices during the depression, Newfoundland could have struggled on without outside aid. In reality, however, it was inconceivable that the royal commission would recommend default when the Newfoundland government itself had failed to do so when it had the opportunity.

On the other hand, since the British government regarded the prevention of Newfoundland's default as important to its own interests – which were not necessarily the same as those of Newfoundland – could the Commission have asked it to give Newfoundland sufficient financial aid in the form of loans to enable it to meet its payments to bondholders without demanding the surrender of self-government? Theoretically it could have, but in practice it must have known that the Dominions Office would have been unsympathetic, and the Treasury positively hostile, to such a suggestion. And even if bureaucratic approval could have been obtained, the cabinet might well have found the idea politically embarrassing. A recent biographer of Aneurin Bevan has written: 'When bankers or finance houses as far away as Newfoundland or Austria were in difficulties, loans were voted for their salvation in a matter of hours; but night after night he [Bevan] had to argue about every penny due to the people drawing transitional [unemployment] benefits.'[1] As the Newfoundland government could have testified, such loans were not without a price attached. Nor is it easy to see why the national government, or its Labour critics, should have found the prospect of granting financial aid to Newfoundland – which need not have been large in British terms and which could have been accompanied by close supervision and, if need be, strong pressure – more burdensome than the larger responsibility of complete administrative and political control. But in the crisis atmosphere of the 1930s politicians were understandably anxious to avoid the charge that they were squandering public funds to prop up foreign governments while neglecting the hardships of their own people. And this pressure was felt in Ottawa perhaps even more strongly than in London. Already the Canadian government

1/ Michael Foot, *Aneurin Bevan* (London, 1962), p. 166.

had made it clear that it would neither assist Newfoundland financially, nor encourage it to seek entry into confederation, nor purchase the territory of Labrador.

Hence, taking into account the composition of the royal commission, as well as the fact that it was appointed by Britain, and the known attitudes of the British and Canadian governments, all of which were factors circumscribing the Commission's range of options as surely as anything they found in Newfoundland, it was practically inevitable that their report would recommend the surrender of self-government and the transfer of administrative and financial control to Whitehall. The fact that democratic politics had no strong defenders in Newfoundland, and that the commissioners themselves evidently saw nothing in the old system that they considered worth preserving, no doubt made their task easier. But, in a sense, their detailed analysis of Newfoundland's predicament was little more than window-dressing – necessary, perhaps, to legitimize their recommendations, but not essential to them.

Finally, it may be asked, could the Commission, had it taken a less extreme view of the iniquities of the political system, have found some means of reconciling Whitehall control with the continuation of at least *one* freely elected body in Newfoundland, however limited its actual powers? Since the report does not discuss any alternative constitutional forms to the one proposed, it would be pointless to raise such theoretical possibilities. It is obvious, however, that no authoritarian system could have permitted an elective body to exist without running the risk of having it develop into a focus of dissent and opposition, perhaps in time capable of overthrowing the new régime itself. Those who believed in the value of democratic institutions, and hoped to see their early restoration in Newfoundland, might well have regarded this as a risk worth taking. All that can be said is that in 1933 the members of the royal commission, rightly or wrongly, did not.

15 Government by commission:
the apotheosis of the bureaucrat

THAT A 'rest from politics' was the best solution to Newfoundland's political problems was a belief by no means confined to the members of the Amulree royal commission; it was, by all accounts, widely held by the people themselves. There was indeed a widespread revulsion against the excesses and corruption which were believed to spring from the operation of open electoral politics. Yet the opposite of open politics is not the absence of politics: it is closed politics. The fundamental question which was not answered, nor even asked, was *how* – in an imperfect world of scarce resources and endemic social conflict – the diverse demands of even a society as small as Newfoundland could be resolved without some form of politics, whether open or closed. In fact, what Lord Amulree and his colleagues were advocating, whether they knew it or not, was the substitution of a closed system of bureaucratic politics for the more open though much abused system of parliamentary democracy.

One outstanding merit of the new system was thought to be its impartiality. The assumption was that a group of appointed commissioners who would (in practice) be responsible to permanent civil servants in the Dominions Office, who would in turn be responsible to a cabinet minister, who would in turn be responsible to the House of Commons, would be practically immune to local political pressures. The Commission would thus be able to make decisions and formulate policies 'objectively.' To ensure that local interests were not unrepresented, however, three of the commissioners were to be Newfoundlanders – and this naturally raised the question of who should hold these posts. Already, though unknown to the public, the circumstances surrounding the death of the old régime had ensured that at least some traditional political considerations would not be absent from the birth of the new. In particular, the unanimous consent of the governing party in the Newfoundland House of Assembly to the surrender of dominion status, to which considerable importance had been attached by observers in Britain and elsewhere, had been obtained on the understanding that certain of its leaders would obtain places on the Commission and that others would be given appointments in the public service.

This at least was the impression given to Prime Minister Alderdice by Lord Amulree in their private conversations. But nothing was put in writing, and once the necessary legislative sanction had been obtained, and the House of Assembly dissolved, the British government was unwilling to admit even privately that any such impression had been intended – though as long as no such admission had to be made, they were willing to go a considerable distance to placate Alderdice, whose co-operation they felt they would need. Hence, when the composition of the new government was under consideration, the only names on the list submitted to the secretary of state for dominion affairs for possible appointment to the 'Newfoundland' posts were those of members of the previous government. This, however, was merely a matter of form. Effectively, the matter had already been settled between Alderdice and Governor Sir Murray Anderson. In December 1933 the latter wrote as follows to Sir Edward Harding, permanent secretary of the Dominions Office:

I think Mr. Alderdice should be one Commissioner and Mr. Puddester another, the former taking Home Affairs and Education. Mr. Alderdice has, I think, the confidence of the people and is known to be thoroughly honest in matters of finance ...

Mr. Puddester was formerly business Manager of the 'Daily News' and still holds shares in it. I think his knowledge of relief work, Health and Employment problems, and his general knowledge would be valuable and necessary. He is probably 75% honest and can be kept in check.

While both these have the stigma which attaches to all Politicians in Newfoundland I can see no better choice available.

The third Commissioner must be a Roman Catholic. This we cannot get away from as the Roman Catholic Archbishop has backed up the idea of Commission Government. Hence there is a difficulty – Judge Higgins was approached by the Prime Minister but declined ... The present Minister of Justice, the Honorable L. E. Emerson, K.C., is available but I cannot recommend him ... He is not popular, is very much inclined to split hairs and I am told by the Prime Minister is very bumptious and self-opinionated ... and there are also certain doubts about his strict honesty.

A Roman Catholic gentleman whom I can recommend is Mr. W. R. Howley, K.C., who has been sounded and would accept the position of Commissioner ...

I have consulted Mr. Alderdice on the appointment of the Newfoundland Commissioners. He agrees with me that the best choice would be Mr. Alderdice, Mr. Puddester and Mr. Howley.

The governor, who was well aware that Alderdice would not be satisfied unless the other commitments he felt he had obtained from Lord Amulree were honoured, also took care to advise the permanent secretary as to how he might best be handled if he attempted to press his demands on a visit to London. His letter continued:

From conversations I have had with Mr. Alderdice he is very determined some of the ex-Ministers should be employed for a time and very assertive that Lord Amulree agreed to the necessity.

Mr. Alderdice when he visits the Dominions Office will psychologically be a very different man from Mr. Alderdice with 'his foot on his native heath' ... I think if I may suggest it that the best course to follow would be to pat him on the back for having got the Bill through in Newfoundland and at the same time make it clear to him that any *appearance* of having got the Bill through by the promise to some members of his Party of employment under the new Government would give a very bad impression and be a bad start for Commission Government.[1]

The issue, however, was still unresolved when the Commission took office on 16 February 1934 with Alderdice, Puddester, and Howley as its Newfoundland members. Immediately, Alderdice was faced with a clamour for appointments from those who expected employment under the Commission; and among these were some to whom he had made unequivocal promises. As he wrote to Lord Amulree on 26 February, he had had to assure his ministers 'that their support of Government by Commission would not involve them being cast adrift,' and there were four to whom he was specifically obligated: 'Before the House of Assembly convened, and before I had called a meeting of my party, I discussed the position of these four Ministers with each of them separately. They accepted my promise in good faith and largely through their influence I was successful in putting the necessary legislation through the House of Assembly.' He also reminded Lord Amulree:

You saw no good reason why these particular Ministers, four in all, should not be retained for at least a year at their regular salaries, in some nominal or advisory capacity, in connection with their respective Departments. After-

1/Public Record Office, Dominions Office Papers, series 35, vol. 489, N1004/7, Anderson to Harding, 26 Dec. 1933, 'Private & Personal' (emphasis in original).

wards, or before the twelve months had elapsed, they might be fitted into some position such as the Outport Magistracy or the like.[2]

Lord Amulree denied that he had given any assurance on the matter, but in consultation with Secretary of State J. H. Thomas, who, as a politician, was sympathetic to Alderdice's position and also concerned to prevent the dispute from causing a rift between Newfoundland and United Kingdom members of the Commission, he privately agreed that if possible the point should be stretched to meet Alderdice's interpretation.[3] The 'hard line' opposition came mainly from Sir Edward Harding and Governor Anderson and their advice eventually prevailed over the inclination of their political 'master.' The governor reported in April that he had been told that 'all the ex-ministers were confidently expecting letters from the Dominions Office informing them that they would be placed in Government positions.'[4] If so, they waited in vain. In the end Alderdice was left in the humiliating position of having made promises he was not permitted to keep, in spite of a final plea in person to the Dominions Office. Nothing more clearly reveals where power lay under the new régime than Sir Edward Harding's note on their conversation:

I thought it wise to tell Mr. Alderdice quite firmly that it seemed to me that what the suggestion amounted to was, in reality, a bribe to some of the ex-Ministers to induce them to accept the Royal Commission's Report. This was a step which I felt no Secretary of State could possibly have agreed to in any circumstances ...[5]

The appointment of the United Kingdom commissioners raised problems of another kind. Newfoundland was not exactly the brightest jewel in the imperial crown, and there were few civil servants of any standing in Whitehall who would look upon a tour of duty there as anything but a penitential exile – a mark of failure rather than a promotion, even if as commissioners their responsibilities and salaries would be larger. As one commissioner later wrote, 'I had no particular desire to go to Newfoundland. The Treasury brought to bear upon me as much pressure as they normally do in regard to appointments of less than first-class importance, and in the end I agreed.'[6] The Treasury, however, in the Britain of 1933, could be certain of finding no shortage of worthy candidates who could

2/DO 35/499/N1024, Alderdice to Amulree, 26 Feb. 1934.
3/DO 35/499/N1024/4, Thomas to Anderson, 21 March 1934.
4/DO 35/499/N1024/7, Anderson to Harding, 11 April 1934.
5/DO 35/499/N1024/9, note on talk [by Sir Edward Harding], 9 Nov. 1934.
6/T. Lodge, *Dictatorship in Newfoundland* (London, 1939), p. 1.

be thus persuaded, or who for personal financial reasons were willing, and in some cases almost pathetically eager, to accept.

The three who were finally selected were Sir John Hope Simpson, a retired ex-member of the Indian civil service; E. N. R. Trentham, a Treasury official who had spent the prevous two years in Newfoundland as financial adviser to the government; and Thomas Lodge, whose previous career had been divided between the civil service and business.[7] Though not of the first rank in the British bureaucratic hierarchy, they were all competent and experienced administrators. Whether they were also politicians, or could learn to be politicians, was another matter, yet crucial to the success or failure of the new Commission government. As commissioners, they could not confine themselves to administrative matters; but unlike their civil service colleagues in Britain, they would have no political ministers to act as spokesmen for their policies, or to tell them what the public would not stand. Nor could they safely rely upon the political judgment of their Newfoundland colleagues, for this would be tantamount to putting themselves in a minister-bureaucrat relationship with the Newfoundlanders – and this was not the way it was intended the Commission should operate. Moreover, since all three Newfoundland commissioners had been prominent members of the previous régime, their political judgment was in any case suspect.

An alternative policy which was obviously more attractive to the English commissioners, and which was soon adopted, was to shield all the deliberations and executive functions of the Commission behind a cloak of secrecy – in effect, to make the whole political process subject to the same convention of administrative secrecy under which they had been accustomed to work as civil servants. This also had the additional advantage, from their point of view, of concealing from the public their true relationship with their Newfoundland colleagues, which they had reason to fear would turn out to be less than happy. The Newfoundlanders were expected to be sensitive about their reduced status and perhaps resentful. Already Governor Anderson had forewarned Whitehall of what to expect. Alderdice, he wrote, 'undoubtedly suffers from an inferiority complex and is afraid the United Kingdom Commissioners may adopt a superior attitude,

7/He had been an administrative class official in the Ministry of Shipping. Sir Edward Harding wrote of him: 'He left the Civil Service some 12 years ago, and was for a good long time engaged in business in France. Latterly, about three years ago, he was selected to be the U.K. representative on the Phosphate Commission which works the deposits at Nauru and Ocean Island. In this work he has been completely successful, and has worked well with his Australian and New Zealand colleagues. He is a strong personality ...' DO 35/489/N1004/7, Harding to Anderson, 10 Jan. 1934.

although I have endeavoured to assure him to the contrary. He is most anxious to avoid a staff of Englishmen coming out with the Commissioners as he thinks they might form an English 'Colony' who would look down on the Newfoundland people generally and be unpopular.'[8]

This, indeed, was only one of several uncertain relationships which had been built into the new constitution, and which were certain to test the resources of even the most adept and experienced of politicians. Most seriously, the position of the governor and his constitutional relationship to the Commission as a whole was particularly unclear. Under the Letters Patent and Royal Instructions issued under the authority of the Newfoundland Act, 1933, which formed the basis of the new constitution, the governor was to preside over the meetings of the Commission and was empowered to act upon its 'advice.' In other words, the governor was not given the same powers as the governor of a Crown colony, where, typically, the governor was assisted in the discharge of his executive functions by an executive council whom he was directed to consult but whose advice he was not compelled to take. Nor was he given the same powers as the governor general of a dominion, where, typically, the governor general had no personal executive power and acted only on the advice of his ministers. His position, in fact, was somewhere between the two – though exactly where was not defined.

Subsequently, when the ambiguity surrounding the governor's rôle had become a source of difficulty, the secretary of state for dominion affairs justified the position on the ground that 'the acceptance by His Majesty's Government here of a form of Government in which the Governor's powers would be limited in this way was one of the conditions on which self-government was surrendered by Newfoundland.' He went on to state what he believed the governor's position to be:

In point of fact ... I am satisfied that the Governor is not prevented in practice by those limitations of his constitutional powers from being the effective head of the administration. The fact that he presides as Chairman at each meeting of the Commission of Government makes all the difference to his authority and influence. He is given under the Letters Patent the right to vote which is exercisable on all occasions when there is a difference of opinion in the Commission, and not merely on those occasions when the Commission is divided 3 and 3. The possession of this right implies a right to speak and to take an active part in the proceedings of the Commission. This indeed is brought out in Clause IV of the Royal Instructions, in which the Governor is directed in all cases to *consult* with the Commission, and though he is also directed in the

8/*Ibid.*, Anderson to Harding, 26 Dec. 1933.

same clause to act in accordance with the decision of the Commission, the use of the word 'consult' clearly implies that it is open to him to express his own views and take the lead in guiding the Commission's deliberations. In short, he is in a position to exercise his influence to the end that in any given case the 'decision' eventually arrived at by the Commission may be such as commends itself to him.[9]

This, however, is a statement of what the governor's rôle *could* be, and while legally and constitutionally correct, it does not accurately describe how the Commission in fact operated in the crucial first two years of its existence. Governor Sir Murray Anderson, perhaps because of his previous experience as governor under the dominion constitution, tended to play a part more nearly like that of a neutral chairman, acting on the advice of the Commission, and exercising a decisive influence only in the event of a deadlock. Moreover, there were both constitutional and organizational factors which made it difficult for the governor to dominate the new government. For policy-making on the 'grand' scale was in the hands of the Dominions Office and the Treasury, while at the local level it was in the hands of the commissioners, each of whom, by virtue of being the head of a department and hence responsible for the administration of policy, commanded resources of information which the governor could not easily challenge. In practice, the major policy-making departments, finance, natural resources, public utilities, were all headed by United Kingdom commissioners, and in the pattern which developed in the first years of the Commission it was the most forceful of these, and not the governor, who exercised the greatest influence upon the decisions of the government. This was to be a source of dissension from the very beginning, and grew into a bitter conflict when a new governor arrived who believed that his position should be closer to that of the governor of a Crown colony.

Of the United Kingdom commissioners, the most outstanding was undoubtedly Thomas Lodge. Lodge's failure to rise to the heights of the British civil service, and hence his appointment to Newfoundland, should perhaps be attributed more to his unorthodox and abrasive personality than to any lack of intelligence or administrative ability. He was energetic, articulate, and intellectually arrogant. He did not 'suffer fools gladly' – and among the latter he evidently counted the bulk of mankind, including most of his fellow commissioners. These qualities alone would not have made him exceptional in Whitehall, but in him they were combined with

9/DO 35/492/N1005/8, Secretary of State Malcolm MacDonald to Lord Winterton, 9 April 1936 (emphasis in original).

others which were frowned upon in that tight little world of administrative-class civil servants. There, the approved fencing weapons were calculated rudeness and subtle snubs; Lodge's behaviour on the other hand was characterized by toughness and directness. Though his mind was 'Whitehall' his instincts were more like those of a type of businessman best described as a 'rugged entrepreneur.' Like the latter, he was 'goal-oriented': he wanted to take action, get results, achieve something immediately, while his English colleagues were more conventional civil service types. They were basically 'agreement-oriented,' had internalized the norms of Whitehall, and thus placed a higher premium on caution and conformity than on boldness and imagination.[10]

The background, training, and personalities of the English commissioners clearly determined the 'style' of the new government. This was most strikingly reflected in its early years of operation. In contrast to the highly personal but chaotic administration which had been typical of Newfoundland governments in the past, the Commission's administration was a model of bureaucratic efficiency. In all matters requiring experience and expertise, the English commissioners were almost instantly effective. They undertook a major reorganization of government departments, replacing the unwieldy existing structure with a compact and rational regrouping according to function, with each new department headed by a commissioner (for example, the old departments of Marine and Fisheries and Agriculture and Mines were combined into a single Department of Natural Resources). Within each new department further internal reforms were imposed to make administration more uniform and systematic. With the aid of expert advisers from the United Kingdom, the operations of the Post Office and Customs and Excise Department were sharply improved, and the entire tariff system revised. The effect of the latter was not only to remove some of the glaring anomalies of the old system but also to make the burden of indirect taxation generally less regressive, to the benefit of the poor. Other significant improvements were made in the administration of the 'dole' and in the organization of public health and welfare services. In other areas, such as education, denominational pressures prevented any major reform, but even here teachers' salaries were raised and an attempt made to improve existing facilities for the training of teachers.

The changes introduced were well within the competence of the English commissioners since, for the most part, they consisted of bringing Newfoundland practices into line with those of the United Kingdom and its

10/For an interesting interpretation of the interaction of 'Whitehall' and 'business' rôles in British society, see J. P. Nettl, 'Consensus or Elite Domination: The Case of Business,' *Political Studies*, vol. 13, no. 1 (Feb. 1965).

colonial territories. Unfortunately, the success of the commissioners as administrators was more than matched by their failure as politicians and policy-makers.

Nothing in their previous training or experience had given them either the ability or the inclination to communicate with the people, to understand their fears and sensibilities. These are the qualities of politicians, not bureaucrats. And to the latter, political blunders come easily when they are unrestrained by political ministers. Upon taking office the commissioners, in the interest of economy, proceeded to attack the few remaining symbols of Newfoundland's lost independence. The trappings of parliamentary government were stripped from the legislature and the building converted to office use; the national museum was closed and its contents carelessly dispersed to places where they could no longer be exhibited. Actions communicate as loud as words, and the message was: 'We are the masters now.' Thus, in spite of their valuable administrative reforms, the commissioners speedily dissipated the goodwill which had originally existed towards them. Nor were matters helped by their policy of meeting criticism by silence and secrecy. As the St John's *Daily News* complained in 1936:

From an early loquaciousness the Government has turned to sphinx-like silence leaving the public to conjecture as best it can if there is any special policy in effect or in contemplation and what the nature of that policy may be.

The communiques issued after meetings of the Commission are chiefly notable for what they do not contain. Nothing of importance is revealed in them. They do bear evidence of ample padding for the purpose of giving the public something to read. But the public wants more than a sop to its natural curiosity. It wants facts ... We may have abused the privilege of responsible government, but that does not alter the fact that we had it and that, therefore, we expect full and detailed information of the course of administrative action ...[11]

The failure of the commissioners as policy-makers, however, was due more to the impossible nature of the task they had been set than to any factors over which they had personal control. According to the Amulree royal commission's report, they were to be responsible for bringing about the financial, and indeed even the moral and political, rehabilitation of Newfoundland. Yet to the extent that Newfoundland's financial difficulties

11/5 Nov. 1936, as quoted in R. L. Clark, 'Newfoundland 1934–49 – A Study of the Commission of Government and Confederation with Canada,' unpublished PH D dissertation, University of California, Los Angeles, 1951.

were caused by the world depression, they were no better able than the previous Newfoundland government, or the government of any other country, to produce in isolation an economic miracle. In fact, their limits of manœuvre were severely restricted, and they can be faulted only for their failure to operate successfully within those limits.

Nevertheless, their position was considerably more flexible than that of the Newfoundland government they had replaced. This was due partly to direct financial assistance from the British Treasury, but even more to the Treasury's guarantee of a new conversion issue of Newfoundland bonds which in effect amounted to a lowering of the interest rate payable to holders of old Newfoundland bonds and consequently a reduction of $1,750,000 in the amount the island's government had to pay annually in interest. There was thus some easing of financial pressure on the new Commission, and consequently the possibility that they would be able to make at least a modest beginning on a policy of economic reconstruction. This, after all, was to be the practical justification for Newfoundland's surrender of self-government. But no such beginning was made, for no policy was forthcoming.

The reason why is explained in the following letter from Governor Anderson to the permanent secretary of the Dominions Office, in response to the latter's request that the Commission produce 'a considered report on the economic situation':

First, the Commission as a body are as yet by no means in agreement as to the precise means to be found for the solution of Newfoundland's economic difficulties. It may be, as stated in the Royal Commission's Report, that reliance must continue to be placed on the fishery as the main industry of the country; but there is a good deal to be said for the view that Newfoundland can never hope to obtain a sufficient livelihood from the fishery and that the proper course would be to acquiesce in this industry being perhaps not wiped out but at least becoming a purely subsidiary occupation, and that the Commission should concentrate instead primarily on the development of agriculture. If a report has to be written during the next few months this cleavage of opinion would undoubtedly appear; indeed it might well be necessary to come to such conclusions as would conflict seriously with those of the Royal Commission in regard to the country's industrial future.[12]

The Amulree royal commission had stated in its report that 'the codfishery has always been, and must continue to be the mainstay of the island,' a view which to most Newfoundlanders, including the Newfoundland mem-

12/DO 35/504/N1051/1, Anderson to Harding, 13 Aug. 1934.

bers of the Commission, was practically self-evident. But the English commissioners, when confronted with what seemed to be the hopelessly depressed state of the industry, were less certain. And one of them in particular, the forceful Thomas Lodge, quickly became convinced that the development of agriculture, not the fishery, offered the best prospect of making Newfoundland self-supporting.

In his view, Newfoundland was suffering from overpopulation, and 'if surplus population cannot be absorbed in fishing or mining or industry, if emigration is impracticable, the only alternative is settlement on the land.'[13] The idea of resettling the unemployed on the land was not new. It was being tried in Britain, and a small scheme for the resettlement of ten men and their families was proposed to the Commission by a group of St John's philanthropists early in 1934. The ten selected were, according to Lodge, 'undernourished, ill-clad and with obviously lowered *morale* due to years of partial or complete unemployment.'[14] But the Commission agreed to support the experiment to the extent of the bare cost of relief maintenance, and when two months later Lodge again saw the men, he was 'profoundly impressed by the moral transformation which had taken place.'[15] From that moment he alone of the commissioners was absolutely convinced of the rightness of a particular economic policy.

By sheer force of intellect and personality, combined with the psychological advantage he obtained from the inability of the others to propose positive alternatives, he succeeded in pushing his reluctant colleagues into acceptance of a government land settlement scheme. As he cryptically put it, 'departmental responsibility for land settlements was, for reasons of no material importance, transferred to me in September 1935.'[16] He could not, however, persuade them to devote sufficient financial resources to the scheme to make any significant contribution to the economy as a whole. Even in the case of skilled and experienced farmers, agriculture in Newfoundland's harsh climate and rocky soil is at least as precarious a livelihood as fishing, and it seems to have been obvious to all but Lodge that the cost of turning the urban unemployed of St John's and the thousands of underemployed fishermen into pioneer homesteaders would be prohibitive, and even then they would be unlikely to be able to survive without subsidies. The major economic effect of land settlement, therefore, was to place a sufficient drain on the Commission's finances to render impossible any major reforms in the structure of the fishery, on which the vast majority of Newfoundlanders continued to depend for their livelihood, beyond the

13/Lodge, *Dictatorship in Newfoundland*, p. 172.
14/*Ibid.*, p. 173.   15/*Ibid.*
16/*Ibid.*, p. 184.

introduction of a regulated system of marketing similar to that which William Coaker had unsuccessfully tried to implement in 1920.

Politically, the impact upon the Commission was disastrous. After acting with such initial decisiveness in such matters as the occupation of the legislature, they then lapsed into a secret internal struggle over policy, to the bewilderment of the Newfoundland public and interested members of the British House of Commons.[17] Moreover, the quarrel over land settlement spilt over into other areas of policy and became as well a source of much personal friction between individual commissioners.

The year 1935 marked a critical turning point. The commissioners, unable to agree but under pressure to act, discovered that they were unbound by any such convention as 'cabinet solidarity' and began, in their individual capacities, to communicate directly with the officials of the Dominions Office, pressing their own viewpoints and attacking and discrediting their fellow commissioners with whom they disagreed. Relations between Alderdice and Lodge were particularly strained. In January Lodge produced a 'Memorandum on General Policy' in which he said of Newfoundland that 'with the possible exception of Russia and a couple of the Balkan States, I doubt whether there is any purely white community in the world on such a low cultural level or where complete ignorance of anything outside the daily task is so widespread,' and concluded with a plea for land settlement as a means of rehabilitation.[18] An unsigned Dominions Office minute attached to the memorandum noted: 'Sir M. Anderson told us yesterday that Mr. Alderdice had lately been crabbing [sic] the Markland [land settlement] experiment and had to be reproached for being generally unhelpful. It is possible that the Memorandum was designed to commit him to the Commission's policy.' A month later, Lodge, anticipating complaints about his action in dismissing the captain of a government steamer for smuggling beaver skins, an offence not regarded as particularly serious in Newfoundland, and aware of Alderdice's hostility, wrote to Sir H. Batterbee of the Dominions Office: 'I emphasise the unanimity of the

17/The Dominions Office went to considerable pains to avoid provoking awkward questions from opposition MPs, including redrafting the Commission's innocuous annual report to make it even more obscure and uninformative. Sir John Hope Simpson could appreciate the artistry of a master craftsman: 'My dear Clutterbuck, I have read the Report of Newfoundland with a certain feeling of admiration. It would be difficult to draft anything less colourful, and the amount of detailed information given is negligible except in the Finance Sections' (DO 35/504/N1051/3, Simpson to P. A. Clutterbuck, 7 Jan. 1935). Clutterbuck was a Dominions Office official who had served as secretary to the Amulree royal commission and was probably the major author of its report. He eventually rose to become Sir Alexander Clutterbuck, GCMG, permanent under secretary of state, Commonwealth Relations Office.
18/DO 35/504/N1051/7, 25 Jan. 1935.

Commission's decision [regarding the dismissal] because I strongly suspect Alderdice of telling his cousin Walter Monroe – a personally honest but incredibly stupid ex Prime Minister – that the poor Newfoundlanders can't prevail against these stiff necked Englishmen!'[19]

Meanwhile, the poor of St John's, their hopes turned into desperation by the grim fact of another winter of hunger, were beginning to stir. By May the mob of the city's unemployed was again a political force. Under the leadership of a five-man committee, they put forward a number of demands to the government, including the recognition of the committee as their official representatives and the acceptance of the committee's list of the names of those actually unemployed. After an interview with J. C. Puddester, commissioner for public health and welfare, who promised that the government would consider their demands, the leaders issued a statement which in its concluding paragraphs caught well the atmosphere of the time:

In view of our deplorable and inexcusable living conditions (which by this hour have been prolonged beyond human endurance) we must therefore consider such demands of the unemployed in St. John's (whose spokesmen we are) as most fair and just, as well as extremely simple and wonderfully expedient.

We mean business. We the Committee of the unemployed have the facts of our brothers' miseries and will leave no stone unturned to see they are given a square deal. It is with us now – One for All! and, All for One!

We want work, not dole – which is poison to an independent industrious people as ours is.

We will call for the answer of the Hon. Gentlemen of the Newfoundland Commission of Government at 3 p.m. tomorrow Thursday May 9th.[20]

The government answered promptly with a curt refusal of all the committee's demands. On the following day, 10 May, several hundred of the unemployed marched on the Colonial Building, where a similar demonstration three years before had brought down the government of Richard Squires. Again the result was riot:

Stones were thrown and when it became apparent that the mob would enter the building the police numbering about 70 drew batons and charged them. A few policemen were injured by stones and several of the demonstrators were

19/DO 35/504/N1051/9, Lodge to Batterbee, 2 Feb. 1935.
20/DO 35/506/N1101/1, petition from 'Committee of the Unemployed,' 8 May 1935.

struck by police batons. They were soon dispersed and the whole affair occupied only a few minutes. Later in the evening a further demonstration took
place after a meeting which was addressed by the ringleaders and others. As a
result of this some shop windows were broken, one shop window looted but
no food shops were disturbed.[21]

Four of the five members of the leadership committee of the unemployed
were subsequently arrested and tried, but were acquitted before a jury.

Thereafter, however, the commissioners had to live with the uncomfort-
able fact that they, though supposedly 'non-political,' were not immune
from political violence. This inevitably introduced into their behaviour an
additional element of internal stress, but even more importantly it also
shook the confidence of the Dominions Office in the Commission's ability
even to maintain public order. The fear of an uprising, and the embarrass-
ment that this would cause to the British government, consequently became a matter of grave concern to Whitehall. In spite of soothing words
from the governor, other intelligence sources strongly indicated that the
situation in St John's remained explosive. One of these sources was P. D.
H. Dunn, a British civil servant who had been seconded to the Newfoundland Customs Department. In an interview in London with a senior Dominions Office official he reported that 'he had been very much surprised
at the way in which former supporters of the Commission appeared now
in the role of critics' and, with an unfortunate choice of words, that 'there
seemed little doubt that the Commission had lost ground lately with the
man in the street.' He also said it was 'common knowledge' that 'dis-
gruntled political elements were exploiting the present economic troubles
for all they were worth and ... were meeting with considerable success.'
So much so, he believed, that 'people of all kinds seemed now to take it
for granted that the Commission could not last very much longer.'[22]

Of all the politicians of the old régime, the one the commissioners – and
the Dominions Office – feared most was Richard Squires. A close watch
was kept on the activities of William Coaker, but it was Squires who in
their eyes constituted the major threat to the government. Without elections, they had no way of knowing how much support he could rally round
him; all they knew was that he was actively plotting their downfall:

Continuing, Mr. Dunn said that it had been reported before he left Newfoundland that Sir R. Squires was shortly to address a public meeting with a view to

21/DO 35/500/N1029/8, secret quarterly report, 1 July 1935.
22/DO 35/500/N1029/9, note of a talk with Mr Dunn, secretary for customs,
1 Oct. 1935.

rallying opposition to the Commission. Personally, however, he did not think that Sir R. Squires would choose to come into the open yet. His most likely course of action would be to continue for a while to foment disaffection by the underground methods of which he was a master with a view to its boiling over during the winter in a series of riots on a grand scale. An orgy of window-smashing, looting of food shops, police charges and general disturbances, ostensibly directed against the 'Dictatorship' would be calculated ... to impress public opinion in England. Sir R. Squires was probably counting on staged agitation of this sort to weaken the position of the Government within and without.

He also indicated that a shadow government was in existence, for he personally had already been approached by an ex-minister who told him that he expected the Commission to fall during the winter, and asked him whether he would be willing 'to stay under the new regime, or would he have to go with the Commissioners.'

The prevailing uncertainty over the future of the government, Dunn believed, was having a damaging effect upon its operation: By way of further illustration he said that the present unsatisfactory manner in which the Department of Justice is being run was due to Mr. Dunfield's ... belief that a change of regime was to be expected before long; he naturally did not want to take any action which would offend those likely to be prominent in a new regime. [Mr Brian Dunfield, a Newfoundland lawyer, was the senior permanent official in the Justice Department.]

The concern of the Dominions Office was that the Commission should not sit idly by while Richard Squires arranged its overthrow. Dunn was therefore asked 'whether it would not be possible for some scheme to be devised which would get most of the permanent unemployed out of St. John's and distribute them, possibly in labour camps, at selected spots out of reach of political influence.' There was no doubt as to whose political influence: 'the removal of these men and their dispersion into small groups would deprive Sir R. Squires of his chief weapon.' Dunn, however, discouraged the idea. He replied that the men would probably refuse to go, and that in any case it was too late to take such action before the winter set in.[23]

As predicted, Squires remained in the background but his supporters became increasingly active. On 30 October 1935 a public meeting was organized in St John's to consider a resolution demanding the abolition of the Commission and a return to responsible government. The *Evening*

23/*Ibid.*

Telegram, which continued editorially to give qualified support to the Commission, reported that the Majestic Theatre, where the meeting was held, was filled to capacity and that 'a crowd as large as that inside the building congregated on the Duckworth Street front and listened to the addresses from a loudspeaker.' The resolution stated that 'the sufferings of our destitute people since the inception of Commission Government have been quietly borne' but that 'rumblings of discontent and unrest are now being heard in every town, village and hamlet.' One of its proposers, E. D. Elliott, protested that 'we are subservient to an autocracy that has no material interest in us ... We are worse off than the Kaffirs of Africa and a people without any political status in the Empire.'[24] The resolution was enthusiastically adopted and marked the beginning of what promised to be a full-scale political campaign. In the following months meetings were held at Placentia and Conception Bay which endorsed the original St John's resolution. But, in a situation reminiscent of the struggle for representative institutions in the 1820s, public enthusiasm diminished in inverse ratio to the distance from the capital. In the hope of overcoming this communication barrier, Peter Cashin, who had emerged as the leading anti-Commission agitator, obtained permission to broadcast over the government-controlled radio station, but a single broadcast could have little effect and the campaign failed to spread beyond the Avalon Peninsula. Squires therefore made no public move, and the tense winter of 1935–6 passed quietly.

Poverty in the outports meanwhile was as widespread as at any time in the island's history. According to the estimate of Commissioner Sir John Hope Simpson, there were '30,000 families of fishermen of whom the large majority will, this year, have nothing';[25] but whether politicians who were less discredited by their past records than Squires and Cashin could have rallied mass support will never be known.

The Commission had survived, though not through any effort of its own. It remained internally paralysed and divided. The only response of the Newfoundland commissioners to the political threat was to warn their English colleagues against taking any step which might disturb the existing class structure. Again, the diary-like correspondence of Hope Simpson is particularly revealing. In view of the poverty of the fishermen, he wrote,

... it is remarkable to note the apparent prosperity of the mercantile community in St. John's. There are a large number of apparently wealthy firms,

24/*Evening Telegram*, St John's, 31 Oct. 1935.
25/DO 35/500/N1029/10, Simpson to Harding, 24 Sept. 1935, 'Personal and Confidential.'

each of whom has a large number of highly paid partners or directors, who live in luxury and seem to have money for everything they want. I was dining last night at the home of one of these merchants, and after dinner the men – three merchants, one of my Newfoundland colleagues and myself – sat talking round the table. I raised the problem of the fishermen. The three merchants were agreed that the standard of comfort was very low but that the fisherman wanted nothing more, and was happy struggling along in the circumstances in which he found himself. My Newfoundland colleague took the opportunity to warn me that we (that is the U.K. Commissioners) must be careful not to attempt to create in the minds of the people of this country a demand for a higher standard of comfort. The opinions of the merchants there, and the remarks of my colleague, are typical of the St. John's attitude towards this problem.[26]

The Newfoundland commissioner had nothing to fear: his English colleagues were not intent upon radicalizing the people. Instead, their response to the political threat was to withdraw even further from public involvement – which for them was not difficult. At the time of their arrival in Newfoundland they had been installed in suites of the fortress-like Newfoundland Hotel, and two years later they were still there, forming, together with the civil service advisers who had joined them, a tiny community of bureaucrats in exile. Their living quarters placed them in easy communication with one another, though not with their Newfoundland colleagues, and this, when personal relations became strained, was inevitably a source of friction. In December 1935 Commissioner W. R. Howley took the occasion of a visit to London to complain to the secretary for the dominions that 'the Newfoundland members do not feel that their views are really sought' and that this 'was getting known to the public outside [and] derogating from the authority of the Administration.'[27] Thomas Lodge, on the other hand, maintained that the Newfoundlanders were 'so easy-going and unbusiness-like that the Commission would never get anywhere at all if its pace had to be accommodated to that of the Newfoundland members.'[28] The Dominions Office note, however, concluded with the observation that 'it is essential in practice that everything should be done to raise the status of the Newfoundland members in the eyes of the public, otherwise we shall have difficulty in obtaining suitable candidates to replace them when the time comes.'[29]

26/Ibid.
27/DO 35/490/N1004A/18, memorandum of a conversation between Mr MacDonald and Mr Howley, Dec. 1935, 'Secret.'
28/DO 35/490/N1004A/19, note on main points raised by Mr Howley, Dec. 1935.
29/Ibid.

The future of the governor and the English commissioners was also by this time in serious doubt. The officials in the Dominions Office were uncomfortably aware of the Commission's failings and the need to make changes in its personnel if not in its structure. Lodge, meanwhile, was taking advantage of the Commission's weakness to urge changes in both. In particular, he was placing an awkwardly narrow interpretation upon the constitutional powers of the governor, maintaining that however undesirable it might be in practice, the latter was not legally empowered to act as a political executive. 'I think what Lodge would like,' wrote an exasperated Governor Anderson, 'would be the U.K. Commissioners acting as "Mussolinis" and the Governor acting the part of the King of Italy.'[30] What the Dominions Office evidently decided *they* would like, however, was a governor with a more forceful personality than Anderson, someone who would place his own stamp upon the Commission and give it personal direction.

Their entirely predictable choice for the job was another naval officer, Vice-Admiral Sir Humphrey Walwyn, a bluff and hearty sea-faring man, totally innocent of any experience in government or public administration. But for an accident of birth, he could as easily have become governor in 1736 as 1936. He was neither intelligent nor educated (indeed, if his letters are any guide, he was no more than passably literate), and possessed to a degree bordering on parody a simple-minded faith in the shibboleths of the quarter-deck. Long years of command, moreover, had given him a massive self-confidence: Newfoundland for him was merely another ship and the Commission another unruly crew to be whipped into shape by leadership and discipline. A head-on clash between the new governor and Thomas Lodge was thus inevitable. Their first meeting is recorded, in characteristic style, by Walwyn:

Lodge returned on Wednesday night and I had a long talk to him on Thursday. We are perfectly friendly and I appreciate his brain.

He rather surprised me by taking the line that I was not a Governor in an administrative position.

He is, of course, at the back of it all, has practically run the Commission, and openly said he had got them all in his pocket because he had the brains.

He expected me to be a passive sort of puppet who would take no part in debates nor express any opinion at the Commission meetings (he was at the meeting on Thursday).

I very soon explained to him who was the captain of the ship out here.[31]

30/DO 35/490/N1004/45, Anderson to Harding, 22 June 1935, 'Secret and Personal.'
31/DO 35/490/N1004/77, Walwyn to Harding, 22 Feb. 1936.

Nothing could have been more calculated to infuriate Lodge, who immediately set out to force a major change in the constitution of the régime. Curiously, his proposal would, if implemented, have given the office of governor considerably greater power, including 'a measure of control over individual departments sufficient to ensure that they are efficiently administered.' He also maintained that the assumption of such control would be 'incompatible with the retention of the Newfoundland Commissioners in executive, as distinct from advisory positions,' and that 'the logical consequence is that all the executive responsibility should fall into English hands.' Newfoundlanders could serve as advisers, in the hope that 'in a somewhat distant future [the Commission] could evolve into a legislative council partly nominated and partly elected by the people.'[32] The catch, as even Walwyn could see, was that the new governor's responsibilities would be such that he would practically have to be an experienced professional administrator – such as Thomas Lodge!

Hence, in forwarding Lodge's proposal for a new constitution to the Dominions Office Walwyn rather obviously added a note of warning: Lodge, he wrote, 'may want to create a billet for himself, but he is not wanted out here in that capacity, because of his inherent rudeness to people with a lower intelligence than himself.'[33]

In fact, there was no possibility that Lodge's proposal would be accepted in London, for it would have meant calling attention to Newfoundland in the House of Commons, which was something the Dominions Office was anxious to avoid. Any request for constitutional revision was bound to be viewed by the Labour opposition as tantamount to a confession of failure. The secretary for the dominions, moreover, was in the exposed position of having recently made a statement to the House to the effect that economic conditions in Newfoundland were 'improving,' which was patently untrue. Walwyn, while privately admitting that the statement 'would give a wrong impression,' had suppressed a devastating critique of it which Lodge had prepared for circulation to the Commission, but the issue remained potentially embarrassing to the British government. Lodge's attempted criticism thus further damaged his personal standing in Whitehall.

'I am really rather sorry for Walwyn,' he wrote to a confidant in the Dominions Office. 'It is not his fault that he wasn't brought up to sell dried codfish and that he cannot disentangle the truth out of the volumes of nonsense which this collection of seventh-rate grocers [the St John's merchants] pours steadily in his ear. He would be better for the healthy scepticism which life in Whitehall inculcates in the civil servant and which

32/DO 35/490/N1004A/24, copy of paper by Lodge [March 1936].
33/DO 35/490/N1004/79, Walwyn to Harding, 9 March 1936.

my sojourn among the lower classes of commerce has not entirely eradicated!'[34] But, ironically, according to Whitehall's ethical code, it was Lodge and not Walwyn who had behaved irresponsibly.

Lodge, indeed, had played his last card: either he or the governor would have to go, and he was clearly losing. Walwyn, meanwhile, in his own bumptious way had made a favourable impression upon the Newfoundland public. He, at least, was not a colourless bureaucrat; he was energetic and outgoing, and, though he could provide no bread, he could provide a passable imitation of a circus. A bit of pomp and ceremony and a touch of old-fashioned British jingoism still went a long way in the St John's of 1936. This further undermined Lodge's influence, for previously he had been the only English member of the Commission with even a limited public following, mainly among trade unionists to whom he was always particularly sympathetic and considerate.[35] By October, Walwyn was in a sufficiently strong position to make sure that the Dominions Office would remove Lodge from the Commission at the expiry of his first term of office in the spring of 1937.

The personnel of the Commission had already begun to change. Alderdice had died in the previous year and had been replaced by J. A. Winter, a member of the St John's élite who was scathingly described by Sir John Hope Simpson as a 'Sahib' who was 'quite colourless and would be of no value in council.'[36] The other Newfoundland commissioners, Howley and Puddester, stoutly maintained that Alderdice (now safely out of the way) had promised them what amounted to life tenure on the Commission, and at first resisted all suggestions that they should retire. Howley was eventually enticed out by a time-honoured method: he was appointed to the sinecure post of registrar of the Supreme Court. Puddester, who had been described by Sir Murray Anderson as the most 'useful' of the Newfoundland commissioners and 'by far the most unpopular' with his Newfoundland colleagues 'as he is inclined to side with the U.K. Commissioners,' was kept on.[37] The problem of finding replacements for the other British com-

34/DO 35/504/N1051/21, Lodge to Machtig, 11 July 1936.

35/Upon learning that Lodge was likely to be removed from the Commission, the officers of the Longshoremen's Protective Union protested to the governor. They praised Lodge for his knowledge of local labour conditions and his willingness to listen to labour representatives, and requested the extension of his term by at least one year. Walwyn, however, deplored 'the action of any public body in seeking to influence the selection, or the extension of office of members of the Commission.' He concluded: 'I feel bound to state that I should be much averse to any extension of Mr. Lodge's time as Commissioner here.' DO 35/490/N1004/114, Walwyn to the secretary of state for dominion affairs, 12 Oct. 1936.

36/DO 35/490/N1004/80, Hope Simpson to Harding, 9 March 1936.

37/DO 35/490/N1004/45, Anderson to Harding, 22 June 1935, 'Secret and Personal.' A visiting Treasury official reported that 'of the three Newfoundland

missioners was also a matter of some concern. Anderson had given some thought to the matter as early as 1935 when he noticed that Trentham had become 'rather under the weather and rather seedy' (Newfoundland, no less than the tropics, was evidently a 'white man's grave').

Trentham [the governor wrote] leads a lonely life and undoubtedly sometimes gets rather hipped with life, living in the Hotel cannot be cheerful and he has not many friends and plays no games and he certainly does not wish to stay too long out here, but he also dislikes the idea of going back to work at the Treasury in London ... I would sooner trust his judgement than that of either Hope Simpson or Lodge, the first of whom is too impulsive and sometimes carried away by people who are not too reliable and the latter of whom lacks consideration of the human element and the 'custom of the country' and wishes to work out everything as a mathematical calculation, and is also very self opinionated not to say pig headed ... I think Hope Simpson is prepared to remain for a long time but I am doubtful if he will be able to continue ... I have the impression that he wishes to hang on to obtain a fairly high honour to 'round off his career.'[38]

The search for new United Kingdom commissioners typically involved a thorough scouring of the Colonial Office lists, but the appointments were themselves of no consequence. One mediocre overseas civil servant succeeded another, care was taken to avoid appointing another disruptive nonconformist such as Lodge, and the Commission continued its aimless drift.

Governor Walwyn occasionally muttered that 'the old politicians here, with Squires in the background, are assiduously spreading propaganda as to their return to office' and once even sought permission to issue 'some semi-official statement to the effect that the present form of Government will continue until the country is financially sound and stable, which will, I understand, be a matter of at least 15 to 20 years.'[39]

But nothing happened. Economically, Newfoundland was no better off than under responsible government, and in some respects worse. 'My impression,' wrote a new United Kingdom commissioner in the fall of

Commissioners, Mr. Puddester ... is probably the best, and would certainly be the most difficult to replace. He is no flier, but he gave me the impression of being keen on his job which, since it includes the administration of the dole, is a most distasteful one ... Mr. Lodge told me that Mr. Puddester was upset at being asked to continue for only a year, and that he feared he might begin to "play politics." ' DO 35/504/ N1051/26, notes on a visit to Newfoundland, Aug.–Sept. 1936 [by Mr Hale].

38/DO 35/490/N1004/45, Anderson to Harding, 22 June 1935, 'Secret and Personal.'

39/DO 35/490/N1004/100, Walwyn to Harding, 6 July 1937.

1936, 'is that the economic position of the labouring classes ... is not improving, but on the contrary perhaps still deteriorating. I am appalled by the growing poverty in the outports.'[40] Nor did conditions subsequently improve, as the average monthly number of persons on relief indicates:[41]

1934	31,899
1935	31,542
1936	38,467
1937	31,610
1938	36,517
1939	58,187
1940	39,802

By the end of the winter of 1938 there were no fewer than 85,000, out of a total population of 290,000, on relief – that is, they were receiving a dole at the rate of six cents per day. And though the economic position was equally bad in the following year, the United Kingdom commissioner for finance announced in November that grants-in-aid from the British government 'should be limited to the amount which the Newfoundland Government themselves spend in the U.K. for the service of the Public Debt.'[42] Taxes and import duties were therefore to be increased in order to save the United Kingdom Treasury the full amount of £300,000 per year. Moreover, so as not to add to the dollar exchange burden of Britain, the grants-in-aid would not be convertible; Newfoundland's annual deficit on dollar expenditure would have to be made up by further taxes and economies.

By 1939 Britain was at war, and so, automatically, was Newfoundland. The first impact upon the island, however, was to further impoverish the people. In 1940 the finance commissioner again raised taxes and announced a drastic retrenchment in public expenditure. Whatever the social cost, Newfoundland was once more 'self-supporting.'

Relief, however, was not long in coming. Newfoundland has always prospered during times of war, and the Second World War was no exception – only this time a large share of the prosperity was not earned in foreign fish markets but was instead brought directly to the island by the armed forces of the United States. In 1941 the British government had reason to be pleased that it had taken over the government of Newfoundland in 1934: for a minimal expenditure it had obtained control of an

40/DO 35/500/N1029/15, R. B. Ewbank to Clutterbuck, 12 Sept. 1936.
41/Clark, 'Newfoundland, 1934–49,' p. 152.
42/The Times, 22 Nov. 1939.

island which was strategically important to the Americans, to whom territorial concessions could be made without having to deal with the awkward question of local sovereignty. Ignoring the apprehension of the Newfoundland commissioners, the British government negotiated an agreement with the United States in September 1940 which placed three substantial areas of the island under complete American control for a period of ninety-nine years, for use as military bases. In return Britain obtained fifty over-age destroyers.[43] For Newfoundland the economic impact of the exchange was immense and almost immediate. On 29 January 1941 the troopship *Edmund B. Alexander* became the largest vessel ever to squeeze through the narrows of St John's harbour, bringing the first of many thousands of American servicemen and the beginning of an economic boom which has been compared to 'frontier days on the American continent.'[44]

Full employment, rising prices, and increased imports quickly pushed the revenue of the government to an all-time high of $23 million by 1942, producing a budget surplus of nearly $7,250,000.[45] (In 1934 the *total* revenue of the government had been only $8,718,979.) Some valuable and long overdue improvements were made in the public services of the island, notably in the fields of public health and education, but the surplus funds were mainly transferred to London to be added to Britain's reserves ($38 million by June 1942) or given to the British government in the form of interest-free loans ($10,300,000 by January 1944).[46] This could be done without public protest for the people of Newfoundland were for the most part too grateful for the measure of prosperity the Americans had brought them, and too patriotic, to complain.

The outbreak of war had saved the Commission. Whereas previously it had governed without purpose or ideas, now all its efforts could be directed towards maximizing Newfoundland's war effort. The difficult problems of domestic policy which had so confounded it could thus be set aside 'for the duration.' Moreover, the dramatic American military presence in the island – which was virtually tantamount to occupation – diverted attention from the civil government. In the eyes of Newfoundlanders the Commission régime merged into the background, becoming but one more facet of the abnormal state of wartime life – like ration books, the black-out, men in uniform, and 'Victory' tea.

43/See A. J. P. Taylor, *English History, 1914–1945* (Oxford, 1965), p. 496.
44/G. S. Watts, 'The Impact of the War,' in R. A. MacKay, ed., *Newfoundland: Economic, Diplomatic, and Strategic Studies* (Toronto, 1946), p. 221.
45/*The Times*, 16 July 1942.
46/*Ibid.*, 14 Jan. 1944.

16 The return to open politics

In 1945 Britain's newly elected Labour government, faced with an enormous task of domestic reconstruction and reform, had neither the capacity nor the desire to continue to govern a far-flung colonial empire. And among the bits and pieces it most ardently wished to dispose of was Newfoundland. The case for restoring responsible government to the island had by this time become undeniably strong: in 1934 it had been understood that the suspension of responsible government would last only 'until such time as the Island may become self-supporting again.'[1] But throughout the war, Newfoundland had not only been self-supporting but had even given financial assistance to Britain.

There were, however, other considerations the British government had to take into account. The war had not brought about any basic structural changes in the Newfoundland economy, which, if it ran true to form, was very likely to collapse in the event of a post-war depression in world trade. Independence might therefore prove to be short-lived: another economic catastrophe could produce another political débâcle, and Britain might find itself once again in the position of having to provide financial assistance. The only way in which Britain could be quite sure that it would be finally relieved of all responsibility for Newfoundland's affairs was for the island to become part of another country – and given its geographical location, this meant either the United States or Canada.

Union with the United States was, for practical purposes, out of the question. Even if Newfoundlanders could have been persuaded to accept

1/Cmd 4480, *Newfoundland Royal Commission 1933 Report* (London, 1933), p. 201.

the idea, which is doubtful, the United States might well have refused to take any further responsibility for a territory in which it already possessed all the military rights it could conceivably need. Moreover, Canada would undoubtedly have been hostile to the suggestion that Newfoundland be turned into an 'eastern Alaska.' This left only one alternative: union with Canada. This would be an ideal solution from Britain's point of view, it would appeal to Canada by enabling it to secure its Atlantic seaboard and 'round out' confederation, and presumably it would be acceptable to the United States. The only question was whether it would be acceptable to Newfoundlanders. All previous attempts to bring the island into the Canadian federation had failed, and there was no evidence of any pro-confederation upsurge during the years of Commission rule. On the contrary, all political agitation had been directed towards bringing about a return to independent dominion status.

Until the public records in both London and Ottawa are opened, the nature of the correspondence between the two capitals on the question of Newfoundland's future must remain a subject for conjecture. But whatever the part played by Ottawa, it is plain that the British government was determined to aid the cause of confederation in every way possible.

On 11 December 1945 Prime Minister Clement Attlee announced that his government had decided to

set up in Newfoundland next year, as early as climatic conditions permit, an elected National Convention of Newfoundlanders. Elections to the Convention will be held broadly on the basis of the former Parliamentary constituencies. All adults will be entitled to vote, and candidates for election will be required to be bona fide residents in the districts they seek to represent.

The terms of reference of the Convention were to be as follows:

To consider and discuss ... the changes that have taken place in the financial and economic situation of the Island since 1934, and bearing in mind the extent to which the high revenues of recent years have been due to wartime conditions, to examine the position of the country and to make recommendations to His Majesty's Government as to possible forms of future governments to be put before the people at a national referendum.[2]

Though the British government could plausibly maintain that their policy was merely to set up the machinery by which the people of Newfoundland could request the restoration of responsible government, in effect both the

2/*Parliamentary Debates*, House of Commons, 5th Series, vol. 417, cc. 210–11.

Convention's proposed composition and its terms of reference opened the door to a new confederation movement. The restriction of membership to those who were residents in the districts they represented was certain to weaken the influence of the anti-confederate professional classes of St John's, while the terms of reference were so broad as to allow *any* future form of government – including confederation – to be considered. But most important of all, Attlee's statement determined that in spite of previous pledges and understandings there would be no return to responsible government without a prior debate and a national referendum.

It took no special political percipience to realize that if responsible government was restored *first* it was extremely unlikely that an independent Newfoundland would choose to become a province of Canada through the normal operation of its political process. It might have been forced to do so in the long run, for economic reasons, but there was no telling how long this might take. A referendum, on the other hand, coming before the old political system could be revived, meant that confederation could be considered as an alternative to Commission rule on more or less equal terms with responsible government, that is, if confederation were placed on the ballot paper – a question the National Convention was supposed to decide.

THE NATIONAL CONVENTION

On 21 June 1946 Newfoundlanders went to the polls for the first time in fourteen years. They were not electing a government, nor voting for a political party, nor in any sense deciding an issue. They were merely electing a group of local notabilities, men who for one reason or another had made themselves fairly widely known in the electoral districts in which they lived and who wished to sit as members of the National Convention. They could campaign only on the strength of their own reputations and were in no position to make promises to their constituents. Interest in the election was therefore relatively slight: eight of the forty-five members elected were returned by acclamation, while the voter turnout for the island as a whole was less than 50 per cent.[3]

In spite of the strict residential qualification that had been applied, in terms of occupation the convention was scarcely more representative than the pre-war legislature. Apart from thirteen merchants who formed the

3/In St John's it was approximately 60 per cent. See R. L. Clark, 'Newfoundland, 1934–49: A Study of the Commission of Government and Confederation with Canada,' unpublished PH D dissertation, University of California, Los Angeles, 1951, p. 196.

largest single group, there was a fairly heterogeneous collection of members from other non-manual occupations. There were, in addition, two trade unionists and three co-operative field workers – but no fishermen. Only three members had held seats in the old House of Assembly: Peter Cashin, St John's West; F. Gordon Bradley, Bonavista East; and Roland Starkes, Green Bay. The latter two had been the only followers of Richard Squires to survive the general election of 1932.

The Convention opened in September 1946 and closed its deliberations some sixteen months later. Inevitably, given the circumstances of its creation and the tasks set before it, its proceedings were almost from beginning to end an exercise in the politically bizarre. Without the substance of parliamentary government the procedures of parliament provided no adequate guide to the conduct of debate. Members were at first uncertain as to the rôle they were expected to play, for there were no parties or leaders to give them direction. Gradually, however, factions began to emerge to fill the vacuum and these in due course turned the Convention into a turbulent and unruly political cockpit.

Basically, the Convention was divided into three groups. First, there was the sizeable group dominated by the mercantile and professional element. Though they had no leader or organization, they naturally expected to dominate the proceedings by virtue of their social standing. The Convention they regarded as an unnecessary preliminary to the restoration of responsible government; but, since the British government had seen fit to call it together, they were not above using it as an opportunity to flail the Commission government for sins both real and imagined. They were determined, in other words, that the Convention should avenge Lord Amulree's strictures on the merchant community, which they had bitterly resented, by 'turning the tables' on the régime that Lord Amulree had been responsible for creating.

When the Convention divided into nine committees to investigate and report on various aspects of Newfoundland affairs, with a view to determining the future needs of the island and the means by which they could be supplied, machinery was created by which a detailed attack could be made upon the whole of the Commission's administration. The Convention demanded powers to examine papers and personnel comparable to those exercised only by the Public Accounts Committee in the British House of Commons; but in this the commissioners, who understandably had no wish to face such an inquisition, flatly refused to co-operate. The first to be summoned, Ira Wild, a United Kingdom commissioner of finance, refused to attend. 'It was not the intention ... of the British Government,' he announced, 'to have officials in the [Commission] Government subjected to examination by this Convention. But though members of the Government and officials cannot be compelled to come before this Convention they are willing and anxious to give any information they may be able to give.'[4] This, however, did not stop the committees, and especially the finance committee under the chairmanship of Peter Cashin, from using whatever information they could gather to attack the Commission and all its works.[5]

A second group in the Convention consisted of those who were less hostile to the Commission than the merchants and who were genuinely uncommitted as to the future form of government which Newfoundland should adopt. They numbered about a dozen, came mainly from the outports, and for the most part were passive rather than active participants.

Finally, there was a third group, the smallest of all, which consisted of a handful of delegates from outport constituencies who, like the merchants and their followers, came to the Convention with their minds fully made up. They, however, were not interested in either defending or condemning the record of the Commission government: their eyes were on the future and their goal was confederation with Canada. One of these was the member for Bonavista Centre, Joseph Roberts Smallwood.

THE FATHER OF CONFEDERATION

In 1946 'Joe' Smallwood, as he was then known – later he changed the diminutive of his name to 'Joey' – was forty-five years old.[6] His life up to this point had been varied and adventurous, and though by no stretch of the imagination could he be considered a 'success,' he was no ordinary failure. His ambitions had been grandiose, and had all come to nothing, but at least he had had the courage to pursue them. From an early age the only career he had followed with any consistency had been journalism; but in 1943 he had abandoned even that to strike out in yet another new direction – this time as a pig farmer in the new airport town of Gander. His idea was to use the swill collected from the various messes at the local RAF base to raise hogs to supply the same messes with pork.

He was still engaged in this peculiar enterprise when in 1946 it was announced that elections would be held to choose a Newfoundland National Convention. The British government had stipulated, in an effort to prevent 'carpet-bagging' by St John's merchants and lawyers, that candi-

4/ *Daily News*, St John's, 18 Sept. 1946.
5/ See Peter J. Cashin, 'My Fight for Responsible Government,' in J. R. Smallwood, ed., *The Book of Newfoundland* (St John's, 1967), III, 105–18.
6/ For an outstandingly perceptive biography of Smallwood, see Richard Gwyn, *Smallwood: The Unlikely Revolutionary* (Toronto, 1968).

dates would have to be bona fide residents of the districts they sought to represent. Thus at a single stroke Joe Smallwood's move to Gander, which had seemingly brought his fortunes to their lowest ebb, turned out instead to be the luckiest move he had ever made. Had he stayed in St John's, where he had been raised and spent most of his adult life, he would have been eligible to stand only for a city seat, with very little chance of winning. But his piggery in Gander had made him a resident of Bonavista Centre, a mainly coastal district he knew well for he had spent three lean pre-war years in the area as a co-operative organizer.[7]

He was already a man of considerable political experience, even though he had been only thirty-three years old when the beginning of the Commission régime had put a damper on his political ambitions. His background was a curious one: by instinct and training he was a product of the old political order, having been apprenticed at an early age as a party hack and political journalist in the unruly and mendacious world of St John's politics – yet he was not a typical product of that world. He was also excited by *ideas*, which perhaps accounts for his remarkable record of devotion to lost causes and lost leaders. He became a convert to socialism through the initial influence of George Grimes, the radical Unionist MHA, and was carried by his faith first to New York and the service of the American Socialist party and briefly to London and the British Labour party. The equivalent of these in Newfoundland was the Fishermen's Protective Union of William Coaker, who became Smallwood's idol. Thereafter, as Coaker's star faded, he transferred his allegiance to Richard Squires and his grandiose promise of industrial development, going down to defeat in the general election of 1932 as a Squires candidate in Bonavista South. Not for the first time, he had enthusiastically flung himself aboard a sinking ship.

By 1946, however, he had already adopted a new cause: confederation with Canada. It was on this policy that he campaigned for election to the National Convention and won by the impressive margin of 2,129 votes to 277,[8] giving him 89 per cent of the votes cast and the largest majority of any of the delegates. Already he had formed an alliance with the member for Bonavista East, F. Gordon Bradley, who was one of the few survivors of the last Squires government. The basis of their co-operation was simple and farsighted: at Smallwood's insistence they agreed that if their confederation venture ended in success Bradley would get a seat in the Canadian cabinet and Smallwood would become provincial premier.[9]

7/*Ibid.*, pp. 49–50.
8/*Ibid.*, p. 75.
9/J. R. Smallwood, 'The Story of Confederation,' in his *The Book of Newfoundland*, III, 16.

Bradley was a useful ally, not least because he was a former grand master of the Orange Order; but he was no match for Smallwood, for whom the National Convention represented the centre of the political stage he had yearned to occupy and which had for so long eluded him. Confederation, moreover, was a cause in which he passionately believed. In his eyes it was the panacea for all Newfoundland's economic ills, the only hope of providing the island people with a decent future in the post-war world.[10] In retrospect, the only wonder is that so obvious a cause was left to Smallwood, a man from nowhere, to pick up and become its champion. But in reality, those who were most likely to emerge in political rôles after the departure of the Commission felt they had too much to lose, or not enough to gain, from promoting confederation. They were St John's merchants or professional men, comfortably off, out of touch with the people in the outports, and sentimentally, nationalistically, attached to the old Newfoundland. They of course had every reason to be, for the old régime had generally suited them well. There were practically no other sources from which new political leaders could be recruited. There were no political parties, the FPU was no longer a force, the labour movement was weak, and the co-operative movement generally unsuccessful and lacking a popular base. The Commission had done nothing to encourage the development of a new political élite, apart possibly from the training of a corps of bureaucrats – who turned out to have learned their lesson well: they prudently waited until a winner emerged before committing themselves. The field was therefore free for Smallwood, a self-recruited renegade from the old régime, a political *sans-culotte*.

When the National Convention convened in St John's in September, Smallwood found that he had among the outport delegates around ten staunch pro-confederation allies, together with four or five others who were sympathetic and could possibly be converted. Over the Confederates he quickly and without difficulty established his personal ascendancy, but it was obvious from the start that no less than two-thirds of the members were opposed to union with Canada and unlikely to change their minds. Therefore no matter how cohesive and effective a party the Confederates might become in the Convention, they were bound to lose if their efforts were confined to the debating chamber. To have any chance of success they had to appeal beyond the Convention and reach the people directly. This was the tactic which Smallwood quickly adopted.

What made it possible for him to do so was the decision of the Com-

10/His case was first presented to the public in a series of eleven lengthy, powerfully argued, letters to the editor of the *Daily News*, 1–14 March 1946. These, together with three subsequent letters in reply to his critics, are reprinted as 'The Gospel of Confederation: Book One' in *ibid.*, III, 38–62.

mission, or the Dominions Office, to have the powerful government-owned radio station, VONF, which was listened to in all parts of the island, record for rebroadcast each evening the entire proceedings of the Convention.[11] This vitally important decision was taken shortly after the Convention opened, by which time it had become clear that a majority of the delegates were opposed even to including confederation with Canada as a possible choice to be put before the people in a referendum. The intervention of the Commission government was in one sense blatantly partisan, for, in a country which had no other effective media of mass communication, it gave the Confederates a public platform they could have obtained in no other way. On the other hand, how could those who favoured a return to independent dominion status and responsible government legitimately complain when the broadcasting of the Convention's proceedings gave them an equal chance to reach the people?

Their chances, however, were equal only in theory. The decision to put the proceedings on the air gave an enormous advantage to Joe Smallwood, the best-known radio voice in all of Newfoundland, who for several years before embarking upon his Gander hog-raising venture had been a professional broadcaster. He was known as 'The Barrelman,' producing daily an entertaining and original programme based upon a form of listener participation: he would invite listeners to send him stories out of Newfoundland's past, folk tales, adventure yarns, eye-witness accounts of shipwrecks and sealing disasters, of rescue and heroism, all generally of a sort to rekindle the battered national pride of Newfoundlanders. These he would edit and read, with much flair and a natural sense of dramatic timing. He alone among the delegates to the Convention was a master of the new medium of radio.

The parallel with the early journalistic career of William Coaker, writing his own tales of piracy and romance for the *Telegrapher*, is striking. And equally striking is the way that Smallwood and the Confederates, like Coaker and the Unionists in the Assembly of 1914, dominated the proceedings of the Convention from beginning to end. It has been said of Smallwood that in him the spirits of William Coaker and Richard Squires struggled for control – and that Squires came out on top. But such a view, while in the long perspective not unjust, ignores the fact that in the early years the spirit of Coaker was dominant.

The 'left' in politics is a notoriously difficult thing to define, but whatever meaning is given to it, even if it is simply Victor Hugo's 'Je suis contre,' Joe Smallwood in the National Convention unquestionably be-

11/In 'The Story of Confederation' (*ibid.*, p. 14) Smallwood states 'I have never known how and why the decision to broadcast the proceedings was made, or by whom.'

longed to it. For the first time since before the First World War a voice
was heard which could dispel the apathy of the poor, and express their
resentment, anger, and hopes. Smallwood, as he once wrote of Coaker,
spoke to the people in a language that they understood. Hence, while his
brutally realistic descriptions of life in the old Newfoundland earned him
nothing but vituperation from the 'patriots,' for the great bulk of outport
Newfoundlanders his words had the ring of simple truth. And, like Coaker,
he convinced them that their hardships were not ordained by Providence
but were the result of an exploitative man-made political and economic
order that could be changed. That the vision of the new messiah was not
of socialism as such but of union with a Canada governed by the Liberal
party of Mackenzie King was an odd touch, but it did not alter his message: confederation would mean a new dignity for the 'little man,' or, in a
vivid phrase coined by another Confederate, William Keough, for 'the
last forgotten fisherman off the bill of Cape St. George.'

The Confederate minority in the Convention soon discovered they had
another advantage of considerable importance: their opponents were un-
organized and leaderless. The only personality to emerge as a spokesman
for responsible government to rival Smallwood was the irrepressible Peter
Cashin. He had battled the Commission government with courage and
persistence during the years when no other voice of protest could be heard.
He also understood earlier than most that confederation and Joe Smallwood were serious threats to the dream of a restored Dominion of Newfoundland. Yet he was unable to establish himself as the effective leader of
the anti-Confederates. There were a variety of reasons for this: he was no
match for Smallwood in the give-and-take of debate, while his oratory
tended to be blustery and illogical; but most of all he was not an acceptable
spokesman in the eyes of the St John's merchant-lawyer élite. His stormy
political career as a minister in the Squires cabinet and subsequently as a
violent critic of his former leader, as well as the fact that he was a Catholic,
were handicaps he might have overcome had he been willing to conform to
their code of behaviour. He preferred, however, to remain his own man,
one of nature's extremists, as unpredictable as he was volatile.

The inability of the anti-Confederates to act like a political party made
it relatively easy for Smallwood to outmanœuvre them at every turn. Some
of their number, among whom the most notable was the much-respected
and very elderly R. B. Job, a merchant and former member of the Legislative Council, were attracted by the idea of a specially negotiated tariff
arrangement with the United States, whereby the free entry of Newfoundland frozen fish would make a return to responsible government economically viable. By encouraging Job in his belief in this almost pure political

'red herring,' Smallwood was able to split the anti-Confederate forces: Job agreed to support a move to seek information on the possible terms of union with Canada in return for Smallwood's support of a move to have the Commission government approach the United States on the question of a tariff arrangement. Accordingly, the National Convention, having previously voted against seeking terms of union from Ottawa, nevertheless passed the following resolution asking the Commission for information:

1 What steps if any can be taken for establishing improved economic or fiscal relationships between the United States ... and Newfoundland, particularly bearing in mind the present occupation of certain Newfoundland territory and the fact that free entry is given to the United States for its importations into Newfoundland.
2 What financial or fiscal relationships could be expected between the Government of the United Kingdom and Newfoundland
    1 Under continuation of Commission Government in its present form;
    2 Under a revised form with elected representatives thereon;
    3 Under Responsible Government in approximately its previous form;
    4 Under any other suitable form of Government.
3 What could be a fair and equitable basis for Federal Union of the Dominion of Canada and Newfoundland, or what other fiscal, political or economic relations may be possible.[12]

The Commission, predictably, ruled that the question of a tariff agreement with the United States lay outside the National Convention's terms of reference; but, with Job's support, the Convention eventually passed a motion to send fact-finding delegations to both London and Ottawa.

For Smallwood it was triumph; he now had the opening he needed to begin negotiations with the Canadian government. In August 1946, before the Convention had opened, he had travelled privately to Ottawa and had there succeeded in meeting various ministers, including the then acting prime minister, Louis St Laurent; but even more importantly, he had made the acquaintance of J. W. Pickersgill, the senior civil servant in the Prime Minister's Office. The Canadian high commissioner in St John's had reported (accurately, at the time) that Smallwood was 'of slight consequence and without political following,'[13] but he evidently impressed Pickersgill and the two became political allies.

In contrast to the London delegation, which received an icy reception in Whitehall, the Ottawa delegation, led by Gordon Bradley and including

12/*Ibid.*, pp. 17–19.
13/Gwyn, *Smallwood*, pp. 76–7.

Smallwood, were hospitably received – and stayed for ninety-nine days, in spite of a mounting clamour of protest from St John's. What had detained them was the indecisiveness of the Canadian cabinet and, once their decision to offer Newfoundland terms of union was finally made, the secret negotiation of those terms in great detail.

In November 1947 Canada's preferred terms were tabled in the National Convention. From that moment until the Convention was dissolved at the end of January 1948, the question of confederation was almost the sole subject of debate, with Smallwood's powerful advocacy reaching out to the people, who night after night in crowded kitchens breathlessly followed each word on the radio.

They were to be his final court of appeal, his political trump card. For when it came to the final vote in the Convention on Smallwood's motion to include confederation with Canada on the ballot paper in a future referendum, the motion was lost by a vote of 29 to 16. The anti-Confederates could hardly have made a more serious political blunder. By defeating the motion they left themselves wide open to the charge that they were 'twenty-nine dictators' who were denying the people the right to choose. Bradley went on the air, with a speech written for him by Smallwood, to attack them in precisely these terms, and appealed for a mass petition of protest to the governor. This was quickly forthcoming, and contained a total of nearly fifty thousand signatures.

The British government was now faced with something of a dilemma. The purpose of the National Convention, the very reason it had been set up in the first place, was to 'make recommendations to His Majesty's Government as to possible forms of future governments to be put before the people at a national referendum.' The convention had now made its decision and recommended that the people be asked to choose between the restoration of responsible government as it had existed prior to 1934 and a continuation of government by Commission. However perverse such a decision may have appeared in the eyes of the British government, could they now simply refuse to accept the recommendation and substitute one of their own which included confederation? Their answer appears to have been that they could, providing such a move were acceptable to the government of Canada – which it was. Accordingly, on 2 March 1948 the secretary of state for Commonwealth relations, Philip Noel-Baker, informed the governor of Newfoundland that:

The terms offered by the Canadian Government represent ... the result of long discussion with a body of Newfoundlanders who were elected to the Convention, and the issues involved appear to have been sufficiently clarified to enable the people of Newfoundland to express an opinion as to whether Confederation with Canada would commend itself to them. In these circumstances, and having regard to the number of members of the Convention who supported the inclusion of confederation with Canada in the ballot paper, His Majesty's Government have come to the conclusion that it would not be right that the people of Newfoundland should be deprived of an opportunity of considering the issue at the referendum and they have, therefore, decided that confederation with Canada should be included as a third choice on the referendum paper.[14]

For all the effect of its decision, the National Convention might just as well never have met.

THE REFERENDA CAMPAIGNS

The National Convention died ignominiously, castigated at home and ignored in London, but during its life it had provided the Confederates with a unique platform from which to launch their campaign. Their opponents had naïvely and complacently believed that confederation could be stopped before it became a public issue, and now found themselves ill-equipped to wage open political warfare against it. The Confederates, on the other hand, had aimed at the electorate from the beginning. They also had in the person of Joe Smallwood a leader with a genius for political communication who had used the Convention to imprint his personal image on the public mind. His voice, and, as the campaign progressed, his appearance, were instantly recognizable: he was the tough, brainy, passionate, little man who spoke often of the 'toiling masses' and addressed them as though they mattered.

    The Newfoundland Confederate Association, with Bradley as figurehead president and Smallwood as 'campaign director,' provided the organizational framework for the enlistment of supporters, the direction of volunteer activists – and the receipt and disbursement of party funds. In his biography of Smallwood, Richard Gwyn estimates the Confederate campaign fund as 'close to $150,000,' a small proportion of which was raised through public subscription, a more substantial proportion through contributions from the Liberal party of Canada:

Smallwood made the first approach by calling on two key contacts: C. D.

14/ As quoted in St John Chadwick, *Newfoundland: Island into Province* (Cambridge, 1967), p. 203.

Howe and Senator McLean, the party treasurer in the Maritimes. They in turn introduced him to Senator Gordon Fogo, the National Liberal Treasurer. Since from this point on discretion, which was never a Smallwood virtue, was an imperative, negotiations with Fogo were taken over by Ray Petten, later a Senator and Newfoundland Liberal fund-raiser, a mantle of delphic succession now descended on his son. From Fogo, Petten received the most sacrosanct of all political documents, a list of pliable Liberal donors, including, unsurprisingly, most of Canada's liquor, beer, and wine manufacturers and importers.[15]

Though skilfully cultivating the image that they were the party of the 'little man' bravely confronting the vast wealth and power of 'Water Street,' in fact the Confederates were far better financed than their opponents.

The outcome of the election, however, was not determined simply by money: the Confederates were also the better organizers, politicians, and propagandists. A comparison of their rival campaign newspapers, the *Confederate* and the *Independent*, reveals the difference between effective professionalism (for example, the political cartoons in the *Confederate* were drawn to Smallwood's order by the cartoonist of the Toronto *Globe and Mail*) and uninspired amateurism. Moreover, the anti-Confederates, so far from uniting their forces under Cashin's leadership, actually split into two mutually antagonistic factions. In opposition to the Responsible Government League, which supported Cashin, a new party was formed under the leadership of Chesley Crosbie, a wealthy St John's merchant, to promote a vaguely defined 'economic union' with the United States. In the hands of two skilled professional publicists, one of whom, Donald Jamieson, was eventually to become a minister in a federal Liberal government, this bogus issue for a time turned the inarticulate Crosbie into a serious political force.[16] One of the side-effects of their campaign, however, was to raise confusions and doubts concerning the loyalty to the Crown of those who urged a return to responsible government for whatever purpose, thus enabling Smallwood to steal their patriotic clothes. In the end it was the Confederates who campaigned under the Union Jack with the slogan 'Confederation – *British* Union.'

15/*Smallwood*, p. 100. Harold Horwood, who was closely involved in the Confederate campaign, has estimated that the total take from these sources was 'approximately a quarter of a million dollars.' Local sources were also tapped: 'I don't know to how many people he [Smallwood] promised senatorships, but it was his method of lining up supporters – I think he would admit this himself now after all these years. He went around to everyone and promised them senatorships if they would join the Confederate faction.' Peter Cashin, Harold Horwood, and Leslie Harris, 'Newfoundland and Confederation, 1948–49,' in Mason Wade, ed., *Regionalism in the Canadian Community, 1867–1967* (Toronto, 1969), pp. 247–51.
16/See Donald C. Jamieson, 'I Saw the Fight for Confederation,' in Smallwood, *The Book of Newfoundland*, III, 70–104.

Yet in spite of all their advantages of money, leadership, and organization the Confederates failed to win even a plurality of votes in the referendum held on 3 June 1948. The result was as follows:[17]

For responsible government	69,400	44.5%
For confederation	64,066	41.1%
For commission government	22,311	14.3%

The British government had stipulated that a clear majority was required for victory, and that if a second ballot should be necessary the form of government receiving the smallest number of votes should be dropped from the ballot paper. The run-off poll was accordingly fixed for 22 July.

There were no new issues of substance, almost nothing that anyone could add to what had already been said. The outcome was a violent sectarian struggle of a sort that had been common in Newfoundland's past but which had remained no more than a strong undercurrent in the first referendum campaign. In the second the old order reasserted itself and returned with all its ancient religious bigotry and viciousness. In general, the returns from the first poll showed that Protestants had tended to support confederation and Catholics responsible government. This in itself would probably not have triggered off an outburst of religious sectarianism, but it did provide a situation conducive to its growth if it were once sparked by other incidents and personalities. The incident was the publication in a St John's tabloid of the news that for the first time members of Catholic religious orders in Newfoundland had gone to the polls; and the personality was Archbishop Roche.

The archbishop was a Newfoundland patriot and an unrelenting enemy of confederation, which, he believed, would destroy the distinctive Newfoundland way of life. To save it, he threw all of his very considerable influence into the fight; the *Monitor*, his church magazine, became an openly political instrument in the cause of responsible government. Ironically, in many respects the clerics presented a more honest and better reasoned case for independence than any of the politicians. In language strikingly similar to that of traditional French-Canadian nationalists in Quebec, they did not deny that an independent Newfoundland would be poor but argued against material blandishments and in favour of the preservation, in isolation, of simple spiritual values:

We must consider what is best for the country ... We do not necessarily mean best in the material sense, but rather wherein lies the best chance of continuing

17/ *Report of the Chief Electoral Officer Relating to the First Poll of the Referendum Held June 3, 1948.*

to live decently and soberly and honestly, continuing to recognize that there has grown up with us during the past four and a half centuries a simple God-fearing way of life which our forbears have handed down to us and which we must pass on untarnished to posterity.[18]

Inevitably, the partisanship of the archbishop provoked a strong re-action from those Confederates who were also militant Protestants; and, predictably, the organization through which Protestant sectarianism found expression was the Orange Lodge – of which Gordon Bradley was an eminent leader and former grand master. On 16 July, five days before the second ballot, the circulation to all members of a letter from the grand master attacking the Catholic Church for its effort 'to dominate the right of free choice of the individual elector'[19] brought sectarianism to a fever pitch. Since Protestants outnumbered Catholics by approximately two to one, a further sharpening of denominational lines in the second ballot could only benefit the Confederates.

A further variable of major, and perhaps crucial, importance was the way the 22,311 supporters of Commission government would cast their ballots when given a chance to express a second preference, or even whether they would vote at all. Once again, however, the Commission government intervened on behalf of the Confederates. Two of the three Newfoundland commissioners, Herman Quinton, commissioner of health, and Herbert Pottle, commissioner of education, came out openly on the Confederate side and were allowed to make speeches over the government radio station in favour of confederation.[20] To their flagrant abuse of office the British government turned a blind eye, but since the days of the Commission were drawing to a close there was probably little that they could have done to stop them. Possibly even more influential with the former supporters of the Commission was the sudden intervention in the campaign of a small group of the wealthiest St John's merchants, of whom the most prominent was Sir Leonard Outerbridge. These gentlemen had previously remained aloof from politics but were assumed to be supporters of responsible government. Now, at the eleventh hour, they came out in favour of confederation. Outerbridge in particular was a considerable asset to any cause: he was a highly respected member of the establishment, a pillar of the Church of England, a figure straight out of the 'Imperial sun-

18/The *Monitor*, St John's, Nov. 1947, as quoted in Gwyn, *Smallwood*, pp. 108–9.

19/The 'Orange Letter' is reproduced in Jamieson, 'I Saw the Fight for Con-federation,' p. 103.

20/Both were subsequently rewarded, Quinton with a senatorship and Pottle with a portfolio in the provincial government.

set,' the epitome of all things British. To those who had supported the Commission out of loyalty to the Crown, or simply out of conservatism or timidity, his presence in the Confederates' camp must have helped allay the fears that the 'radical' Smallwood aroused. In 1949 he was appointed lieutenant governor.

In the second ballot the final result was as follows:[21]

For confederation	78,323	52.3%
For responsible government	71,344	47.4%

The turnout was 84.9 per cent, only slightly less than in the first ballot.

An analysis of the voting in the referenda by electoral district suggests that religious sectarianism played a considerable part in determining the outcome. Protestant solidarity was stronger in the second ballot than in the first, while the six electoral districts with Catholic majorities continued to divide along the same lines, four supporting responsible government and two confederation.

	For confederation	For responsible government
First ballot		
Protestant	14	5
Catholic	2	4
Second ballot		
Protestant	16	3
Catholic	2	4

A simple tabulation, however, cannot convey the full complexity of the voting pattern. Religion was undoubtedly an important factor, but not the only one. Even in St John's there were many Catholics who voted for confederation, while in even the most solidly Protestant outport areas there were pockets of staunch responsible government support. There was also an economic aspect to the referendum vote: those areas where fishing was the sole or predominant occupation tended to be most solidly for confederation while the merchant and professional classes of St John's tended to be most strongly opposed. Yet there were so many exceptions that it would be a gross oversimplification to interpret the referendum result as primarily the product of a merchant-fisherman cleavage.[22] The fact is that

21/*Report of the Chief Electoral Officer Relating to the First Poll of the Referendum Held July 22, 1948.*

22/Such an interpretation (as it appears, e.g., in Chadwick, *Newfoundland*, pp. 205–6) has been effectively refuted by George C. Perlin, 'The Constitutional Referendum of 1948 and the Revival of Sectarianism in Newfoundland Politics,' *Queen's Quarterly*, vol. 75, no. 1 (Spring 1968), pp. 155–60.

no simple explanation of the result is possible. Voters were subject to a variety of influences and pressures, but there is no reason to suppose that their rational weighing of the issues was not also an important, and perhaps decisive, determinant of their behaviour.

Many who voted for confederation did so with regret, and only because they could see no realistic economic alternative. The Confederate case was strong; it was ably and at times brilliantly presented. The case for responsible government was by contrast weak and presented with almost pathetic ineptitude. That it so very nearly succeeded is an indication of the powerful hold which the idea of a separate national life had upon the minds and hearts of Newfoundlanders.

THE TERMS OF UNION

Any fears (or hopes) that the slender majority in favour of confederation would be regarded in Ottawa as unsatisfactory were quickly dashed by the announcement on 30 July that the Canadian government was willing to proceed with the negotiation of the final terms of union. Thus, in the autumn of 1948, while the responsible government die-hards fought on to the end with a series of forlorn appeals to the British House of Commons and the Privy Council, discussions were begun in Ottawa between representatives of Newfoundland and Canada. The chairman of the Newfoundland team was Albert Walsh, a St John's lawyer. The other members were Gordon Winter, a St John's businessman; Philip Gruchy, the manager of the Grand Falls paper mill; J. B. McEvoy, a former chairman of the National Convention; Chesley Crosbie, the leader of the movement for economic union with the United States; and the Confederate leaders, Smallwood and Bradley. All were appointed by the Commission government.

The new terms turned out to be more financially advantageous to Newfoundland than those originally negotiated in 1947 for presentation to the National Convention. It is possible that the Canadian government was concerned with the extreme narrowness of Newfoundland's verdict in favour of confederation or wished to avoid the impression of niggardliness which had ruined negotiations for union in the nineteenth century, or that the Newfoundland negotiators astutely used the threat of embarrassing the Canadian government by refusing to sign an agreement in order to extract better terms.[23] The result in any event was a 50 per cent increase in the

23/See Gwyn, *Smallwood*, p. 115.

Canadian offer of transitional grants 'to facilitate the adjustment of New-foundland to the status of a province.' These were to be paid over a twelve-year period, beginning with the payment of the sum of $6.5 million annually for three years and thereafter reducing progressively to $350,000 in the twelfth and final year.

Term 29 of the Terms of Union, however, provided as follows:

In view of the difficulty of predicting with sufficient accuracy the financial consequences to Newfoundland of becoming a province of Canada, the Government of Canada will appoint a Royal Commission within eight years from the date of Union to review the financial position of the Province of Newfoundland and to recommend the form and scale of financial or additional financial assistance, if any, that may be required by the Government of the Province of Newfoundland to enable it to continue public services at the levels and standards reached subsequent to the date of Union, without resorting to taxation more burdensome, having regard to the capacity to pay, than that obtaining generally in the region comprising the Maritime Provinces of Nova Scotia, New Brunswick, and Prince Edward Island.[24]

This non-committal clause was later to become a source of acute controversy. In 1957 the promised federal royal commission, under the chairmanship of Chief Justice McNair of the New Brunswick Supreme Court, produced a report which recommended the payment to Newfoundland of the sum of $8 million in perpetuity. The refusal in 1959 of the Conservative government of John Diefenbaker to extend these special payments beyond 1962 provoked a furious clash between St John's and Ottawa over what had actually been intended in 1948.[25] But at the time future difficulties were for the most part unanticipated: only one member of the Newfoundland delegation, Chesley Crosbie, refused to sign the final Terms of Union. The others placed their signatures on the historic document on 11 December, with Louis St Laurent and Brooke Claxton signing for Canada. The agreement was scheduled to come into effect on 31 March 1949. It had originally been scheduled for 1 April, the beginning of the Canadian fiscal year, but was changed to avoid holding the anniversary of confederation on April Fool's Day.

24/ For the complete Terms of Union see Appendix c.
25/ See Gwyn, *Smallwood*, pp. 181–98.

17 Post-confederation society and politics

Newfoundland in 1949, in spite of the many forces of change and modernization introduced during the war, was still very much a 'traditional' society. The bulk of the people still lived in tiny isolated outports where their way of life was not essentially different from that led by their forefathers. The fishery, with its antiquated technology and financial structure, remained their basic source of livelihood; such amenities as motor roads and hydro-electric power were practically unknown; while in their homes a simple nineteenth century world of large patriarchal families, Victorian manners and morals, oil lamps and wood stoves, remained anachronistically alive. The outports were still tightly knit communities, bound together by the homogeneity of their economic life, by extended patterns of kinship, by inherited customs and folkways, and, in Catholic and Protestant outports alike, by the acceptance of stern religious authority. It was, however, a traditional society on the verge of momentous change.

There can now be no doubt that in choosing union with Canada rather than a return to responsible government and dominion status the people of Newfoundland were determining not only their island's constitutional future but also the speed and direction of its future social and economic development. The implications of this were naturally spelled out in greater detail by the Confederates, for it was they who could paint the rosier picture of what they had to offer; but in general the significance of the choice was well understood by both sides and lent a peculiar emotional intensity to their struggle. Thus, a vote for responsible government was also in effect a vote for the maintenance of the old Atlantic-oriented Newfoundland, poorer than its North American neighbours but also different from them, holding to more conservative values, and preserving a culture historically rooted in the pre-industrial societies of Ireland and the west of England. A vote for confederation, on the other hand, was also in effect a vote to integrate Newfoundland into the more prosperous, dynamic, and competitive system of North American industrial capitalism with its 'consumer culture' and liberal values. This is not to suggest that an independent Newfoundland would not in any case have been drawn more closely into its continental environment; on the contrary, the die had already been cast in that direction by influences introduced during the war. But it is to suggest that the whole inevitable process of post-war social change would have been slowed down by independence and hence would have been more easily absorbed and adapted without fundamentally disturbing existing patterns and institutions.

Already by 1945 thousands of Newfoundland workers who during the war had found temporary employment in the construction of American and Canadian military bases had returned to their outport homes to earn their living once again in the traditional way as inshore fishermen. Fortunately, improved shipping conditions in the North Atlantic in the latter part of the war, combined with a high level of demand for Newfoundland salt cod, enabled the industry in the short run to absorb this growth in the numbers it had to support,[1] though in the long run it was unlikely to be able to continue to do so once the war-disrupted Icelandic and Norwegian fisheries returned to full production. This shift of labour back to the fishery, however, clearly revealed how fleeting the war's impact had really been. The construction boom had been spectacular while it lasted, but had produced no new productive capacity to help sustain the economy in peacetime. Thus the Second World War, like the First, brought Newfoundlanders no more than a tantalizing taste of a standard of living they could not really afford. But whereas the First, in which Newfoundland maintained its own regiment in Europe, encouraged the growth of a spirit of national pride and independence, the Second, in which the island was virtually occupied by North American troops, opened the way for its subsequent political integration with the mainland. For although the economic effect of the war was neither profound nor lasting, its residual cultural and political effects were nevertheless important. The Newfoundlanders who returned to their traditional occupations in the fishery as the war drew to a close did so because there were no alternative sources of employment available to them. But they took with them an awareness of their continental neighbours that was lacking in 1939. The war had brought them

1/G. S. Watts, 'The Impact of the War,' in R. A. MacKay, ed., *Newfoundland: Economic, Diplomatic, and Strategic Studies* (Toronto, 1946), p. 225.

into face-to-face contact with "mainlanders,' both American and Canadian, and encouraged even those whose homes were on the east coast to take an unaccustomed look westward. After the war they could be persuaded to see their political future in that direction: before it they almost certainly could not have been.

In voting for confederation the outport people were voting for change, but few could have imagined, especially in view of the narrow margin of the Confederate victory and the concentration of the opposition in St John's, that within twenty years their society would be changed almost beyond recognition. Some idea of the sheer magnitude of this change is suggested by the crude statistical indicators shown in Table 1. But such figures, however significant, cannot adequately convey the qualitative changes that have occurred in the Newfoundland way of life; yet it is in the latter that the transformation has been most dramatic.

Since 1949 the traditional outport community has all but disappeared. Many outports have literally disappeared from the map, having been abandoned by all their residents in favour of resettlement in the larger towns. To a certain extent this demographic trend has been the result of a natural and spontaneous rejection of outport life, with its isolation and hardships, by those who had become newly aware of the attractions of urban living and for the first time could see it as a viable alternative for themselves. They had found, after confederation, that the worst economic risks of moving to a larger community were cushioned by the Canadian social security system and the growing welfare services of the provincial government. Compared with underemployment in some remote hamlet, unemployment in a town, 'Canadian style,' was positively attractive: even the unemployed could enjoy the advantages of better educational opportunities for their children, better medical services, and the availability of such amenities as roads and electricity. To the Newfoundland government the advantages were no less obvious, for it could not hope to raise the standard of public services in the island to a level approaching even that of the Maritime provinces while its population remained so widely scattered. Thus, though the first wave of centralization occurred spontaneously, an even greater movement of population occurred as a result of deliberate government policy. Under the provincial government's first centralization programme in the period 1954–65, 115 outport communities were abandoned and their populations totalling 7,500 resettled in larger centres with the aid of government grants. Since 1965 at least a further fifty to sixty outports have been abandoned under a new Fisheries Household Resettlement Programme, the cost of which is shared with the federal Department of Fisheries, making a total, including those which

TABLE 1

Post-confederation social and economic change: some statistical indicators*

	c. 1949	c. 1965
Total expenditure of the Newfoundland government, 1950–65, on:	$30,011,000	$157,628,000
Education	$4,012,000	$82,000,000
Health	$5,538,000	$28,580,000
Social welfare	$8,620,000	$19,009,000
Transportation and communications	$3,978,000	$47,371,000
Per capita personal income, 1949–63	$472	$1,029
Population, 1951–61	361,416	457,853
Population of incorporated areas, 1949–67	85,000	338,000
Number of municipalities, 1949–67	23	152
Road mileage, 1949–66	2,296	4,627
Number of motor vehicles	13,765	91,165
Number of public libraries	27	53
Number of books	127,000	311,000
Circulation	264,000	693,000
School enrolment	75,086	144,000
University enrolment, 1949–67	307	4,762
Number of television and relay stations, 1955–65	0	11
Number of radio stations	4	11
Number of telephones, 1949–62	18,688	69,777
Number of working doctors, 1949–64	150	330
Number of hospital beds, 1949–64	2,000	5,000
Percentage of reduction in mortality rates, 1948–64		
General	25	
Tuberculosis	95	
Diphtheria	95	
Infant	40	
Maternity	80	

*Constructed from data contained in R. I. McAllister, ed., *Newfoundland and Labrador: The First Fifteen Years of Confederation* (St John's, n.d. [1965]); *Report of the Royal Commission on the Economic State and Prospects of Newfoundland and Labrador* (St John's, 1967); and J. R. Smallwood, ed., *The Book of Newfoundland* (St John's, 1967), III and IV.

have been abandoned without any government assistance, of well over two hundred settlements which have disappeared since confederation.[2]

Other outports have 'disappeared' in the sense that they are no longer fishing villages but have become small towns, providing their residents with a range of municipal services which twenty years previously had been available only in St John's and two or three other centres. Such communities are as different from the traditional outport in character as they are in appearance: inevitably, as they grew in size, the old intimate and

2/C. M. Lane, 'Centralizing Our Population,' in J. R. Smallwood, ed., *The Book of Newfoundland* (St John's, 1967), III, 564–7.

cohesive pattern of village life became submerged beneath the more anonymous semi-urban patterns of the town, just as the original random tangle of fishermen's cottages gave way to regular streets and new housing, the latter built for the most part in the same monotonously ubiquitous styles that are the marks of low-cost housing throughout much of North America.

The fishery has remained the economic mainstay of approximately 20 per cent of the population, but in the larger settlements modern fish freezing and processing plants have rendered obsolete the traditional family unit of production. Women are employed under industrial conditions in the plants, but the centuries-old scene of women and children working on the fish-flakes turning the salt cod in the process of sun-drying has all but vanished. Even in the small outports which remain, and which are still largely dependent economically upon the production of salt fish (which in 1963 still accounted for 40.1 per cent of the total landings of cod), the conditions of life and labour are vastly different from what they were in 1949. Partly the change has been brought about by technological innovation, the outstanding example of which is the artificial drying kiln which is now widely in use in the major salt fish producing areas. This device, by eliminating the fisherman's dependence upon the weather for good drying conditions, and also by freeing him from the final laborious stage of the productive process, has stabilized both the quantity and quality of production and increased productivity per man in the industry. Also, since confederation there has been substantially increased capital investment in marine works and harbour facilities of all kinds, many of them built by the federal government.

Perhaps most important of all, however, has been the dramatic increase in the standard of living. Canadian transfer payments in the form of family allowances and old age pensions in particular have been instrumental in bringing this about. Moreover, they have contributed in no small measure to the undermining of the ancient and pernicious truck system, for there are today no communities left where cash does not circulate. As a result, fishermen and their families who once had practically no disposable income, but were carried from year to year 'on the merchant's books' with the inevitable semi-feudal relationship which this entailed, have come to enjoy a new status and dignity as independent consumers; if merchants want their custom they have now to earn it, for no outport kitchen is complete without two bulky mail-order catalogues – Eaton's and Simpson's, twin symbols of the new economic order.

After twenty years the initial impact of confederation is slowly but surely fading as the first generation of 'Canadian' Newfoundlanders comes to maturity; yet in the society as a whole the relentless process of modernization shows no sign of slackening. Rather, the disappearance of old objects and old ways of behaviour and even of speech has become – in the North American fashion – an accepted condition of everyday life. The social and psychological consequences of change, moreover, have been compounded many times over by the widespread effect of developments in three fields in particular: education, transportation, and mass communication.

Educational systems are today universally regarded by social scientists – and, to a greater or lesser degree, consciously used by governments – as vehicles of social change and adaptation. For schools, universities, polytechnics, and other such institutions not only supply the economy with the pattern of skills it requires but also in large measure shape the values and aspirations of those who possess the skills. Formal education, in other words, is a potent instrument of pre-adult socialization as well as a factor in economic growth. Newfoundland is a prime example of this. Nothing since confederation has more dramatically modernized, and 'Canadianized,' the island, and nothing will have a more profound and far-reaching effect upon the whole outlook of the society than the developments which have taken place in the field of education, at all levels from primary school to university.

Prior to 1949 Newfoundland educationally (as in so many other ways) still belonged to the nineteenth century. As noted earlier[3] the Commission government had, within the narrow confines of its limited financial resources, succeeded in introducing a number of improvements and reforms, but in general the system as a whole was much as it had been in the 1890s. This meant that not only were educational facilities divided vertically among the various religious denominations who owned and controlled them; they were also, within each of the three main denominational systems (Roman Catholic, Church of England, and United Church), horizontally stratified on the basis of socio-economic class. Though this latter feature of Newfoundland education has received less attention than denominationalism, it was no less important in its effects, for in practice the churches were remarkably in agreement in designing their respective school systems to serve and perpetuate the existing class structure of the island. Their organizations were hierarchical and practically identical, and in each the range in the quality of education from top to bottom was immense. At the one extreme there were the church 'colleges' in St John's. These were substantial and well-endowed foundations which functioned both as day-schools for the children of the commercial and professional

3/See above, p. 228.

élite of St John's (or in some cases, especially after 1945, the members of the petite bourgeoisie of the city who were willing to make financial sacrifices for their children's education) and as boarding schools for the children of prosperous outport merchants. Their high fees put them beyond the reach of the vast majority of families, but those who could afford them obtained for their children an undoubtedly superior quality of academic education that was roughly comparable, in style as well as in content, with that provided by a minor English public school (though the Roman Catholic college perhaps more closely resembled a mixture of seminary and Irish boarding school).

In all three church school systems the dominant social ethos was élitist: their pupils were encouraged to believe, what few of them would have doubted in any case, that they were entitled to and were being trained for 'leadership.' In this, as in so much else, these schools were typical relics of an imperial age. Their counterparts could be found dotted around the British colonial empire, in such places as Southern Rhodesia and Malaya, or wherever a 'white settler' community existed. The justification of the system in Newfoundland, however, was not that it segregated the 'whites' from the 'natives' but that it segregated the religious denominations. Yet, ironically, the pupils of the church colleges competed exclusively with one another at games, and even, to the extent that the social conventions of St John's would allow, mixed with one another socially – though with their lower class co-religionists they mixed hardly at all. The old Newfoundland educational system was often defended as representing the triumph of religion over the state: what it also represented, in practice, was the triumph within each denomination of class interests over religion.

For at the other extreme of the educational scale, standing in stark contrast to the church colleges with their fine stone or brick buildings, qualified teachers, laboratories, gymnasia, and playing fields, were the hundreds of one-room outport schools. These were for the most part primitive wooden shacks, without even the most basic facilities. Their teachers (when teachers could be found, and it was not unknown for a school to remain closed for a whole year or more for lack of a teacher) were often little better than semi-literate themselves. Of the children attending such schools, about one in seven hundred ever obtained matriculation (Grade 11). The remainder dropped out, usually at a much earlier stage, having acquired at most no more than the rudimentary skills of reading and writing. For them, the advantages of Christian denominational education were of necessity purely spiritual.

In between these two extremes there were good modern schools in Grand Falls and Corner Brook (in education as in most other respects these two industrial towns were atypical); large but generally poor and overcrowded schools for the children of the St John's working class; and, in the larger outports, schools of five or more classrooms in which the quality of education varied widely. Unfortunately, in the latter type of community the denominational system often produced a wasteful overlapping of school facilities (unlike St John's which could support a multiplicity of schools, or the small outports which were commonly unidenominational). Hence, instead of one large- or medium-sized school serving the whole community, each church would supply its own small, ill-equipped school for the children of its own adherents.

Even in the larger outport schools, however, it was rare to find a teacher with a university degree. In the whole province at the time of confederation, out of a total of 2,375 teachers there were only fifty-seven with degrees,[4] and of these the majority were concentrated in St John's, particularly in the church colleges.

One of the effects of such a system of education upon Newfoundland society was to restrict the utility of education as a channel of upward social mobility. The gross inequality of educational opportunity inherent in the system meant that in practice a person's class and status were fixed practically at birth. For a child born in a small outport, and destined to be educated in a one-room school, of whatever denomination, the only place open in the social hierarchy was at the bottom, as a fisherman. A few who were exceptionally lucky or exceptionally gifted might occasionally escape, but in general there was no such thing as 'a career open to talent.' Recruitment into the commercial, professional, and political élite was therefore confined largely to entrants from a narrow social stratum who had the good fortune to enjoy the best that the educational system could offer. The consequences of this are difficult to judge, but it is at least possible that the catastrophic incompetence of the Newfoundland élite in the 1920s and 1930s was due less to the heavy losses it suffered in the First World War (as is sometimes claimed) than to its closed nature, arising in part from the educational system which ensured that positions of power and responsibility would be inherited, often by those of weak character or limited intelligence, rather than earned by those of lowly origin but high ability. (The apotheosis of the system was undoubtedly Frederick Alderdice, who in 1928 inherited the premiership itself from his uncle, Walter Monroe.) Newfoundland, it would seem, in the absence of a good and relatively open educational system, was deprived of the main social mechanism by which the constant renewal or (in Pareto's famous phrase) 'the circulation of elites' could be achieved.

4/F. W. Rowe, 'The Rise of Education,' in *ibid.*, IV, 114.

Since education in Canada is a provincial responsibility, it was not generally anticipated at the time that confederation would have much of an impact in this field, especially since the continuation of the denominational system was specifically guaranteed under article 17 of the Terms of Union. In fact, however, there were indirect consequences of confederation which had the almost immediate effect of straining the system to the point of breakdown. The most important of these arose from the introduction of family allowances and other federal social security payments, which produced a sudden increase in school enrolment. School attendance up to the age of fourteen had been compulsory since 1944, but the regulation had never been widely enforced – the average attendance rate for the whole country in 1948 was 76 per cent; in some areas it was below 50 per cent. The payment of family allowances, however, was conditional upon school attendance and this positive inducement proved far more effective than any negative penalty. Moreover, the introduction of all forms of Canadian social security clearly revealed the extent to which the children of the poor were being denied even the minimal educational opportunities supposedly provided for them by their churches. Even after the relatively prosperous wartime years, there were still many children in Newfoundland who were prevented from attending school by lack of shoes or winter clothing, and even more by the appalling physical and psychological disabilities caused by malnutrition, disease, and lack of medical treatment.[5] There can be little doubt that the poor in general have used their social security payments wisely and to good effect. The average rate of school attendance has risen to more than 90 per cent and it has become rare to find children who are hungry or ill-clothed.

These improvements, together with a sharp decline in the death rate, a high birth rate with reduced infant mortality, and a fall in emigration meant that the highest priority in the immediate post-confederation period had to be given simply to expanding the school system to meet the pressure of numbers, while leaving the archaic organizational structure of education virtually intact. This policy was pursued with considerable success – between 1948–9 and 1956–7 the number of classrooms grew from 2,286 to 3,215.[6] Increasingly, however, the problem became one of reform. It was obvious from the beginning that though some defects, such as the low level of teachers' salaries, could be remedied without fundamentally disturbing the status quo, others, such as the poor quality of education

5/F. W. Rowe, *The Development of Education in Newfoundland* (Toronto, 1964), pp. 155–6.
6/F. Kirby, 'The School System,' in R. I. McAllister, ed., *Newfoundland and Labrador: The First Fifteen Years of Confederation* (St John's, n.d. [1965]), p. 32.

in the smaller schools, could only be remedied by a major reorganization of the entire system. Yet, for essentially political reasons, this could only be achieved within the limitations imposed by the denominational system; for the Liberal government, whatever its wishes in the matter, and in spite of its large majority, refrained from challenging the power of the churches for fear of reawakening the sectarian conflict that had been so marked a feature of the confederation campaign. Hence government policy was directed instead mainly towards improving and reorganizing each of the existing denominational systems. In particular, it was with government encouragement that each of the churches launched major schemes of school centralization. New denominational regional high schools, financed almost entirely out of public funds, have since 1954 proliferated around the province. By 1964 there were ninety such schools, including a number that were 'Protestant amalgamated,' which accommodated approximately 70 per cent of the high school population.[7]

The implications of this development are wider than might be at first apparent. Not only have these large modern high schools gone a long way towards improving the quality of education and equalizing educational opportunity, their introduction by each of the denominations has also had the effect of undermining the old church colleges of St John's which, in the face of considerable opposition, have been abolished and their buildings absorbed into their respective denomination's newly centralized system covering the children of all its adherents in the city.

Moreover, by taking measures to improve the pay, status, and training of teachers the government has enabled the churches to staff their new schools with better qualified teachers than would otherwise have been possible. Between 1949–50 and 1966–7 student enrolment in the Memorial University of Newfoundland, which is a non-denominational institution (though it has certain denominational aspects) has grown from 307 to 4,762, a large proportion of whom are teachers in training under the Faculty of Education. Though it is still the case that the percentage of the relevant age-group reaching university in Newfoundland is substantially lower than in most other provinces, the government has been unique in Canada in attempting to ensure reasonable equality of access to higher education by a programme of free tuition and student grants. Before it could be fully implemented, however, this programme was drastically curtailed as a government economy measure in 1968.

Thus, in spite of the rigidities and anomalies of the denominational system, the whole educational structure of Newfoundland has been profoundly altered since confederation. In terms of opportunity, quality of

7/*Ibid.*, p. 31.

instruction, and physical environment, Newfoundland children are for the first time in the island's history recognizably part of a Canadian educational pattern, even if gaps and deficiencies still remain. Also, with the increased concern shown for educational matters by a new generation of better-educated parents, the popularity of the denominational system has noticeably declined, at least among Protestants. This may be in part a reflection of the growing secularization of Newfoundland society generally, but, whatever the reasons, the implementation of a comprehensive public school system has at last become a viable possibility.

It is noteworthy also that what is perhaps the most significant educational development of all – school centralization – was only made possible by a simultaneous development in another, seemingly unrelated, field: that of road transportation. The familiar yellow schoolbus of rural Canada, which in 1949 was practically unknown in Newfoundland, has since become a commonplace sight. There is no more vivid symbol of the breakdown of the centuries-old isolation of the outports: children from villages which a mere twenty years before could be reached only by sea now daily take entirely for granted the fact that a modern bus will transport them to and from their large new central and regional schools. Over 2,300 miles of new roads have been built since confederation, with the federal government paying approximately 30 per cent of the cost of all road expenditures. The result is that there are today very few settlements remaining that are not connected with the main provincial highway system. There is already approximately one car to every five inhabitants and the ratio is steadily dropping.

Yet paradoxically, while the widespread introduction of motor cars has made the outports less isolated, it has also tended to erode the old patterns of community life which in the past made the isolation bearable. Other social and economic forces have naturally contributed to this as well, especially the migration of men away from the outports and the fishery to undertake seasonal employment in the logging, mining, or construction industries; but it has been the car that has most directly transformed the situation. The young in particular are no longer bound to their home communities, either physically or psychologically, the way their parents were. Further, apparently, outport life has little to offer compared with the liberty of the open road or the public entertainments of the nearest town. In a complex way, too, the car has become both a cause and a reflection of the gap between the old and the new Newfoundland, affecting in various ways such widely divergent matters as employment, education, church attendance, and patterns of dating, courtship, and sexual behaviour. While Newfoundland could scarcely be considered unique in this respect, in few societies has the break with the past been quite so sharp. The young, moreover, appear to share the general mainland preference for the urban way of life; for many, the real significance of a new road is that it offers a quick and easy exit, to Corner Brook, or St John's – or Toronto.

Finally, the pace and direction of social change has been immeasurably affected since confederation by the rapid growth of the media of mass communication, particularly radio and television. In 1949 the government-owned Broadcasting Corporation of Newfoundland was absorbed into the Canadian Broadcasting Corporation, which modernized and expanded its facilities and increased the Canadian content of its programming; at the same time, it was careful to maintain the tradition of public service broadcasting which had made the old BCN such a valuable institution to the people of the outports. A far more important development, however, in terms of its cultural impact, occurred in the private sector. Under the Commission Newfoundlanders had been spared the experience of American-style commercial radio,[8] but in 1951 a new private station was established in St John's with a powerful transmitter that enabled it to reach a large proportion of the population. Its basic formula was the well-tried one of local broadcasting from Wheeling, West Virginia, to Boise, Idaho – western and 'hillbilly' music, aggressive 'spot' commercials, quiz programmes, sports scores, news 'flashes,' and the breast-beating promotion of its own 'personalities.' It was of course immensely successful. It also set the style of the subsequent expansion in private broadcasting.

The same company expanded its activities to commercial television in 1955 and operated without a competitor in the field until 1964 when, after considerable public pressure, the CBC network was extended to St John's. Since that time Newfoundland has been liberally blanketed by both public and private radio and television transmitters and local relay stations.

The overall influence of this development has been not only to put Newfoundlanders more closely in touch with North America but to make them part of it. The instantaneous appearance on their television screens of mainland scenes and events undoubtedly tended to foster the growth of a 'continental consciousness' to a degree, especially among the young, that their more insular or Atlantic-oriented forefathers would have found inconceivable. At the same time, television's vivid and repetitious promotion, by means both crude and subtle, of the materialistic values and high level of consumption of American society has tended inevitably to arouse

8/There was one small commercial station operating in St John's, but it was scarcely touched by the influence of American broadcasting.

aspirations, if not yet fully articulated demands, which Newfoundland's relatively meagre economy is unlikely to be capable of satisfying.

Thus, in each of these three vitally important areas – education, transportation, and mass communication – the great changes that have taken place since, if not always directly as a result of, confederation have operated to push Newfoundland society in a single direction: towards closer integration with the mainland. They have, in other words, worked on the social plane to reinforce and translate into everyday reality the political integration that was formally achieved by the act of confederation itself. Culturally, partly as a result of these forces, Newfoundland is in the process of being homogenized into North America, and this for some is a cause of regret.[9] But local dialects and customs are everywhere on the way to extinction, and this fact is as evident in the 'mainlandized' speech and outlook of young Newfoundlanders as it is in the rather comic efforts of the ageing 'professional Newfs' of St John's, who periodically try – by such means as organizing massed choirs to sing folk ballads on television – to revive them. The old 'distinctive island culture' was in any case largely a culture of poverty, a product of ignorance or necessity, and a means of making unendurable deprivation slightly less unendurable. It is hardly surprising therefore that those who were part of it, as distinct from those who romanticize it, are able to view its disappearance with unconcern or even pleasure.

Finally, it is important to note the general context of political values and attitudes within which these momentous post-confederation social changes took place. Contrary to what often seems a general belief in Newfoundland, 1949 was not politically the Year One: in fact, the novelty of confederation overshadowed a great deal of continuity with the past, both in terms of revived institutions, such as the House of Assembly, and – more subtly – in the reassertion of the traditional norms of the political culture.[10] For the only political tradition which existed in 1949 was basically that which had survived from the old days of independent dominion status, the values inherent in it being transmitted without fundamental change across the long hiatus of Commission rule. The Commission had neither changed the political outlook of the people generally nor facilitated the emergence of new élites holding different social values from the old. It had operated according to the traditional precepts of British bureaucracy

9/ For a sensitive essay and pictorial lament, see Farley Mowat and John de Visser, *This Rock within the Sea: A Heritage Lost* (Boston, Toronto, 1968).
10/ See Peter Neary, 'Democracy in Newfoundland: A Comment,' *Journal of Canadian Studies*, vol. 4, no. 1 (Feb. 1969), pp. 37–45.

– secrecy, hierarchy, anonymity – and when confederation came it simply faded away, leaving no lasting impression on the society it had governed for fifteen years. Hence, when elective government was eventually restored, it naturally came to be operated in a manner and style which unconsciously reflected the political orientations of Newfoundlanders in the twenties and thirties, for this was the period in which most adult Newfoundlanders, including the political leaders of the new province, had first become politically active, or at least aware of politics. Thereafter the very success of the new provincial political order in 'delivering the goods,' in the sense that the benefits of joining the Canadian federation did in fact materialize as promised, combined with the Newfoundlander's understandably weak sense of identification with federal politics, tended to produce a climate in which assumed political values and norms could not be easily challenged.

Thus, in the first post-confederation decade in particular, substantial social and economic developments took place without fundamentally disturbing the sectarian-factional nature of the political culture. The 'denominational principle' remained as strongly held and widely shared a value as it had been in the nineteenth century, the Smallwood government being as careful as any of its predecessors not to offend any religious group by giving it less than its proportional share of offices and patronage. The attitudes of the people towards their representatives in the House of Assembly were little different from those described by Governor Sir Ralph Williams in 1913[11]; a member was expected to barter personal favours and services in return for electoral support. It was still widely held that a person who 'got something out of the government' was not really doing anything wrong; and that if he was actually *in* the government, but did not gain financially from it, then 'there must be something wrong with him.' The notion of 'to the victor the spoils' was generally accepted as right and just by people and politicians alike, though the latter now risked prosecution if they asserted it too zealously – after the first provincial election Premier Smallwood was threatened with a court action for allegedly intimidating the electors of Ferryland during the campaign by stating what was no more than a well-understood precept: if they did not vote for the government candidate 'not one red cent' of government money would be spent in their district.[12]

The old outport – St John's antagonism, which the referenda cam-

11/See above, p. 20.
12/Richard Gwyn, *Smallwood: The Unlikely Revolutionary* (Toronto, 1968), pp. 125–6.

paigns had exacerbated, continued to be a source of political cleavage only a little less significant than in the days of William Coaker and the FPU. The political symbols of the 'Empire connection,' the monarchy and the Union Jack, were still commonly displayed and widely revered. And, perhaps most significant of all, there was even a return to Newfoundland's traditional spirit of financial optimism. In spite of the highest rate of unemployment and the lowest per capita income in Canada, economic conditions were so immeasurably better than they had ever been before confederation that Newfoundlanders again eagerly embraced that curious intoxicating myth which runs like a thread through their history – that their land, underneath its harsh and unproductive exterior, is really a shining El Dorado, awaiting only the right leader to unlock its treasures. Flights of fancy about the new province's 'vast economic potential,' the alleged existence of which was used to justify the expenditure of public funds on a variety of highly dubious private development schemes, thus became the rhetorical stock-in-trade of the governing Liberal party, whose leader excelled even Edward Morris and Richard Squires in his ability to tell the people what they loved to hear.

The problem of economic development, however, was not solved by confederation. The basic dilemma remains the one which has plagued the island ever since the first Reid contract in the 1890s: outside capital can be attracted neither for the establishment of secondary industry in a small market nor for the exploitation of natural resources, which in North American terms are economically marginal, without extraordinary guarantees and concessions by the provincial government. And the terms which investors are able to extract are typically so severe as to make the investment of dubious benefit to the community. In the immediate post-confederation period the main effort of the government was directed towards the creation of labour-intensive light industries, a programme undertaken under the direction of a Rasputin-like economist and former minister in pre-war Latvia, Dr Alfred Valdmanis, who had impressed Smallwood by his imaginative plans and acquired a position of great trust and influence as director general of economic development. It was hoped that a combination of Newfoundland government capital, European (mainly German) technical and entrepreneurial skill, and cheap local labour would be able to overcome the disadvantage of remoteness from large markets. A few of the new enterprises eventually succeeded but most quickly failed. The development scheme itself was abandoned in 1954 when Dr Valdmanis was convicted of fraud and imprisoned.

After this strange and costly episode the Smallwood government returned with enthusiasm to the economic dream of Richard Squires: not local manufacturing but large-scale exploitation of forest, mineral, and hydro-electric resources would be the path of economic progress. In the 1950s the resources of Labrador, particularly its water power and plentiful supplies of low-grade iron ore, were potentially marketable – if investors could be offered sufficient financial inducements to develop them. In its determination to do so the government was prepared to offer concessions which made even the Reid contract seem niggardly. The result was a major construction boom in Labrador, opportunities for speculators unmatched since the days of Edward Morris, and the growth of new extractive industries. Unfortunately, the economic benefits to Newfoundland have been less than the size of the investment would suggest, for the new industries are capital-intensive and automated, and the processing of the new materials is done elsewhere. Similarly, the development of the hydro-electric generating capacities of Churchill Falls is mainly of benefit to Quebec. The alternative was probably no development whatever. Hence, the government's defence of its policies is not basically different from A. B. Morine's defence of the 1898 Reid contract. Nor is John C. Doyle, the premier's chief associate in these enterprises, very different from Robert Reid himself. A buccaneering American stock promoter, he as much as Smallwood is for better or worse the architect of the new Labrador. His contribution was the raising of capital, a function now perhaps somewhat reduced by his inability to set foot in the United States – in 1964 he skipped bail in Connecticut to avoid a prison sentence for a breach of United States securities regulations.[13]

In the 1960s, however, there were signs that certain aspects at least of the old political culture were slowly being altered by the infiltration of outside ideas and values, rising levels of education, and a generally more sophisticated understanding of Canadian politics. The latter is especially noteworthy. Not surprisingly, for some time after confederation many Newfoundlanders were confused by the practical implications of federalism, in the operation of which they had had no previous experience, and particularly by the federal-provincial division of powers. Their new rulers, for obvious reasons, preferred to make no sharp distinction between the two levels of government, suggesting instead that all the multifarious benefits of confederation flowed directly from the provincial régime – and would cease if the Smallwood Liberals lost office. Such claims, however, have now lost much of their credibility. The functions of the federal gov-

13/For accounts of the careers of Valdmanis and Doyle, see *ibid.*, 140–68, 240–54.

ernment have become more clearly differentiated and federal standards of administrative and political behaviour have become more widely known, thus inviting popular evaluation of provincial institutions and practices according to criteria which are at least some improvement on those which had so disastrously prevailed in the old Dominion of Newfoundland.

POLITICAL PARTIES

One of the provisions of the Terms of Union which brought Newfoundland into confederation was that the House of Assembly should be restored to its original position under the pre-1934 constitution, thus practically assuring the revival of parliamentary politics and political parties after their long period of suspension. None of the old parties, and almost none of their leaders, had survived: Richard Squires, William Coaker, Frederick Alderdice, were all dead; Walter Monroe alone lived on in retirement. It was inevitable, therefore, that the new provincial parties would grow out of the existing organizations which had so recently fought two referenda campaigns, the Newfoundland Confederate Association and the Responsible Government League. Nor was there any doubt that the victorious Confederates would adopt the Liberal label, or that Joseph Smallwood would be the party leader. For him, confederation had been a personal triumph, making his ascendancy in the movement so complete that he could have given it almost any party label he wished. (There was only one other potential leader, Gordon Bradley, but according to Smallwood's own published account, there was never any possibility of a rivalry developing between them because of their private pact to the effect that should confederation succeed Bradley would become Newfoundland's representative in the federal cabinet and Smallwood would become premier.)[14] However, in 1949 it was obviously advantageous for the Confederates to adopt the Liberal colours; the Liberal party was in power in Ottawa and close contacts with the federal leaders had already been established; moreover, though both Bradley and Smallwood had been 'Squires' Liberals in pre-Commission days, the name Liberal also retained certain older and more favourable historical associations – with Carson and Bond – which made it still, on balance, an electoral asset.

The correct procedure to be followed in the creation of a new provincial government, it was eventually decided in Ottawa after some uncer-

14/Gwyn states that Bradley later had doubts and wanted the premiership himself, but was angrily reminded of his promise by Smallwood (*ibid.*, p. 117).

tainty, was that a lieutenant-governor should first be appointed[15] and that it should be clearly indicated to him that it was the Canadian government's wish that he should call upon Joseph Smallwood to form a government.[16] Under the Terms of Union, the House of Assembly was required to meet within four months, thereby necessitating an early general election, Newfoundland's first since 1932.

The Confederate Liberals under Smallwood, who, having already become premier, was formally endorsed as leader at the Liberal party's founding convention in April, entered the contest with everything in their favour; not only were they carried forward by the momentum of their referendum victory, but their leaders were now endowed with the prestige and power of ministerial office, and control of all the patronage that this traditionally entailed. The supporters of the Responsible Government League, on the other hand, were in disarray even in their eastern strongholds. Once the main issue of confederation had been finally and irreversibly settled, the League's raison d'être had vanished, leaving its leaders with no credible claim to govern the new province whose creation they had tried so strenuously to prevent. The provincial Progressive Conservative party which was formed to fight the general election therefore laboured from the beginning under unique handicaps: it had neither a popular following, nor an organization, nor even an identity of its own; Newfoundlanders generally were unfamiliar with its well-established place in Canadian national politics; and its new leader, H. G. R. Mews, was politically inexperienced and unknown outside St John's. Most damaging of all, it was clearly the party of the anti-Confederate 'die-hards.'

This was largely unavoidable in 1949 – former supporters of responsible government naturally transferred their allegiance to the opposition party – but it was also an identification positively encouraged by the Conservatives who no doubt saw it at the time as a means of avoiding complete electoral eclipse, for it assured them of at least some seats in the new House of Assembly. Hence, at a rally in St John's, even the national leader of the Progressive Conservative party of Canada, George Drew, spoke out strongly against the fact that confederation had been brought about without the British government first restoring independence to Newfoundland. Yet had the party leaders looked beyond the immediate election campaign, to the party's long- or even medium-run prospects, they

15/Sir Albert Walsh was chosen (instead of Sir Leonard Outerbridge, who succeeded him) because Prime Minister St Laurent was anxious to appoint a Catholic in view of the denominational split revealed by the second referendum result.
16/Gwyn, *Smallwood*, pp. 118–19.

could hardly have failed to see that an anti-Confederate appeal was bound to yield sharply diminishing returns, especially once the social welfare and other benefits of confederation began to pour in. Had they therefore suppressed their procedural qualms and wholeheartedly welcomed confederation they might have alienated their 'die-hard' supporters (though even this is uncertain, for the latter would have had nowhere else to go) while at the same time establishing their future credibility as an alternative pro-confederation party. Instead, by what in retrospect can only be judged a major blunder of electoral strategy, they ensured only that for at least a generation, and in spite of all their subsequent disclaimers, they would suffer the stigma of being identified as 'the party that would undo Confederation.'

The result of the first provincial general election held on 27 May 1949 was a landslide Liberal victory. The government was returned with 22 out of the 28 seats in the legislature, the Conservatives managed to win only 5, and Peter Cashin was returned as an independent anti-Confederate in Ferryland.[17] Three districts, Harbour Grace, Port de Grave, and St John's West, which in the second poll of the referendum had voted for responsible government, now elected Liberals. The Conservatives were successful only in St John's East and Harbour Main–Bell Island, both of which were two-member constituencies, and Placentia–St Mary's. The Conservative leader, H. G. R. Mews, was among the defeated candidates. All the Conservatives elected were Catholics and represented predominantly Catholic and hard-core responsible government districts. Thus, to their already disadvantageous anti-Confederate image, the Conservatives – like the FPU in 1913 which elected only Protestants – inadvertently acquired a sectarian image as well.

In the six provincial general elections which have taken place since confederation the pattern which emerged in 1949 has been repeated with remarkably little variation (see Tables 2 and 3). At the same time there has been little variation in the districts which have returned opposition members. Of the aggregate of 30 seats won by opposition candidates in the six elections, no less than 19 have been in St John's (see Table 4). With the exception of Harbour Main–Bell Island, no district outside the capital city has returned members to the opposition side more than once; and in two of the five districts, Ferryland and Labrador West, the successful candidates were Independents. Thus, the urban base of Conservative support has been even more pronounced than its Catholic base – and more of a handicap, for the Newfoundland electoral system, while designed to

17/W. Millman, 'Election Results since Confederation,' in Smallwood, *The Book of Newfoundland,* III, 172–3.

TABLE 2

Party standing in the House of Assembly, 1949–66

	1949	1951	1956	1959	1962	1966
Liberal	22	23	32	31	34	39
Prog. Conservative	5	5	4	3	7	3
Independent	1	0	0	2[a]	1	0
Total seats	28	28	36	36	42	42

[a]United Newfoundland party.

TABLE 3

Percentage distribution of the popular vote in provincial general elections by party, 1949–66

	1949	1951	1956	1959	1962	1966
Liberal	65.5	63.6	66.3	58.0	58.7	61.8
Prog. Conservative	32.9	34.4	30.9	25.3	36.6	34.0
CCF/NDP	—	—	1.7	8.0	3.5	1.8
UNP	—	—	—	8.2	.5	—

TABLE 4

Constituencies electing opposition members, 1949–66

Constituency	1949	1951	1956	1959	1962	1966
St John's East[a]	xx	xx	x	x	x	x
St John's East Extern[b]					x	x
St John's West[a]		x	x			
St John's Centre[c]			x	x	x	x
St John's South[c]			x	x	x	
Harbour Main–Bell Island[a]	xx	xx				
Harbour Main[cd]				x		
Bell Island[c]				x		
Ferryland	x					
Placentia–St Mary's[e]	x					
Grand Falls					x	
Humber East[c]					x	
Labrador West[b]					x	
St Barbe South[b]					x	

[a]Two-member constituency in 1949 and 1951.
[b]Created by Redistribution Act, 1961.
[c]Created by Redistribution Act, 1955.
[d]Two-member constituency, 1956–66.
[e]1949 and 1951 only.

achieve 'denominational balance,' is also, as a matter of government policy, deliberately weighted in favour of rural areas.[18]

The dominant position of the Liberal party, however, cannot be adequately explained by these factors alone, for they ignore the extent to which post-confederation Newfoundland politics have revolved around the personality of one man: Joseph Smallwood. Indeed, in so far as there has been any consistent issue in provincial elections, it has been simply 'Are you for Joey or against him?' The Conservatives have put forward a succession of leaders but never one who could polarize opinion around himself like the diminutive heir of Richard Squires.

Federal politics have been, in practice, an extension of provincial politics – a further test of the premier's popularity. National issues, and to a large extent national party leaders, have been overshadowed by 'a lingering preoccupation with old feuds.'[19] The federal Liberal party has had no independent existence in Newfoundland and there have been no public selection procedures for its candidates. Though a greater degree of intra-party democracy was promised in 1968, up to that time the premier had made no secret of his ability to nominate candidates as part of his personal prerogative. Thereafter, once their appointments were confirmed by election, they tended to be regarded both by the premier and the public more as 'ambassadors' of the provincial régime than as members of a Parliament with any direct responsibility for matters affecting Newfoundland. For fourteen years, from 1953 to 1967, Newfoundland's most authoritative spokesman in Ottawa and in the highest councils of the national Liberal party was J. W. Pickersgill,[20] a former federal civil servant whose path to ministerial office had been cleared by Smallwood. A Manitoban, with no personal connection with Newfoundland, he had been given the safe seat of Bonavista-Twillingate in the justifiable expectation that a representative in the cabinet who had once served as secretary to Mackenzie King would know better than any local member how to loosen federal purse-strings. The first Liberal member of the House of Commons to acquire a political standing in the province which is not owed directly to Smallwood is Donald Jamieson, a popular St John's television personality who was first elected in Burin-Burgeo in 1966 – and who in 1949

18/See G. O. Rothney, 'The Denominational Basis of Representation in the Newfoundland Assembly, 1919–1962,' *Canadian Journal of Economics and Political Science*, vol. 28, no. 4 (Nov. 1962), pp. 557–70.

19/George Perlin, 'St. John's West,' in John Meisel, ed., *Papers on the 1962 Election* (Toronto, 1964), p. 3.

20/Secretary of state, 1953; minister of citizenship and immigration, 1954–7; secretary of state, 1963; minister of transport, 1964–8.

had been an advocate of economic union with the United States. As minister of transport he is also the first Newfoundlander to hold a major federal portfolio.

The Conservative party has generally been willing to fight federal elections on the premier's own ground. As in provincial elections, after confederation the only seats they had any hope of winning were in the predominantly Catholic, anti-Confederate, anti-Smallwood districts of St John's and the Avalon Peninsula, and in these any concentration on 'Canadian' issues would in the short run have alienated their most active supporters. Moreover, even St John's East, the party's 'safest' seat, includes within its federal boundaries a substantial rural area and is in fact marginal, returning Liberals in three out of eight federal general elections. Conservative electoral strategy has therefore tended to be defensive: its major goal being to avoid extinction from the provincial scene while waiting for the political tide to turn federally, or for Smallwood's popularity to fade. Tables 5 and 6 show the party standings in federal elections since 1949.

Neither federally nor provincially can there be said to be a party system in Newfoundland if the term is taken to imply the operation of party structures and organizations. Contrary to what mainland commentators often assume, the durability of the Smallwood régime cannot be attributed to the existence of a highly organized Liberal party 'machine,' for no such machine exists. The party of Smallwood has remained as organizationally embryonic as the party of Squires, a loose network of people held together

TABLE 5

Newfoundland representation in the Canadian House of Commons, by party, 1949–68

	1949	1953	1957	1958	1962	1963	1965	1968
Liberals	5	7	5	5	6	7	7	1
Progressive Conservatives	2	0	2	2	1	0	0	6

TABLE 6

Percentage distribution of the popular vote in federal general elections, by party, 1949–68

	1949	1953	1957	1958	1962	1963	1965	1968
Liberal	71.9	67.3	61.9	54.4	59.0	64.5	64.1	42.7
Prog. Conservative	27.9	28.1	37.8	45.2	36.0	30.0	32.4	52.8
CCF/NDP	.2	.6	.3	.2	4.9	4.2	1.2	4.4
Social Credit	—	—	—	—	.1	—	1.6	.1

by personal relationships, old loyalties, and the multifarious rewards and deprivations that Liberal ministers have it in their power to bestow.

Party organizations are not merely vehicles for the acquisition of power: they can also operate to check the power of party leaders. Thus, a political leader such as Smallwood, whose authority flowed directly from his relationship with the people, had no need of a formal party organization; he could operate more freely without it, as long as his popularity held. This is not to suggest that at election time the Liberal government has not been able to mobilize men and resources for the purpose of the campaign – indeed, at such times it can be formidably effective – but its organization has been *ad hoc*, an electoral task force rather than a party, lacking in even the rhetoric of internal democracy, and fading away once it has served its immediate purpose. The Conservative party has not been basically different; only weaker in leadership, more St John's oriented, and, except for the period when the Conservatives were in power in Ottawa, with no tangible rewards to attract party 'volunteers.'

The result has been to restore the traditional system of intensely personal politics, almost wholly confined to the capital city, and marked by intrigues of Byzantine obscurity. As in the days before the rise of the FPU in 1913, practically all members of the Assembly are residents of St John's, and often have only the most tenuous connections with the constituencies they represent. For most outport electors it has been enough to know that their Liberal candidate, even if he happened to be yet another St John's lawyer who had never seen their district before, has been sent to them as 'Joey's man.' Thus the premier has had no difficulty in treating a number of districts as 'rotten boroughs,' as in pre-1832 England, nominating as their candidates the sons of cabinet ministers or of prominent party supporters, or others more eccentrically selected for political preferment.

The outcome of the 1968 federal election, in which all but one of the seven Newfoundland seats were won by Conservatives, may be seen as an indication that the period of Smallwood's complete ascendancy in the province is over, for again the only real 'issue' in the election was 'Are you for or against Joey?' Some of the underlying economic and social factors, such as the rise in educational levels and the closer integration of the island with the mainland, which contributed to this reversal have been discussed elsewhere. It need only be noted here that the Liberal defeat classically demonstrates one of the inherent weaknesses of personal rule. That is, the leader's reluctance to encourage the growth of democratic political infrastructures, combined with the tendency of politicians to congregate in the capital (phenomena found in many of the newly independent countries of the world), produces a political system in which the 'feedback' of information from the people to the government becomes increasingly weak and distorted – even when the leader (an Nkrumah or a Smallwood) is one who could once legitimately claim to understand the discontents and aspirations of the 'toiling masses.'

In a unitary state, when the popular reaction comes, it tends to erupt suddenly and sweep the leader out of office. In a federal system, however, it is possible for the leader of a provincial régime to receive an advance warning from the electorate in federal elections which, from the provincial point of view, can perform a vital function of political communication. For a provincial premier, the loss of his party's seats in Ottawa is a small price to pay for the invaluable message that his own political fences need mending.

In Newfoundland, for the first time since confederation, politics have become competitive. Yet competitive politics are by no means new to Newfoundland's experience. Sharp electoral swings were common occurrences in the past, and most were hailed at the time, at least by the victors, as marking the dawn of a new era. Whether the ending of a unique period of personal rule will lead to the emergence of a new and more democratic political order or a return to the rancorous political instability of the past, must therefore remain an open question.

APPENDICES

Appendix A

NEWFOUNDLAND MINISTRIES, 1900–34

Bond's cabinet
November 1900–March 1909

Prime minister and colonial secretary: Sir Robert Bond
Minister of justice and attorney general: Sir Edward Morris
Minister of finance and customs: E. M. Jackman
Minister of agriculture and mines: J. A. Clift
Minister of marine and fisheries: E. Dawe
Ministers without portfolio: G. Knowling, MLC,* J. S. Pitts, MLC, H. Gear, G. Shea

Outside cabinet:

Minister of public works: G. Gushue

Changes:

Sir Edward Morris resigned on 26 July 1907 and his place was taken by J. M. Kent on 6 August 1907.

Morris' cabinet
March 1909–July 1917

Prime minister: Sir Edward Morris
Colonial secretary: R. Watson
Minister of justice and attorney general: D. Morison
Minister of finance and customs: M. P. Cashin
Minister of agriculture and mines: S. D. Blandford
Ministers without portfolio: R. K. Bishop, MLC, M. P. Gibbs, MLC, C. H. Emerson, J. C. Crosbie

    *Member of the Legislative Council

Outside cabinet:

Minister of public works: W. Woodford
Minister of marine and fisheries: A. W. Piccott

Changes:

J. R. Bennett replaced R. Watson as colonial secretary and R. Squires, MLC, replaced D. Morison as minister of justice and attorney general in November 1913.

Morris' National government
July 1917–January 1918

Prime minister: Sir Edward Morris
Colonial secretary: R. Squires, MLC
Minister of justice and attorney general: W. F. Lloyd
Minister of finance and customs: M. P. Cashin
Minister of agriculture and mines: W. W. Halfyard
Minister of militia: J. R. Bennett (appointed August 1917)
Ministers without portfolio: W. F. Coaker, J. C. Crosbie, J. A. Clift,
A. E. Hickman, M. P. Gibbs, MLC, W. J. Ellis, MLC

Outside cabinet:

Minister of public works: W. Woodford
Minister of marine and fisheries: J. G. Stone

Lloyd's National government
January 1918–May 1919

Prime minister: Sir William Lloyd
Colonial secretary: W. W. Halfyard
Minister of finance and customs: Sir Michael Cashin
Minister of agriculture and mines: J. A. Clift
Minister of militia: J. R. Bennett
Minister of shipping: J. C. Crosbie
Ministers without portfolio: W. F. Coaker, A. E. Hickman, W. J. Ellis, MLC

Outside cabinet:

Minister of public works: W. Woodford

Changes:

J. C. Crosbie was briefly minister of militia in January 1918, but was replaced by J. R. Bennett on January 18, at which time the new portfolio of shipping was created.

Cashin's cabinet
May 1919–November 1919

Prime minister and minister of finance and customs: Sir Michael Cashin
Colonial secretary: J. R. Bennett

Minister of justice and attorney general: A. B. Morine
Minister of shipping: J. C. Crosbie
Minister of militia: A. E. Hickman
Minister of marine and fisheries: J. G. Stone
Minister of public works: W. Woodford
Ministers without portfolio: W. J. Ellis, MLC, J. S. Currie, A. W. Piccott

Outside cabinet:

Minister of agriculture and mines: W. J. Walsh

Squires's first cabinet
November 1919–July 1923

Prime minister and colonial secretary: Sir Richard Squires
Minister of justice and attorney general: W. R. Warren
Minister of finance and customs: H. J. Brownrigg
Minister of marine and fisheries: W. F. Coaker
Minister of agriculture and mines: A. Campbell, MLC
Minister of education: A. Barnes (appointed 1920)
Ministers without portfolio: S. J. Foote, G. Shea, MLC

Outside cabinet:

Minister of shipping: W. H. Cave
Minister of public works: W. B. Jennings

Changes:

In April 1923, T. Bonia replaced H. J. Brownrigg as minister of finance and
customs, W. W. Halfyard replaced W. F. Coaker as minister of marine and
fisheries, and A. W. Piccott replaced W. B. Jennings as minister of public
works. In June 1923 W. H. Cave replaced T. Bonia as minister of finance and
customs, T. Bonia, MLC, was appointed minister of posts and telegraphs, and
Sir Marmaduke Winter, MLC, was appointed minister without portfolio.

Warren's cabinet
July 1923–May 1924

Prime minister and minister of justice and attorney general: William Warren
Colonial secretary: W. W. Halfyard
Minister of finance and customs: W. H. Cave
Minister of agriculture and mines: J. F. Downey
Minister of education: A. Barnes
Minister of posts and telegraphs: M. E. Hawco
Ministers without portfolio: Sir William Coaker, G. Shea, MLC,
Sir Marmaduke Winter, MLC, S. J. Foote

Outside cabinet:

Minister of marine and fisheries: G. F. Grimes
Minister of public works: A. W. Piccott

Warren's 'four-day' cabinet
3 May–7 May 1924

Prime minister and minister of justice and attorney general: William Warren
Colonial secretary: W. J. Higgins
Minister of finance and customs: J. R. Bennett
Minister of posts and telegraphs: M. E. Hawco
Ministers without portfolio: W. S. Monroe, J. A. Robinson, MLC,
M. S. Sullivan, C. P. Ayre, W. Roberts

Outside cabinet:

Minister of marine and fisheries: W. C. Winsor
Minister of agriculture and mines: W. J. Walsh
Minister of public works: C. E. Russell

Hickman's cabinet
10 May–9 June 1924

Prime minister: A. E. Hickman
Colonial secretary: W. W. Halfyard
Minister of justice and attorney general: Sir William Lloyd
Minister of finance and customs: W. H. Cave
Minister of agriculture and mines: J. F. Downey
Minister of education: A. Barnes
Minister of posts and telegraphs: M. E. Hawco
Ministers without portfolio: L. E. Emerson, H. M. Mosdell, C. A. Forbes

Outside cabinet:
Minister of public works: R. Hibbs
Minister of marine and fisheries: F. C. Archibald

Monroe's cabinet
June 1924–August 1928

Prime minister and minister of education: Walter Monroe
Colonial secretary: J. R. Bennett
Minister of justice and attorney general: W. J. Higgins
Minister of finance and customs: Sir John Crosbie
Minister of posts and telegraphs: W. Woodford
Ministers without portfolio: A. B. Morine, MLC, M. S. Sullivan, R. Cramm,
F. G. Bradley, J. J. Long

Outside cabinet:
Minister of agriculture and mines: W. J. Walsh

Minister of marine and fisheries: W. C. Winsor
Minister of public works: C. E. Russell

Changes:

In May 1926 F. G. Bradley and C. E. Russell resigned. Russell was replaced as minister of public works by W. McK. Chambers. In June 1926 R. Duff was appointed minister without portfolio.

Alderdice's first cabinet
August 1928–November 1928

Prime minister: Frederick Alderdice
Colonial secretary: M. S. Sullivan
Minister of justice and attorney general: W. R. Howley
Minister of finance and customs: S. J. Foote
Minister of agriculture and mines: W. J. Walsh
Ministers without portfolio: J. A. Robinson, MLC, H. A. Winter, J. S. Ayre, J. A. W. McNeilly, W. S. Monroe (appointed September 1928)

Outside cabinet:

Minister of public works: W. McK. Chambers
Minister of marine and fisheries: J. G. Stone
Minister of posts and telegraphs: H. N. Burt

Squires's second cabinet
November 1928–June 1932

Prime minister and minister of justice and attorney general:
Sir Richard Squires
Colonial secretary: A. Barnes
Minister of finance and customs: P. J. Cashin
Minister of posts and telegraphs: W. W. Halfyard
Ministers without portfolio: Sir William Coaker, A. Campbell, F. G. Bradley, H. M. Mosdell, P. J. Lewis, Tasker Cook, MLC

Outside cabinet:

Minister of agriculture and mines: J. F. Downey
Minister of public works: R. Hibbs
Minister of marine and fisheries: H. B. C. Lake

Changes:

F. G. Bradley was appointed to the new portfolio of solicitor general in June 1929. In February 1932 P. J. Cashin resigned from the cabinet. In May 1932 H. B. C. Lake and R. Cramm were appointed to the cabinet, the latter as minister without portfolio, replacing H. M. Mosdell.

Alderdice's second cabinet
June 1932–February 1934

Prime minister, minister of finance and customs, and minister of education:
Frederick Alderdice
Secretary of state: J. C. Puddester
Minister of labour: K. M. Brown
Minister of marine and fisheries: J. G. Stone
Minister of agriculture and mines: W. J. Walsh
Ministers without portfolio: H. Mitchell, H. A. Winter, W. J. Browne,
F. MacNamara, J. S. Ayre

Outside cabinet:

Minister of posts and telegraphs: W. C. Winsor

Changes:

In July 1932 H. A. Winter was appointed minister of justice and attorney
general. In August 1932 W. J. Browne was appointed minister of finance and
customs. In March 1933 W. C. Winsor was appointed to the cabinet.

Appendix B

Seats in House of Assembly, by party, 1900–66

Date of election	Party forming government	Main opposition party
1900	32 Liberal	4 Conservative
1904	30 Liberal	6 United Opposition party
1908	18 Liberal	18 People's party
1909	26 People's party	10 Liberal
1913	21 People's party	15 Liberal-Union
1919	23 Liberal Reform	13 People's party
1923	23 Liberal Reform	13 Liberal-Labour-Progressive
1924	25 Liberal Conservative	11 Liberal Progressive
1928	28 Liberal	12 Conservative
1932	24 United Newfoundland	3 Liberal
1949	22 Liberal	5 Progressive Conservative
1951	23 Liberal	5 Progressive Conservative
1956	32 Liberal	4 Progressive Conservative
1959	31 Liberal	3 Progressive Conservative
1962	34 Liberal	7 Progressive Conservative
1966	39 Liberal	3 Progressive Conservative

Appendix C

Memorandum of agreement entered into on the eleventh day of December, 1948, between Canada and Newfoundland.

WHEREAS a delegation appointed from its members by the National Convention of Newfoundland, a body elected by the people of Newfoundland, consulted in 1947 with the Government of Canada to ascertain what fair and equitable basis might exist for the union of Newfoundland with Canada;

WHEREAS, following discussions with the delegation, the Government of Canada sent to His Excellency the Governor of Newfoundland for submission to the National Convention a statement of terms which the Government of Canada would be prepared to recommend to the Parliament of Canada as a fair and equitable basis for union, should the people of Newfoundland desire to enter into confederation;

WHEREAS the proposed terms were debated in the National Convention in Newfoundland and were before the people of Newfoundland when, by a majority at a referendum held on the twenty-second day of July, 1948, they expressed their desire to enter into confederation with Canada;

WHEREAS the Governments of the United Kingdom, Canada, and Newfoundland agreed after the referendum that representatives of Canada and Newfoundland should meet and settle the final terms and arrangements for the union of Newfoundland with Canada;

AND WHEREAS authorized representatives of Canada and authorized representatives of Newfoundland have settled the terms hereinafter set forth as the Terms of Union of Newfoundland with Canada;

It is therefore agreed as follows:

TERMS OF UNION

UNION

1 On, from, and after the coming into force of these Terms (hereinafter referred to as the date of Union), Newfoundland shall form part of Canada and

shall be a province thereof to be called and known as the Province of New-foundland.

2 The Province of Newfoundland shall comprise the same territory as at the date of Union, that is to say, the island of Newfoundland and the islands adjacent thereto, the Coast of Labrador as delimited in the report delivered by the Judicial Committee of His Majesty's Privy Council on the first day of March, 1927, and approved by His Majesty in His Privy Council on the twenty-second day of March, 1927, and the islands adjacent to the said Coast of Labrador.

APPLICATION OF THE BRITISH NORTH AMERICA ACTS

3 The British North America Acts, 1867 to 1946, shall apply to the Province of Newfoundland in the same way and to the like extent as they apply to the provinces heretofore comprised in Canada, as if the Province of Newfound-land had been one of the provinces originally united, except insofar as varied by these Terms and except such provisions as are in terms made or by reason-able intendment may be held to be specially applicable to or only to affect one or more and not all of the provinces originally united.

REPRESENTATION IN PARLIAMENT

4 The Province of Newfoundland shall be entitled to be represented in the Senate by six members, and in the House of Commons by seven members out of a total membership of two hundred and sixty-two.

5 Representation in the Senate and in the House of Commons shall from time to time be altered or readjusted in accordance with the British North America Acts, 1867 to 1946.

6 (1) Until the Parliament of Canada otherwise provides, the Province of Newfoundland shall for the purposes of the election of members to serve in the House of Commons, be divided into the electoral divisions named and de-limited in the Schedule to these Terms, and each such division shall be entitled to return one member.

(2) For the first election of members to serve in the House of Commons, if held otherwise than as part of a general election, the Governor General in Council may cause writs to be issued and may fix the day upon which the polls shall be held, and, subject to the foregoing, the laws of Canada relating to by-elections shall apply to an election held pursuant to any writ issued under this Term.

(3) The Chief Electoral Officer shall have authority to adapt the provisions of The Dominion Elections Act, 1938, to conditions existing in the Province of Newfoundland so as to conduct effectually the first election of members to serve in the House of Commons.

PROVINCIAL CONSTITUTION

7 The Constitution of Newfoundland as it existed immediately prior to the sixteenth day of February, 1934, is revived at the date of Union and shall, subject to these Terms and the British North America Acts, 1867 to 1946,

continue as the Constitution of the Province of Newfoundland from and after the date of Union, until altered under the authority of the said Acts.

Executive

8 (1) For the Province of Newfoundland there shall be an officer styled the Lieutenant-Governor, appointed by the Governor General in Council by instrument under the Great Seal of Canada.

(2) Pending the first appointment of a Lieutenant-Governor for the Province of Newfoundland and the assumption of his duties as such, the Chief Justice, or if the office of Chief Justice is vacant, the senior judge, of the Supreme Court of Newfoundland, shall execute the office and functions of Lieutenant-Governor under his oath of office as such Chief Justice or senior judge.

9 The Constitution of the Executive Authority of Newfoundland as it existed immediately prior to the sixteenth day of February, 1934, shall, subject to these Terms and the British North America Acts, 1867 to 1946, continue as the Constitution of the Executive Authority of the Province of Newfoundland from and after the date of Union, until altered under the authority of the said Acts.

10 The Lieutenant-Governor in Council shall as soon as may be after the date of Union adopt and provide a Great Seal of the Province of Newfoundland and may from time to time change such seal.

11 All powers, authorities, and functions that under any statute were at or immediately prior to the date of Union vested in or exercisable by the Governor of Newfoundland, individually, or in Council, or in Commission,

(*a*) as far as they are capable of being exercised after the date of Union in relation to the Government of Canada, shall be vested in and shall or may be exercised by the Governor General, with the advice, or with the advice and consent, or in conjunction with, the King's Privy Council for Canada or any member or members thereof, or by the Governor General individually, as the case requires, subject nevertheless to be abolished or altered by the Parliament of Canada under the authority of the British North America Acts, 1867 to 1946; and

(*b*) as far as they are capable of being exercised after the date of Union in relation to the Government of the Province of Newfoundland, shall be vested in and shall or may be exercised by the Lieutenant-Governor of the Province of Newfoundland, with the advice, or with the advice and consent, or in conjunction with, the Executive Council of the Province of Newfoundland or any member or members thereof, or by the Lieutenant-Governor individually, as the case requires, subject nevertheless to be abolished or altered by the Legislature of the Province of Newfoundland under the authority of the British North America Acts, 1867 to 1946.

12 Until the Parliament of Canada otherwise provides, the powers, authorities, and functions vested in or imposed on any member of the Commission of Government of Newfoundland, as such member or as a Commissioner charged

with the administration of a Department of the Government of Newfoundland, at or immediately prior to the date of Union in relation to matters other than those coming within the classes of subjects by the British North America Acts, 1867 to 1946, assigned exclusively to the Legislature of a province, shall in the Province of Newfoundland be vested in or imposed on such person or persons as the Governor General in Council may appoint or designate.

13 Until the Legislature of the Province of Newfoundland otherwise provides, the powers, authorities, and functions vested in or imposed on any member of the Commission of Government of Newfoundland, as such member or as a Commissioner charged with the administration of a Department of the Government of Newfoundland, at or immediately prior to the date of Union in relation to matters coming within the classes of subjects by the British North America Acts, 1867 to 1946, assigned exclusively to the Legislature of a province, shall in the Province of Newfoundland be vested in or imposed on such person or persons as the Lieutenant-Governor in Council may appoint or designate.

Legislature

14 (1) Subject to paragraph two of this Term, the Constitution of the Legislature of Newfoundland as it existed immediately prior to the sixteenth day of February, 1934, shall, subject to these Terms and the British North America Acts, 1867 to 1946, continue as the Constitution of the Legislature of the Province of Newfoundland from and after the date of Union, until altered under the authority of the said Acts.

(2) The Constitution of the Legislature of Newfoundland insofar as it relates to the Legislative Council shall not continue, but the Legislature of the Province of Newfoundland may at any time re-establish the Legislative Council or establish a new Legislative Council.

15 (1) Until the Legislature of the Province of Newfoundland otherwise provides, the powers, authorities, and functions vested in or imposed on a Minister or other public officer or functionary under any statute of Newfoundland relating to the Constitution of the Legislature of Newfoundland as it existed immediately prior to the sixteenth day of February, 1934, shall, subject to these Terms and the British North America Acts, 1867 to 1946, be vested in or imposed on such person or persons as the Lieutenant-Governor in Council may appoint or designate.

(2) Until the Legislature of the Province of Newfoundland otherwise provides,

(*a*) the list of electors prepared pursuant to The List of Electors Act, 1947, shall be deemed to be the list of electors for the purposes of The Election Act, 1913, subject to the provisions of The Election Act, 1913, respecting supplementary lists of electors;

(*b*) the franchise shall be extended to female British subjects who have attained the full age of twenty-one years and are otherwise qualified as electors;

(*c*) the Coast of Labrador together with the islands adjacent thereto shall constitute an additional electoral district to be known as Labrador and to be represented by one member, and residents of the said district who are otherwise qualified as electors shall be entitled to vote; and

(*d*) the Lieutenant-Governor in Council may by proclamation defer any election in the electoral district of Labrador for such period as may be specified in the proclamation.

16 The Legislature of the Province of Newfoundland shall be called together not later than four months after the date of Union.

EDUCATION

17 In lieu of section ninety-three of the British North America Act, 1867, the following Term shall apply in respect of the Province of Newfoundland:

In and for the Province of Newfoundland the Legislature shall have exclusive authority to make laws in relation to education, but the Legislature will not have authority to make laws prejudicially affecting any right or privilege with respect to denominational schools, common (amalgamated) schools, or denominational colleges, that any class or classes of persons have by law in Newfoundland at the date of Union, and out of public funds of the Province of Newfoundland provided for education,

(*a*) all such schools shall receive their share of such funds in accordance with scales determined on a non-discriminatory basis from time to time by the Legislature for all schools then being conducted under authority of the Legislature; and

(*b*) all such colleges shall receive their share of any grant from time to time voted for all colleges then being conducted under authority of the Legislature, such grant being distributed on a non-discriminatory basis.

CONTINUATION OF LAWS

General

18 (1) Subject to these Terms, all laws in force in Newfoundland at or immediately prior to the date of Union shall continue therein as if the Union had not been made, subject nevertheless to be repealed, abolished, or altered by the Parliament of Canada or by the Legislature of the Province of Newfoundland according to the authority of the Parliament or of the Legislature under the British North America Acts, 1867 to 1946, and all orders, rules, and regulations made under any such laws shall likewise continue, subject to be revoked or amended by the body or person that made such orders, rules, or regulations or the body or person that has power to make such orders, rules, or regulations after the date of Union, according to their respective authority under the British North America Acts, 1867 to 1946.

(2) Statutes of the Parliament of Canada in force at the date of Union, or any part thereof, shall come into force in the Province of Newfoundland on a day or days to be fixed by Act of the Parliament of Canada or by proclamation

of the Governor General in Council issued from time to time, and any such proclamation may provide for the repeal of any of the laws of Newfoundland that

(*a*) are of general application;

(*b*) relate to the same subject matter as the statute or part thereof so proclaimed; and

(*c*) could be repealed by the Parliament of Canada under paragraph one of this Term.

(3) Notwithstanding anything in these Terms, the Parliament of Canada may with the consent of the Legislature of the Province of Newfoundland repeal any law in force in Newfoundland at the date of Union.

(4) Except as otherwise provided by these Terms, all courts of civil and criminal jurisdiction and all legal commissions, powers, authorities, and functions, and all officers and functionaries, judicial, administrative, and ministerial, existing in Newfoundland at or immediately prior to the date of Union, shall continue in the Province of Newfoundland as if the Union had not been made, until altered, abolished, revoked, terminated, or dismissed by the appropriate authority under the British North America Acts, 1867 to 1946.

Supply

19 Any statute of Newfoundland enacted prior to the date of Union for granting to His Majesty sums of money for defraying expenses of, and for other purposes relating to, the public service of Newfoundland, for the financial year ending the thirty-first day of March, one thousand nine hundred and fifty, shall have effect after the date of Union according to its terms, until otherwise provided by the Legislature of the Province of Newfoundland.

Patents

20 (1) Subject to this Term, Canada will provide that letters patent for inventions issued under the laws of Newfoundland prior to the date of Union shall be deemed to have been issued under the laws of Canada, as of the date and for the term thereof.

(2) Canada will provide further that in the event of conflict between letters patent for an invention issued under the laws of Newfoundland prior to the date of Union and letters patent for an invention issued under the laws of Canada prior to the date of Union

(*a*) the letters patent issued under the laws of Newfoundland shall have the same force and effect in the Province of Newfoundland as if the Union had not been made, and all rights and privileges acquired under or by virtue thereof may continue to be exercised or enjoyed in the Province of Newfoundland as if the Union had not been made; and

(*b*) the letters patent issued under the laws of Canada shall have the same force and effect in any part of Canada other than the Province of Newfoundland as if the Union had not been made, and all rights and privileges acquired

under or by virtue thereof may continue to be exercised or enjoyed in any part
of Canada other than the Province of Newfoundland as if the Union had not
been made.

(3) The laws of Newfoundland existing at the date of Union shall continue
to apply in respect of applications for the grant of letters patent for inventions
under the laws of Newfoundland pending at the date of Union, and any letters
patent for inventions issued upon such applications shall, for the purposes of
this Term, be deemed to have been issued under the laws of Newfoundland
prior to the date of Union; and letters patent for inventions issued under the
laws of Canada upon applications pending at the date of Union shall, for the
purposes of this Term, be deemed to have been issued under the laws of Canada prior to the date of Union.

(4) Nothing in this Term shall be construed to prevent the Parliament of
Canada from providing that no claims for infringement of a patent issued in
Canada prior to the date of Union shall be entertained by any court against
any person for anything done in Newfoundland prior to the date of Union in
respect of the invention protected by such patent, and that no claims for infringement of a patent issued in Newfoundland prior to the date of Union shall
be entertained by any court against any person for anything done in Canada
prior to the date of Union in respect of the invention protected by such patent.

Trade Marks
21 (1) Canada will provide that the registration of a trade mark under the
laws of Newfoundland prior to the date of Union shall have the same force and
effect in the Province of Newfoundland as if the Union had not been made,
and all rights and privileges acquired under or by virtue thereof may continue
to be exercised or enjoyed in the Province of Newfoundland as if the Union
had not been made.

(2) The laws of Newfoundland existing at the date of Union shall continue
to apply in respect of applications for the registration of trade marks under the
laws of Newfoundland pending at the date of Union and any trade marks registered upon such applications shall, for the purposes of this Term, be deemed
to have been registered under the laws of Newfoundland prior to the date of
Union.

Fisheries
22 (1) In this Term, the expression 'Fisheries Laws' means the Act No. 11
of 1936, entitled 'An Act for the creation of the Newfoundland Fisheries
Board', the Act No. 14 of 1936, entitled 'An Act to Prevent the Export of Fish
Without Licence', the Act No. 32 of 1936, entitled 'An Act to Amend the Newfoundland Fisheries Board Act (No. 11 of 1936)', the Act No. 37 of 1938,
entitled 'An Act further to Amend the Newfoundland Fisheries Board Act,
1936', the Act No. 10 of 1942, entitled 'An Act Respecting Permits for the
Exportation of Salt Fish', the Act No. 39 of 1943, entitled 'An Act Further to

Amend the Newfoundland Fisheries Board Act, 1936', the Act No. 16 of 1944, entitled 'An Act Further to Amend the Newfoundland Fisheries Board Acts, 1930–38', and the Act No. 42 of 1944, entitled 'An Act Further to Amend the Newfoundland Fisheries Board Act, 1936', insofar as they relate to the export marketing of salted fish from Newfoundland to other countries or to any provinces of Canada.

(2) Subject to this Term, all Fisheries Laws and all orders, rules, and regulations made thereunder shall continue in force in the Province of Newfoundland as if the Union had not been made, for a period of five years from the date of Union and thereafter until the Parliament of Canada otherwise provides, and shall continue to be administered by the Newfoundland Fisheries Board; and the costs involved in the maintenance of the Board and the administration of the Fisheries Laws shall be borne by the Government of Canada.

(3) The powers, authorities, and functions vested in or imposed on the Governor in Commission or the Commissioner for Natural Resources under any of the Fisheries Laws shall after the date of Union respectively be vested in or imposed on the Governor General in Council and the Minister of Fisheries of Canada or such other Minister as the Governor General in Council may designate.

(4) Any of the Fisheries Laws may be repealed or altered at any time within the period of five years from the date of Union by the Parliament of Canada with the consent of the Lieutenant-Governor in Council of the Province of Newfoundland and all orders, rules, and regulations made under the authority of any Fisheries Laws may be revoked or altered by the body or person that made them or, in relation to matters to which paragraph three of this Term applies, by the body or person that under the said paragraph three has power to make such orders, rules, or regulations under the Fisheries Laws after the date of Union.

(5) The Chairman of the Newfoundland Fisheries Board or such other member of the Newfoundland Fisheries Board as the Governor General in Council may designate shall perform in the Province of Newfoundland the duties of Chief Supervisor and Chief Inspector of the Department of Fisheries of the Government of Canada, and employees of the Newfoundland Fisheries Board shall become employees in that Department in positions comparable to those of the employees in that Department in other parts of Canada.

(6) Terms eleven, twelve, thirteen and eighteen are subject to this Term.

FINANCIAL TERMS

Debt

23 Canada will assume and provide for the servicing and retirement of the stock issued or to be issued on the security of Newfoundland pursuant to The Loan Act, 1933, of Newfoundland and will take over the Sinking Fund established under that Act.

Financial Surplus

24 (1) In this Term the expression 'financial surplus' means the balances standing to the credit of the Newfoundland Exchequer at the date of Union (less such sums as may be required to discharge accounts payable at the date of Union in respect of appropriations for the public services) and any public moneys or public revenue (including loans and advances referred to in Term twenty-five) in respect of any matter, thing, or period prior to the date of Union recovered by the Government of the Province of Newfoundland subsequent to the date of Union.

(2) Newfoundland will retain its financial surplus subject to the following conditions:

(*a*) one-third of the surplus shall be set aside during the first eight years from the date of Union, on deposit with the Government of Canada, to be withdrawn by the Government of the Province of Newfoundland only for expenditures on current account to facilitate the maintenance and improvement of Newfoundland public services, and any portion of this one-third of the surplus remaining unspent at the end of the eight-year period shall become available to the Province of Newfoundland without the foregoing restriction;

(*b*) the remaining two-thirds of the surplus shall be available to the Government of the Province of Newfoundland for the development of resources and for the establishment or extension of public services within the Province of Newfoundland; and

(*c*) no part of the surplus shall be used to subsidize the production or sale of products of the Province of Newfoundland in unfair competition with similar products of other provinces of Canada, but nothing in this paragraph shall preclude the Province of Newfoundland from assisting industry by developmental loans on reasonable conditions or by ordinary provincial administrative services.

(3) The Government of the Province of Newfoundland will have the right within one year from the date of Union to deposit with the Government of Canada all or any part of its financial surplus held in dollars on the thirty-first day of March and the thirtieth day of September in each year to receive with respect thereto interest at the rate of two and five-eighths per centum per annum during a maximum period of ten years from the date of Union on the minimum balance outstanding at any time during the six-month period preceding payment of interest.

Loans

25 (1) The Province of Newfoundland will retain its interest in, and any securities arising from or attaching to, any loans or advances of public funds made by the Government of Newfoundland prior to the date of Union.

(2) Unless otherwise agreed by the Government of Canada, paragraph one of this Term shall not apply to any loans or advances relating to any works, property, or services taken over by Canada pursuant to Term thirty-one or Term thirty-three.

Subsidies

26 Canada will pay to the Province of Newfoundland the following subsidies:

(*a*) an annual subsidy of $180,000 and an annual subsidy equal to 80 cents per head of the population of the Province of Newfoundland (being taken at 325,000 until the first decennial census after the date of Union), subject to be increased to conform to the scale of grants authorized by the British North America Act, 1907, for the local purposes of the Province and the support of its Government and Legislature, but in no year shall sums payable under this paragraph be less than those payable in the first year after the date of Union; and

(*b*) an additional annual subsidy of $1,100,000 payable for the like purposes as the various fixed annual allowances and subsidies provided by statutes of the Parliament of Canada from time to time for the Provinces of Nova Scotia, New Brunswick, and Prince Edward Island or any of them and in recognition of the special problems of the Province of Newfoundland by reason of geography and its sparse and scattered population.

Tax Agreement

27 (1) The Government of Canada will forthwith after the date of Union make an offer to the Government of the Province of Newfoundland to enter into a tax agreement for the rental to the Government of Canada of the income, corporation income, and corporation tax fields, and the succession duties tax field.

(2) The offer to be made under this Term will be similar to the offers to enter into tax agreements made to other provinces, necessary changes being made to adapt the offer to circumstances arising out of the Union, except that the offer will provide that the agreement may be entered into either for a number of fiscal years expiring at the end of the fiscal year in 1952, as in the case of other provinces, or for a number of fiscal years expiring at the end of the fiscal year in 1957, at the option of the Government of the Province of Newfoundland, but if the Government of the Province of Newfoundland accepts the latter option the agreement will provide that the subsequent entry into a tax agreement by the Government of Canada with any other province will not entitle the Government of the Province of Newfoundland to any alteration in the terms of its agreement.

(3) The offer of the Government of Canada to be made under this Term may be accepted by the Government of the Province of Newfoundland within nine months after the date of the offer but if it is not so accepted will thereupon expire.

(4) The Government of the Province of Newfoundland shall not by any agreement entered into pursuant to this Term be required to impose on any person or corporation taxation repugnant to the provisions of any contract entered into with such person or corporation before the date of the agreement and subsisting at the date of the agreement.

(5) If the Province of Newfoundland enters into a tax agreement pursuant

to this Term the subsidies payable under Term twenty-six will, as in the case of similar subsidies to other provinces, be included in the computation of tax agreements payments.

Transitional Grants

28 (1) In order to facilitate the adjustment of Newfoundland to the status of a province of Canada and the development by the Province of Newfoundland of revenue-producing services, Canada will pay to the Province of Newfoundland each year during the first twelve years after the date of Union a transitional grant as follows, payment in each year to be made in equal quarterly instalments commencing on the first day of April, namely,

First year	$6,500,000
Second year	6,500,000
Third year	6,500,000
Fourth year	5,650,000
Fifth year	4,800,000
Sixth year	3,950,000
Seventh year	3,100,000
Eighth year	2,250,000
Ninth year	1,400,000
Tenth year	1,050,000
Eleventh year	700,000
Twelfth year	350,000

(2) The Government of the Province of Newfoundland will have the right to leave on deposit with the Government of Canada any portion of the transitional grant for the first eight years with the right to withdraw all or any portion thereof in any subsequent year and on the thirty-first day of March and the thirtieth day of September in each year to receive in respect of any amounts so left on deposit interest at the rate of two and five-eighths per centum per annum up to a maximum period of ten years from the date of Union on the minimum balance outstanding at any time during the six-month period preceding payment of interest.

Review of Financial Position

29 In view of the difficulty of predicting with sufficient accuracy the financial consequences to Newfoundland of becoming a province of Canada, the Government of Canada will appoint a Royal Commission within eight years from the date of Union to review the financial position of the Province of Newfoundland and to recommend the form and scale of additional financial assistance, if any, that may be required by the Government of the Province of Newfoundland to enable it to continue public services at the levels and standards reached subsequent to the date of Union, without resorting to taxation more

burdensome, having regard to capacity to pay, than that obtaining generally in the region comprising the Maritime Provinces of Nova Scotia, New Brunswick, and Prince Edward Island.

MISCELLANEOUS PROVISIONS

Salaries of Lieutenant-Governor and Judges
30 The salary of the Lieutenant-Governor and the salaries, allowances, and pensions of the judges of such superior, district, and county courts as are now or may hereafter be constituted in the Province of Newfoundland shall be fixed and provided by the Parliament of Canada.

Public Services, Works and Property
31 At the date of Union, or as soon thereafter as practicable, Canada will take over the following services and will as from the date of Union relieve the Province of Newfoundland of the public costs incurred in respect of each service taken over, namely,

(*a*) the Newfoundland Railway, including steamship and other marine services;

(*b*) the Newfoundland Hotel, if requested by the Government of the Province of Newfoundland within six months from the date of Union;

(*c*) postal and publicly-owned telecommunication services;

(*d*) civil aviation, including Gander Airport;

(*e*) customs and excise;

(*f*) defence;

(*g*) protection and encouragement of fisheries and operation of bait services;

(*h*) geographical, topographical, geodetic, and hydrographic surveys;

(*i*) lighthouses, fog alarms, buoys, beacons, and other public works and services in aid of navigation and shipping;

(*j*) marine hospitals, quarantine, and the care of ship-wrecked crews;

(*k*) the public radio broadcasting system; and

(*l*) other public services similar in kind to those provided at the date of Union for the people of Canada generally.

32 (1) Canada will maintain in accordance with the traffic offering a freight and passenger steamship service between North Sydney and Port aux Basques, which, on completion of a motor highway between Corner Brook and Port aux Basques, will include suitable provision for the carriage of motor vehicles.

(2) For the purpose of railway rate regulation the Island of Newfoundland will be included in the Maritime region of Canada, and through-traffic moving between North Sydney and Port aux Basques will be treated as all-rail traffic.

(3) All legislation of the Parliament of Canada providing for special rates on traffic moving within, into, or out of, the Maritime region will, as far as appropriate, be made applicable to the Island of Newfoundland.

33 The following public works and property of Newfoundland shall become

the property of Canada when the service concerned is taken over by Canada, subject to any trusts existing in respect thereof, and to any interest other than that of Newfoundland in the same, namely,

(*a*) the Newfoundland Railway, including rights of way, wharves, dry-docks, and other real property, rolling stock, equipment, ships, and other personal property;

(*b*) the Newfoundland Airport at Gander, including buildings and equipment, together with any other property used for the operation of the Airport;

(*c*) the Newfoundland Hotel and equipment;

(*d*) public harbours, wharves, break-waters, and aids to navigation;

(*e*) bait depots and the motor vessel Malakoff;

(*f*) military and naval property, stores, and equipment;

(*g*) public dredges and vessels except those used for services that remain the responsibility of Newfoundland and except the nine motor vessels known as the Clarenville boats;

(*h*) the public telecommunications system, including rights of way, land lines, cables, telephones, radio stations, and other real and personal property;

(*i*) real and personal property of the Broadcasting Corporation of Newfoundland; and

(*j*) subject to the provisions of Term thirty-four, customs houses, and post-offices and generally all public works and property, real and personal, used primarily for services taken over by Canada.

34 Where at the date of Union any public buildings of Newfoundland included in paragraph (*j*) of Term thirty-three are used partly for services taken over by Canada and partly for services of the Province of Newfoundland the following provisions shall apply:

(*a*) where more than half the floor space of a building is used for services taken over by Canada the building shall become the property of Canada and where more than half the floor space of a building is used for services of the Province of Newfoundland the building shall remain the property of the Province of Newfoundland;

(*b*) Canada shall be entitled to rent from the Province of Newfoundland on terms to be mutually agreed such space in the buildings owned by the Province of Newfoundland as is used for the services taken over by Canada, and the Province of Newfoundland shall be entitled to rent from Canada on terms to be mutually agreed such space in the buildings owned by Canada as is used for the services of the Province of Newfoundland;

(*c*) the division of buildings for the purposes of this Term shall be made by agreement between the Government of Canada and the Government of the Province of Newfoundland as soon as practicable after the date of Union; and

(*d*) if the division in accordance with the foregoing provisions results in either Canada or the Province of Newfoundland having a total ownership that is substantially out of proportion to the total floor space used for its services an adjustment of the division will be made by mutual agreement between the two Governments.

35 Newfoundland public works and property not transferable to Canada by or under these Terms will remain the property of the Province of Newfoundland.

36 Without prejudice to the legislative authority of the Parliament of Canada under the British North America Acts, 1867 to 1946, any works, property, or services taken over by Canada pursuant to these Terms shall thereupon be subject to the legislative authority of the Parliament of Canada.

Natural Resources

37 All lands, mines, minerals, and royalties belonging to Newfoundland at the date of Union, and all sums then due or payable for such lands, mines, minerals, or royalties, shall belong to the Province of Newfoundland, subject to any trusts existing in respect thereof, and to any interest other than that of the Province in the same.

Veterans

38 Canada will make available to Newfoundland veterans the following benefits, on the same basis as they are from time to time available to Canadian veterans, as if the Newfoundland veterans had served in His Majesty's Canadian forces, namely,

(*a*) The War Veterans' Allowance Act, 1946, free hospitalization and treatment, and civil service preference will be extended to Newfoundland veterans who served in the First World War or the Second World War or both;

(*b*) Canada will assume as from the date of Union the Newfoundland pension liability in respect of the First World War, and in respect of the Second World War Canada will assume as from the date of Union the cost of supplementing disability and dependants' pensions paid by the Government of the United Kingdom or an Allied country to Newfoundland veterans up to the level of the Canadian rates of pensions, and, in addition, Canada will pay pensions arising from disabilities that are pensionable under Canadian law but not pensionable either under the laws of the United Kingdom or under the laws of an Allied country;

(*c*) The Veterans' Land Act, 1942, Part IV of the Unemployment Insurance Act, 1940, The Veterans' Business and Professional Loans Act, and The Veterans' Insurance Act will be extended to Newfoundland veterans who served in the Second World War;

(*d*) a re-establishment credit will be made available to Newfoundland veterans who served in the Second World War equal to the re-establishment credit that might have been made available to them under The War Service Grants Act, 1944, if their service in the Second World War had been service in the Canadian forces, less the amount of any pecuniary benefits of the same nature granted or paid by the Government of any country other than Canada;

(*e*) Canada will assume, as from the date of Union, the cost of vocational and educational training of Newfoundland veterans of the Second World War on the same basis as if they had served in His Majesty's Canadian forces; and (*f*) sections six, seven, and eight of The Veterans' Rehabilitation Act will be extended to Newfoundland veterans of the Second World War who have not received similar benefits from the Government of any country other than Canada.

Public Servants

39 (1) Employees of the Government of Newfoundland in the services taken over by Canada pursuant to these Terms will be offered employment in these services or in similar Canadian services under the terms and conditions from time to time governing employment in those services, but without reduction in salary or loss of pension rights acquired by reason of service in Newfoundland.

(2) Canada will provide the pensions for such employees so that the employees will not be prejudiced, and the Government of the Province of Newfoundland will reimburse Canada for the pensions for, or at its option make to Canada contributions in respect of, the service of these employees with the Government of Newfoundland prior to the date of Union, but these payments or contributions will be such that the burden on the Government of the Province of Newfoundland in respect of pension rights acquired by reason of service in Newfoundland will not be increased by reason of the transfer.

(3) Pensions of employees of the Government of Newfoundland who were retired on pension before the service concerned is taken over by Canada will remain the responsibility of the Province of Newfoundland.

Welfare and Other Public Services

40 Subject to these Terms, Canada will extend to the province of Newfoundland, on the same basis and subject to the same terms and conditions as in the case of other provinces of Canada, the welfare and other public services provided from time to time by Canada for the people of Canada generally, which, in addition to the veterans' benefits, unemployment insurance benefits, and merchant seamen benefits set out in Terms thirty-eight, forty-one, and forty-two respectively, include family allowances under The Family Allowances Act, 1944, unemployment insurance under The Unemployment Insurance Act, 1940, sick mariners' benefits for merchant seamen and fishermen under the Canada Shipping Act, 1934, assistance for housing under The National Housing Act, 1944, and, subject to the Province of Newfoundland entering into the necessary agreements or making the necessary contributions, financial assistance under The National Physical Fitness Act for carrying out plans of physical fitness, health grants, and contributions under the Old Age Pensions Act for old age pensions and pensions for the blind.

Unemployment Insurance

41 (1) Subject to this Term, Canada will provide that residents of the Province of Newfoundland in insurable employment who lose their employment within six months prior to the date of Union and are still unemployed at that date, or who lose their employment within a two-year period after that date, will be entitled for a period of six months from the date of Union or six months

from the date of unemployment, whichever is the later, to assistance on the same scale and under the same conditions as unemployment insurance benefits.

(2) The rates of payment will be based on the individual's wage record for the three months preceding his loss of employment, and to qualify for assistance a person must have been employed in insurable employment for at least thirty per centum of the working days within the period of three months preceding his loss of employment or thirty per centum of the working days within the period since the date of Union, whichever period is the longer.

Merchant Seamen

42 (1) Canada will make available to Newfoundland merchant seamen who served in the Second World War on British ships or on ships of Allied countries employed in service essential to the prosecution of the war, the following benefits, on the same basis as they are from time to time available to Canadian merchant seamen, as if they had served on Canadian ships, namely,

(*a*) disability and dependants' pensions will be paid, if disability occurred as a result of enemy action or counter-action, including extraordinary marine hazards occasioned by the war, and a Newfoundland merchant seaman in receipt of a pension from the Government of the United Kingdom or an Allied country will be entitled, during residence in Canada, to have his pension raised to the Canadian level; and

(*b*) free hospitalization and treatment, vocational training, The Veterans' Land Act, 1942, and The Veterans' Insurance Act will be extended to disability pensioners.

(2) Vocational training, Part IV of The Unemployment Insurance Act, 1940, and The Veterans' Insurance Act will be extended to Newfoundland merchant seamen who were eligible for a Special Bonus or a War Service Bonus, on the same basis as if they were Canadian merchant seamen.

(3) The Unemployment Insurance Act, 1940, and The Merchant Seamen Compensation Act will be applied to Newfoundland merchant seamen as they are applied to other Canadian merchant seamen.

Citizenship

43 Suitable provision will be made for the extension of the Canadian citizenship laws to the Province of Newfoundland.

Defence Establishments

44 Canada will provide for the maintenance in the Province of Newfoundland of appropriate reserve units of the Canadian defence forces, which will include the Newfoundland Regiment.

Economic Survey

45 (1) Should the Government of the Province of Newfoundland institute an economic survey of the Province of Newfoundland with a view to determining what resources may profitably be developed and what new industries may be established or existing industries expanded, the Government of Canada will

make available the services of its technical employees and agencies to assist in the work.

(2) As soon as may be practicable after the date of Union, the Government of Canada will make a special effort to collect and make available statistical and scientific data about the natural resources and economy of the Province of Newfoundland, in order to bring such information up to the standard attained for the other provinces of Canada.

Oleomargarine

46 (1) Oleomargarine or margarine may be manufactured or sold in the Province of Newfoundland after the date of the Union and the Parliament of Canada shall not prohibit or restrict such manufacture or sale except at the request of the Legislature of the Province of Newfoundland, but nothing in this Term shall affect the power of the Parliament of Canada to require compliance with standards of quality applicable throughout Canada.

(2) Unless the Parliament of Canada otherwise provides or unless the sale and manufacture in, and the interprovincial movement between, all provinces of Canada other than Newfoundland, of oleomargarine and margarine, is lawful under the laws of Canada, oleomargarine or margarine shall not be sent, shipped, brought, or carried from the Province of Newfoundland into any other province of Canada.

Income Taxes

47 In order to assist in the transition to payment of income tax on a current basis Canada will provide in respect of persons (including corporations) resident in Newfoundland at the date of Union, who were not resident in Canada in 1949 prior to the date of Union, and in respect of income that under the laws of Canada in force immediately prior to the date of Union was not liable to taxation, as follows:

(*a*) that prior to the first day of July, 1949, no payment will be required or deduction made from such income on account of income tax;

(*b*) that for income tax purposes no person shall be required to report such income for any period prior to the date of Union;

(*c*) that no person shall be liable to Canada for income tax in respect of such income for any period prior to the date of Union; and

(*d*) that for individuals an amount of income tax for the 1949 taxation year on income for the period after the date of Union shall be forgiven so that the tax on all earned income and on investment income of not more than $2,250 will be reduced to one-half the tax that would have been payable for the whole year if the income for the period prior to the date of Union were at the same rate as that subsequent to such date.

Statute of Westminster

48 From and after the date of Union the Statute of Westminster, 1931, shall apply to the Province of Newfoundland as it applies to the other Provinces of Canada.

Saving

49 Nothing in these Terms shall be construed as relieving any person from any obligation with respect to the employment of Newfoundland labour incurred or assumed in return for any concession or privilege granted or conferred by the Government of Newfoundland prior to the date of Union.

Coming into Force

50 These Terms are agreed to subject to their being approved by the Parliament of Canada and the Government of Newfoundland; shall take effect notwithstanding the Newfoundland Act, 1933, or any instrument issued pursuant thereto; and shall come into force immediately before the expiration of the thirty-first day of March, 1949, if His Majesty has theretofore given His Assent to an Act of the Parliament of the United Kingdom of Great Britain and Northern Ireland confirming the same.

Signed in duplicate at Ottawa this eleventh day of December, 1948.

On behalf of Canada:

LOUIS S. ST LAURENT
BROOKE CLAXTON

On behalf of Newfoundland:

ALBERT J. WALSH
F. GORDON BRADLEY
PHILIP GRUCHY
JOHN B. MCEVOY
JOSEPH R. SMALLWOOD
G. A. WINTER

Bibliography

MANUSCRIPT SOURCES

Newfoundland Archives, St John's
State papers
    Records of the administrations from Morris to Alderdice, 1914–33
    Governor's Correspondence, 1914–33
    Papers relating to Labrador, 1928–33
Private papers
    William Warren Papers

Public Record Office, London
    Colonial Office Records, Newfoundland, series 194, vols. 239–85
    Foreign Office Records, Diplomatic Correspondence, series 371, vols 185, 388–90
    Dominions Office Records, Newfoundland, series 35, vols. 488–506

Public Archives of Canada, Ottawa
    Earl Grey Papers (correspondence, 1906–7)

Bodleian Library, Oxford
    James Bryce Papers (correspondence, 1907)

Bonar Law–Bennett Library, University of New Brunswick
    Sir R. B. Bennett Papers (correspondence, 1931–4)

Privately held
    Sir Robert Bond Papers (in the possession of Professor F. F. Thompson, Royal Military College of Canada, Kingston, Ontario)

PRINTED SOURCES

Primary

Proceedings of the Newfoundland House of Assembly and Legislative Council,
   1909–34
Journals of the Newfoundland House of Assembly and Legislative Council,
   1900–34
Newfoundland Census, 1901, 1911, 1921, 1935
Consolidated Statutes of Newfoundland, 3rd series to 1916, 4 vols.,
   St John's, 1919
Rules and Orders for the Proceedings of the House of Assembly of New-
   foundland, St John's, 1920
Year Book and Almanac of Newfoundland, St John's, 1911–31
British Parliamentary Papers
          Cd 2383, *Convention between the United Kingdom and France*
          Respecting Newfoundland and West and Central Africa, London, 1904
          Cd 2737, *Agreement between His Majesty's Government and the French*
          Government for the Constitution of an Arbitral Tribunal ..., London,
          1905
          Cd 3262, *Correspondence Respecting the Newfoundland Fisheries,*
          London, 1906
          Cd 3523, *Correspondence Respecting the Newfoundland Fisheries,*
          London, 1907
          Cd 3765, *Further Correspondence Relating to the Newfoundland Fishery*
          Question, London, 1908
          Cmd 4479, *Newfoundland, Papers Relating to the Report of the Royal*
          Commission, London, 1933
          Cmd 4480, *Newfoundland Royal Commission 1933 Report,* London,
          1933
British Parliamentary Debates, 5th series, 1933, vol. 284, cc. 215–308
Canada, House of Commons Debates, vol. CVI, cc. 6528–43, 29 March 1912
United States Congressional Record, vol. 42, part 3, pp. 2986–8, 60th Con-
   gress, 1st session, 10 February 1908

Memoirs and contemporary works
Coaker, W. F., ed., *The History of the Fishermen's Protective Union of*
   Newfoundland, St John's, 1920
—   ed., *Twenty Years of the Fishermen's Protective Union of Newfound-*
   land, St John's, 1930
—   *Past, Present, and Future,* St John's, n.d. [1932]
Kean, A., *Old and Young Ahead,* London, 1935
Morine, A. B., *The Railway Contract, 1898, and Afterwards,* St John's, n.d.
   [1933]
Smith, N., *Fifty-two Years at the Labrador Fishery,* London, 1936

Stansford, J., *Fifty Years of My Life*, Ilfracombe, Devon, n.d.
Williams, Sir R., *How I Became a Governor*, London, 1913
Winter, J. S., *et al.*, *The Case for the Colony Stated by the People's Delegates*, London, 1890

Newspapers

Newfoundland
Daily Globe, St John's
Daily News, St John's
Daily Mail, St John's
Daily Star, St John's
Evening Advocate, St John's
Evening Chronicle, St John's
Evening Herald, St John's
Evening Telegram, St John's
Fishermen's Advocate, St John's and Port Union
Free Press, St John's
Harbour Grace Standard
Liberal Press, St John's
Mail and Advocate, St John's
Twillingate Sun
Royal Gazette, St John's

British
The Times, London

Canadian
Gazette, Montreal

Select list of secondary works

Ammon, Lord, *Newfoundland: The Forgotten Island* (Fabian Society Research Series, no. 86), London, 1944
Birkenhead, Lord, *The Story of Newfoundland*, London, 1920
Bonneycastle, R. H., *Newfoundland in 1842*, London, 1842 (2 vols.)
Brebner, J. B., *North Atlantic Triangle*, Toronto (Carleton Library Edition), 1966
Campbell, C. S., *Anglo-American Understanding, 1898–1903*, Baltimore, 1957
Chadwick, St J., *Newfoundland: Island into Province*, Cambridge, 1967
Clark, R. L., 'Newfoundland 1934–49 – A Study of the Commission of Government and Confederation with Canada,' unpublished PH D dissertation, University of California, Los Angeles, 1951
Crosbie, J. C., 'Local Government in Newfoundland,' *Canadian Journal of Economics and Political Science*, vol. 22, no. 3, 1956, pp. 332–46
Devereux, E. J., 'Early Printing in Newfoundland,' *Dalhousie Review*, vol. 43, no. 1, 1963, pp. 57–66

Digby, M., *Report on the Opportunities for Co-operative Organization in Newfoundland and Canada*, London, 1934
— *Newfoundland and Iceland: A Parallel*, London, 1935
Encyclopedia of Canada, Newfoundland Supplement, Toronto, 1949
Fay, C. R., *Life and Labour in Newfoundland*, Cambridge (Heffer), 1956
Feltham, J., 'The Development of the F.P.U. in Newfoundland (1908–1923),' unpublished MA thesis, Memorial University of Newfoundland, 1959
Gosling, W. G., *Labrador*, London, 1910
Grenfell, W. T., *A Labrador Doctor*, London, 1919
— *Labrador*, New York, 1922
— *Labrador's Fight for Economic Freedom*, London, 1929
Gunn, G. E., *The Political History of Newfoundland, 1832–1864*, Toronto, 1961
Gwyn, R., *Smallwood: The Unlikely Revolutionary*, Toronto, 1968
Harmsworth, G., and Pound, R., *Northcliffe*, London, 1959
Howe Green, W., *Wooden Walls among the Ice Flows*, London, 1933
Innis, H. A., *The Cod Fisheries: The History of an International Economy*, rev. ed., Toronto, 1954
Junek, O. W., *Isolated Communities – A Study of a Labrador Fishing Village*, New York, 1937
Keith, A. B., *Responsible Government in the Dominions*, Oxford, 1928 (2 vols.)
Little, J., *The Constitution of the Government of Newfoundland in its Legislative and Executive Departments*, London, 1855
Lodge, T., *Dictatorship in Newfoundland*, London, 1939
— 'Oligarchy in Newfoundland,' *Fortnightly Review*, vol. 144, 1938, pp. 475–84
McAllister, R. I., ed., *Newfoundland and Labrador: The First Fifteen Years of Confederation*, St John's, n.d. [1965]
McGrath, P. T., 'Newfoundland and the Paper Supply,' *Dalhousie Review*, vol. 3, 1924, pp. 483–91
— *Newfoundland in 1911*, London, 1911
— 'Will Newfoundland Join Canada?' *Queen's Quarterly*, vol. 36, 1929, pp. 253–66
MacKay, R. A., ed., *Newfoundland: Economic, Diplomatic and Strategic Studies*, Toronto, 1946
McLintock, A. H., *The Establishment of Constitutional Government in Newfoundland, 1783–1832*, London, 1941
Mayo, H. B., 'Municipal Government in Newfoundland,' *Public Affairs*, March 1941, pp. 136–9
— 'Newfoundland and Canada: The Case for Union Examined,' unpublished D PHIL thesis, Oxford University, 1948
— 'Newfoundland and Confederation in the Eighteen-Sixties,' *Canadian Historical Review*, vol. 29, no. 2, 1948, pp. 125–42

Meekins, L. W., *Newfoundland: Commercial and Industrial Survey* (United
    States Department of Commerce, Trade and Information Bulletin,
    no. 409), Washington, 1929
Mitchell, H., 'The Constitutional Crisis of 1889 in Newfoundland,' *Canadian
    Journal of Economics and Political Science*, vol. 24, no. 3, 1958,
    pp. 323–31
—— 'Canada's Negotiations with Newfoundland, 1887–1895,' *Canadian
    Historical Review*, vol. 40, no. 4, 1959, pp. 277–93
Morton, W. L., 'Newfoundland in Colonial Policy, 1775–93,' unpublished
    B LITT thesis, Oxford University, 1935
Neary, Peter, 'Democracy in Newfoundland: A Comment,' *Journal of
    Canadian Studies*, vol. 4, no. 1, 1969, pp. 37–45
Newfoundland Social and Economic Studies, Institute of Social and Economic
    Research, Memorial University of Newfoundland, St John's, 1966–
    1 Tom Philbrook, *Fisherman, Logger, Merchant, Miner: Social Change
    and Industrialism in Three Newfoundland Communities*
    2 John Szwed, *Private Cultures and Public Imagery: Interpersonal
    Relations in a Newfoundland Peasant Society*
    3 Jim Faris, *Cat Harbour: A Newfoundland Fishing Settlement*
    4 Shmuel Ben-Dor, *Makkovik: Eskimos and Settlers in a Labrador
    Community: A Contrastive Study in Adaptation*
    5 Melvin M. Firestone, *Brothers and Rivals: Patrilocality in Savage Cove*
    6 Noel Iverson and D. Ralph Matthews, *Communities in Decline:
    An Examination of Household Resettlement in Newfoundland*
    7 Cato Wadel, *Marginal Adaptations and Modernization in Newfound-
    land: A Study of Strategies and Implications of Resettlement and
    Redevelopment of Outport Fishing Communities*
    8 Robert L. DeWitt, *Public Policy and Community Protest: The Fogo
    Case*
    9 Ottar Brox, *Maintenance of Economic Dualism in Newfoundland*
Newfoundland's Who's Who, St John's, 1930
Newfoundland and Labrador Who's Who, St John's, 1968
Nicholson, G. W. L., *The Fighting Newfoundlander: A History of the Royal
    Newfoundland Regiment*, Ottawa, 1964
Noel, S. J. R., 'Politics and the Crown: The Case of the 1908 Tie Election in
    Newfoundland,' *Canadian Journal of Economics and Political Science*,
    vol. 33, no. 2, 1967, pp. 285–91
Panting, G. E., 'The Fishermen's Protective Union of Newfoundland and the
    Farmers' Organizations in Western Canada,' *Canadian Historical
    Association Report*, 1963, pp. 141–51
Prowse, D. W., *A History of Newfoundland from the English, Colonial, and
    Foreign Records*, London, 1895, rev. ed., 1896
—— 'Local Government in Newfoundland,' *University of Toronto Studies,
    History and Government*, vol. 2, no. 4, 1907, 271–8

*Report of the Royal Commission on the Economic State and Prospects of
    Newfoundland and Labrador*, St John's, 1967
Rogers, J. D., *Newfoundland: Historical and Geographical*, Oxford, 1911
Rothney, G. O., 'The Denominational Basis of Representation in the New-
    foundland Assembly, 1919–1962,' *Canadian Journal of Economics and
    Political Science*, vol. 28, no. 4, 1962, pp. 557–70
Rowe, F. W., *The History of Education in Newfoundland*, Toronto, 1952
—   *The Development of Education in Newfoundland*, Toronto, 1964
Seitz, D. C., *The Great Island*, London, 1927
Smallwood, J. R., ed., *The Book of Newfoundland*, St John's, 1937 (vols.
    I and II) and 1967 (vols. III and IV)
—   *Coaker of Newfoundland*, London, 1927
—   *The New Newfoundland*, New York, 1931
Stanley, G. F. G., 'Sir Stephen Hill's Observations on the Election of 1869 in
    Newfoundland,' *Canadian Historical Review*, vol. 29, no. 3, 1948,
    pp. 278–85
Thompson, F. F., *The French Shore Problem in Newfoundland: An Imperial
    Study*, Toronto, 1961
Travers, D. H., 'The Problem of Taxation,' *Newfoundland Quarterly*,
    April 1927
Wade, Mason, ed., *Regionalism in the Canadian Community, 1867–1967*,
    Toronto, 1969
Whiteway, A. R., 'The Commercial Collapse of Newfoundland,' *National
    Review*, February 1895

Index